A History of the Personal Social Services in England

Ray Jones

A History of the Personal Social Services in England

Feast, Famine and the Future

Ray Jones
Kingston University
Kingston, Surrey, UK

ISBN 978-3-030-46122-5   ISBN 978-3-030-46123-2   (eBook)
https://doi.org/10.1007/978-3-030-46123-2

This Palgrave Macmillan imprint is published by the registered company Springer Nature Switzerland AG.
The registered company address is: Gewerbestrasse 11, 6330 Cham, Switzerland

Contents

1

Introduction: History and Hints

This book is published in 2020 at a time of the 50th anniversary of the creation of unified local authority personal social services in the UK and of a UK-wide unified profession of social work. Different UK national administrations have increasingly diverged in the shaping of their personal social services during the past half century, and especially since the pace of devolution has accelerated, and this text focuses on the developments in England and, for much of this time, Wales.

From 1970 until 2004 care and protection services for children, families, and disabled and older people were primarily planned, provided and purchased in England and Wales through local authority social services departments. These personal social services were largely shaped and defined by legislation set by the national government, and it was funding from national government that mainly determined the extent of these services. As funding ebbed and flowed so did the services which had a major impact on the life experiences, and quality of life, of children and families in difficulty and of disabled and older people needing assistance.

© The Author(s) 2020, corrected publication 2021
R. Jones, *A History of the Personal Social Services in England*,
https://doi.org/10.1007/978-3-030-46123-2_1

Prior to 1970, and since 2004, local councils personal social services responsibilities were and are now spread between different departments, with in particular a separation of social care services for children and for adults. How and why have these changes occurred are explored in this book. But the significance of this story is greater than just a reflection on the personal social services for as Vaclav Havel noted 'the basic measure of the general state decency is how a society cares for its children, its sick, its elderly, and its helpless. In other words how it looks after its own' [1].

I am a social worker, not a professional historian. This account of the history of the personal social services is heavily influenced by my own participation and observation of an unfolding history over the past 50 years as a social work practitioner, manager and academic, and by personal experiences within my family and community of the use of personal social services. This is not *THE* history of the personal social services. It is *A* history determined by a view which at any one time has inevitably had a constricted horizon and a restricted vision.

It is also a view shaped by personal values which themselves are built on personal and professional experience over time and by a selective recalling and understanding of the past. It is, therefore, a personal history as much as a history of politics, policy and practice, and the people who shaped them, within the personal social services. As such, occasionally memories and anecdotes are shared from my personal and professional experience over more than 50 years, but this sharing is as much to locate my own perceptions as to illustrate a more general commentary.

This history is, however, not only informed by my own experiences and recollection. It draws on and quotes from what were then contemporary records and writings prepared and published at or close to the time practice and policies were developing and changing. Importantly, the book is heavily influenced, illuminated and illustrated by interviews with key players within the history of the personal social services over the past 40–50 years. More than 30 interviews have been undertaken with key politicians, policy makers, academics, senior managers and professional leaders. They have had influence and often been at the centre of the changes which have occurred within the personal social services. They give an insider's perspective about what has happened and why and how. Their quotations bring to life in the here-and-now the then-and-when.

They have provided a richness of recollection which enlivens the story now to be told.

Those interviewed, for example, range from a member of the Seebohm Committee in 1967 and others who were active in campaigning for the implementation of the Committee's recommendations, to the chief inspectors of the personal social services from the 1970s onwards, key civil servants who were in the midst of the shaping of the landmark 1989 Children Act and 1990 NHS and Community Care Act, leaders in the disability movement, those who have given professional leadership within social work, and politicians and others who have shaped the personal social services during the 2000s. Some of those I have interviewed over the past ten years have since died—and capturing their experience, expertise and wisdom has therefore been especially important.

There is an importance in looking back and remembering history. As attention is justifiably and importantly concentrated on forward planning with strategies and targets generated to seek improvements for the future, there is a danger that the past is forgotten and not known. This is of significance within the personal social services. For example, just consider three points within the age range of people's life spans.

Firstly, for older people who are living in care homes their average age of admission is in the mid-80s. They would have been born and had a childhood in the context of the Poor Law with its policies of deterring people from seeking assistance and stigmatising those who received help. The Poor Law was only ended by the 1948 National Assistance Act. Their expectations and anticipations of welfare and the personal social services would, in its early foundations, have been built on the public fear and threat of the Poor Law and the workhouse, albeit a fear and threat which was already being ameliorated before its formal ending with, as will also be shown later, practice leading to rather than following legislative change [2].

And if the older person now in their mid-80s were admitted to a care home straight from hospital it may well be that the hospital was converted from a former Poor Law workhouse, as with the community hospital in Redruth in Cornwall where my parents grew up, where we lived and where my mother was an in-patient before her death a few years ago. Even when policies change, bricks and mortar tend to endure and to be recycled and reinvented as a resource for the new policies, but their previous usage and reputation are likely still to be recalled by some.

Secondly, many of the new students starting their social work degree programmes would have been born in the late 1990s and early 2000s. For them Thatcherism and the Conservative governments of 1979–1997 are unknown in their lived experience. They are history. Their personal knowledge of politics and policy will have been within the context of New Labour and Blair and Brown and then the Coalition and Conservative governments of Cameron, May and Johnson. Without a knowledge of policy and practice before they were born they would not, for example, know about how the personalisation programme within adult social care had its roots within the lobbying of disabled people in the 1970s and 1980s. They would not know how cash transfers to disabled and older people through direct payments were initially established and promoted by some local authorities before the permissive 1996 Community Care (Direct Payments) Act gave the legal power and then duty to local councils to provide direct payments. They would not know about the prompts and processes, and the debates on principles and practice philosophy, which led to the 1989 Children Act which is still the statutory foundation for their social work practice with children and families.

Thirdly, the current context for local authority personal social services is one of funding reductions and cuts in services and assistance whilst at the same time charges are increased for service users who have to contribute financially to meet the cost of more heavily rationed assistance. This has become a subject of public comment and concern [3, 4]. But this is not the first, nor no doubt the last, time that public services, including the personal social services, will be confronted with imposed reductions in funding.

It might be wise to recall and reflect on the previous periods of funding cuts. The current national and international economic crisis, largely created by a banking system and bankers who became reckless and greedy [5], will not continue forever. A sensible strategy for local politicians and managers may be to do as little fundamental damage as possible whilst awaiting the upturn in the economy and changed national political priorities.

The current impact of politically chosen austerity targeted at poor children and families and disabled people, and at public services and public servants is, however, deeper and more dramatic than at any time over the past 50 years. Indeed, it was 70 years ago in the late 1940s at a time of post-war austerity that the Labour government introduced the public services that formed the infrastructure of the welfare state. It was a government led by Clement Attlee. One hundred years ago in 1920 he wrote a book titled *The Social Worker* [6] based on his experience of working in a settlement in East London. The message from the post-war 1920s and 1940s is that economic difficulties do not necessarily require cuts and retrenchment—and they should not be accepted as an excuse for politically chosen austerity targeting poor people and public services.

Reflecting on the past is not, however, as the comments above probably signify, a neutral and value-free activity. As we speculate about the future, what might be called 'thought experiments' [7], we might also recall that all thought is 'action in the mind' [8], including our reflections on the past. The events and ideas from history are glimpsed through our more recent and contemporary experiences and through our selective and incomplete recall. There is also a power held by the historian, the power of interpretation, as once noted by Winston Churchill:

> 'History', Winston Churchill once told Stanley Baldwin during an exchange in the House of Commons in the 1930s, 'will say that the right honourable gentleman was wrong in this matter'. He then paused and added with a grin, 'I know it, because I will write that history'. [9]

Historians are partisan, taking sides as they structure the story they tell [10], and their structuring of the story is for relatively recent history (as with this book) likely to be influenced from where they viewed events as they unfolded [11].

This is a history which is intended to illustrate and illuminate the journey for the personal social services and for social work in England (with comparative reflections on Scotland, Wales and Northern Ireland within increasingly devolved political administrations) which has brought us to the present day and where the context is particularly challenging for social workers and for those they seek to assist.

It is sensible to remember and recall, however, that the current context will not remain static—it will continue to evolve, change and potentially re-route. If there are two messages from this book they are that, firstly, social work has and always should and will have a relevance within a caring society and, secondly, the future is still to be shaped and created and social workers, as they have done over the past 50 years, have a role to play in creating that future.

Part I

Creating the Personal Social Services

2

Seizing the Moment: The Seebohm Committee

The formation and focus of the Seebohm Committee in the late 1960s might be seen as an adventure of intrigue and personalities. And what in retrospect, and from a considerable distance 50 years on, might be seen as logical step change for the personal social services was at the time neither so obvious nor necessarily welcomed and agreed. Professional and political vested interests all played a part in the discussions and debates, along with the continuation, but also the refining and re-shaping, of the script that was already beginning to flow.

The Drivers for Change

By the mid-1960s, there were a number of drivers for change which led to the Seebohm Committee and its recommendations. This was truly a gestation period for a new concept of the personal social services and for their future organisational home within local authority social services departments.

© The Author(s) 2020, corrected publication 2021
R. Jones, *A History of the Personal Social Services in England*,
https://doi.org/10.1007/978-3-030-46123-2_2

The drivers for change included, firstly, the refocusing of children's services from care away from families to assisting families to care for their children. The role of child care officers had started to change in the 1950s [1] and following the 1963 Children Act. They were now more engaged in work with families to improve and maintain their care of children, including children and young people involved in offending, rather than primarily arranging placements in children's homes and, increasingly, foster care, for children in the care of local councils. This was to be of particular significance in leading, probably unseen and unexpectedly in the early 1960s, to the ending of children's departments, separate children's services and child care officers, as noted by Jean Packman:

> Developments in prevention and work with delinquency not only strained, modified and redefined the original aims and methods of the child care service; they also contributed directly to its eventual demise ... [As] the prevention of neglect [was] seen more and more as a key means of forestalling delinquency, [there was] pressure to change ... and to provide an integrated 'family service' ... In the event, the form of reorganisation was much more radical than the early child-centred blueprints envisaged, so that the service lost its identity in a way that was not anticipated. [2]

A Family Focus in the Midst of Demographic Change

The family focus led to the argument that there should be a family service, with social workers working with all family members. It would also tackle the issue 'that David Donnison's research in Salford and Manchester found that some families had had ten different kinds of social workers' [Bob Holman interview].

What was less easy to define, however, was where a family started and where it ended. Did a family's boundary include or exclude extended family members? Within families, and indeed within family homes, there might not just be parents and their children but also grandparents and may be uncles and aunts and nieces and nephews. And what about people who lived alone or in relationships but with no children? Were they to be included or excluded from a potential family social work service?

One aspect of emerging democratic change was that the traditionally constituted nuclear family of parents and children, with maybe granddad but more likely granny also present, was only one model of family life as increasing rates of divorce, remarriage and reconstituted families became more prevalent.

Secondly, demographic change also included an increasing number of people living into old age, albeit that old age in the 1960s was still seen to start at age 65 (with pensions payable at age 60 for women). How was an expanding older population to be responded to and assisted within whatever future arrangements might be made for social work services?

Amongst the options available were retaining separate local authority welfare departments, with their antecedents in the old Poor Law; merging welfare services into health services, but the focus of discussions and developments within the National Health Service were still largely about hospitals and hospital care and treatment; or seeing a new family service as spanning the age range from birth to death and with a focus on care and assistance outside of the big institutions of geriatric hospitals and wards which still existed.

Thirdly, there was the demographic change of younger disabled adults living for longer and the service change of people with mental health difficulties no longer being incarcerated in the large asylums, partly as a consequence of pharmacological advances. But within the existing tripartite council arrangements of children's, welfare and mental health services, there had been less development of services in the community for disabled and older adults, and for people with mental health difficulties, compared to children.

Children's services had benefitted from having their own legislative focus in 1948 and with their legislation being upgraded in 1963 along with developing professional practice. Services for disabled and older adults were still framed by the 1948 National Assistance Act which had replaced the Poor Law and with the Act still having a focus on institutional and residential care. Mental health services, although re-set by the 1959 Mental Health Act away from an overwhelming orientation towards hospital care, were still largely undeveloped and remained dominated by the large institutions.

So, demographic and social changes were a part of the changing landscape to be considered by whatever policy and organisational social welfare arrangements might be made. But there were also already professional changes and expansion emerging which contributed to the shaping of the landscape for social welfare in the mid-1960s. They were in part a response to and represented a much more diverse society, as noted by Richard Titmuss, a professor at the London School of Economics (LSE) and a prominent advisor to the Labour governments of the 1960s:

> It is an interesting and often overlooked fact that, during the last twenty years, whenever the British people have identified and investigated a social problem there has followed a national call for more social work and more trained social workers. Consider, for one moment, the history of twenty years of Royal Commissions, central and local committees of inquiry, working parties, conferences and Government task forces concerned with: the mentally ill, the schizophrenic discharged from hospital, the mentally subnormal, the maladjusted child, the physically handicapped, the blind and the deaf, the chronically ill and bedridden, the long-stay patient in hospitals and other kinds of residential accommodation, neglected and deprived children, young delinquents and those brought before the juvenile court, youth unemployment, the after-care of prisoners, the prevention of venereal disease, and the after-care of those who have contracted it, the problems of prostitution, unmarried mothers, unsupported wives, marital breakdown and the roles of the courts, drug addiction, alcoholism, homeless families, immigrants from the Commonwealth, and so on. [3]

Unifying the Social Work Profession

There were already underway the argument and arrangements for the development of an integrated and unified profession of social work. Common core characteristics of social work were being identified which spanned and transcended the separate occupational groupings of social workers working in different settings (e.g. within hospitals compared to those working within the community) and with different client groups.

Kenneth Brill, a children's officer who in 1970 would become the first general secretary of the British Association of Social Workers, noted that there was 'a trend towards a coherent philosophy of casework seen as a form of treatment' [4], and Webb and Wistow commented:

In the years before Seebohm at least eight groups of field social workers, or potential social workers, could be identified: psychiatric social workers; medical social workers (almoners); probation officers; mental welfare officers; welfare officers; housing welfare officers; and education welfare officers. Of these, only the first four were well down the road towards something like full professional standing. The types of training offered to each group had traditionally varied, as had the proportion of practitioners with professional qualifications. Moreover, each group of social workers was located within a different organisational setting and the extent of discretion, of managerial control, and of independence of other—'superior'—professions, also differed greatly … The search for a common professional identity rested on two pillars, that of organisational change to bring the professional sub-groups together and that of a common training structure able to produce the set of generic skills necessary for the performance of all types of social work. [5]

This variety and variation of social work and social welfare occupational groups was seen at the time as more of a 'dog's dinner' than an opportunity to 'let every flower bloom'. The solution was to have a common education and training curriculum leading to one qualification, and with one major agency and organisational home-base for statutory social work to tackle the concern that 'social workers [had] found themselves limited in the help they could give by the functions of their agencies and sometimes by their peripheral status within them' [6].

But there were also rivalries and vested interests, especially for high status psychiatric social workers and medical social workers benefitting from the glow of being associated with doctors and of not being directed by local and central government politicians [7].

A further concern was about deskilling and losing the ground gained, especially by child care officers, with welfare officers still usually untrained, and with their roots as Poor Law visiting officers still remembered, as noted by several interviewees for this book:

My experience before Seebohm was that the children's departments were considered to be the crème de la crème. The welfare departments were really considered to be by many people, in comparison, rather pedestrian and completely overshadowed by the chief medical officer who operated within local authorities in those days and really was a prima donna in my view. And then the mental health services were very much under the control of the hospital-based psychiatric services. [Herbert Laming interview]

The welfare departments were not on the same levels of sophistication as the children's departments. Quite a high proportion of the welfare officers had started their [working] lives as workhouse clerks. [Bleddyn Davies interview]

In the welfare services there were a much larger proportion of people who'd been part of the Poor Law until 1948 when the National Assistance Act was passed and they were still there with some of the old welfare attitudes and were much more reticent about what they saw as 'new fangled ideas' … But in child care there was an increasingly large number of people who said 'We're doing the job, we know what's going on, we need to use that knowledge to influence the actual policy that affects the services provided. [Tom White interview]

The welfare officers, with their roots in the Poor Law and with a tradition as local authority officers rather than as professionals with special expertise, were however within a service working with disabled and older people which was 'big business':

The number of people employed [in welfare departments] was enormously greater than children's departments. They employed more fieldworkers than children's departments. Few of them were qualified, but there were more of them … [There was also] the extent to which the chief welfare officers were well embedded into local government traditions more than the children's officers. [Keith Bilton interview]

It was noted in the Seebohm Report [8] that local authority welfare services employed 3513 full-time equivalent (FTE) welfare officers and large numbers of other workers, including, for example, almost 32,000 workers in residential homes and over 30,000 home helps. This was much greater than children's departments with 2341 field workers and 5600 workers in children's homes and nurseries. Other services employing social workers were also much smaller than the welfare departments with 176 FTE psychiatric social workers employed across England and Wales in school health services and child guidance clinics [9], 1794 largely unqualified mental health social workers [10], and the probation service, a national service accountable to the Home Office, had 2549 basic grade and senior probation officers [11].

The Climate for Change

But there were other developments in the 1960s, in addition to the aspirations of the developing social work profession, which set the ground for the Seebohm Committee. One was the great hope that science and technology would find and deliver solutions to problems, including social problems. This was the era of the 'white heat of technology' [12], a phrase coined by Harold Wilson as prime minister in the incoming Labour government of 1964 after 14 years of Conservative government. Change was in the air and this was to be a time of renewal, including a re-energising and resurgence of the welfare state 20 years on from its incarnation. Pressure groups, academics and researchers were all a part of fuelling up this revitalisation of political and social action.

Keith Bilton, who with Tom White was to take a leading role in pressing for the soon to be established Seebohm Committee's recommendations to be implemented, was the secretary of the Association of Child Care Officers. He became one of the first assistant secretaries of the British Association of Social Workers when it was formed in the early 1970s. He commented that the roots of the Seebohm Committee were in part grounded in the aspirations and energy of the new incoming Labour government:

> Harold Wilson won the 1964 election and talked about thirteen wasted years of Tory rule, and I think there must have been quite a strong consciousness in that new government that they needed to revisit the achieve-

ments of setting up the welfare state and that something needed to be done to make the bits of it work together better. [Keith Bilton interview]

And Tom White commented:

I remember being in Scarborough for the Labour Party Conference and Harold Wilson made his speech [about the 'white heat of technology']—I mean there were more scientists alive that day in 1964 than there had been ever in the whole world. So it was a time when people were thinking about change and modernising everything. [Tom White interview]

Although the outgoing prime minister had recently claimed that 'you have never had it so good' [13], there was an emerging recognition of and increasing attention given to poverty and deprivation [14] and also about how care services were less than adequate with a remaining stigmatising and shaming poor quality legacy of the Poor Law, including in care homes for older people (Townsend) [15], in 'subnormality' hospitals for people with learning disabilities [16] and mental asylums [17], and in institutions generally [18]. And it was the expanding base of social science, including in the increasing number of new universities converted from colleges of advanced technology, which provided the capacity, competence and commitment to stimulate and inform the discussions about driving improvements in social welfare.

'Big Bureaucracies Are Beautiful'

A further contribution to setting the landscape within which the Seebohm Committee was to operate was that big was seen as beautiful, especially for organisations:

The Maud Report on Management in Local Government (published in 1967) deplored the proliferation of committees and small departments, which made efficient management so difficult. One of its proposals was a drastic reduction in such departments. [19]

Within these organisations, bureaucracy and bureaucratic structures were the means of generating performance. This was despite the counter-current within some sociological research which argued that bureaucracy was not necessarily efficient, primarily because the concept was too mechanistic and rule-determined, whereas in real life organisations were organic with employees generating their own subcultures and meaning and were more motivated when they could control and shape their working lives and contributions [20, 21].

However, even in the mid-1960s, there were challenges about what much later will be seen as the concerns about the 'bureaucratisation' of social work:

> Are local authorities quite certain that they are making the most effective use of trained social work staff? How much unnecessary form-filling, record-keeping and report writing is there? … To what extent are social workers undertaking tasks that might be delegated to other and less trained staff? Are social workers at all levels being given the clerical help they need? [22]

This 1965 comment from Richard Titmuss could easily be cut-and-pasted into the debates about social work in the 2000s, for example in the report of the Social Work Task Force [23] and in the Munro Review of child protection social work [24].

'Big is better', however, was the main mantra of the 1960s. Titmuss' questioning about the form-filling and record keeping did not deter him from advocating an even bigger expanded family service bureaucracy, although even at that time some had concerns about a big bureaucracy being built within local government:

> One of the reservations I did have was that I did not share the sort of current optimism that was the kind of apotheosis of social work in this country, because from my perspective [in the probation service] from outside of local government, it seemed very difficult to me for social work to flourish as an activity inside a local authority politically led, bureaucratically structured organisation. [Bill Utting interview]

But organisational change was not only about scaling up. It was also about tidying up. Just take, for example, the account in Appendix F of the Seebohm Report [25] of the complexity in the mid-1960s of the various arrangements within local authorities for the delivery of the 1948 National Assistance Act welfare responsibilities for disabled and older people:

> 129 authorities have a welfare committee responsible solely for welfare services; in 28 authorities the health committee are responsible for the provision of those services; and 18 authorities have combined health and welfare committees ... A few councils do not divide their health functions neatly from their welfare functions, even though there are separate health and welfare committees. For example, the health committee and not the welfare committee may be responsible for services for handicapped people.

So there were a wide range of local authority committee arrangements for the welfare services. There were also a wide range of management arrangements:

> There is no requirement on a welfare authority to appoint an officer directly responsible for its welfare services. In those authorities with a combined health and welfare department, the medical officer of health is in overall charge of the welfare services. In total, in 56 authorities the services are the responsibility of the medical officer of health, in 116 authorities of a chief welfare officer or a director of welfare, and in 3 authorities of the clerk of the council ... In the pattern of departmental responsibility also the exact division between health and welfare functions is not the same in all authorities. Even when there is a chief welfare officer he may be subordinate to the medical officer of health ... On the other hand, in at least two areas the chief welfare officer, and not the medical officer of health, is responsible for running the home help service which is provided under the National Health Service Act.

Twenty years on from the mid- and late 1940s foundation of the welfare state, it does seem that some tidying up might have been required following two decades of incremental growth and development. And a specific aside about home help services—at this time they were not primarily about assisting older and disabled people. Instead, they were mainly a 'lying in' service for mothers who had recently given birth, with most babies delivered at home rather than in hospitals.

The Creation of the Seebohm Committee

So with all of this as the scene setting landscape of the mid-1960s how was the Seebohm Committee spawned? The genesis of the Seebohm Committee are described in two accounts published in the late 1970s and early 1980s, both based on extensive access to those who were involved at the time. In her account, Hall notes that:

> By October 1964, when Labour was returned to power, there were two major reports, advocating very similar changes, awaiting the reactions of the incoming ministers. Both documents suggested the formation of new structures for the treatment of offenders and the reorganisation of the local authority social work services so that one department took primary responsibility for the welfare of the family. The immediate reaction of Alice Bacon, who became minister of state at the Home Office, was to begin planning a policy for young offenders based on the advice of the Longford Committee (of which she had been a member). As an Under Secretary at the Scottish Office, Mrs Judith Hart began working on the proposals of the Kilbrandon Report and a third minister, Douglas Houghton, who made his debut in the newly created role of coordinator of the social services, started to develop his own ideas on a family service. [26]

There are several issues to note from this account by Hall. Firstly, it was a concern about tackling youth offending, then called juvenile delinquency, which had led to the Longford report in England and the Kilbrandon report in Scotland. Both reports extended their concerns to concentrate on the child in the family and with recommendations that encouraged thinking about how families might be assisted through what became canvassed as a family (social work) service.

Secondly, although being developed at the same time, the discussions in Scotland and England (and Wales) would diverge and become differentiated, with contrasting arrangements to be put in place by the early 1970s which have continued to the present day. Why this was so will be discussed below.

Thirdly, Hall notes the names of key politicians who were central to how the discussions were shaped and how arguments were championed. Throughout this book, people and personalities will be seen to be important alongside politics and policies. Indeed, it is key players who over and over again are decisive in determining what happens.

And fourthly, one option in driving improvement in change in social welfare in the 1960s was seen to be better coordination across services. Indeed a particular role had been created within the newly elected Labour government to lead on this coordination. But better coordination was not, as will be seen, the route to be taken, with more radical and fundamental change ahead instead.

Hall was a social policy academic. Her account was informed by talking with those involved at the time. Joan Cooper, however, gives an insider's perspective. She had been the children's officer for East Sussex County Council from the foundation of children's departments in 1948 until she became, in 1965, the chief inspector at the Home Office's Children's Department [27]. She was, therefore, in the midst of the deliberations about child care services which were central to, and indeed largely generated, the agenda which led to the Seebohm Committee. Cooper noted:

> When it came to power in October 1964 the Labour Party was already committed to an embryonic family policy as a minor item on its political agenda, but it did not have a social services policy. The Party had a majority of only four seats and a financial crisis on its hands but despite these problems Lord Longford, who was made Lord Privy Seal and Leader of the House of Lords (in which post he remained until 1968), was determined to persuade the government to push through the machinery for the implementation of a family policy. [28]

But how and why did this interest in a family policy, what Hall calls a family service, come to lead to the formation of the Seebohm Committee and what led to the brief of this committee being widened beyond a focus on families with children?

Differing Routes for England and Wales and for Scotland

It was not obvious or inevitable that a committee of enquiry should be established to consider whether a 'family service' should be established. Other ways forward might have included the government itself preparing and publishing a consultative green paper detailing options or a white paper with clear proposals. Indeed, as already noted, in relation to children there were two white papers published in the 1960s. Alternatively, the government could have moved directly to the publication of a bill which, following debate and amendment, may have led to legislation. Indeed the route forward in Scotland was different and quicker as:

> At the Scottish Office, Judith Hart decided, in preference to a formal enquiry, to appoint three expert advisers [one of whom was Richard Titmuss, whose significance in relation to the Seebohm Committee is noted below] to work with civil servants on plans for Scotland. This process achieved legislative change [The Social Work (Scotland) Act] two years ahead of that in England and Wales. [29]

Why this difference between England and Scotland? In England, responsibilities for social welfare and social work services were shared between three central government departments. Responsibility for children's social care policy was held by the Home Office. Responsibility for welfare policies for disabled and older people was held by the Ministry of Health. And there was also an interest from the Ministry of Housing and Local Government as the services were primarily provided by local councils. Because of the initial focus in the discussions on children the Ministry of Education also had an interest in how a potential family service might evolve. If the services were fragmented within local councils between children's, health and welfare departments the fragmentation across central government was at least equally as great and with vested interests to be protected:

> There was a very strong feeling within these departments that whatever happened you didn't concede to the other departments. And it's interesting

that one of the big battles internally wasn't so much about 'Is this a good idea or not [to bring services together]?' but 'What's this going to do to my department? [Tom White interview]

But not so in Scotland where there was one Scottish Office and one Secretary of State for Scotland. So in Scotland there was no requirement to have to manoeuvre around the minefield of ministerial and departmental rivalries. In England, the setting up of a committee of enquiry was one way of handling political and civil service vested interests in an apparently neutral forum.

And Scotland was different in how local government was organised on the ground and where it looked for its reference point:

I think there's always a desire in Scotland to be different. In Scotland there were a great many small borough/town councils, and this meant that some of the children's departments were far too small, so you did have some very small and not very good departments. But partly because of this failure there arose some very good civil servants and there were also a number of social work trainers, like Vera Hiddleston at Jordan Hill College, who pressed very strongly for much more social work training, because it was lagging behind England, and their drive led to the setting up of the Kilbrandon Committee. [Bob Holman interview]

Vera Hiddleston noted that, as in England, it was a re-setting of the views taken about children and young people and delinquency which in part shaped the agendas of the Seebohm and Kilbrandon Committees. Scotland went further than England in re-shaping its response to children and young people involved in delinquency. There was a process of decriminalisation with children's hearings being introduced in Scotland rather than juvenile courts in England, and there was a driver to provide a 'matching fieldwork organisation'—social work departments—which included what had previously been the separate probation service [30].

The chair of the Kilbrandon Committee was to be a lawyer (Seebohm in England was a banker) and its reference point was different:

I think Kilbrandon, I met him and heard him speak a couple of times, did have a tremendous grasp of the issues, social work issues, and I don't know who it was on the Kilbrandon Committee, but somebody was obviously drawing on the Scandinavian experience, and some of them did go out to Scandinavia to look at the systems there, and of course there is this historical link between Scotland and Scandinavia. So the result was Scotland then got a different system, which they called social work departments. Then, of course, in Scotland we had local government reorganisation and some of these very small boroughs disappeared and the standard of social work I think improved enormously. [Bob Holman interview]

David Donnison commented:

I think that the Scots have always been more of a public sector society and still are. More people work in the public sector, more people use public sector services, private education and healthcare is smaller than in England. They always have been a society which believes in qualifications. They are always joking that 'in England it's who you know and in Scotland it's what you know'. [David Donnison interview]

Hall also argued that it was 'deep divisions of opinion between professional groups within the social services as to the preferred patterns of reorganisation, whereas in Scotland the groups were less well developed', [31] which led to the larger and longer Seebohm Committee process in England compared to the work of Kilbrandon in Scotland.

So despite the creation in England at the London School of Economics in 1954 of the first generic training course for social workers, and the establishment in 1963 of the Standing Conference of Organisations of Social Workers (SCOSW), with the objective of establishing a unified national association of social workers, there were still considerable rivalries in the 1960s between these associations and the different specialist occupational groupings of social workers.

The Contribution of the London School of Economics

Several of the interviewees for this book who were involved and active in the 1960s spoke of these rivalries and frictions which were exemplified by personal as well as professional positioning, especially at the LSE [32]:

> To work with Eileen Younghusband, Kay MacDougall, and Claire Britain, as she was when I arrived but who became Claire Winnicott, was an amazing privilege. They were three very good people. But they fought like cats. It was my baptism of fire. Richard [Titmuss], who was not very good at dealing with angry women, had tried to bring about some fusion of these [separate professional] traditions having secured funds from the Carnegie United Kingdom Trust to launch the generic course, led by Eileen. He was at his wits end and he asked me, a very innocent young reader, would I get all of them together and try to work out a solution. [David Donnison interview]

A less sympathetic view of Titmuss' actions and struggles at this time, based on correspondence within the Younghusband Archives at Warwick University, has been given by Ann Oakley, Titmuss' daughter:

> People made observations about Titmuss's 'insensitive leadership', his ignorance and ambivalence about professional social work, his refusal to recognise the close links that existed between Eileen Younghusband and the Carnegie Trust, and his blindness about the fact that the Course depended on very close working partnerships with employment and fieldwork training agencies, including government departments, who therefore saw themselves as equals in the experiment, and who objected to LSE's unilateral action to merge the course with others and deposing Younghusband and Lewis from their positions of authority over it. [33]

But students of the 'Carnegie' generic course were generally positive about it, despite an awareness of staff and university conflicts:

I was confident in my own mind that we had got a sound theoretical case to argue for generic social work, and all that stuff at the LSE between the different courses and staff was really a diversion. [Olive Stevenson interview]

I did the year on the [LSE] social admin course, and then went on to the professional course. Claire Winnicott I think was the most inspiring teacher. It was a good course and the practical placements I thought were of a good standard, and you got plenty of supervision and I was like quite Freudian, but I think it was a good training because it was a generic course, but you did in fact split into a medical social work stream, a child care stream, or mental work, or whatever it was. [Bob Holman interview]

Overall, the LSE was a considerable influential powerhouse in the 1960s. For example, Tom White commented:

There was a kind of movement that led to the establishment of the generic social work course at the LSE, there was academic thinking that there wasn't that much difference between the teaching of social work in different settings ... There was also a great deal of concern, both in the profession and more widely, and people in the political and social [administration] world generally, about the duplication and waste that went on when one family—a real problem family—would have multiple involvement with every agency under the sun. That obviously was a recipe for either duplication or everybody leaving it to everybody else and nothing being done. [Tom White interview]

Tom White also noted that:

And then there was the [issue] of 'do you drain the swamp or pull people out of it'? There was a real feeling amongst the intellingencia that we should really be thinking again about how we provided our services, and did we need to be doing something to prevent the problems that occurred rather than providing a fire brigade service. [Tom White interview]

And many within this intelligencia were within the LSE. Seven of the interviewees for this book—all of were chosen to interview because they were influential in their later careers—had been social work students at the LSE—Olive Stevenson; Bob Holman; Peter Westland; John Rea Price; Tom White; Herbert Laming; Denise Platt—and three further interviewees had worked at the LSE during the 1960s—David Donnison; Roy Parker; Bleddyn Davies. And the LSE staff also included several further academics who had close links with the Labour Party and who were also engaged and influential in the debates and discussions about social work and social services:

> [Richard] Titmuss was a major player. David Donnison was very interested in a fascinating way about how services interacted with each other. There was Brian Abel-Smith who was very engaged in health and social security and pensions. [Peter] Townsend was more of a sociologist and was working on the family life of older people. John Grieve was very much a housing man. And there was a junior lecturer [Roy Parker] who I didn't at that time know very well who was on the Seebohm Committee. [John Rea Price interview]

> I mean LSE, Titmuss, Abel-Smith, Townsend … all of them were thinking about the [family service] issue … They were all seeing a need for more integration but within a much smaller total span than Seebohm eventually proposed. [Tom White interview]

The importance and influence, and prestige and power, of the LSE in the 1950s and 1960s was noted by Reisman in his, not uncritical, 1977 book looking back posthumously over Titmuss' career and contributions:

> The London School of Economics in 1950 … was almost entirely a social science college, and the resultant continuous and stimulating debate on social issues was valuable to the new, largely self-educated professor … Titmuss was, of course, not a trained social worker, a fact which brought him into conflict with some of his colleagues; but this conflict was to some extent resolved by the demonstration effect of his strong commitment to vocational social work education. [34]

But although LSE was an influential power house, not all who were there as students in the mid-1950s thought it was necessarily a centre of excellence for education:

> There was Eileen Younghusband and [Herschel] Prins, and I can't remember all the names, but it wasn't actually a very good course. Eileen was not a very good teacher although I was very fond of her and we got on well. [Roy Parker interview]

> In 1952 to 1954 I did my training at LSE with Claire Winnicott, that's my teacher in the second year. The course was invaluable but the preceding social science year was not in my view looking back strong even by the standards of the time, because we had virtually nothing about sociology or social policy as a way of looking at things as distinct from simply a story ... I suspect that the course was not given the kind of serious attention that it should have been given. I think there were a lot of eminent people building their careers. [Olive Stevenson interview]

But ten years later, by the mid-1960s, these careers had become well established and the careerists had become much respected and influential. They were well networked, especially with the Labour Party in the early 1960s and then with the post 1964 Labour government, and this was especially so of Titmuss [35].

The Contribution of the National Institute for Social Work Training

It was not, however, only the LSE that was a centre of influence within the discussions about a possible family service. The National Institute for Social Work Training (NISWT) also provided a base and network for those within social work to have an input and impact.

NISWT had been established in 1961 following a recommendation of the 1959 Younghusband report on social workers in local authority health and welfare services [36]. Robin Huws Jones was director of the social science courses at Swansea University and was a member of the

Younghusband Committee. He was to be the first director of NISWT. NISWT's chair was Lord Frederick Seebohm, a member of the Seebohm Rowntree family of Quakers. He was to become the chair of the Seebohm Committee.

How key players networked and linked at this time, with overlapping relationships and roles, was quite extraordinary. Here, for example, is a comment from Tom White, who in the 1960s was chair of the Association of Child Care Officers and Deputy Children's Officer in Lancashire. He was to become chair of the Seebohm Implementation Action Group, of which more later, and was the first person to take up an appointment as a post-Seebohm director of social services (in Coventry):

> In 1965 Sir Frederick Seebohm, Chairman of Barclays Bank, was invited to chair a joint departmental committee on the future of the social services. I was delighted to find I knew quite a number of the members of the committee—two of them quite well. (i) Robin Huws Jones was Principal of the National Institute for Social Work. Robin had been director of my social science course at Swansea. I had kept in close touch with Robin and was a member of the board of NISWT. (ii) Bee Serota, a former chair of the LCC [London County Council] Children's Committee, was now a Labour member of the House of Lords. I had worked closely with Bee when she was on the Longford Committee and had maintained contact. [37]

The role of NISWT in relation to the Seebohm Committee was extensive. Peter Leonard, a lecturer at NISWT, was to be a member of the Committee, as was Lady James, whose husband was president of NISWT—and the Committee met at the NISWT's premises, although as Joan Cooper noted that this was not without its consequences:

> The use of the National Institute for Social Work Training for the majority of the Committees meetings was no more than a matter of convenience since there was a scarcity of government meeting rooms, and particularly those where food could be supplied and evening meetings held. This convenient but inept use of the National Institute premises on the part of the Committee laid it open to suspicion of bias which may have later impeded a ready acceptance of its proposals by central and local government and professional staff. [38]

However, as Tom White had noted, Joan Cooper at the time was embedded in the Home Office and 'Joan was advocating a joint Home Office and Health Department. So there were those in government circles with a kind of concern with protecting the departmental interests' [Tom White interview].

This comment about differing departmental interests within central government was also referred to by Webb and Wistow, who noted that it was the Home Office that was first driving an argument for a family service, albeit one which would be focused on families with children and would, therefore, stay within the Home Office's remit:

The Home Office began to run with its proposals for change almost before the Ministry of Health had realised that play had begun: a draft white paper was ready for discussion early in 1965. Nevertheless, the possibility of quick reform which would produce a family service was soon halted. Whether inter-departmental rivalries or external pressures for a wider policy review were the more important is not clear. However, this does appear to be one of those occasions when an external group of outsiders—mainly academics and professional social workers active or sympathetic to the Labour Party—was a key factor. The case put by the group hinged around two points: that the future development of the welfare services ought to be considered in conjunction with that of the child-care services and that any proposals for reform ought at least to consider the possibility of bringing the scattered subsections of the social work profession together. The first was politically astute, the creation of a Family Service could have drained away reforming zeal and left the lower priority welfare services with little hope of making up ground. The second was professionally astute and it was no accident that the majority of the experts in the group were closely involved in the newly created National Institute for Social Work. [39]

There is more below on the influence of 'outsiders' and of NISWT, but what is described by Webb and Wistow as a pausing of the process, which was being driven by the Home Office to promote a more limited child-focused family service, was of significance. If it had progressed it would have led to an enhanced children's and families' service, not the cradle-to-grave social services which were to be created through the recommendations of the Seebohm Committee.

But as White also noted the recommendations and outcome of the Seebohm Committee were not a foregone conclusion at the time it was established:

> No, I don't think so at all. Some people may have had a very clear idea but I doubt if anyone thought it exactly as it came out. I think there was a genuine convincing of each other as they went along, which doesn't always happen in such committees. [Tom White interview]

Tom White's comment echoes the view of Joan Cooper:

> When it came to power in October 1964 the Labour Party was already committed to an embryonic family policy as a minor item on its political agenda, but it did not have a social services policy. [28]

The Impact and Importance of Richard Titmuss

But even before the Seebohm Committee was established and starting to meet there was a re-setting and re-shaping of the focus of discussion and debate, and this itself set a direction of travel for the Committee. Two people were central to this re-setting of the focus—Richard Titmuss (LSE) and Robin Huw Jones (NISWT). They might be seen as the original parents of the future personal social services and local authority social services departments, although the term 'personal social services' was not as yet in use.

Roy Parker commented that:

> [Richard Titmuss] was the power behind the throne, absolutely no doubt about that, and I'm pretty sure that it was he who recommended me as a member of the Seebohm Committee. He was invited but decided he did not want to serve.[1] And his influence, together with Robin Huw Jones and one or two others, was very important in shaping [the focus for the committee]. And what Titmuss of course was trying to alert the world to was

---

[1] Maybe Titmuss decided not to become a member of the Seebohm Committee as he was unwell with cancer at this time.

the demographic explosion that was coming with the elderly, a generation that would carry with them disabilities of all kinds. [Roy Parker interview]

It was Titmuss who, in effect, expanded the debate and focus beyond a concern for children, and families with children, to encompass a much broader territory of all who might need help from social workers. It took the debate beyond an argument for a family service. In essence, Titmuss, in a speech given in April 1965 to a Royal Society of Health Conference, was setting out the ground for what were to become known as the personal social services:

It is fashionable at the present time to argue for Family Service Departments. As I understand it, the core of this new Department would be the Children's Department to which would be transferred other responsibilities at present carried in many areas by welfare departments. I must say, I am not happy about this proposal, and for the following reasons. In the first place it is too family-centred and child-centred ... We have to remember that a large number of needs arising in the community are not essentially 'family needs'; mentally ill migrants, elderly widows and widowers, the isolates and childless, unmarried mothers and other categories of people who, in an increasingly mobile society might well hesitate before turning to a 'Family Department' ... Secondly, I suggest that the conception of a Family Service Department is not broad enough. Important welfare responsibilities both residential and domiciliary might remain well outside the province of a Family Service Department ... Thirdly, I am doubtful whether a Family Service Department would effectively bring together within one administrative structure all social workers in the employ of a single local authority. [40]

As Cooper commented:

[Titmuss] made an alternative proposal: departments of social services should be created and organised around the services to be provided rather than around 'categories of clients or particular fragments of need'. [41]

A working group of nine people was formed to consider the case against a narrowly defined family service. Hall noted that the membership included six members or governors of the NISWT and with two of the working group members, Robin Huws Jones and Jerry Morris (professor of social medicine at the University of London), soon to become members of the Seebohm Committee.

This was all something of a game changer. No longer was the agenda to be set exclusively by a concern about families with children. The script now was about all—or almost all—who might receive a social work service. This fitted well with the focus of the NISWT on social work rather than any occupational group of social workers, such as child care officers. Hall noted that the group prepared a proposal for

> an enquiry into the integration of social work services at the local level, the reasons cited for such a proposal reading rather like parts of the Seebohm Report itself. The rationale included the ad hoc expansion of social work since 1948, the overlapping of services, the problem of pin-pointing responsibility for services, the wastage of resources, the difficulty in providing effective preventative services and of improving professional skills. [42]

It was therefore a concern for the integration of services and a concern for the evolving social work profession which came together to expand the focus beyond the concept of a family service. But the actual brief given in 1965 to the Seebohm Committee by the Government still concentrated on a family service. As noted in paragraph 1 of the Seebohm Report:

> We were appointed on 20th December, 1965 'to review the organisation of the local authority personal social services in England and Wales, and to consider what changes are desirable to secure an effective family service'. [43]

A moment's reflection on this brief for the Committee would be timely at this point. First, the phrase 'personal social services' is now introduced. It is not about social welfare services, nor about social work services. A new term has been given currency. Secondly, the scope is to be 'local authority personal social services'. This would seem to exclude, for example, social work services provided in hospitals by the National Health

Service (NHS) and probation services directly accountable to the Home Office. And thirdly, it is about securing a 'family service', and as noted above this had previously been narrowly defined as being about families with children.

But the door was soon opened to the Committee taking a wider brief and Titmuss and Huw Jones were recalled as being influential in generating this wider brief:

> Remember that when the Seebohm Committee was set up it was called the *family* services committee and the emphasis in that sense would have been more on children. Various people, I think Titmuss perhaps, Robin Huw Jones and one or two others—I quite liked Robin, but he was a real wheeler-dealer, you know, he was a fixer of things, a little word here and little word there, and the title got changed to the 'Personal Social Services'. This was quite significant because that brought in a wider review than I think was at first intended, because it then covered the elderly, disabled, mental illness and a whole range of things like that. [Roy Parker interview]

Keith Bilton also noted the part played by Titmuss and Huw Jones in widening the scope of the Committee's considerations and that 'Huw Jones was a very wily and influential man, if not as well known as Titmuss' [Keith Bilton interview].

The widening of the scope of the Committee was noted in paragraphs two and three of its final report where it recommended the setting up within councils of 'a new local authority department, providing a community based and family service, which will *be available to all*' [paragraph 3; italics added] and that 'the new department will have *responsibilities going beyond those of existing local authority departments*' [paragraph three; again italics added].

The Membership of the Seebohm Committee

So the Committee came to give itself a wider scope than initially described in its terms of reference. But who were the members of this committee and how were they chosen? Essentially, it was about trying to cover a range of vested organisational and professional interests so that the committee had a credibility and legitimacy that spanned the wide territory of local government and of the social work profession:

> The formula was for membership to reflect local government, academia, medicine, the voluntary sector, social work training and penal interests. The main contenders in government, the Home Office and the DHSS [Department of Health and Social Security], looked for a balance of interests to be reflected in the membership. The secretary, a civil servant, was drawn from the Ministry of Housing and Local Government to provide neutrality since that department customarily managed central and local government relationships and was not a contender in the issue of allocation of responsibility among government departments. The committee membership counterbalanced the powerful political influence of Lord Longford, Alice Bacon and the Home Office in that it over-represented health and welfare interest, and this exacerbated professional rivalries within the various separated services. [44]

The view of Joan Cooper that health and welfare (as compared presumably to children's) interests were over represented was not shared by Hall:

> The committee was composed of a group whose views and allegiances were fairly well known to those conversant with the key academics and practitioners within the social services. Their backgrounds and any published work available at the time suggest that two members could be associated with the interests of local government, two with those of the Home Office and children's services, two less closely identified with the Home Office, two having close links with the Ministry of Health and one with more tenuous links but still broadly concerned with health and welfare services. In terms of probable departmental affiliations, therefore, the committee was fairly balanced. [45]

Hall goes on to note that the membership of the committee was criticised because of 'the lack of field-level workers and representatives of social work organisations'. Hall comments that this may have been because the committee membership 'comprised those not actively opposed by any one ministry which may explain why a number of prominent names from the social services field were omitted'. Hall also noted that the medical lobby 'perhaps not without justification, pointed to the imbalance of medical and social work representation'.

Two reflections on Hall's comments. Firstly, in the 1960s, it would have been exceptional and unexpected to have the users of services engaged formally in discussing and shaping services. For example, the first research in the UK on users' experiences and perceptions of social work was not published until 1970—'The Client Speaks' by Mayer and Timms [46] was seen as a ground-breaking and novel study for directly capturing and quoting the views of users. Secondly, the assumption that when considering the personal social services there should be a balance of medical and social work interests highlights the dominance and pre-eminence of the medical professionals at the time, including medical officers of health in local councils.

If there was an imbalance within the membership of the committee, it was about the weighting of its membership who had affinities and allegiances with the NISWT. As John Rea Price, who was then a probation officer but who later was a director of social services, commented, 'I think [the Seebohm Committee was very much propelled from within the NISWT' [John Rea Price interview]. The Committee included Sir Frederick Seebohm as the chair of committee was also chair of NISWT; Huws Jones the director of NISWT; the husband—the vice chancellor of York University—of Lady James of Rusholme was president of NISWT; and a then young soon-to-be NISWT lecturer, Peter Leonard, was also a member of the Seebohm Committee.

Another possible bias, or at least influence, with the committee was Richard Titmuss, including the medical member of the committee, Dr Jerry Morris, being Richard Titmuss' general medical practitioner (GP). And how did Roy Parker, a young LSE lecturer and researcher, come to be a committee member? He commented that:

> I don't know. It was one of those little mysteries. I mean, I think, Titmuss said 'Why don't you try Roy Parker?'. And Robin Huws Jones probably suggested Peter Leonard who was then on his staff, so there was a coterie to begin with and the coterie I think was Huws Jones, Jerry Morris, Titmuss

[who was not actually a Committee member] and probably Seebohm himself, who was very interested in these issues. [Roy Parker interview]

Such is the means and process through which major policy is made:
people, networks, contacts and relationships as much as ideas, argument
and evidence. Indeed the hard evidence was limited when considering the
way forward:

And of course remember in 1965 we didn't have much information. I
mean that little appendix that Michael Power and Jean Packman wrote at
the end [of the Seebohm Report] on children. I mean nowadays you
wouldn't think of anything of that, but that was the first thing of its kind
to get some ideas about numbers. [Roy Parker interview; see also
Packman] [47]

Evidence to the Seebohm Committee

But the Seebohm Committee did invite and receive evidence and some of
it was informed by research:

One of the things I showed in my evidence—I was one of the two people
which Seebohm got to do some research for them—was that the authorities which had a separate chief welfare officer responsible directly to the
council spent much more and performed better [than those where the welfare department was within the range of responsibilities of the medical
officer of health]. [Bleddyn Davies interview]

Most of the evidence considered by the Committee was not, however,
based on research but on the submissions and statements from organisations and interested parties, including those representing different sectors
within local government, other public services (including the probation
service and NHS interests) and the various professional associations of
social workers.

The submissions from the various parties, not surprisingly, reflected their own concerns, but some moved beyond existing vested interests to argue for change (which might also be seen to be generated by seeing future opportunities to promote or enhance particular interests). For example, John Rea Price, a former probation officer and, at the time, a relatively new child care officer who was later to be the director of social services in Islington, commented that:

> Seebohm was very much in the wind, and so we decided—me and three or four other people—to set up a committee which would prepare evidence for the Seebohm Committee based on how we saw the services in Islington being organised within a restructured [organisation]. And apparently this was unique. We were the only group of grassroots workers who prepared and organised that material. [John Rea Price interview]

Roy Parker recalls that professional associations of social workers were varied in the evidence they submitted, possibly reflecting differing views of their professional interests, and the evidence from the Association of Child Care Officers was seen, even now by one of its authors at the time, as 'remarkably self-centred':

> It was saying 'Yes, we would like something along the lines of the Social Services Department with all these services for adults and mentally ill people and so on and so forth as well, but we want it done in a phased way with the children's department at the middle, gradually sort of taking other people in bit by bit. And it wasn't until the Seebohm Report came out that one saw what it was … you know, it's the muck or the nettle, you've got the report, you're either for it or against it by then really. [Keith Bilton interview]

But the Seebohm Committee was not a passive receiver of information and evidence. For a start, the committee actively sought information for itself, as noted above by Bleddyn Davies, and as Keith Bilton noted it was active in starting to structure the thinking of others:

> I think in a way one of the things the Seebohm Committee did was actively shape the debate themselves and tried to gently lead the people who gave

evidence to them into the kind of evidence they wanted to receive really. [Keith Bilton]

The Seebohm Committee and Probation Officers

Some, however, were not up for shaping. In particular, probation officers, as one occupational group of social workers in England and Wales, fought hard to ensure that they were not merged into any sort of 'family service'. In Scotland probation was to become integrated into what were to be local authority 'social work departments'. In England and Wales the probation service was to remain as a service with local committees accountable to the Home Office. This was much later to leave it vulnerable, with probation officers in England and Wales to become a part of a National Offender Management Service (NOMS) with their training and identity being distanced from social work. In 2013, much of what had been the probation service was taken out of the public sector and privatised [48].

The tension and dilemma for probation officers at the time of the Seebohm Committee was captured by Joan Cooper:

> The probation opposition [to the potential integration into a family social service] was powerful but by no means unanimous. There was conflict between a reluctance to dilute their special role and legal status as officers of the court, and some nervousness about the influx of graduate social workers, but there was the wider aspect of client need and for social work as an emerging profession. A group of Scottish probation officers saw that by isolating themselves in the Scottish scene they would isolate their clients too, but this group was not in an easy position. [49]

As noted below in two quotes from probation officers who would become directors of social services and later chief social services inspectors in the Department of Health, probation officers in England and Wales argued that their role would not be appropriately merged into a family service:

I had been a probation officer for a number of years and then I was a senior probation officer, and then I was the number two in the Probation Service ... the Home Office persuaded me to do additional training ... and I did mental health training at the LSE and qualified as a psychiatric social worker ... I felt myself to be very much a social worker; I mean I was in the Probation Service but social work was my values and what I thought about. So when Seebohm came along I was very interested in it from a personal point of view, but the Probation Service was not remotely interested in it because they thought this is all about local authority services. Just towards the end [of the Seebohm committee's deliberations] the Probation Service got extremely upset and worried because they thought that Seebohm might swoop the Probation Service into the new social services departments. And so my boss sent me off (a) because I was a qualified psychiatric social worker and (b) I'd worked in other units and had very close relationships with the local children's department and the welfare department. He sent me off to meet members of the committee. I think they had already finished taking their formal evidence so it wasn't a question of giving evidence, it was I just met informally members of the committee to talk about keeping Probation out of it. My boss and I certainly felt there was a strong argument that the biggest impact we should have should be on the courts and sentencing, and on the prison service ... if we went into social care we wouldn't be able to do that. [Herbert Laming interview]

In the mid-1960s the probation service had taken on the responsibility for all aftercare of prisoners and by the end of the decade the majority of clients of the probation service were in fact adults, so it was getting pretty heavy into real crime as against what people regarded as youthful delinquency. I thought then that if there were going to be combinations, the logic would take it to join up with the prison department rather than the local authority. [Bill Utting interview]

This logic was followed through 40 years later when the probation service was merged with prison services in to a National Offender Management Service (NOMS) and the training and education of probation officers was distanced from social work. Probation officers came to concentrate on the supervision and management of offenders rather than what had been their long-standing role, even as far back to the pre-probation officer days of court missionaries, to 'advise, assist and befriend'.

In the 1990s Mr Blair as prime minister said that he wanted to be 'tough on crime, and tough on the causes of crime'. The refocusing of the probation service concentrated on the first more so than the second of Mr Blair's stated intentions.

But it was not only probation officers in the 1960s who wanted the probation service to remain separate and outside a possible family service. As Roy Parker said when interviewed, 'That was I think probably one of the Home Office's little victories' at the time it was losing its responsibility for children's services.

The first draft of the Home Office's Probation Division's evidence to the Seebohm Committee was written by Peter Westland, then a Home Office inspector of probation services:

> What I tried to do was to sort of have the essence of social work being relevant, whether you are talking about delinquency, mental illness, physical handicap and so on. I wrote a beautiful piece about the Children's Department in the Home Office and its objectives and it came back with lots of it crossed out with a note from some under-secretary saying 'The Probation Division of the Home Office does not comment on the work of any other division in the Home Office'. [Peter Westland interview]

So the civil service rivalries were not only between departments but also within departments. What was to be intriguing, however, was that although the argument was won that in England and Wales the probation service should remain separate from the new social services departments, many probation officers and probation service senior managers moved to join the social services departments. There was already some transfer from the probation service to local authority services, as noted in the Seebohm report:

> A high proportion of probation officers take professional training before entry [into the service]; of those, some have received training at universities on similar lines to that received by local authority social workers, and there is some movement between the probation and after-care services and the local authority services. In 1965, 43 probation officers, out of a total strength of 2319, entered the local authority services. The figure in 1966 was 25 out of 2557. [11]

But the advent of large social services departments within local government opened up a career and advancement opportunity for senior probation officers and their managers, who were mainly male but also professionally trained. Of those interviewed for this book, four who had been probation officers in the 1960s were to become directors of social services in the 1970s (Bill Utting; Peter Westland; John Rea Price; Herbert Laming).

The Seebohm Committee and the Medical and Health Professions

So probation officers and the Home Office were active and successful in arguing that the probation service should not be merged within the Seebohm-recommended local authority social services departments. But another interest group, the medical profession were late in recognising the direction and potential destination of travel of the Seebohm committee. The consequence was that local authority medical officers of health lost power and influence, and the NHS as a possible home for a new health and social care integrated (family) service was never given much attention, as was noted by Cooper and by Hall:

> The health view was neither coordinated nor precise and it had to represent interests outside local government as well as within it. The BMA [British Medical Association] argued for a unified health and welfare department which would include the children's department under the over-all control of medical officers of health … [But] the representatives of the medical and nursing professions did not present a unified front with clear-cut proposals … the health professionals were far more preoccupied with the proposed reorganisation of the NHS than with the arrangements for small local government departments. [50]

> In contrast to the evidence from social worker organisations, where a basic similarity in the proposals for reorganisation could be found, the medical and para-medical organisations wanted a variety of outcomes. The first was to argue that no structural change was necessary; increased co-ordination

could prevent the overlapping of services and fill existing gaps. The second was to propose reorganisation in various forms with the medical officer of health in overall command. This lack of unanimity undoubtedly lessened their chances of success. There was no solution open to the committee which could satisfy them all. Why was there no consultation between groups over possible strategies? It appears that at the stage of evidence presentation many of them did not regard the existence of the committee as any great threat to their preserves. [51]

Roy Parker noted that the medical professions 'thought if you're going to unify, it should all be unified under a much expanded medical officer of health kind of thing' [Roy Parker interview], but that the medical professions were focused elsewhere along with the Ministry of Health as there was also running at the same time as the Seebohm Committee a major review of the NHS:

There was this reform [of the NHS], the Green Papers and so forth on the reform of the National Health Service and the structures that were being envisaged didn't really see a place for this [a unified health and social services], and if you take on all this stuff, its expenditure implications are considerable. 'We've got enough on our plate in the NHS' was I think the thinking at the top at a political level. [Roy Parker interview]

The attention of the medical professions being elsewhere and not on the Seebohm committee was also commented upon by Tom White:

I don't think [the medical lobby] realised the significance [of the Seebohm Committee] at all. They came very, very late into the business. I don't think [the changes] would have happened if the medical professions had woken up much earlier to what was likely to be proposed. The medical officers of health, only at a really late stage did they put any effort into it ... I don't think they saw it as really being of great significance. There were more important debates going on in terms of the NHS and the argument about where public health should be more generally, and I think they took their eye off the ball. [Tom White interview]

There was, however, one member of the Seebohm Committee who was a medical doctor. Bleddyn Davies, when interviewed, described him as 'the dog who failed to bark', but Tom White's recollection was that:

He was genuinely open to listen to arguments, and I think he became convinced that what was proposed made sense. He had a hell of a tough time [from other medical professionals] when the report was published. [Tom White interview]

But such was the assumption within parts of the NHS that health services changes would lead to an integration of, at least, local authority welfare services into an expanded NHS that some in the health service moved into local authorities to get experience of welfare services before they were—as they assumed—transferred to the NHS:

I actually moved in 1967 into the old welfare department in a health and welfare department, and the reason I did that was that I was a health services manager, and I thought that the health services changes would subsume community health services, and possibly community welfare services, into the old NHS hospital structures. I wanted to position myself so I knew something about it and would move back [into the NHS] better equipped to deal with the new world. [Anne Parker interview]

In such ways are illustrious and influential careers made! In 1971, Anne Parker became an assistant director in Berkshire's new social services department, later became its director, was in the early 1990s honorary secretary of the Association of Directors of Social Services, and was later chair of National Care Standards Commission. And she launched on this career route because she inaccurately predicted that council welfare services would be transferred in the late 1960s to the NHS.

So, medical officers of health (MOHs) and NHS managers and other health professionals missed the opportunity to argue early enough that the Seebohm Committee should recommend the integration of health and social services within the NHS or, less radically, that MOHs should head up an integrated public and community health and social services department within local authorities.

Probation officers and the probation service, on the other hand, had largely successfully argued that probation should remain a separate service, serving the courts, and outside of the local government. They were, however, only 'largely' successful as the debates and white papers about young offenders throughout the 1960s culminated in the 1969 Children and Young Persons Act which transferred to local authorities from the Home Office and the probation service responsibility for children aged under 14 years who had committed offences. The Act was to make the supervision of these children the responsibility of local authority social services departments and social workers.

And children and young people up to the age of 18 years were to be placed in the care of local authorities if it was considered by the courts that they should live away from their parents, including those young people who would previously been resident in Home Office registered 'approved schools' which were now to be redesignated as 'care homes with education' (CHEs). The managers of the approved schools were no more accepting than probation officers of being encapsulated in the new post-Seebohm social services departments. Joan Cooper commented:

> I was deeply involved in the Children and Young Persons Act (1969) and if I was to try to defend myself I would say that my energies went into legislation to do something about the approved schools. Approved schools disliked it, abused it, they were antagonistic. I had to spend a lot of time meeting their association's committee. But they clung to their traditions and the military model because it was what they knew. [52]

So after all the debates and deliberations what did the Seebohm Committee report and recommend? The next chapter gives information about what might be called the anatomy of the report, its anatomical structure, before moving on to its physiology—its philosophy and how it saw the new social services working.

3

Scripting the Future: The Seebohm Report

The Seebohm Report was published in July 1968. The front page noted that it was 'Presented to Parliament by the Secretary of State for the Home Department, the Secretary of State for Education and Science, the Minister for Housing and Local Government, and the Minister for Health'. Here was what might be seen as a cross-cutting report of relevance to, and with implications for, several government departments. It was 370 pages long, had 206 'conclusions and recommendations', and was structured into six parts with 22 chapters. In addition, there were 20 appendices of background and statistical information considered by the committee and nine pages of an extensive index. It certainly justified its chairman's statement in his foreword to the report that:

> An accurate comparison of the work of the Committee with others is clearly not possible. Nevertheless, I am assured that it has worked as hard and conscientiously as any and that the two and half years we have taken to submit our report compares favourably with most committees. [1]

© The Author(s) 2020, corrected publication 2021
R. Jones, *A History of the Personal Social Services in England*,
https://doi.org/10.1007/978-3-030-46123-2_3

Supporting Frederick Seebohm's statement that the committee had worked 'hard and conscientiously' is the information on page 21 of the report that the committee had met 74 times, and that 12 of these meetings had lasted for two days. There were visits to 17 local authorities, and committee members also met in subcommittees and working groups. Two hundred and nineteen bodies and individuals were invited by the committee to provide evidence, evidence was received from 160 organisations and 79 individuals, and the committee held discussions with 42 organisations and 54 individuals.

This is all a considerable amount of activity, with over a two-year period meetings held by the full committee on average every one and half weeks, plus all the other meetings and visits, alongside the preparation and consideration of background and briefing papers.

The Seebohm Report can be seen, 50 years on, as the missing chapter of the 1942 Beveridge Report. The Beveridge Report, with its concentration on the then contemporary 'five giants' of want, ignorance, idleness, sickness and squalor, never confronted the still to emerge and yet to be identified sixth 'giant' of neglect, abuse and the need for care.

At the time the Beveridge Report was written few people lived to an old age and people with long-term conditions often died young. Those who needed care were either cared for within their families by women who in the 1940s were still at home and not in paid employment or were placed in large institutions, such as the big 'mental asylums' or 'mental subnormality' hospitals. Children were looked after within their nuclear and extended families or where placed in children's homes or foster homes, with only a limited identification of issues of abuse of children within families (or within institutions).

By the 1960s, however, there was a concern about the poor quality and appropriateness of care in big, often isolated, institutions. There was also an increasing emerging awareness of the needs of a growing number of disabled and older people and of difficulties within families, all within the context of changes in demography, with an ageing and more mobile population and more women in paid employment. The Seebohm Report, therefore, as with the Beveridge Report, can be seen as a creature of its times addressing recently identified concerns and needs.

The Seebohm Report includes a rich account of the state and shape of the range of social work and welfare services in the mid-1960s, services which had grown incrementally and opportunistically since the 1940s, and with an analysis of their strengths and weaknesses. Although specifically tasked 'to review the organisation and responsibilities of the *local authority personal social services in England and Wales*, and what changes are desirable to secure an effective *family service*' (paragraph 1, emphasis added) the committee, as noted in the previous chapter, expanded its brief beyond what might have been the traditional concept of a family to cover all people who might use what it came to call the 'personal social services'. It also took into its purview services beyond those provided by local authorities and beyond parents and their children:

> We decided very early on in our discussions that it would be impossible to restrict our work solely to the needs of two or even three generation families. We could only make sense of our task by considering also childless couples and individuals without any close relatives: in other words, everybody. (Paragraph 32)

The Committee saw its starting point as the 'personal social services' within local authorities and to include the whole of the work of children's and of welfare departments and the social work elements in health, education and housing departments (paragraph 31).

However, although the Committee saw its starting point as the 'personal social services' within local authorities it recognised that in considering these services there were implications for other non-personal social services within local government such as schools and housing. It went further and decided that it had to give some attention and consideration to what might be seen as related services provided outside of local authorities by central government departments, such as the National Assistance Board [which dealt with cash income support payments], the probation and after-care service and voluntary organisations (paragraph 33).

Links with Health Services

Staying restricted to a focus on local authority personal social services was clearly a struggle for the Committee as 'it soon became clear that any substantial changes which might be proposed for the local authority services were bound to affect these and other local services, including in particular the general practitioner services, the hospitals and their medical social workers' (paragraph 34).

The recommendations for other services included that 'we are in no doubt that the organisation and the responsibilities of social work departments in hospitals should be reviewed urgently in the light of our proposals'. Hospital and medical social work services subsequently transferred in 1974 to local authorities and their social services departments.

Joan Baraclough had been a medical social worker and in the early 1970s was an assistant general secretary of the British Association of Social Workers (BASW). She recalled:

> The debate was all around whether local authorities would agree to have medical social workers still based in hospitals ... [BASW] sent the message to the Department [of Health and Social Security] that they 'must' stay [in hospitals] and the Department changed it to 'may'. [Joan Baraclough interview]

She noted that 'it was a really fraught time and BASW lost a lot of members over this'.

With regard to primary health care and general medical practice, however, the 1968 Seebohm Report made recommendations which might just as readily and relevantly be made in the 2020s:

> Social service departments and local general practitioners should make a determined effort to co-operate with one another ... A variety of experiments in joint working between general practitioners and social workers should now be started, on central initiative if necessary... As soon as doctors in a health centre or sizable group practice feel they want a social worker of the social service department to be attached to them to become

also a member of their team, the department should do all it can to meet the request. (p. 217)

But the Seebohm Report was pretty scathing about cooperation and collaboration within health services as much as between health and social services, and it tracked these difficulties back to the complexity of arrangements within the NHS introduced in the 1940s:

> To do its work the social service department must be able to co-operate with an effective department of community medicine. All the local medical services, the district general hospital and executive council [which oversaw GP services] as well as the local health authority, together with the social services are mutually concerned in providing care and treatment for handicapped children, for the chronic sick, the mentally disordered, the infirm aged, families that are failing; in questions of hospital stay and discharge, of treatment in institutions or at home ... However, services are not structured to require or promote this. (Paragraph 383)

The NHS has not been short of inquiries, reviews and organisational change and churn over the past 50 years which, in themselves, have undermined health and social care integration, cooperation and partnership working. The Seebohm Committee in 1968 saw the review of the NHS which was then underway as a possible solution to the fragmentation within the NHS as well as for the difficulties of working well across the NHS-social services boundary. Possibly one of the lessons of the past 50 years is that there may be no perfect solution and that what might be more constructive is to allow organisational stability so that relationships, trust, joint agendas and commitments can be built locally which will span the divides within the NHS and with social services. Structural and organisational change often, in effect, destroys foundations and infrastructures being built between organisations.

In 1968, the Committee was arguing that amidst the tripartite NHS arrangement of GPs, hospitals and community health services, it was community health services which were often the Cinderella service. This particularly impacted on marginalised groups who were given little priority, and it was argued that this was more likely to be addressed and rectified if responsibility for them was passed to the new social service departments. The concern about these Cinderella services for mental health, learning disability, and older people with clusters of long-term conditions, still continues in the 2020s. But there is little doubt that the move away from the disempowering symptom-focused medical model and from long-term confinement in big institutions has positively changed the life experiences of many.

Should There Be Major Organisational Change?

It was the issue of boundaries between organisations and services, an issue which will always exist as it will never be possible in terms of size and span to include all responsibilities and resources within one organisation, which inevitably taxed the Committee. It was resolved in part, as noted by Cooper, by the Committee taking a view about the 'social component' within the work of other services and agencies:

> While the over-all picture gave some prominence to the 'allied' [the Seebohm Committee's full title was 'The Committee on Local Authority and Allied Personal Social Services'] as well as to the local authority services, these wider ramifications never became of significant political or legislative concern. If there was a dream of a monopoly of 'public welfare' in the hands of local government, it was not to be realised. If the aim was to expose the chaos of a number of parallel systems it was undoubtedly achieved, but it was the exercise of boundary setting that was the crucial test of the Committee's strategy. In a case-by-case determination, it was the extent of the social component in a service which tipped the balance in favour of inclusion or exclusion as a personal social service. [2]

Within the Seebohm Report there is discussion of the arguments against any major organisational change in the arrangements for the personal social services. It is noted that reorganisation is disruptive and that there was the risk that service users may have breaks and changes in the care they were receiving. There was also the argument that the contemporaneous Royal Commission on Local Government in England might lead to larger local authorities and that this would address the limitations of too small local government departments which would increase in size in larger councils. It was also suggested that the difficulties within and across local government personal social services were not created by structural divisions but by difficult people with personalities which generated conflict, and that this would not be remedied by reorganisation. Finally, it was noted that to date changes in the arrangements for the personal social services had largely been evolutionary, gradually responding to changing and newly emerging needs, and that this should continue rather than resort to what was described as 'theoretical revolution', and that better publicity about and access to existing services would suffice in terms of the improvement immediately required.

All of these arguments, whilst noting that they had some value, were dismissed by the Committee. The conclusion was that there were significant difficulties with the existing structural and organisational arrangements for the personal services, which they noted to be inadequacies in the amount and quality of provision, poor coordination, difficult access and insufficient adaptability. These difficulties were understood to be the result of a lack of resources, an inadequate knowledge base, and divided responsibility across often competing council departments. The Committee's conclusion was that 'substantial improvements can be made to the local authority personal social services, and that organisational change and changes in the distribution of responsibilities will be important means to this end' (paragraph 110).

The Aims of the Seebohm Committee

The Committee then listed what it saw as a 'strong case for reorganisation so that services may meet needs on the basis of the overall requirements of the individual or family rather than on the basis of a limited set of symptoms' (paragraph 37). It also concluded that reorganisation gave the opportunity to provide a clear and comprehensive pattern of responsibility and accountability over the whole field, attract more resources, use those resources more effectively, and generate adequate recruitment and training of workers. It argued that the reorganised services would be more able to meet needs which were being neglected, adapt to changing conditions, and be more accessible and comprehensible to those who need to use the services, as well as helping the collection of information to inform the development of services.

So what was it, reflecting on the list above, that the Seebohm Committee was seeking to achieve?

Firstly, it wanted to reduce the complexity, fragmentation, duplication and rigidity within the then current arrangements of several local government departments providing personal social services and employing social workers. One family could be visited by several workers who were separately managed, deployed and located, and yet still some people went without help and their needs were unrecognised.

Secondly, it wanted to create a more powerful and influential base within local authorities for the personal social services so that a stronger and successful argument could be made to increase resources and to entice more workers into the personal social services.

Thirdly, it wanted to improve economy, efficiency and effectiveness (although terms such as the 'three Es' and 'value for money' would only come to gain currency two to three decades later) and that this would be assisted by a better trained workforce and by building an information (what might now be termed a knowledge) base.

Organisational Options

This was all to be achieved through a reorganisation of the personal social services. But what form was this to take and how radical would it be? There was the option of leaving current organisational structures in place but improving coordination between departments and services. This did happen throughout the 1970s and beyond for NHS health and local government personal social services. Joint consultative committees, joint planning teams, joint plans and joint finance were all created as mechanisms to get health and social care to be more coordinated locally and to work better together [3]. The Seebohm Committee did not see this, however, as an adequate or good enough solution for the fragmentation across local government personal social services.

The Committee gave consideration to creating two social services departments—one for services for adults and one for children and families with children. The Committee argued that this was not a viable or desirable way forward because:

> First, it would inevitably split responsibility for the social care of individuals or families between the departments, interrupt the continuity of care, and perpetuate a symptom-centred approach. Second, as a corollary, it would be difficult to treat the needs of an individual or family as a whole ... In addition, such a reorganisation would offer little or no additional attraction to recruits to the service from any of the professions, and no advantage over the existing situation in attracting additional resources. There would be no simplification of the present structure in terms of departmental organisation. (Paragraph 125)

This argument largely held good until the 1989 Children Act and the 1990 NHS and Community Care Act introduced increasing complex and centrally defined separate requirements for children services and adult services which led to social services departments fragmenting internally into separate divisions for children and for adults, and the 2004 Children Act generated an unwinding of the integrated local authority personal social services and the creation of separate children's and adults' services. In 1968, however, integration and genericism were seen as the solution to existing complexity and fragmentation.

An imaginative possibility, beyond changing departmental structures and responsibilities, considered by the Committee would have involved creating a 'social casework department acting on an agency basis for other departments'. All the social workers would be brought together with their own professional manager and would provide a service to the children's, health and welfare departments which would still manage children's homes, care homes for adults, and day centres. This radical option was rejected because, it was argued, the 'social casework department would not have enough control of the residential and other services to enable it to do its work. The relationships between departments would still be confusing to the public and to other agencies. The boundaries of the department would be uncertain because social work does not consist only of casework' (paragraph 131).

There was one further and final model considered by the Committee ... remove personal social services responsibilities from local authorities and transfer them to central government. It was a model rejected by the Seebohm Committee which saw 'a high level of citizen participation as vital to the successful development of services which are sensitive to local needs, and we do not see, at present, this participation can be achieved outside the local government system' (paragraph 137).

So what did the Seebohm Committee propose? As Cooper noted, 'only an integrated department maximised opportunity and overcame duplication' [4]. The Committee proposed a social service department[1] within each local authority with personal social services responsibilities. It was a solution which was to have a life span of over 30 years—from 1970 until 2004—and through the terms of office of six prime ministers. The Committee noted:

> The basis of the department, in our view, should in most parts of the country be teams of upwards of a dozen social workers, each team serving populations of between 50,000 and 100,000, and with the maximum amount of responsibility delegated to them from the headquarters of the social service department. For the time being, the social service department should be run by a separate committee of the local authority, with a separate principal officer reporting directly to the council. We envisage that in the course of time most of the principal officers at the heads of the new departments would be professionally qualified social workers with training in management and administration or administrators with qualifications in social work. We emphasise the importance of close links between the social ser-

---

[1] The reference throughout the Seebohm Report is to a social service department, not a social services department, although the plural is always used for the personal social services. Why? It may have been because a major thrust of the Committee's argument and intention was to emphasise unification and integration across the personal social services and possibly this was seen to be signalled and exemplified by describing a single social service department. The 1970 Local Authority Personal Social and Allied Services Act which implemented the Seebohm Committee's recommendations, however, referred to social services and not social service, so the new departments became social services departments.

vice department and other departments, notably health, education and housing departments. (Paragraph 19)

This one, relatively short, statement is rich in detail and assumptions. Firstly, it promotes the primacy of social work within the personal social services. In the 1960s, social work and social workers were definitely seen as a part of the solution to tackling social problems. Secondly, although it recognises the need for administrative and management competence in leading the new social service departments it again emphasises that the leadership needs itself to be rooted in social work. Thirdly, it sees teams and team work as the foundation of social service delivery, a tradition and expectation which has continued within social work and the personal social services. Fourthly, it sees localisation and delegation to teams working close to communities as a central concept for the proposed social service departments. And, finally, it reinforces that social service departments are to be embedded within local government and democratic accountability, and with the senior manager of the social service department accountable to the full council, albeit with a separate social service committee dealing with specific social service issues. None of this was inevitable. But it did have a coherence which created an organisational and governance arrangement which was to be long standing.

In its making of the argument for an integrated and unified social service department within each local authority with personal social services responsibilities the Seebohm Committee focused on how this would assist in tackling social need and social problems:

There is a realisation that it is essential to look beyond the immediate symptoms of social distress to the underlying problems. These frequently prove to be complicated and the outcome of a variety of influences. In many cases people who need help cannot be treated effectively unless this is recognised. Their difficulties do not arise in a social vacuum; they are, have been, or need to be involved in a network of relationships, in social situations. The family and community are seen as the context in which problems arise and in which most of them have to be resolved or contained. Similarly, residential establishments are no longer asylums, separated and insulated from the outside world. They are increasingly expected to maintain contacts with the families of those for whom they care and the communities in which they are located. (Paragraph 141)

Community and Community Work

So what was being proposed went beyond a 'family social service' to a family and community social service, with one of the tasks of the proposed social service departments to engage in and lead on community development. There was a separate chapter in the report on 'the community' which stated that:

> At many points in this Report we have stressed that we see our proposals not simply in terms of organisation but as embodying a wider conception of social service, directed to the well-being of the whole community and not only of social casualties, and seeing the community it serves as the basis of its authority, resources and effectiveness. Such a conception spells, we hope, the death knell of the Poor Law legacy and the socially divisive attitudes and practices which stemmed from it. (Paragraph 474)

The conception of 'community' and community development in the Seebohm Report, with community seen as a resource to assist those in difficulty, was not as radical, however, as the 'community development projects' (CDPs) introduced in the late 1960s in several areas of high social deprivation. These projects had a concept not only of 'community development' but much more of 'community action', empowering rather than only engaging communities, and about leadership, power and control being embedded within communities.

John Rea Price, a probation officer who was to become one of the early directors of social services, noted:

> Derek [Morrell, the senior civil servant in the Home Office who both led on the CDP policy development, and who also was the driver and champion for the 1969 Children and Young Persons Act which saw 'bad' children involved in delinquency as the same as 'sad' children who had been abused and neglected] was wanting a more radical concept of community than the Seebohm Committee. [John Rea Price interview]

But whether it was 'community development' or 'community action' the focus on communities as well as individuals and families was an extension of interest of the Seebohm Committee which was of its time. As Herbert Laming commented:

> As time has gone by, social care in my view has become the most important function of a local authority, it's a key element to the well-being not just of individuals and families, but of the community as a whole. So I think that Seebohm was actually a remarkable document. Unlike for example earlier committees of enquiries and individual cases which had an impact on legislation, I think Seebohm was one where it looked at the big agenda, and so I have great regard for the Seebohm Report. [Herbert Laming interview]

But what Cooper calls 'the community dimension' in the Seebohm Report was not widely anticipated:

> The surprise element in the Committee's humane but mainly bureaucratic perception of personal social services was their responsiveness to the resurgence of 'community' as an undervalued network in society. The notion of community, the ideology of the time, represented an underlying philosophy that the Committee hoped would inform the future service pattern. It was a notion that grew in dimension as the thinking developed, and it seemed that the community could supply human and social support as an extra resource. In one sense, community-derived authority was both anti-professional and anti-bureaucratic. In another, it was the source of extra resources that would be needed. [5]

But 'community' as an issue was a potential cause of controversy and of conflict. Controversy because, as Cooper noted, 'whether or not community work was a part of or distinct from social work continued to remain a controversial question throughout the next decade' [6], and within higher education institutions there were social work courses having modules on community work but also completely separate community work courses and qualifications. And there was conflict because, as Cooper who was in the Home Office at the time noted, 'the Home Office children's department wanted ... any subsequent legislation to deal with delinquency [to be] not only through the judicial system but in the context of preventive work, and with community development as the means of promoting social growth and reducing antisocial behaviour' [7]. So was 'community development' to be within the remit of the new local authority social services departments (with the Department of Health and Social Security as the relevant central government policy department) or to be a central government Home Office responsibility? It became both. Social services departments in the 1970s employed community development officers. Separately, the Home Office moved ahead with its programme of CDPs. Neither survived into the 1980s.

Research and Training

Within the Seebohm Report there was an explicit focus on research. The Committee stated that they saw the personal social services as 'large-scale experiments in ways of helping those in need' and that 'it is both wasteful and irresponsible to set experiments in motion and omit to record and analyse what happens' [8]. The research agendas referred to in the report related to 'basic descriptive data about the personal social services and the communities they serve' and 'evaluation and analysis' which would 'establish the usefulness of different methods of treating people in obvious need and the effects upon different individuals, families and communities of different forms of care' [9].

The influence on and within the Committee of the London School of Economics and Political Sciences, and of the National Institute for Social Work Training, might be seen to have been influential in giving such a profile to research within the Committee's report. The same is probably true for the separate chapter on 'Training' and when social services departments were formed in the early 1970s they often had both research and training sections within their overall structure and capacity. This was only to become much less prevalent when local government reform in the late 1990s led to smaller local authorities which were unable to retain what was often seen as the additional and unaffordable overhead cost of separate research and training sections.

The Committee stressed the importance of training for social workers:

If the country is to have effective personal social services, those who staff these services must have the knowledge, attitudes and skill which will enable them to respond appropriately and sensitively to people in need … In close co-operation with other services, the staff will have to develop new ways of meeting individual, family and community needs through a comprehensive social service department; they will need constantly to draw upon the results of relevant work in the behavioural sciences and they must be trained to assess the effectiveness of different ways of meeting needs (paragraph 528) … [and that] The responsibilities of the social service department point to the need for professionally trained social workers to receive additional training during their careers. (Paragraph 548)

The Seebohm Committee noted that there were, in 1968, three national councils for training in social work—the Central Training Council in Child Care, the Council for Training in Social Work and the Advisory Council for Probation and After-Care. It also noted that in addition to university and college of further education courses in social work, courses were also provided by bodies such as Institute of Medical Social Workers. It seems from the Committee's report that this was all something of a minefield where it was risking treading too far. The consequence was that the report is less decisive or radical in recommending a simplification and unification of the training and education basic qualifying courses for social workers, although it did firmly recommend that 'a single new central advisory council on the personal social services should be established which would have a standing committee on training' (paragraph 533).

What actually happened post-Seebohm was that one unified body for social work education and training was established, the Central Council for Education and Training in Social Work (CCETSW) with the Certificate of Qualification in Social Work (CQSW) as the one basic qualification for professional social workers in the UK and, separately, a Personal Social Services Council (PSSC) was created in 1973 (it ended in 1980) to advise central and local government and the voluntary sector on the development of the personal social services.

The Seebohm Committee also gave attention to other workers who would be within the new social service departments, including home help organisers, social work aides and, especially, residential workers, and that they should have access to education and training programmes with a national qualification. This was to come to fruition with the introduction of the Certificate in Social Services (CSS) which in 1988 was merged with the CQSW into the Diploma in Social Work .

Prevention

Within the Seebohm Report particular attention is given to 'prevention' as 'an effective family service must be concerned with the prevention of social distress. Morally, socially and economically this makes sense. In principle, by taking timely and appropriate measures much human suffering and family breakdown can be avoided' (paragraph 427).

Prevention of 'social distress' was seen as being dependent on knowledge of what action is really preventive (and the Report noted this is not always clear), the ability to identify early those people who are at particular risk of increasing social distress, and how much agencies and workers are able to do preventative work beyond what the Report calls 'the care and "casualty" service which at present absorbs most of their resources' (paragraph 430).

Housing

The Seebohm Report also had a separate chapter on housing, may be because it was a local authority responsibility. The attention paid to housing issues may also have been because one of the members of the Seebohm Committee, Roy Parker, had a particular (academic and research) interest in housing issues. He along with Peter Leonard (the other young academic social worker on the Committee) were each given the substantial responsibility to draft separate sections of the report. Indeed, as noted by Cooper:

> [The] wide-ranging task for members [of the Committee] whose voluntary service had to be fitted into their normal work commitments was exacting

and possibly overambitious. It was aided by the work of one member, Roy Parker, who used a year's sabbatical leave from the London School of Economics to ensure that the report contained the detail to support its case. [10]

The importance and power of the minute taker and report writer often seems to be ignored today. It was probably influential then. It still is.

Housing, housing policy and housing regeneration were generally gaining political and public and political attention in the 1960s. There was research on slum clearance, urban renewal and the impact on social life and communities of housing policy [11, 12, 13] and on housing policy and race [14]. However, as noted by Hall, the Seebohm Committee decided that although related to social needs 'The full range of housing responsibilities was to remain with [separate housing departments within councils] but the provision of recuperative units and social services for homeless families should be provided by the latter' [15].

Medical and Psychiatric Social Work

There were other services 'allied' to local authority personal social services which the Committee considered, including medical social work and psychiatric social work, both within the remit of NHS and hospitals:

> Some organisations and individuals have taken the view that it is vital that hospitals (including psychiatric hospitals) should retain and even extend their own social work departments … [But] it is said that the present pattern fails to provide continuity of care, and it is not well placed to help with repercussions of illness on the family or to contribute fully to the community care of patients … It would not be proper for us to offer specific recommendations on this subject but we are in no doubt that the organisation and the responsibility of social work departments in hospitals should be reviewed urgently in the light of our proposals for a unified social service department. (Paragraphs 688 and 689)

There can be little doubt what was wanted by the Seebohm Committee. A 'unified social services department' would not be unified if key elements of social work within the overall personal social services remained elsewhere. However, at the same time as the Seebohm Committee was doing its work, a separate review of the NHS was underway. It meant that the Seebohm Committee had to be careful for fear of treading into the territory that was already allocated to and occupied by others.

This was an issue for the Committee on several fronts. It was not operating in a stable vacuum. The NHS was subject to a separate central government review. So was local government. And even responsibilities and services which were not in the midst of major discrete reviews were also changing. This was true, for example, for income support social security responsibilities which were now within the remit of a relatively new Supplementary Benefits Commission introduced by the 1966 Social Security Act.

Social Security and Social Work

In the UK, there was and is a stronger separation between the assessment, administration and payment of income support cash benefits and social work services than in many other countries. The separation has its roots in the Liberal government introduction of separate national administration arrangements for pension and other welfare cash payments in the early twentieth century, arrangements which were distinct from the local Poor Law responsibilities. The welfare state reforms of the 1940s reinforced the responsibility of central government to administer a national social security scheme of cash benefits whereas social work and other personal social services responsibilities were assigned to local authorities.

What was the view of the Seebohm Committee, recognising that it could not be too deliberate or directive about a service which was outside of local government? The Committee commented that:

> It seems to us that a natural and helpful division of responsibility emerges between the [Supplementary Benefits] Commission and the new social service department. The Commission's functions in ascertaining need and

referring clients to the social service department should be helpful to both organisations and should we believe ensure the most effective help for the clients. We consider that the Commission's officers should refer cases to that department and should not undertake social work themselves. (Paragraph 685)

However, the interface between the Supplementary Benefits officers and local authority social work was seen as a continuing difficulty and dilemma, as noted by Hall:

> The major problem—a perennial one—was the desirability of attempting to retain the distinction between the provision of cash benefits and welfare services. When the SBC [Supplementary Benefits Commission] was formed in 1966, the introduction of a 'visiting service', which would represent a considerable extension of the rudimentary welfare functions of the old NAB [National Assistance Board], was seriously considered. The [Seebohm] committee looked with disfavour on this proposal, arguing that it cut across its attempts to unify social work and avoid divisions of responsibility … Partly as a result of this opposition, the suggestion for a visiting service was dropped but debates about the boundary between the SBC and the social services departments continued. [15]

How the relationship between social work and the Supplementary Benefits Commission was to be handled was, in part, a task allocated to Olive Stevenson. She was a reader in social work at Oxford University and was appointed from 1968 to 1970 as the social work advisor to the Commission:

> I was given a very clear assignment, which was to write at double quick speed papers on the problematic groups in the supplementary benefits eye. That was lone parents, the cohabitation rule, voluntary unemployed and so on. I had a series of these things to do. And it involved hurtling around the country and interviewing all sorts of people. [Olive Stevenson interview]

The Different Client Groups

In addition to considering how the proposed social service department should relate to other 'allied services' the Seebohm Committee gave attention to each of the main 'client groups', which would receive help from the proposed local authority social service department.

For *children's services*, in 1967 in England and Wales there were 69,000 children and young people in the care of local authorities plus 8000 children who had committed criminal offences and had been ordered by the juvenile courts to reside in 'approved schools' (which were large residential institutions accountable to the Home Office). This total of 77,000 children is similar to the March 2019 figure of 78,150 children looked after by local authorities in England. But what is different is that in 1967 '150,000 children and their families were helped in their own homes by preventive or rehabilitative work' (Seebohm Report, paragraph 172) whereas in March 2019 there were 399,500 children in need with whom local authority children's social services were in contact [16]. Not only has the workload increased over the years but the pattern of the work has also changed. In 2019 a much higher proportion of children in contact with social workers were living at home.

A further difference between 1967 and 2013 is that in 1967 31,547 children in care were in foster care ('boarded out' was the term used in the 1960s and before), and this is 54% of the children in care; and there were 27,932 children in residential care (40% of all children in care) (Seebohm Report, Appendix F, para 48). In March 2019, 9630 (12%) of children 'looked after' in England by local authorities were in residential care and 56,160 (72%) were in foster care, and with 5200 children and young people whilst formally still looked after by local authorities placed at home with their parents.

With regard to *older people*, a significant concern of the Seebohm Committee was how the numbers of older people would increase over the coming years (a perennial concern running and continuing into the twenty-first century). In 1966, there were 6,021,000 people in England and Wales aged 65 years and older, with 2,131,000 aged 75 years or older. In total, this was 12.5% of the population. By 1991, it was anticipated that there would be 7,535,000 people aged 65 years and older (13% of the total population) of whom 3,062,000 would be 75 years or older (Seebohm Report, paragraph 295). In England alone (excluding Wales) in 2017 there were 4.5 million people aged 75 years and older [17].

But it was not only the increasing numbers of older people that the Seebohm Committee saw as an issue for the proposed social services departments. There was also discussion about how older people were perceived and how they were helped or hindered to participate. This was a radical and ground-breaking agenda being set by the Committee in the 1960s. It may have much more currency under the headings of 'empowerment' and 'personalisation' in the 2000s but it was not an established concern or commitment in the 1960s. The Report noted that:

> In the provision of social services the users are seldom consulted, nor as things are at present, does the retired person often enough play a significant part in the management of any scheme designed to help him ... We believe that enforced retirement, with nothing to replace many years of regular work, can sometimes be detrimental to old people and incidentally increase the demand on the social services. (Paragraph 314)

The themes here of participation and active retirement, with older people as contributing citizens with influence and control within their lives, was not a mainstream agenda in the 1960s. Service users were largely seen as dependent recipients of care, with the care shaped and determined by others. In the 2010s, the move may be towards enforced employment into older age as the age of pension entitlement is extended, but the Seebohm Committee was visionary in its view which was resetting how older people should be seen.

The Committee also urged that more recognition and attention should be given to *younger physically impaired people*. It was noted, using the jargon and terminology of the time, that as with older people the number of physically impaired younger people would increase and that:

> A number of strong voluntary organisations, operating both nationally and locally, are concerned with services for the physically handicapped. It is natural that the public should be more sympathetic towards the develop-

ment of services for the blind and for cripples than towards services for other groups of people in need [it refers, for example, to 'epileptics' and 'chronic bronchitics'], whose disability is less evident or less acceptable. Nevertheless, we are clear that services for the physically handicapped, no less than services for other groups, are in urgent need of development. [Paragraphs 318 and 319]

And reflecting issues of the 2020s as much as the 1960s the Seebohm Committee were concerned that 'physically handicapped people are often poorly or inappropriately housed and their incomes are generally low compared with those of the rest of the population' (paragraph 319).

The Seebohm Committee grouped together 'social services for the *mentally sub-normal and mentally ill people*' reflecting the combining of these two client groups in the 1959 Mental Health Act. In considering how to improve services for people with a 'mental disorder' the Seebohm Committee focused on the favoured themes of team work and coordination across health and social services, and that mental health social services should be the responsibility of the social service department. But in relation to mental health services the Committee went one step further. It also argued that 'the areas of local social and medical services should be coterminous; and nowhere is this more important than in the field of mental health where services will often have to contend for a long time ahead with the geographical isolation of the Victorian mental hospitals from the communities they serve' (paragraph 350).

Coterminosity between health and social services was to be a cherished dream and aspiration for the next 50 years, but one which was often thwarted by frequent changes imposed by central government which redefined health services boundaries and which did not necessarily take local authority boundaries as the geographical building blocks for health organisations.

Generic or Specialist Workers and Services?

The Sebohm Report gave detailed attention as to how the proposed social service department should be organised, how it should work and how workers should be deployed. One particular issue, which ran and ran as a debate through the 1970s and beyond, as will be discussed in later chapters, was about specialisation within social work. Indeed, this is a debate—in relation to the professional training and education of social workers—which still generates much energy in 2020.

There is a quote in the Seebohm Report from the evidence submitted to the Committee by the British Medical Association:

> There is too high a degree of specialisation early on in a social worker's career with consequent isolation of groups of social workers according to departmental aims. Furthermore, the development of numerous specialities encourages differentiation in title, status and salary scale and this, in turn, causes dissatisfaction among staff who essentially undertake duties of a similar nature contributing to the general welfare of the family. (Paragraph 510)

In the 1960s too early specialisation within social work was seen as a problem. It was seen to undermine social work as a unified profession and with social workers as primarily agents of 'departmental aims'. It was seen to cause friction between social workers and to fail to recognise that all social workers should be aware of, informed about and concerned for the 'general welfare of the family' and all family members.

These are all still pertinent issues in the 2020s, where those social workers who work in services primarily with adults, such as mental health, drug and alcohol, learning disability, and domestic violence services, need to be alert to any concerns about child development and the care of children by the adults. Those social workers working within children's services need to have an understanding and awareness of adult behaviours and how these might be influenced.

The Seebohm Report noted that:

We consider that a family or individual in need of social care should, as far as is possible, be served by single social worker. In support of this proposition it can be argued that the basic aim of a social service department is to attempt to meet all the social needs of the family or individual together and as a whole. The new department, by escaping from the rigid classifications implied in the present symptom-centred approach, will provide a more effective 'family' service ... It follows that a single worker, and through him [although most were 'hers'!] the social service department as a whole, can be held accountable for the standard of care the family or individual receives (or fails to receive) much more easily than if responsibility is fragmented between several workers ... The comprehensive planning of help for a family or individual should be easier if the primary professional responsibility lies with a single worker. (Paragraphs 516 and 517)

The arguments put forward in favour of genericism as compared to specialism were that, first, it would better address all the needs of a family or individual and, second, would simplify and make explicit single worker and single agency accountability. The argument was not made on the basis of economy, that having one worker visiting a family rather than several would reduce costs, nor that it would ease the burden on families who would not have to give time to and negotiate between several workers. Both of these arguments, however, might also be seen to have some value, but for the Seebohm Committee it was the drive to develop a 'family service' which drove the genericism argument.

The Seebohm Committee did not, though, ignore the value of specialisation. First, it saw it as acceptable that workers might have a degree of specialisation and weighting within their workloads and, second, that beyond the frontline practitioners there might be experienced professional consultants who would be client group or social need specialists. Practitioners, however, and their supervisors and managers, were to be social work generalists.

It was, amongst all the Seebohm Committee's recommendations, the issue of generic compared to specialist social workers which was to run and run and which was also the thorniest issue at the time. Hall wrote:

The evidence presented to the committee on specialisation was scanty and social worker groups put forward a variety of views on whether it should be encouraged and, if so, in what form ... The decision to recommend the reduction in specialisation, against the weight of the views presented, was particularly contentious. Perhaps more than any other recommendation it armed critics with 'evidence' that the primary aim of the enquiry was to develop a united social work profession. [18]

The Committee recommended that existing separate children's, health and welfare departments in local authorities should be disbanded and should be replaced by one social service department within each local authority. It should be led by a senior manager who should be a qualified social worker, and with teams of generic social workers supervised and managed by senior social workers, and where any individual or family would be the responsibility of one worker. The department should be organised with devolved responsibilities to area offices covering populations of between 50,000 and 100,000. Workers and services should engage with the communities as well as the families and individuals they served, with communities seen as a potential resource in tackling social need. Whilst recognising that other workers, such as home help organisers, residential and day care workers, and administrators would also be employed within social service departments, the overwhelming focus and primacy was given to social workers.

But mid-stream in the Committee's deliberations a warning bell was sounded, as noted by Hall, about the Committee and its report seeming to be primarily an advocacy statement for social work and social workers:

When the Committee were two-thirds of the way through their work, Dr Alvin Schorr, then Deputy Assistant Secretary for Individual and Family Services at the Department of Health, Education and Welfare, Washington DC, flew over at their request to advise them on the credibility of an integrated department ... Schorr offered a stiffener. He encouraged a radical and positive approach to the concept of an integrated department, and urged that it should demonstrate quickly to the public, to professionals and to politicians that it was breaking new ground in family and community interventions, and needed extra resources. He was concerned that the arguments favouring one department were resting too strongly on the needs and wishes of social workers. Overemphasis on these might too easily be interpreted as an overt bid for professional power. It was more important to create an organisational base for professionals and para-professionals to respond to problems effectively in a co-ordinated way and to influence related social systems and professions ... if more individuals, families, households and communities were to be more effectively served by the new departments, then the integration of all staff and all facilities was of more importance than the creation of a new and dominant profession. [19]

So the advice to the Committee, which it took, was to focus on services and the experience of service users rather than the enhancement or empowerment of the profession of social work, although this might be a subsidiary outcome.

National and Local Government

In addition to the focus—albeit to be considered and seen as secondary—on the social work profession, was the focus on local government. This was required by the Committee's terms of reference, but with a recognition that local authority social service departments would need to work closely with the voluntary sector. The private sector was not referred to at all by the Committee—its significant arrival on the personal social services scene was still over a decade and more away.

The Seebohm Report foresaw a change in the power relationship between central and local government. It was recommending the establishment of a large local government department with the intention that this department would be successful in arguing for more resources which would have largely to come from central government grant, albeit its distribution across services and departments would be determined within each local authority.

The Committee also recommended that central government took to itself the power to direct the shape of committee and departmental organisations within local authorities and also who should be the most senior manager in these departments. This was a source of debate and disagreement, reflecting divergent interests, within the Committee, as noted by Hall:

The precise relationship between the central authority and the new departments was an issue the committee found extremely difficult to resolve. There were deep divisions of opinion amongst the members as to the desirability of making recommendations which increased central control over local government. Those primarily interested in the delivery of the services under consideration stressed the need for considerable central control in order to ensure that no authority fell below a reasonable minimum standard. On the other hand, the members with local authority interests argued that this would inhibit experimentation at a local level and, more importantly, that the limitation of local autonomy would conflict with current views on the balance of power between central and local government. They pointed to the recommendations of the Committee on the Management of Local Government (the Maud Committee), where general decentralisation of power was advocated. [20]

The Committee concluded that central government should require that there be a separate, unified social services department, and it also wanted central government to define the accountability and governance arrangements for social services within each local authority and the qualifications (which were expected to be in social work) and acceptability of the director:

> [The Committee] concluded that a statutory duty should be placed upon local authorities to create a separate social services committee and a principal officer with adequate supporting staff … [and with] the ministerial right of veto over the appointment of individual chief officers. [21]

It was not, therefore, to be left to the vagaries and differing views of local authorities. The Committee was determined that its recommendations for a unified family and community social service should not be undermined by local discretion about its organisation, governance or leadership. So this is what the Seebohm Committee in 1968 recommended. What actually happened?

4

Preparing the Platform: The Local Authority Social Services Bill and Act

When the Seebohm Report was published in July 1968, there was every possibility that it might have attracted little attention and interest and that it might have disappeared without trace. There were a number of other policy and service reviews which had been launched by the government. There were committees reviewing primary education [1], the NHS [2], local government [3], planning [4] and with new legislation such as the 1969 Housing Act to promote general improvements in housing, slum clearance and area regeneration. For Richard Crossman, secretary of state for health and social security, his attention was focused on NHS reform and, especially, reform of pensions [5]. Within this wider context, local authority personal social services were a minor concern.

The Response of Government

There was not clear ownership and responsibility for the personal social services within central government, which were everybody's minnow and marginal interest. The Home Office had responsibility for children's social services, but a much more major concern would have been its cluster of criminal justice responsibilities spanning the courts, police and

© The Author(s) 2020, corrected publication 2021
R. Jones, *A History of the Personal Social Services in England*,
https://doi.org/10.1007/978-3-030-46123-2_4

probation. And within the Department for Health and Social Security, which had the central government responsibility for welfare and mental health services for disabled and older people, the much more significant—both in terms of size but also political profile—responsibilities were for the NHS and for social security.

In addition, central government set the legislative frameworks, and through government grant largely funded, the personal social services but the services were provided by local government, unlike many of the other central government departmental responsibilities where ministers were accountable for the delivery of the services.

Each of the above may have led to the Seebohm Report getting very little government attention. Departmental vested interests, such as the Home Office having responsibility for children's services but the Seebohm Committee recommending that these be integrated into a social services department within local councils along with health and welfare services, may have led to inertia as ministers and senior civil servants sought to hold on to territory and the status quo, as noted in Crossman's diaries.

Finally, within local government itself, and across the social work professional groupings, there was no overall consensus that what the Seebohm Committee was proposing was necessarily what was wanted or desired.

Criticisms of the Seebohm Committee's Recommendations

Even some of those who accepted the main thrust of the Committee's proposals that a unified personal social services department should be created within local authorities were less than enthusiastic about the specific recommendations within the report. For example, Peter Townsend, who had been a research fellow at the LSE and was then professor of social policy at Essex University, collated and edited the papers given at a conference organised by the Fabian Society in February 1969 to consider the Sebohm Report. Townsend wrote:

The Seebohm Report is constructive and its chief recommendation to merge the local services in one department is justified. But as an example of planning the report is lacking in analysis, drive and vision, and it gives an insufficient picture of the objectives that should be pursued. [7]

In particular, Townsend criticised the Seebohm Committee for failing to consult with service users:

The implications of failing to find out consumer opinion run deep. Some far-reaching criticisms of professional activity may be either undetected or under-estimated. Some needs which are felt by individuals or groups may be ignored. More important, some of the rights of the consumer to a voice in planning and administration may be unrecognised. [8]

Other damning criticisms from Townsend were that the committee lacked vision and also accepted too readily that resources for the personal social services would not be substantially increased although, as noted in the previous chapter, the committee hoped that a larger unified local authority department would be stronger and successful in making the case for a bigger slice of the local authority cake.

However, may be the Seebohm Committee was being pragmatic as there was the risk of possibly scaring the government about the viability and affordability of the committee's recommendations. Roy Parker noted that whilst:

The drawbacks I think were that we didn't sufficiently calculate the cost, we deliberately didn't do that in the report because Seebohm, as a banker, said we should, 'never tell them what it's going to cost!'. [Roy Parker interview]

A particular concern about the Seebohm Committee's proposals was that they would increase the power of social workers. This may have been welcomed by the social work professions, which as will be noted below campaigned strongly for the implementation of the Seebohm proposals, but Townsend noted that:

The problems which might arise as a consequence of extending the power of officials over a larger area, creating a monopoly of certain kinds of service, weakening some citizens' power to seek redress for maladministration and neglect through alternative organisations, and emphasising the professional power of social work, were not examined critically enough. [9]

Townsend was not alone in this concern as noted in *The Political Quarterly* in 1969 by Brooke and by Wistrich:

The Seebohm proposals, particularly if coupled with the recommendations from the Royal Commission on Local Government for much larger local authorities, will mean a far greater concentration of power in the hands of officials and social workers of the family services. [10]

Some [social workers] are less competent, some seem to the client to be unreceptive to his needs. In this situation, the fact that the social worker provides the only point of access to the services the client needs will be frustrating. [11]

Adrian Sinfield, who had been a student of Townsend at the LSE and was then Townsend's colleague at the University of Essex, argued that the Seebohm Committee never produced the evidence—indeed he argued it did not exist—to support the importance the Committee gave to social work as the lead profession within the personal social services:

The Seebohm report never appears to question the efficacy of social work. Yet this question cannot be ignored if we are to decide whether the Seebohm proposals are adequate. This crucial issue has received scarcely any attention from the social work profession, though without a clear and positive answer the necessity for social workers, and more of them, remains largely a matter of faith. [12]

And not all social workers wanted a unified, generic social worker role within social services departments. There was still a significant lobby for specialism within social work and social work education and training. Here are two expressions of concern, one based on the views of Clare Winnicott, a leading social work child care teacher, and one from Zofia Butrym, who had been a medical social worker, and both of whom had taught at the LSE:

In what can now be called 'code', Clare Winnicott was expressing her fears that the creation of large social work super-departments would lead to administrative functions overshadowing social work ones, to the lessening of a sense of child care identity and skills, and to social work agencies in which many employees would be cut off from personal contact with clients ... She poured scorn on the idea that the needs of children were the same as those of older people and other client groups. [13]

Social workers on the whole appear to have regarded the committee with a disarming degree of trust, as if it had been set up for the explicit purpose of furthering the interests of social work! The most serious important single omission resulting from the combined absence of an adequate social work representation on the Seebohm committee and the political inexperience of social workers was that of a failure to differentiate between social service provision and social work services within the envisaged new local authority unified departments ... One wonders whether, had the concept of a 'personal social service' been more carefully considered, particularly in relation to the function of social work, the advantages of unification of all local authority personal social services (plus the hospital social work services) and the creation of the large new bureaucratic structures with a virtual monopoly of service provision which such a unification entailed, the advantages of the 'one door' would have been quite so overriding. [14]

The concern expressed by Winnicott and Butrym that the new proposed local authority bureaucracies would hinder the delivery of social work was a concern shared by others, including by Bill Utting who, in 1976, replaced Joan Cooper as the government's chief social work officer:

Because of my perspective [as a probation officer] outside the local authority, it seemed very difficult to me for social work to flourish as a professional activity inside a local authority politically led, bureaucratically structured organisation where the resources were predominantly directed towards the provision of material services, so I didn't actually share the optimism that I think a lot of other felt at the time that this was a new dawn for professional social work. [Bill Utting interview]

And for some, such as Bob Holman, there were arguments which could be made for bigger departments but they should still have remained more specialist:

> There were some rubbish children's departments, usually those which were far too small and I won't name them, places in Scotland, with just two or three people, far too small ... Personally I was not against reorganisation, and I can certainly see the case that some children's departments were too small, but I would have done it in a different way in that I think instead of a children's department, I think we should have set up a family department which would have been bigger, and also set up an adult department in that way because I think initially childcare did lose out a bit, partly because of this initial emphasis on being generic. [Bob Holman interview]

However, despite the range of concerns noted above, the Seebohm report was generally positively received by social workers, as noted in 1975 by Jean Packman with 'social workers pressing for implementation when action was delayed' [15]. She commented:

> Doubts and reservations [about the Seebohm Committee's proposals] were still apparent, especially but not exclusively among groups of social workers like the probation officers [who were to remain separate and outside of social services departments] and medical social workers [who in 1974 were integrated into social services departments from the NHS at the same time public health transferred to the NHS], who were not included but looked as though they might be. But the excitement and potential of Seebohm (significantly it was dubbed the 'social workers charter' by some—status and career prospects were clearly going to be much brighter) carried along most of those concerned. [15]

Medical Officers of Health

There were, however, two further stumbling blocks. What to do with public health and, not unrelated, how to stop those local authorities which disliked what was being proposed by the Seebohm Committee from reorganising very quickly to subvert and undermine the Seebohm recommendations of a unified social services department?

With regard to public health, it was a responsibility embedded in the role of the local authority medical officer of health. It had its history in the nineteenth century municipal achievements in improving water quality, sewerage and waste systems, and housing standards. More recently, programmes of vaccination to tackle infectious diseases and tackling malnutrition of children had fallen within the public health remit (and in the 2000s, it is the life-style diseases resulting from obesity, heavy consumption of alcohol and smoking which have become the next-stage public health focus, with the lead responsibility back again within local authorities).

But with the Seebohm Committee recommending the creation of local authority social services departments, and with the corollary of the demise of the medical officer of health's departmental domains of mental health and, in some councils, welfare departments, what was to happen to public health? The solution was to transfer, in 1974 as a part of NHS reorganisation, the lead responsibility for public health to the NHS (it was transferred back again to local authorities, as a part of another NHS reorganisation, in 2013).

Tom White noted:

> While there wasn't immense public interest in the [Seebohm] report, media response and informed opinion was generally favourable—except for the medical profession which indicated strong opposition, as implementation of the proposals would greatly diminish the role and importance of the MOH (medical officer of health), then a statutory appointment in each large authority. [16]

Commenting on the only doctor who was a member of the Seebohm Committee, White noted:

> I think [Jerry Morris] was genuinely intellectually open to listen to arguments, and I think he became convinced that what was proposed made sense, you know. He had a hell of a tough time when the report was published. [Tom White interview]

And Roy Parker, who was a member of the Seebohm Committee, noted:

> Seebohm said, when we finished, 'We can't let this just ride, all of you have got to get out and talk about it … and then I think the trio of Seebohm, Robin Huws Jones, and Jerry Morris, because by then Jerry, who had a real rough time with his medical colleagues for signing, he was the last one to sign [the report], that trio I think then worked hard in the political arena, probably with Titmuss' assistance. [Roy Parker interview]

Campaigning for Implementation

There was a danger for the Seebohm Committee that pre-emptive action might be, and indeed was being, taken within some local authorities to not only safeguard but also to enhance the role and status of medical officers of heath. As medical doctors they were already high status professionals compared to what were seen as local government administrators heading up children's and welfare departments. Parker commented that the medical professions 'thought if you're going to unify, it should all be unified under health, under a much expanded medical officer of health kind of thing' [Roy Parker interview]. This caused concern, especially amongst the social work interest groups, and Packman noted that 'premature reorganisation of welfare services in some boroughs, in advance of legislation, which put Medical Officers of Health in charge, created alarm and increased pressures to reorganise the Seebohm way' [15].

Precipitative action by some local authorities was foreshadowed in local governments' early reaction to the Seebohm report:

> The County Councils Association gave a guarded welcome to the committee's proposals, agreeing with the principle of unified local authority social services but, possibly to placate the county medical officers of health, it made the reservation that 'the importance and scope of the local health authority services … have been insufficiently stressed. [17]

Getting attention and gaining action to the Seebohm Committee's proposals, however, was a continuing struggle. First, there was no political champion, and second there were potentially legitimate reasons for delay. Roy Parker noted that 'There wasn't a strong political patron for the whole thing' and 'the government had its eyes on other rather bigger balls, the Health Service, penal reform, local government reform, [the personal social services were] just a side issue almost' [Roy Parker interview].

Keith Bilton noted:

> We had a line to Callaghan [Home Secretary] which we never had to Crossman [Secretary of State for Health and Social Security] ... [At one meeting] it was ministers from both departments and Crossman was there, but he spent the whole meeting sitting almost horizontally in his chair, usually with his eyes shut and said not a word. Maybe he's very like that, I don't know, it was the only time I ever met him. But I mean, it was Callaghan who more or less said informally 'Look, you really need to fight this business with MoHs taking over, because if it goes too far it will be too much of an uphill struggle to carry this legislation through'. [Keith Bilton interview]

Audrey Callaghan, Jim Callaghan's wife, was seen to be particularly helpful and influential. Bilton commented that 'she knew about Social Services from local government experience, she was a bright lady, and she and her husband were I think very close and actually talked about these things' [Keith Bilton interview]. Audrey Callaghan's involvement was also recognised by White:

> Audrey Callaghan, the wife of Jim Callaghan, the Home Secretary, was a member of the London County Council Children's Committee and well informed on welfare issues. We ensured Audrey was well-briefed and became a strong closet supporter. (Later Callaghan's support in Cabinet in defeating Crossman's opposition was crucial) [18]

White also noted that it was not unhelpful that 'Bee Serota, former chair of the LCC Children's Committee and a member previously of the Seebohm Committee, was now a junior minister in the Department of Health. She was an especially effective advocate on our behalf behind the scenes' [18].

But Hall noted that:

> In January 1969, the future of the Seebohm proposals looked somewhat
> bleak. It was clear to the social work organisations that legislation could
> not be passed during the current Parliamentary session. The rejection of
> the first NHS green paper meant inevitable delays and, what was worse, the
> BMA seemed to be placing much greater emphasis on community medi-
> cine and the use of social workers in medical teams. The introduction of
> social service departments was being further threatened by local attempts
> to reorganise along anti-Seebohm lines by putting the medical officer of
> health in charge of social work services. The fact that no statement indicat-
> ing the government's views on the subject was forthcoming reinforced
> social workers' fears. [19]

The race was now on to implement the Seebohm Committee's recommendations and to ensure that they were not negated by opposition from
doctors' representatives or by wrecking actions within some councils.

There were three driving forces for implementation. Firstly, the
Commmittee and its members. Secondly, allies who had influence. And
thirdly, the social work professions. Tom White noted that 'the Seebohm
Committee were not prepared to leave it [and] they wanted help to move
it forward' [Tom White interview]. White was particularly active at this
time. He became chair of the Seebohm Implementation Action
Group (SIAG):

> It was clear that any hope of implementation required a united front of a
> broad range of welfare professionals, expressed through their professional
> associations. I was able to ensure that ACCO [the Association of Child
> Care Officers] took the lead in bringing together the various groups to
> discuss the issue. NISW (the National Institute for Social Work) was also
> vigorous in its advocacy behind the scenes ... A meeting of all the relevant
> professional associations, with representatives from some of the major
> voluntary organisations in the field, was called by ACCO, which I chaired.
> We agreed to establish a group to campaign for Seebohm implementation,
> hence SIAG, the 'Seebohm Implementation Action Group' was formed—I
> was elected to chair and Keith Bilton, the ACCO general secretary, was
> appointed secretary. [20]

Keith Bilton's recollections were that:

The Standing Conference of Social Workers (SCOSW) was not in a strong position to lead or co-ordinate pressure from social workers for implementation of the report. It was, as its name implies, primarily a meeting ground for its eight member organisations, and had few resources. It had not been in the habit of obtaining general permissive mandates from the associations and acting on them … At the suggestion of Tom White, and SCOSW's approval, the Seebohm Implementation Action Group was formed to add further weight to this campaigning. It brought together the SCOSW members most closely concerned, the Institute of Social Welfare, and the three chief officers groups: the Association of Directors of Children's Officers, the Association of Directors of Welfare Services, and the Society of County Welfare Officers. SIAG organised a range of pressure group activities, including a deputation to James Callaghan [the Home Secretary], a mass lobby of Parliament by social workers, a set of 'speaker's notes' on Seebohm, and numerous contacts between social workers and their MPs. Some ventures were less successful: a planned series of letters to The Times from eminent people stalled after the first letter. [21]

Tom White commented:

There were regional groups set up, hundreds and hundreds of social workers actually had meetings, individual meetings with MPs. It was explained to them how to get to know your MP, get to MPs' surgeries, and get letters [to MPs], they just had to top and tail them. I mean well ahead of its time, it was a genuinely well-organised campaign so it looked very much as if there was mass support for the proposal. And that made a big difference, particularly with the Tory Party. You must remember at this stage social workers were definitely the goodies, they hadn't had these serious tragedies, and to be quite honest they were seen as being totally disinterested. It wasn't that they were arguing for themselves, they were arguing for people in need. [Tom White interview]

The role played by the Seebohm Implementation Action Group, and with the leadership of Tom White, was noted by Judith Niechcial, the biographer of Lucy Faithfull (see below) who in the late 1960s was children's officer for Oxford and was its first director of social services, and later became a Conservative peer in House of Lords and active in legislating the 1989 Children Act:

> Tom White developed a sophisticated campaign. He obtained funding from the National Institute for Social Work [Tom White in his autobiography noted that Robin Huw Jones, the director of the National Institute for social Work Training, helped to obtain financial help from one of the Joseph Rowntree Trusts [20]]. SIAG members visited their MPs in their constituency surgeries to ensure they were properly briefed, and there was a mass lobby of Parliament by social workers. Notes were produced for public speakers. He valued Lucy's contacts with eminent people from Oxford and the Civil Service and they planned a strategy of who should approach whom. Such lobbying was uncommon in those days. [22]

Tom White, in his autobiography, reflected on the contribution at this time of Lucy Faithfull:

> [She was] the Children's Officer for Oxford [and later its first director of social services], and used her contacts with academia and within the Conservative Party to help enlist support, especially from Tory MPs and Lords. [18]

When, in 1975, Lucy Faithful was made a Conservative life peer (she was to be active in the House of Lords in debates about the Bill which led to the 1989 Children Act) by Margaret Thatcher, Lord Seebohm was one of her sponsors introducing her to the House of Lords and she had borrowed a hat from Baroness Serota [23]. The Seebohm fraternity was still alive and well!

But even with the coming together of different social work and welfare constituencies, there were still differences and rivalries, and differing competing ambitions, within the SIAG:

> David Fleet, chief welfare officer in Tower Hamlets, said 'Oh well, the chief welfare officers are going to get these directors' jobs, I mean 80% of the work of these departments is going to be welfare work' ... [and] if you look at ACCO's evidence to the Seebohm Committee, I mean it's remarkably self-centred. It was saying 'Yes, we would like something along the lines of

the Social Services Department with all these services for adults and mentally ill people and so on and so forth as well, but we want it done in a phased way with the children's departments at the middle'. [Keith Bilton interview]

Progress was made when Richard Crossman came to accept the Seebohm proposals as the way forward. Roy Parker noted that:

Although in the Crossman Diaries he thought Seebohm and all its recommendations weren't much, he actually changes his mind, and he was persuaded. This was really I think again, the Titmuss role, Jerry Morris, direct lines. This was important and I think at some point, and I don't quite know when, Crossman put his shoulder to the wheel. [Roy Parker interview]

Crossman's changing stance is also noted by Hall:

Crossman's indifference to the Committee's proposals might have condemned the report to a dusty shelf had there been no vociferous groups and powerful individuals able to persuade him otherwise. The pressure groups were undoubtedly helped by the influence of the civil servants in the welfare division of the DHSS [Department of Health and Social Security]. The latter were firmly of the opinion that the Seebohm proposals should be implemented. In turn, they were supported by Baroness Serota without whom, Crossman has argued, he would have remained unconvinced. [24]

But it was the DHSS which also had the responsibility for the NHS, so why were its civil servants not supportive of the arguments of doctors that social services should be managed within local councils by medical officers of health or integrated into the NHS? Hall notes that:

Whilst the merits of the Seebohm Committee were debated, the medical divisions of the department were preoccupied with the reorganisation of the health service. Hence they had little time to oppose changes within local government which would undermine the medical officer of health's existing preserve. [24]

This was, however, a close call as Crossman himself was inclined to favour, to the extent that he thought it needed any attention at all, an integration of the personal social services within the NHS:

> His interest in, amongst other policies, the reform of the health service had always taken precedence over the considerations of social work issues. This meant that when the boundary between the two services had to be drawn, Crossman's initial preference was to allocate the services in which there was both a medical and social component to the health service. The fact that he was persuaded to change his mind was the final triumph of the pro-Seebohm lobby both inside and outside Crossman's department, but it was the former who achieved it. Only weeks before the Bill was published the civil servants in the welfare divisions of the department, powerfully supported by Baroness Serota, managed to convince Crossman that, using the principle of 'primary skill', social services for the mentally disordered [and people with a learning disability and impairments from long-term chronic illnesses] should be a social service department responsibility. [25]

Ultimately, Hall notes that 'the personal social services did not raise issues for which Crossman felt it was worth fighting' [26], and Keith Bilton commented that 'Crossman, I think, was profoundly uninterested in personal social services and local government issues. I remember when the Local Authority Social Services Bill was going through, his big thing was the National Superannuation and Social Insurance Bill' [Keith Bilton interview].

So it was a close call and a last minute decision by Crossman to support the Seebohm Committee's main recommendations. It could have been that the personal social services, instead of having a separate profile and organisational arrangement within the local government, could have been subsumed within the NHS or under medical officers of health.

In addition to the position of Crossman, Callaghan as Home Secretary also had to change his stance, possibly helped as noted above by the influence of Audrey Callaghan, his wife. Indeed, it was the Home Secretary and the Home Office which had to give the most if the Seebohm proposals were to be accepted. The responsibility for children's services would be lost to the Home Office and transferred to the DHSS. Giving up a slice of political territory, departmental responsibility and down-sizing empires is unlikely to come easily to politicians with concerns about status and political pecking orders:

> Neither James Callaghan, Secretary of State for the Home Office, nor Richard Crossman, who was then Secretary of State designate for the Social Services, was prepared to give up any of the services for which they were responsible ... Many of those involved, civil servants, politicians and professionals, have observed that traditional departmental conflicts were exacerbated by the long-standing political rivalry between Callaghan and Crossman ... The only solution was a compromise; in late September 1968, Crossman enlisted Callaghan's support for replanning the personal social services on the understanding that the children's sector did not leave the Home Office until [Callaghan's] term as Home Secretary had ended. [27]

A way forward, therefore, was found so that Callaghan was not seen to give up departmental territory. There would be no decision or action until Callaghan had moved on from being Home Secretary [24].

Legislating

After the government had accepted the Seebohm Committee's proposals, the proposals still had to be enacted in legislation and time was running out in this Parliament with a general election not far away [28].

The Labour government was coming towards the end of its Parliamentary term of office. It had been busy and energetic with numerous reviews, committees of inquiry and green and white consultative papers. It may be that all this busyness allowed the Seebohm Committee's review of the personal social services to progress without a great deal of party political attention. It may also have been that compared to other areas of government responsibility and attention it was not politically contentious between the political groups.

Joan Cooper, in her detailed account of how the Seebohm Committee's recommendations were turned into a Parliamentary Bill and then shepherded to become an Act, commented that:

Lord Balniel, an MP with a courtesy title, as spokesperson for the Opposition front bench, had announced that the Conservative Party would give the Bill a Second Reading without a vote which is the Parliamentary way of indicating that the Opposition accept a Bill in principle, and that during the line-by-line discussion at the Committee Stage they would not oppose amendments inconsistent with that principle. The tactic was on 'probing' rather than 'wrecking' amendments. He accepted that the organisation of services based on the primary skill was the only 'conceivable logical line of demarcation'. Social workers had competently briefed interested MPs towards swinging a service reorganisation in the direction of assembling services round a profession; 'in layman's language, the Seebohm Report was really asking society to recognise social work as having come of age, of having its place alongside the teaching, medical, nursing and other great professions', explained Lord Balneil. [29]

This is what the social work lobby had sought. This is what those who were concerned about a professional monopoly and hegemony may have feared. Whatever view is taken, it was a considerable achievement to get cross-party support for a proposal which would integrate the personal social services within the local government with social work as the dominant profession.

Hall also noted the general political consensus:

The Bill which implemented many of the Seebohm Committee's proposals was non-contentious in a party-political sense. Although pressure groups lobbied MPs of all persuasions, there was little discernible difference in the official views of the parties ... The overwhelming impression, however, was one of indifference—the debates were extremely poorly attended and they lacked the sparkle of more contentious legislation. It is well known that the social work services fire the imaginations of few MPs but, this apart, it has been suggested that another reason for the poor attendances may have been that time was short and room for manoeuvre consequently limited ... Moreover, other Bills competed for attention in the race for completion before the election. [30]

How much a race this all was is noted by Tom White:

There was a bit of a panic when Wilson decided to call the 1970 general election before the Bill had passed through all its parliamentary stages. Even with frantic activity in Parliament, in the few days after an election is called and before Parliament is dissolved, only bills that are supported by both major parties can hope to get through all the parliamentary processes—would the Tories support its passage? There was much relief in SIAG when they agreed to do so, demonstrating the wisdom of directing our campaign at both major parties. [31]

The importance of having engaged with the Conservative opposition was also recalled by Roy Parker:

Again Robin Huws Jones was quite shrewd politically. I remember going to a meeting at the National Institute where he'd invited Edward Heath [then leader of the Conservative Opposition and in 1970 to be Prime Minister when the Local Authority and Allied Personal Social Services Bill became enacted], because he thought the Conservatives were likely to come in and he was likely to be prime minister, so we had a session bending Edward Heath's ear. He was one of the most deadpan people I've ever met. He just sat there kind of asking us no questions and so forth, but that was kind of the thing [those promoting the Seebohm Committee's recommendations] were doing. [Roy Parker interview]

The Conservative Opposition position on the Bill is described by Keith Bilton:

I always found the Conservative Opposition's view strange. The Conservatives always said they didn't agree with all this dictating to local government. Really, dictating to local government was all that the Act did! But they always made a point of saying that they supported what they called the 'spirit of the bill' and clearly they did not want to be painted as people who were in some way against bringing these services together. [Keith Bilton interview]

Bilton also noted how close the Bill was to failing:

I thought it was touch and go because it had to go through the House of Lords very quickly, there were only days left, so that at that point it was entirely within the gift of the Conservative Party to kill it, once they started to vote against anything it would just run out of time. And there was a guy called Lord Sandford who was leading [for the Conservatives] in the House of Lords on the bill who was a hereditary peer and Anglican clergyman. He called a meeting to discuss what their attitude should be to the bill in the Lords, and I went to that meeting. I've no way of knowing whether it was for forms sake or what, but it felt real, it felt as though he had one or two others sitting there and they had some sort of decision to make as to whether they were going to facilitate its passage or not. [Keith Bilton interview]

Managing Across Government Boundaries

The Conservatives did not disrupt or block and did facilitate passing of the Bill into statute. But there were still some outstanding contentious issues. The first was recognising the differences in style and approach of the two main central government departments which had been the national home and host for the personal social services. The second was the relationship between the central and local government and how pre-scriptive and controlling central government should be. The third was the thorny and fraught issue of finance.

The different styles and traditions of the Home Office and the DHSS were described by Cooper:

[The DHSS] came into the laissez-faire category as regards both health and welfare services; it normally adopted a positive philosophy of non-intervention … The Home Office exemplified the regulatory attitude in its relations with local authority children's departments, especially through its inspectorate which trod the middle ground between checking whether regulations were kept and the giving of informal advice. [32]

This differences of approach … the hands off style of the DHSS com-pared to the more directive style of the Home Office … had to be moulded and merged if one central government department was to take national policy responsibility for the personal social services.

Secondly, and not unrelated, how directive was central government to be towards local government in how the personal social services were to be organised and provided? The Seebohm Committee had wanted central government to be prescriptive and there were still concerns that some councils might undermine the Seebohm proposals. Cooper noted that '[the Association of Child Care Officers] was considering, using the terminology of the time, "blacking" posts in "anti-Seebohm" areas' [33].

Keith Bilton was at the centre of the action at this time as the general secretary of ACCO:

> At ACCO's annual conference, its South Wales branch had proposed that the Association should blacklist any local authority which combined its health, welfare and children's departments [under the medical officer of health]. Following tense behind-the-scenes negotiations, the Branch accepted an amendment giving the Association's Executive Committee discretion on whether to blacklist an authority, and a resolution to this effect was adopted. As a result, there were discussions with about half a dozen authorities which, despite government advice to the contrary, either had carried out or were proposing such amalgamations. Only one, the London Borough of Sutton, was actually blacklisted. This action appears to have been sufficient to stem the tide until February 1970, when the government introduced the Local Authority Social Services Bill. [34]

As noted by Tom White, the government was very prescriptive in what was to be required:

> The crucial elements of the Act which would ensure successful implementation were the establishment of Social Services Committees in each large local authority, with a designated Director of Social Services whose appointment had to be approved by the Secretary of State. This ensured a significant degree of uniformity for England and Wales [Scotland already had their own largely similar arrangements] and prevented those local authorities that disagreed from retaining existing structures or appointing inappropriate people as directors. The hope of some of us that only qualified social workers would be approved for appointment [as was the case in Scotland] was rejected but qualification and relevant experience was taken

into account in approving applications. The 1st April 1971 was the designated date by which time all authorities would have to implement the new arrangements. This was the biggest change in welfare provision in the country for decades and was an immense upheaval for local government, which at that time was largely unused to government imposed reorganisations. [31]

This was a considerable tension between central and local government, represented by its associations. Local government was not used to its internal arrangements being determined and dictated by central government. This was commented on by Hall:

> Determining the exact relationship between central and local agencies required three key decisions: whether to create a statutory [social services] committee [in each local authority], whether there should be a statutory director of social services, and whether to allow the Secretary of State the right to veto chief officer appointments … The local government associations vigorously opposed such restrictions on local autonomy, yet the Bill included all three constraints. We can only speculate as to the reasons, since those involved were unwilling to be very specific about the rationale for their decisions. The most obvious reason is that policy-makers wished to minimise local variations between authorities. The previous structure had accommodated considerable differences and pre-empting by some local authorities before the implementation of Seebohm indicated there could continue to be widespread variation if the structure was determined by local decisions. Moreover, if in many areas health departments took over social services functions, the reorganisation of the health service [which was to largely take local authority health responsibilities such as public health and health visiting away from local councils and place them within the NHS] could cause much greater upheavals than if the social services departments were uniform and separate. Although the local authority associations continued to protest at the controls included in the Bill even up to the committee stage they won no concessions. [35]

This concern about NHS reorganisation and its relationship with the reorganisation of the personal social services was crucial and critical in the political and civil service management of the legislative changes:

By skilful management within the civil service, the Second Green Paper on the NHS was announced in the House of Commons on 11 February 1970, and won considerable approval from the Opposition. The Local Authority Social Services Bill was published on the following day. The relationship between the two was inescapable; in the words of the government press notice, a 'New Bill unifies Social Services partnership with integrated Health Structure'. [36]

The third contentious issue which was outstanding was about the financing of the personal social services. This was an issue to be kicked into the long grass. Too hot to handle, and certainly too complex and controversial to resolve quickly in the immediate run in to a general election, it was, in essence, parked, just as the Seebohm Committee itself (see above) decided to leave it largely unaddressed. Hall noted that:

Unlike the Social Work (Scotland) Act [passed two years before in 1968 and well before the now imminent general election] the counterpart for England and Wales was to place no general duty to promote welfare upon new social services departments and would include no cash-giving functions in addition to those provided in existing statutes. This meant there was no need for a financial resolution to be passed alongside the Bill and hence the complexity of negotiations and especially those with the Treasury could be reduced. [37]

Cooper also commented that to get the Bill enacted within a very tight timescale it was important to keep clear of any debate about finances, and indeed other potentially controversial issues were also kept to one side and left unaddressed:

A Bill had to be introduced and to become law before the summer recess of Parliament about the end of July 1970. Speed and efficiency became the driving forces. To win a place in the competition for inclusion in the government's legislative programme, the Bill had to be short, and as restricted in scope as possible in order to limit the range of amendments that could be proposed during the Committee Stage on behalf of special interest groups, and to reduce the time occupied by that stage. It followed from this legislative strategy that a Bill had to be kept clear of the financial field by omitting any general duty to 'promote social welfare', and to keep clear of the extra consultations and negotiations if education and housing welfare were included. A minimum viability strategy was essential. [38]

When the Bill was published in February 1970 the Seebohm Implementation Action Group issued a handout headed 'Seebohm—Two Cheers'. It applauded the government for its intention to implement most of Seebohm's recommendations but it lamented that there was no general duty to promote welfare, and that school social work and housing welfare services were not included within the Bill [39].

As Hall noted, 'the relative brevity and simplicity of the Social Services Act, 1970, disguised years of complicated decision-making on the part of many diverse individuals and groups' [40], and Cooper concluded that 'the enactment of this machinery Bill ended ten years of uncertainty. In the particular political and economic circumstances the promoters had shaped the Bill on the assumption that half a loaf was better than no bread' [41].

This 'half loaf' had staying power. It was to be the bedrock and platform for the personal social services in England for over 40 years until 2004. In Wales, over 50 years on, social services departments still continue. It may have been a relatively short act, and getting it passed was a race to get it concluded before the 1970 general election. It then became an Act passed under Wilson's Labour government and implemented by Heath's new Conservative government. By April 1971 it was required that all local authorities should have appointed their director of social services, and then the work was really to begin.

Part II

The Personal Social Services in Action

5

Creating the Empires: Promise and Potential (1970–1976)

When Edward Heath's Conservatives won the general election in 1970 there was still the possibility that it might choose not to implement the Local Authority and Allied Personal Social Services Act (LASSA). This indeed happened with key sections of the 1969 Children and Young Persons Act, leaving its intentions partly undermined, but more about the 1969 Children and Young Persons Act (CYPA) later in this chapter. The major danger for the LASSA, as the 1970 social services Act became known, was that the medical lobby were still resistant and fighting a rearguard action. There was every possibility that the high status doctors would ultimately have more influence than the still emerging and somewhat fragmented profession of social work.

The Change of Government

Tom White noted:

© The Author(s) 2020, corrected publication 2021
R. Jones, *A History of the Personal Social Services in England*,
https://doi.org/10.1007/978-3-030-46123-2_5

The Conservatives won the election and the newly elected Government was reported to have given serious consideration to not implementing the Act, following a lot of pressure to take that stance from the medical profession. Fortunately the BMA [British Medical Association] had started their lobbying far too late and the obvious support for implementation on the Conservative backbenches bore fruit, again demonstrating the foresight of the SIAG in seeking all party support. [1]

Tom White was to become only the second director of social services to be appointed across all the local authorities in England and Wales [2]. For those who were to be appointed to the newly created posts of director of social services there was the reward of becoming the chief officer in a large local authority department. They had the trappings of status and salary, but also the responsibility of bringing together services and staff previously scattered across three departments, seeking to build coherence and create a new organisational culture as well as structure.

The political environment, with an incoming Conservative government replacing the Labour government which had, in a rush, shepherded the Local Authority Social Services Act through Parliament, looked as though it would be less sensitive and sympathetic to the personal social services. With the anticipation of storms ahead, it looked as though it would not be plain sailing to set up and embed the new social services departments.

In 'State of Emergency: The Way We Were: Britain 1970–1974', Dominic Sandbrook quoted Heath in the summer of 1970 as promising:

to reorganise the functions of Government, to leave more to the individual or corporate effort, to make savings in Government expenditure, to provide room for greater incentives to men and women and to firms and businesses, [encouraging them] to take their own decisions, to stand on their own two feet, to accept responsibility for themselves and their families … If we are to achieve this task we will have to embark on a change so radical, a revolution so quiet and yet so total, that it will go far beyond the programme for a Parliament to which we are committed and on which we have already embarked: far beyond this decade and way into the 1980s. We are laying the foundations, but they are the foundations for a generation. [3]

The foundations being laid were for a revision and retreat from the welfare state built in the 1940s, a reversal of direction which continued and indeed picked up power and pace throughout the 1980s and beyond.

Sandbrook's title for his retrospective recounting of Britain from 1970 to 1974 was 'State of Emergency'. In summer 1970 the conflicts ahead, and the crisis which was created and which led the collapse of the Conservative government, would not have been anticipated. But a government intent on cutting public expenditure, favouring individualism rather than collectivism, and prioritising the private rather than public sector, was hardly what had been sought or assumed by the Seebohm Committee. The Local Authority Social Services Act was launched just as the political tide was turning and setting up the new social services departments was a task which looked as though it would be swimming against the current being created by a change of government. The Seebohm Committee's report may have been a creature of its time, but times were changing. But as will be seen below, all was not what it seemed and the radical rhetoric of cutting public expenditure and requiring that the state withdraw from welfare was more of a message than reality.

An explanation for the disconnect between rhetoric and reality is given by Marwick:

> Tory radicals in the 1960s had argued that as society became more affluent the need for the welfare state would wither away. In actual fact, as the majority grew more affluent the needs of individuals and groups left behind were more sharply revealed. Conservative and Labour spokesmen voiced differences over the respective weighting to be given to collectivist initiatives or market forces in the provision of welfare facilities; but as far as welfare policies affected individual members of society there was a striking continuity between the policies of the Labour Government which fell in 1970, the Heath Conservative Government which fell in 1974, and the Wilson and Callaghan Labour administrations which lasted till 1979. [4]

Recruiting Directors of Social Services

Recruiting the new heads of social services departments across all the local authorities in England and Wales was itself a considerable and sometimes contentious task. Noted below are the experiences of three of the first directors:

[What was the mood at the time?] Well, in my authority [Bill Utting was the first director of social services in the London Borough of Kensington and Chelsea] there was a combination of excitement and apprehension. I was an outside appointment and there had been a great deal of jockeying and competitiveness between the old welfare department and the children's department and I think it was partly to resolve that that I was brought in from outside. [Bill Utting interview]

I had applied for about 70 directors of social services jobs and hadn't got any of them, but some I was very relieved not to get. Eventually Hammersmith advertised because they had been trying to get the medical officer of health appointed as director of social services and the department [Department of Health] wouldn't let them, so they advertised and I applied. [Peter Westland interview]

The first authority to advertise the post was Leicester—Eileen's (Tom White's wife's) home town and from a family perspective it would be good to move near Eileen's ageing widowed mother, so I applied. Within a few days of the Leicester advertisement another group of authorities advertised including Coventry which indicated an unusual approach. Coventry made clear that the newly appointed Director of Social Services, in addition to the departmental management duties, would be regarded as 'the social adviser' to the authority through the developing corporate management system being established and widely praised in knowledgeable quarters. This approach was very attractive to me, as the Seebohm Committee had acknowledged that social problems in the community would not, in the long run, be solved by the provision of direct services to individuals—necessary as they were—but also by wider social change through education, planning, housing and recreation departments—so I also applied to Coventry ... I took up my appointment on the 1st August 1970—the first

Director of Social Services to take up post in the country and eight months before the designated date by which all authorities would have to have directors in post. [Tom White] [5]

Each of the quotes above is from men who became the first directors of social services in their authorities. As such, this is not unrepresentative of the gender imbalance in the appointments to these top posts, as noted by Niechcial:

There was a cut-throat competition across the country for these jobs, with female Children's Officers pitted against invariably male Chief Welfare Officers in the same authority … Of the 174 Directors appointed, only 21 were women. This was an indication of the ambivalence still felt by councillors about Children's Officers, who were often very able professional women. [6]

Niechcial quotes Lucy Faithfull, who was appointed as Oxfordshire's first social services director:

I realised that being a Director of Social Services one was going to be much more a manager and much less involved with the staff, with the children, and that one would devolve responsibility to people without oneself carrying it out … what you had to do was to see that the Department was so organised that the work was done. [7]

An overview of who was appointed as the first directors of social services was provided by a study carried out in 1971 by the Institute of Local Government Studies at the University of Birmingham:

Their survey of appointments made before 1 April 1971 explored the age, qualifications and experience [but not the gender?] of 136 directors newly in post. Of this group, 34 were graduates, 32 held a social science certificate or diploma and 53 were qualified social workers. Thirty four were without either university or professional qualifications. The 47% of directors appointed in authorities for which they were already working tended to be those without a professional social work training. Younger candidates were predictably more likely to move, and ex-children's officers moved more frequently than ex-welfare officers. [8]

What conclusions to draw? First, 75% of the new directors had a university or professional social work qualification, but the 25% without such a qualification were more likely to be current chief officers, mainly welfare officers, within their local authority. Two types might be seen here: Type 1, about three quarters of the new directors of social services were mainly university or professionally qualified, who were mobile, and appointed through a competitive process to new authorities; Type 2, about a quarter, were established welfare officers, largely men who were not professionally qualified and were appointed within their existing authority.

But whether it was directors, such as Tom White, appointed in summer 1970, or others, such as Lucy Faithful, appointed in January 1971, there was not much time to get the new social services departments established by the go-live date of April 1971 ... at most less than 9 months and for others no more than 3 months.

As Foren and Brown wrote in the midst of all this change:

> Buildings, equipment, physical resources, money—all these things are essential if the personal social services are effectively to be made available to those requiring them, but the most important resource of all is personnel—fieldworkers, residential workers, day-centre staff, ancillary workers, administrators, committee members. And although all these will come together in a differently-shaped, larger yet more complex, and hopefully streamlined organisation which is appropriately geared to the attainment of its objectives, none of these people should be perceived as tabula rasa—as a 'clean slate'. [9]

If the new social services departments were being created from scratch it might have been easier. As it was, they inherited workers from two or may be three separate local authority departments (children, welfare and mental health), and social workers who although aspiring (or may be resisting) to be within one profession had different traditions, experiences and possibly varying views of their position and status within an hierarchy of separate but related social work professionals.

There were also large numbers of employees who were not social workers in fieldwork services to be integrated and moulded into the new departments. The majority of the staff being employed within the new social services departments were working in residential homes and day centres for children and adults with learning disabilities, physical impairments and mental health difficulties, and especially the social care services for an increasing number of older people.

Anne Parker was appointed as the assistant director for research, development and planning in the new Berkshire County Council Social Services Department:

> I'll never forget a meeting between the welfare department staff and some of the children's department staff, and the temperature was absolutely soaring and I couldn't work out why. We'd all been given working groups to work with, and it must have been about setting up area teams, and eventually the penny dropped that the words 'Area Team' meant one thing in the children's department and another thing in the welfare department, and there was a complete misconception as the whole thing was developing into what a new area team would be, and it made me realise the importance of language. [Anne Parker interview]

Bill Utting, within a few years to become the government's chief social work advisor, recalls his task in setting up the new social services department in Kensington and Chelsea:

> I was fortunate in my inheritance in that there was I thought a highly professional children's department there with 90% qualified social work staff in the children's department; by the time we put them altogether of course we were down to about 40% qualified social workers which I think was an indication of the relative priorities in the old departments. And there was also of course the medical officer of health's outfit to get in under the umbrella, all the day nursery set-up and mental welfare officers, so there were three quite distinct strands that were difficult to bring together, and if I had known then what I know now about the difficulties of reorganisation

I think I might have been much more worried myself at the time than I was. [Bill Utting interview]

And if creating a coherent culture and organisation by bringing disparate but existing sets of local authority workers together was not difficult enough, there was the added complication of absorbing into the new arrangements staff and services from outside of local government who following the Seebohm Committee recommendations and the review of the NHS were to be relocated to local government and new social services departments, including the large workforce of home helps.

All this was to be done at the same time as implementing new legislation including the 1970 Chronically Sick and Disabled Persons Act (CSDPA) and the 1969 Children and Young Persons Act (CYPA). The latter included the transfer to local government of what had previously been 'approved schools' for young offenders. Approved schools had been independently managed but accountable to the Home Office. They were now renamed as 'community homes with education' (CHEs) and largely placed within social services departments (some continued as independent trusts or were owned and run by charities, including several by the Catholic church).

The 1970 Chronically Sick and Disabled Persons Act

The Chronically Sick and Disabled Persons Act (CSDPA) was shepherded through Parliament by Alf Morris (his niece, Estelle, was secretary of state for children, school and families in the Labour government in the mid-2000s) as a private members bill. Morris was possibly motivated in part by having a father who had significant impairments from being seriously injured in the First World War, and then living with his wife's parents, both of whom had severe impairments [10]. Successfully shepherding the Bill through Parliament was a considerable achievement by Morris as without time within the government's legislative agenda private members bills rarely got the attention or space to be debated and enacted (a second example to feature later in this chapter was David Owen's Adoption Bill).

The Chronically Sick and Disabled Persons Bill was presented to Parliament at a time when there was campaigning by the recently formed Disablement Income Group (DIG). It was one of several single cause pressure groups set up in the mid- and late 1960s which have had longevity and are still in action 40 years later, including the Child Poverty Action Group, Shelter and Gingerbread. It was also a time when Richard Crossman's National Superannuation and Social Insurance Bill was soon to lead to the introduction of attendance allowances for disabled people and earnings-related invalidity pensions.

Edith Topliss and Bryan Gould, one a lecturer in sociology and the other a recent Member of Parliament (MP) who went on to become a television journalist, gave a detailed account of the how the Chronically Sick and Disabled Persons Bill was shaped, how it was progressed through Parliament, and what happened after it was enacted. They note that:

> It seems very likely that the work of pressure groups of and for disabled people in securing publicity for the Bill played a considerable part in convincing the outgoing Government that the measure should be among the few to be completed as a matter of urgency in the last few days of the [Labour] administration. [11]

The Bill became an Act on the same day (29 May 1970) as the Local Authority Social Services Bill became an Act. They were not just siblings favoured by the outgoing Labour government. They were twins!

The CSDPA had considerable significance. It was, in effect, the first disability rights legislation, giving an entitlement to all disabled people to be assessed in relation to their needs and how they should receive assistance to meet their needs. It required local authorities to keep a register of disabled people which would be used in planning services. It also listed, in paragraph 2 of the Act, the services which local authorities should provide.

The help to be provided went beyond the residential care focus of the 1948 National Assistance Act. It was to include the provision of practical assistance (in the disabled person's home); assistance in obtaining wireless, television, library or similar recreational facilities; the provision of lectures, games, outings or other recreational facilities outside the home; assistance to take advantage of educational facilities; facilities for, or assistance in, travelling to and from his (and her) home for the purpose of participating in any services provided under arrangements made by the authority; adaptations in the home or the provision of any additional facilities designed to secure greater safety, comfort or convenience; facilitating the taking of holidays by the disabled person; the provision of meals in the disabled person's home or elsewhere; and the provision or assistance in obtaining a telephone and any special equipment necessary to enable the disabled person's to use a telephone.

This is a wide-ranging menu of services and assistance to be provided by the new social services departments. What was of particular importance in Section 2 of the 1970 Act was the statement that 'it shall be the duty of that authority to make those arrangements'. A duty to provide this extensive range of assistance and services in the social services halcyon days of the early 1970s, with growth projected and planned at 10% year-on-year for the next ten years, may have been seen as feasible and desirable and even achievable. But later, when growth was curtailed and there were cuts in local authority funding, the CSDPA duty became controversial and a source of conflict between local authorities and disabled people and their organisations. It was a conflict which was only resolved when the courts concluded that councils could take into account the availability of funding and what they could afford in deciding to what extent they could fulfil the 1970 CSDPA duty.

In 1970 the CSDPA and the new expansive duty for the personal social services were largely welcomed. And an open-ended commitment to meet all identified need was not, of course, totally novel as national assistance welfare benefits, what were soon to become social security and national insurance and supplementary benefits, was exactly that, a non-cash limited budget commitment to meet all need assessed to be within the entitlement rules set by the government.

But the 1970 CSDPA went beyond the responsibilities of the new social services departments. It required housing authorities to consider and plan for the special housing needs of disabled people, and also required that buildings and premises to which the public had access should meet the needs of disabled people, including the provision of parking and toilets. However, the 1970 Act reined back from making this a statutory requirement as it was only to apply where 'in the circumstances it is both practicable and reasonable' [1970 CSDPA paragraph 4(1)].

It may not now 50 years later be recognised how radical this all was. Although not always well enforced or provided, disabled parking and disabled access are assumed and accepted as sensible and necessary. Before the 1970 CSDPA, these were largely unrecognised and unaddressed issues. Section 4(1) applied to shops, parks, pubs and clubs as much as to hospitals, health centres and local council offices. It applied to communities and community and commercial resources as much as to specialist health and social services. It was about integration rather than segregation and about community as compared to institutions. It reflected the continuing move away from a dependence on large institutions to care in the community. It was a giant leap on from the old Poor Law but also from the residential focus of the 1948 National Assistance Act. And it matched the aspirations of the Seebohm Committee and of the new social services departments to be positive players in contributing to the life experiences of disabled people [12].

But at the time in 1970, the radical implications of the Act were not always initially widely recognised and local authorities had had little time for preparation. Phelan, who was a social worker working with disabled people, wrote in 1979:

> Simultaneously with their own creation social services committees had their responsibilities for people with handicaps expanded, without anticipation and preparation and it would appear in many cases without realisation … the responsibilities in question were contentious, far reaching, in the majority of local authorities highly innovatory. [13]

Anne Parker, who had previously worked in the NHS and then as assistant county welfare office in Berkshire County Council's, became the assistant director for research, development and planning in the new social services department. She recalled the introduction of the CSDPA:

One of the things I had to do was to work out with other people in the department how we would approach it, and there were great debates about would you publicise it, how would you publicise it, would we be sunk if we publicised it widely? And we ended up doing a very widespread information drop with collars around milk bottles [these were the days before the big supermarkets, and even for some before refrigerators, when most people had their milk delivered in bottles early each morning to their doorstep by a milkman] and things like that to try and get the message across. That piece of legislation has been so powerful for people with disabilities, it just transformed the way we operate in England. [Anne Parker interview]

A personal reflection which I shared with Anne Parker at the time of the interview:

The reason I arrived in Berkshire in 1972 as a newly qualified social worker and a recent graduate is that you advertised a job for a social worker to be partly based on research to identify disabled people. But by the time I'd arrived you gone down the milkman route, so I was then just a full-time social worker and as the only young male in the office built up a caseload weighted to work with the courts and adolescent boys. [Ray Jones]

In such ways are careers changed and shaped!

In 1971, alongside the implementation of the 1970 LASSA and the 1970 CSDPA, there was the implementation of the 1968 Health Services and Public Health Act (HSPHA). Tucked away within the Act was a significant section, Section 45, which gave local authorities a new power 'to make arrangements for promoting the welfare of old people' [1968 HSPHA Section 45(1)]. The Act also made it mandatory for local authorities to provide a home help service. In 1972, it was noted that the requirement for local authorities to create new social services departments, and the anticipation of further local government reform, may have delayed the development of assistance for older people following the 1968 Act:

Various factors contributed to this state of affairs, but inevitably the main one has been the internal reorganisation of local authorities as a result of the Local Authority Social Services Act, 1970, and the consequent preoccupation of new or redeployed staff with matters of administration (or even their own personal position at this time of major upheaval). It has been difficult enough to keep afloat existing services. Shortage of time, money and staff too have added factors which have tied the hands of the new social services departments and caused frustration on the part of those (often voluntary bodies) who have been anxious to see quick action. Not least the spectre of local government reorganisation ahead in 1974 ... made the idea of planning ahead seem unrealistic to staff or authorities who justifiably responded to overtures urging them, to act by pointing out that their position or authority might disappear in three years anyway. [14]

But this did not mean that nothing was happening for older people. Anne Parker gave examples:

We started to have partnerships with the library services so when they were developing a new library we'd be locating a chunk of the site to have a day centre for older people in the community ... and the one I was proudest of was the centre for disabled people on an education campus ... [And] we had a small group of community development workers [but that was] the bit of Seebohm which never really took off all through this period—we hung on to them like grim death but [then] we did lose them ... but we'd built a very strong set of partnerships in Berkshire with the voluntary sector. The voluntary sector mixed economy was very well rooted in the department. [Anne Parker interview]

The intention of community development was to open up universal as much as specialist opportunities for disabled and older people and to pre-empt the 2000s focus on 'personalisation' and choice and control by and for disabled people. In 1975 Topliss wrote:

In fact the provision of such [specialist and segregated] services have expanded little since the passing of the Chronically Sick and Disabled Persons Act, but major expansion may be unnecessary and undesirable. Most disabled people desire to salvage as much as possible of the lives they led, or might have led, without disablement. They want friendships and contacts which reflect their individual interests, not clubs the membership of which shares only disablement in common. They want to pursue those hobbies and pursuits which are compatible with their reduced physical capacities, and share their holidays and recreations with family and friends … the major lack of disabled people and their families is financial. Most of them seem able and willing to devise the most appropriate compromise between limited capacities and their desires, as long as their financial resources are not so straitened … The provision of an adequate income as a right to all disabled people might well reduce still further the already quite small demand for welfare services, making it possible for local authorities to meet, with minimal expenditure, such as still remained. [15]

So as the Seebohm Report's recommended Social Services Departments came into being they were confronted with very new legislation to be implemented concerning disabled and older people. These were substantially increased responsibilities beyond those in force when the Seebohm Committee reported in 1968. There were also substantial increases in responsibilities for children and young people.

1969 Children and Young Persons Act

Earlier chapters have recounted how it was the concern about juvenile delinquency and its causes which had fuelled an argument for a family social service. From the Ingleby Committee's report in 1960 [16], to the Labour Party's early 1960s Lord Longford study group with its report 'Crime—a Challenge to Us All' [17] published in 1964, to the subsequent White Paper 'The Child, the Family and the Young Offender' (1965) [18] published by the Labour government when it came into power, and then the White Paper 'Children in Trouble' in 1968 [19], the direction was all in one direction. Children who were seen as mad or bad were to be seen as essentially sad and children who had been seen as disturbed or delinquent were to be recognised as children who had been disadvantaged and deprived.

Packman noted:

The problem of how to deal with young offenders is the theme of a whole series of reports and reappraisals published in the 1960s and it exercised the magistracy, the probation service, police and political parties alike. Cause for concern sprang not only from the apparent decline in the success of the approved schools in rehabilitating young offenders, but also from the rising incidence of juvenile crime ... A feature of those who pressed for change in the 1960s was their conviction that family-based explanations of delinquency were of prime importance ... This basic assumption naturally led the reformers to stress the connection between prevention of neglect and prevention of delinquency. [20]

The 1969 CYPA introduced several significant changes to be inherited in 1971 by the new social services departments. For children aged 10–14 years they were only to be brought before the courts if they had offended *and* they were assessed as being in need of care and control. The offence alone, unless very serious, was not an adequate ground to bring a child before the juvenile court. The intention was both to decriminalise and to divert from the courts children who might instead, if thought necessary, receive voluntary assistance from the new social services departments. For young people aged 14–17 years the option of a 'caution' was introduced if it was thought a court appearance and sentence would not be helpful or necessary and there were to be enhanced non-custodial and non-care sentences for those who were brought to the court, with 'intermediate treatment' [21, 22, 23] to be attached to a supervision order and which was initially seen to be about diversionary activity and then later became more focused on what became called a 'correctional curriculum' confronting offending behaviours. And when it was deemed by the court necessary to remove a child or young person from their family they were to be cared for by local authorities either in foster care or children homes or in what had previously been Home Office controlled 'approved schools' which now became local authority 'community homes with education'. As noted by Packman 'Taken in its entirety the intentions of the Act are clear. Delinquent children and deprived children are all children "in trouble" and, as far as possible, should be treated alike' [24].

The responsibility for these 'children in trouble' was given to the new local authority social services departments. Their social workers would provide reports to the courts for children aged 10–14 years, would supervise these children if supervision orders were made, would provide 'intermediate treatment programmes' in the community for those who had these conditions attached to a supervision order, and would accommodate, mainly in foster and children's homes, children and young people aged 10–17 years if 'care orders' were made by the courts.

In essence, large chunks of responsibilities were transferred from the Home Office and its probation services to local authorities and their social services departments. Social workers and their managers were given considerable discretion especially regarding what to do with children and young people made subject to care orders, deciding whether they should be allowed to remain or returned to live with their families or should they be cared for away from their families, with the local council deciding where and how this care was to be provided.

This did not sit well with the magistrates in the juvenile courts or with the police. It also was not fully supported or enacted by the Conservative government which was elected in 1970. [25] Not all of the sections of the Act were brought into power. For example, the Act had included that the minimum age for prosecution should be raised to 12 years. This did not happen. Restrictions were also intended to be applied to those who could be prosecuted between the ages of 14 and 17 years, but these were not introduced. As Packman noted:

> The goal of more liberal, less punitive treatment of offenders suffered with the retention of many of the old orders. While magistrates still have power to send offenders to attendance and detention centres and to recommend Borstal training [a form of prison for juvenile offenders] they will continue to do so—the more so, it seems, since their power to make approved school orders has been taken away and replaced by the unpopular 'care order', giving social workers discretion to choose where the offender shall be accommodated. [26]

Berlins and Wansell, writing in 1974, noted:

> One of the most serious general accusations levelled against the way the Act is operating is that children under the age of seventeen are now able to commit almost any kind of offence with impunity. The law has, as a result, been made almost irrelevant and an object of mockery among young offenders. The reason for this is said by juvenile court magistrates to be the taking away of their power by the 1969 Act to make an order to send a

child to an approved school. Many children who should be in a residential institution are left free to commit further offences, because, the magistrates allege, the only order the court can now effectively make is one placing the child into the care of the local authority. [27]

Berlins and Wansell comment specifically about the magistrates' concerns about social workers:

Many of the magistrates' criticisms entre around the character of the 'new breed' of social workers whom the 1969 Act suggested they rely on in its operation. They claim that these new social workers seem to be both young and inexperienced in dealing with troubled children. As one magistrate put it, 'How can these young people, fresh from university departments of sociology, but otherwise completely untrained and inexperienced, possibly understand the needs of a delinquent child from a deprived home in one of the city's slums?' [28]

But, as Berlins and Wansell noted, the magistrates' criticisms directed at social workers were essentially a continuing disagreement about the philosophy and intentions of the 1969 Act:

In essence, therefore, the magistrates in England and Wales were in dispute with the 1969 Act, albeit also concerned about the competence of the social workers and the social services departments implementing the Act. How much even more concerned must have been magistrates in Scotland where as a part of the process of decriminalising children juvenile courts were replaced by children's hearings focused on children's welfare rather than delinquency.

The magistrates were right in some of their views about the 'new breed' of social workers graduating with sociology degrees. I was one. The 'new criminology' [29] introduced deviancy and labelling theory and concepts of deviance amplification by (over)reacting to children and young people who had committed, usually petty, crime. It argued that grouping young people who had offended together, with approved schools seen as having delinquent subcultures, promoted further delinquency and escalated criminal careers.

The 'new criminology' was central to the learning and understanding of the recently qualified and expanding number of young social workers. One of the key texts to which student social workers were introduced was titled *Radical Non-Intervention: Rethinking the Delinquency Problem* [30], with the view that sometimes not intervening at all was more helpful than intervening and creating delinquent identities and stigmatising, stereotyping and segregating children and young people.

In response to the magistrates' concerns about the 1969 CYPA, social workers, and the new social services departments Berlins and Wansell noted:

Social workers accept that the reorganisation of their departments that took place as a result of the Seebohm reforms in January 1971 made it difficult for them to cope as well as they would have liked with the changes brought about at exactly the same time by the Children and Young Persons Act 1969. They accept, for example, that the foundation of generic social work departments has meant that some social workers experienced in children's work have had to work in other fields as well. They also accept that sometimes those with different experience have suddenly found themselves confronted for the first time with difficult delinquent children and have been unable to cope. But they utterly reject the magistrates' implicit criticism that they are in any way 'soft' with the children under their care. Mr Brian Roycroft, the Director of Social Services for Newcastle-upon-Tyne, has summarised the social workers attitude in an article in the *Magistrate*, 'I believe we are getting a new breed of social workers with a tremendous commitment to their work and to reaching into the basic roots of social ills to cure them'. [31]

And on genericism:

Directors of social services deny fiercely that the decision to allow a child to return to his home, against the recommendations of the magistrates, is taken by inexperienced or ill-advised social workers. They point out that the whole concept of a generic social work department is that there should be a team of social workers, all of them having different skills and experience who could combine to consider particular cases together. They maintain that any important decision is only taken after discussion and with the individual social worker's administrative superiors. [32]

So what was the outcome of this running dispute between the magistracy (and the police) versus the social workers and the social services departments? Writing in 1980, Thorpe, Smith, Green and Paley looked back through the 1970s and commented that:

> The tragedy that has occurred since [1971 and the partial implementation of the 1969 CYPA] can best be described as a situation in which the worst of all possible worlds came into existence—people have been persistently led to believe that the juvenile criminal justice system has become softer and softer, while the reality has been that it has become harder and harder. Even before the Act was due to come into operation, the Labour government which had championed it fell from power. The incoming Conservative government of 1970 almost immediately declared that it would not implement the vital decriminalising Sections 4 and 5, which were intended to raise the age of criminal responsibility and to provide diversionary services through local authority social work intervention. [33]

Between 1971, when the 1969 CYPA came into operation, and 1977 supervision orders for 10–13 year olds declined from 28.4% to 21.1% of all sentences, and care orders declined from 12.6% to 9.4%, so the proportion who would have been in contact with social workers reduced contrary to the intention of the 1969 and of Seebohm Committee's 'family service'. The proportion of more punitive sentences, however, increased with fines up from 19.3% to 22.2% and attendance centre orders increased from 12.2% to 13.3%. For 14–17 year olds the move towards more punitive and penal sentencing was even more pronounced with care orders down from 7.9% to 4.2% and supervision orders from 19.4% to 15%, but with attendance centre orders up from 7.5% to 10.2% and detention centre orders increased from 3.3% to 7.3%, with also a small increase from 3.1% to 3.3% in longer Borstal detention orders. Thorpe and his colleagues concluded that 'A system that was intended to produce a shift towards the use of community [children's] homes and supervision in the community [by social workers] has in fact produced a dramatic increase in custodial sentences' [34]. This was despite a raft of publications, including from the Home Office's own research unit, noting the negative impact on children and young people of residential and penal sentences [35, 36, 37]. Norman Tutt (who as a psychologist had worked in approved schools, became a professor of applied social studies and later a director of social services) commented that:

> At present residential treatment fails to alter the behaviour of the majority of offenders ... The failure of institutional treatment is achieved at considerable financial cost—there would be cause for concern if it was only a matter of the taxpayer not getting for money. But this failure more importantly reflects the irreparable damage done to children by the state. [38]

Organisational Structures

Although social workers were not the largest type of workers in the new social services departments (the largest group would have been home helps followed by residential care workers) it was social workers who were often dominant in the thinking about and deciding how to structure the new social services departments [SSDs].

As was noted at the time, there was a flurry of activity in exploring structural possibilities [39]. A whole enterprise developed centred on designing alternative options for the line management structures of the new SSDs with a 'Social Services Organisational Research Unit' at the 'Brunel Institute of Organisational and Social Studies' (BIOSS) established and producing books concentrated on how social services departments should be structured [40, 41].

Two models came to dominate—the 'geographic model' and the 'functional model'. The 'geographic model' would have all the services within one area, neighbourhood, locality or geographical division (the terminology and descriptors varied) under one manager for that territory. The 'functional model' had, under the director of social services, assistant directors who each had the management responsibility for a type of service, usually fieldwork, and then residential, day and domiciliary care. There might also be a separate assistant director for finance and administration and one for research, planning and development. But note what is not here. There are no specialist and segregated management arrangements for children's, welfare and mental health services as in the former separate departments.

For those leading the new large bureaucracies the change was considerable:

> [Lucy Faithful] likened the change from Children's Officer to Director of Social Services to moving from running a little local shop where you'd know what was on every shelf, know every customer, and know the few assistants you've got, to running a big supermarket. [7]

The supermarket analogy actually underplays the complexity of what was within the remit of the newly appointed directors of social services. A supermarket is on one site with one purpose—sell as much and make as much profit as possible. The new social services departments encompassed a myriad of functions, located on a large number of dispersed sites and with several different constituencies all seeking to set the agenda and the business focus, ranging from central and local government's elected representatives to the local public and press and to local and national pressure groups.

Bob Holman noted that these new big organisations became known by some as the 'Seebohm factories':

> With staff in some departments numbered in their thousands, the Social Services Departments were sometimes referred to as Seebohm factories. Like any large organisation, they rapidly developed as bureaucracies with complex administrative systems and layers of management. Bureaucracy is not in itself an evil, it can be a force for efficiency or inefficiency. But the weight of evidence is that within the personal social services it became a source of problems as much as a solution for them. For instance, far from improving communications between different sections, as the Seebohm Report had anticipated, it seemed to make them worse. [42]

The dangers of the new big 'Seebohm departments' being dysfunctional large bureaucracies was noted in 1970 by Peter Leonard, a lecturer in social work at the time who had previously led a Family Service Unit and who had been a member of the Seebohm Committee:

The legislation itself could lead to the development of the personal social services as bureaucratic and remote as ever and the ghost of the Poor Law might never be laid. Whether or not a really *new* social service is created depends upon the extent to which the organisational framework can be seen as the means for mobilising community resources so as to enable radical change to take place. [43]

The quality of leadership of the new departments was, therefore, going to be crucial. Bill Utting commented on the quality of the first directors of social services. Overall, he was not overwhelmingly impressed:

There were 170 of them and most of them I regarded as safe local authority appointments … This sounds sort of snobbish and I don't mean it to be, but the majority were rather humdrum local authority welfare officers. I should say that there were a number of extremely able local authority welfare officers who went on to lead us in the Association [Association of Directors of Social Services], but I couldn't see that the quality of those in 1971 was really up to what Seebohm wanted. I don't think that's necessarily their fault. The way the legislation went through on the nod in 1970 meant that there hadn't been the preparatory work with local authorities that one would have expected with a major piece of legislation like that, and most local authorities saw it as a straightforward administrative reorganisation, we're going to have to cope with all these new Acts of Parliament and so on. But it was administrative and you needed to sort out control of the costs so we would go for safe people rather than the adventurous.

But this was soon to change, prompted and enabled by local government reform which was concluded in 1974:

The 1974 reorganisation I think winnowed out quite a lot of people who frankly weren't up to the job, but I think over the years the calibre of directors of social services remained variable. The proportion of able ones increased, but there were always anxieties about the management of services in a number of authorities partly due to straight managerial problems, perhaps more often than political issues. [Bill Utting interview]

Hall commented on how the 'double reorganisation' (1970, 1974) was disruptive. She also gave the numbers which showed how much change and disruption there was:

Before 1971 there were 173 children's departments and 204 welfare authorities in England and Wales ... In the first [1971] reorganisation, 174 social services departments were created and, in consequence, the number of chief officer appointments was reduced considerably. The second [1974] reorganisation diminished the number of departments still further to 116, creating even larger organisations, taller hierarchies and fewer appointments at the most senior levels. A great many senior personnel in social services departments were displaced; some retired, some left the services and many were, in effect, demoted.

Tom White, in his autobiography, commented how it was not only local government boundaries which were being reorganised but also the culture and workings within local government:

The mood was changing nationally with recognition that decisions in one service could very much affect another and it seemed obvious that there should be a more coordinated approach, at both elected member and officer level. Coventry, as a county borough, was an all-purpose authority and very much in the vanguard of promoting the 'corporate management' of the affairs of the city. The previous traditional officer structure with a legally qualified town clerk as 'primus inter pares' [first among equals] of the chief officers of the authority was replaced by a chief executive who would chair an executive board of chief officers, each of whom would have a shared accountability to him and to a committee of elected members. A strong 'Policy Committee' provided the elected members' political co-ordination for the authority. [44]

The changes to local government in 1974 included the demise of some smaller local authorities and the scaling up to big 'metropolitan counties'. For example, Avon County Council was created by taking top-tier local government responsibilities from Bristol and Bath city councils and territory from Somerset and Gloucestershire county councils. Cleveland and Humberside County Councils were created in the same way. Not only now were social services departments big but they became even bigger within bigger councils. And although, in 1974, public health functions were moved to the NHS, local authorities were given the responsibility for hospital social work services which were transferred from the NHS to social services departments.

The Development of Generic Social Work

Tom White commented that social workers supporting and campaigning for the Seebohm Committee's proposals were 'like turkeys voting for Christmas in the sense that they treasured specialisation, some of them did anyway, and yet they were campaigning for something that was going to remove them from that' [Tom White interview]. And Anne Parker noted:

> The thing I think is important post-Seebohm is how strong the children's teams were and how relatively weak and low in numbers of professionals the welfare department teams were, and what a lot there was to learn, and how the amalgamation really just raised the profile, raised the quality, raised the approach across the piste … In Berkshire the line we took was generic teams, not generic workers, which was the big debate at the time, which I think was the right thing to do … it didn't mean that people didn't cross boundaries, but it meant they were not required to, and I think it just made sense in learning terms And then gradually as we got stronger people became more generic workers with mixed workloads. [Anne Parker interview]

Tom White commented that in Coventry the move to generic social workers was possibly too quick:

> This was an opportunity to establish a family service, but we went too far too fast. I was totally committed to the concept of providing a family service and believed that essentially each social worker was able to meet the whole range of family needs, with extra training. Now perhaps we shouldn't have done that, anything like as quickly as that. [On reflection] I would've maintained specialist provision for a proportion of the service and at the

same time gradually introducing the more generic approach. I think it would've made a very big difference in terms of staff morale. [Tom White interview]

Hall gave an overview of the generic-specialist issue and its impact in the early 1970s:

Many departments and directors of social services pursued genericism with great zeal and implemented the rapid integration of caseloads. The low morale which for several years was a feature of the new departments must in part be attributed to the effects of the loss of specialist labels which, quite apart from the security they provide for the holders, are important as a source of status and prestige. To deny the importance of specialisation— indeed to denigrate specialist knowledge as narrow and out of date—is to devalue the holder. Quite apart from the impact on the morale of staff concerned, the move to the generic worker has also been blamed for a supposed loss of specialist skills for highly complicated tasks, such as working with disturbed adolescents. [45]

The impact on the morale of speedily introduced genericism for social workers was noted by Bilton:

I well remember we had a [British Association of Social Workers Children and Families section] conference in Manchester … the whole atmosphere of that meeting was of people who'd been kind of knocked for six, just a feeling of everybody wandering around in a daze, kind of 'never in our most pessimistic moments did we imagine it would be like this sort' of thing … Many of us had thought it would all happen a bit more gradually, that we would be brought together in teams of your ex-mental welfare officer, your ex-child care officer, a couple of new people with [Secretary of State] Sir Keith Joseph's new money and you would be taking on largely the work that you were used to. [Keith Bilton interview]

Roy Parker gave an explanation as to why social workers as generalists may have been pushed so hard and so quickly:

It was a confused situation … the Seebohm idea of a [social services team] area was 30,000 population. Nobody did the figures [for the Seebohm Committee] of how many of this and how many of that, but there's a limit to how far you can specialise if you're a team serving 30,000 people. [Roy Parker interview]

Bilton, whilst agreeing with Parker, gave an additional different explanation of why generic social work was pushed so hard and so quickly in many of the new social services departments:

One possible reason is that you do need to get control of that department, and you may not be able to afford to have too much of the old order still preserved within the new structure, or if you do you find that it gets increasingly difficult to deal with as time goes on … And more importantly perhaps were the numbers of people available in relation to their previous experience, they didn't stack up with the mix of new work coming through the door. [Keith Bilton interview]

Olive Stevenson, who later in the 1970s wrote a book about specialisation within social service departments [46], commented that when social services departments were forming:

The organisation was not generic friendly, largely because it did not involve proper mechanisms for specialisation which is very complex. But also training arrangements were not in place for helping people who were interested in but scared of moving across [into generic roles]. [Olive Stevenson interview]

Olive Stevenson's reflections on complexity and on training and skills and knowledge development echo those of T.H. Marshall, a leading professor of social administration in the 1960s and 1970:

A welfare service which aims at being preventive, curative and comprehensive poses problems of diagnosis and prognosis of great difficulty and complexity. But the fact that investigation must study the situation as a whole means that no single specialism can cope with it. The choice lies between employing several specialists on one case, or trusting the judgement of a single specialist. The Seebohm Committee advocates the latter course … The expertise should be available at a higher [more senior] level. But it goes on to say it is expected in the future 'as the service develops, specialisations will cluster differently and new types of specialisation emerge', but 'it would be unwise to attempt to define these now'. Perhaps so, but it should be remembered that the role of a social service, especially a personal welfare service, must be tailored to the capacities of those who are to execute it. [47]

However, it was not only the magistrates and the police, as noted above, who bemoaned the loss of specialist child care social workers. Timmins in his overall account of the welfare state and its development stated that this was also the view of doctors about the loss of specialist older and more experienced mental health social workers:

Seebohm's desire for generic social work departments and less rigid divisions between the various practitioners became over-interpreted into generic social workers who acted as jacks of all trades and too often masters of none. Those used to dealing with the mentally ill were suddenly expected to handle the complex canon of child care law and procedures, and vice versa. The rapid expansion, not just of social work but of a whole range of caring services, brought in a flood of young, raw recruits, trained in theory but lacking in experience. Too many were plunged into situations which they had neither the experience nor the back-up to cope. Relations between GPs and social workers in particular deteriorated: family doctors calling in the mental welfare officer to deal with a seriously disturbed patient, for example, would find that the old sweat from the armed forces with a good armlock had been replaced by a slip of a girl who did not believe in principle in sectioning patients and who the doctor felt needed his protection rather than the other way round. [48]

Increasing Management and Managers

It was not only the advent of genericism which stretched and tested the workforce within the social services departments. There was also the creation of more management posts to oil and sustain the large bureaucracies which had been created. This had two impacts. The first was that experienced workers were promoted and clients were left in contact with less experienced workers, as noted by Hey in 1979:

> Many experienced practitioners and managers progressed one or several levels in the structure and the basic conditions for successful generic practice were lost or postponed ... In modelling the new Departments so that they might cope with their corporate and community planning functions and encompass the increased size of the organisation, more senior posts were established and many middle managers moved up a level. Clients of the new Department and the less experienced workers were deprived of colleagues and managers who could provide the help and guidance they needed to implement the new expectations on them. [49]

The second impact of the large and growing bureaucracies was that young, relatively inexperienced graduates were promoted quickly:

> The problem was that we actually needed skills and experience that money couldn't buy so we could provide material services alright, but we sort of lacked the solid middle management that you get with people who have been in the authority for 10 years and worked at it. I mean, in the early 1970s we were promoting to first line managers people who had got two years fieldwork experience after qualification. [Bill Utting interview]

Funding

So the new social services departments had the problems which came with being very large and increasingly bureaucratic and with not having a ready supply of qualified social workers who would and could work generically. But the size of the new departments had one advantage which had been anticipated by the Seebohm Committee. They had the profile and influence to be able to argue successfully for money, both within local authorities and also with central government. This was despite there now being a Conservative government publicly stating that it was on a mission to cut back public expenditure and services, but budgets were increased even in Conservative controlled councils. It was a time of financial feast for local government personal social services as noted by several who were interviewed for this book:

> The annual estimates [on which government grant for the personal social services were based] were exceeded because local authorities were distributing [general grant] resources towards those services. In the first few years year one had 15% real growth, year two 14% real growth, 13% the year after that. [Bleddyn Davies interview]

> It was a time of enormous expansion. I mean Keith Joseph [the Conservative secretary of state for health and social services] said 10%. I don't think there was any area [of activity] in Coventry in those first 10 years when we did not get a 15–20% increase in our budget. [Tom White interview]

> Hammersmith was pretty good and it rapidly became Labour so then I had a Labour Council intent on spending money. They gave me more money than I could cope with. The growth rate was far beyond my capacity to use it after due consideration … I had exponential growth for social services. [Peter Westland interview]

> It was of course the time when we were required [by central government] to produce 10 year plans with an assumption of 10% per annum growth, and so in that sense we [in Berkshire] were very growth orientated. [Anne Parker interview]

Writing in 1981, ten years on from the initiation of the social service departments, Tom White noted that there had been growth but that it was necessary and needed to match and meet the new responsibilities and demands facing the new departments:

> During the past decade political decisions have given increased responsibilities to social services departments (Health Services and Public Health Act, 1968, Children and Young Persons Act, 1969, Chronically Sick and Disabled Persons Act, 1970 and Children's Act 1975). In the same period public expectations of the personal social services have been rising, often encouraged to do so by political comment. The substantial increase in the elderly population of the UK, and changing views about appropriate meth-

ods of care for dependent groups have both contributed to an increased demand for services, which authorities have not been able to satisfy. One may cite changing attitudes to the care of the mentally disordered, as evidenced in the two 'Better Services' White Papers and the general acceptance of community care as the preferred option. In this context the increase in social services spending does not seem to be disproportionate. [50]

The new departments and their directors had had a surprising, and possibly unlikely, ally in the recently appointed Conservative government's secretary of state for social services. It was unlikely as Sir Keith Joseph, the son of a wealthy family which had built the Bovis construction company, was later to be described as 'the power behind [the Thatcherite] throne' [51], and as 'the father of Thatcherism' [52]. Biffen, a Conservative cabinet colleague, noted in his 1994 obituary of Joseph that 'Joseph confessed that his record as a public spender sat ill with his subsequent exhortations for retrenchment' [51].

Tom White recalls his contacts with Joseph:

It was vital that the new administration was convinced of the need for change and a willingness to make resources available to ensure the changes were effective. Sir Keith Joseph, the new secretary of state for health and social services, was the key person in this process. I was involved with Sir Keith in many meetings. He had a unique style—conducting more a seminar than a typical government meeting or an interview. Always excessively polite, he would nevertheless frequently challenge views put to him and demand evidence, preferably backed by research. Once persuaded of the case he was an influential and effective patron of our services and amazingly, in a Conservative government bent on 'smaller government' and cutting back on local council expenditure, he secured real increases in spending on social services of ten per cent a year, each year he was Secretary of State—a previously unheard of period of sustained growth in social service expenditure. [53]

And Bilton noted:

In the first half of the 1970s it played out rather well because we had a committed Secretary of State in Sir Keith Joseph, however much he may subsequently have come to regard his views of those days as misguided, but at the same time he introduced ten year Social Services plans, which we all had to write, based on an assumption of 10% annual growth. [Keith Bilton interview]

Biffen commented that Joseph 'specialised on social issues—not always the most favoured topic with Tories—and soon won recognition. Looking back on this period he later commented "my main motivation was then as it has been since, the escape of a society and individuals from poverty"' [51].

Sir Keith Joseph's explorations into the causes of poverty, and its transmission for families across generations, focused on what became called 'the cycle of deprivation', which is discussed in the next chapter. Herbert Laming stated:

If you talked to someone like Sir Keith Joseph, I mean he was a chap who was Tory through and through, he was actually concerned when you got him talking about the cycle of deprivation. He was actually talking about a lot of things that I think that Seebohm was actually [concerned about], in a different language but actually he'd got that vision. [Herbert Laming]

Bob Holman had also met Joseph:

[I met Keith Joseph a number of times and I must admit I liked him.] Once, when I was in Birmingham [as a lecturer in social work at Birmingham University] I got up at a public meeting, I think BASW had organised it, and said my usual stuff, you know, 'you're public school/ Oxbridge, you're completely removed from clients', as we used to call them, and to his credit he said 'you're quite right, bring me some', and I did. I brought them from Handsworth, took them to his office in London, and he was incredibly welcoming, slightly patronising, but really interested and in fact took up some of their cases, their social security complaints. He was just the opposite of Richard Crossman who was very arrogant, really dismissed clients just like he dismissed the Seebohm report … [But] Sir Keith with his cycle of deprivation, which I think is fundamentally flawed, believed it is caused by a minority of very inadequate parents who have lots of children. [Bob Holman second interview]

However, as will be noted in the following chapter, it was not a concern with poverty and deprivation which came to have a major impact on the personal social services and the developing social services departments and their social workers. It was the death of a little child, Maria Colwell. There was also a quick end of the funding feast which had promised 10% year-on-year growth.

6

The Seismic Shifts of the Mid-1970s

The Maria Colwell Inquiry was one of two significant, indeed seismic, events which reset the ground for the personal social services and re-charted the course to be followed over subsequent years, with new routes which are readily recognisable and still trodden 50 years later.

The Colwell Inquiry was the first of many media-driven frenzies about child abuse which have become more common since the 1970s. The family-orientated and family support aspirations for children within the white papers of the 1960s, and of the 1963 Children Act and the 1969 CYPA, were replaced by an emphasis on rescuing and removing children from poor care and from families in difficulty.

The second significant change was that the anticipation of year-on-year financial growth for the personal social services hit the economic and political buffers. The 1970 Chronically Sick and Disabled Persons Act's focus on expanding assistance for disabled people was to be replaced by retrenchment and rationing. The hopes and aspirations of the Seebohm Report that there might be time and attention given to preventing social

© The Author(s) 2020, corrected publication 2021
R. Jones, *A History of the Personal Social Services in England*,
https://doi.org/10.1007/978-3-030-46123-2_6

need arising, with resources for community development and early help, were increasingly put on the back-burner as social services departments had to respond to a growing aged population and more very impaired young people living longer and well into adulthood. They also had to provide services to respond to the closure of the long-term institutions such as 'mental asylums', 'subnormality hospitals' and geriatric wards in general and cottage hospitals. All of this was to be tackled with no commensurate budget increase to match the expanding responsibilities for community care and the increasing numbers of disabled and older people needing assistance.

The legacies of these two seismic shifts still have impact within social services in the 2000s. Children's social services are dominated by a focus on child protection. Adult social services are dominated by a focus on rationing scarce resources. Both are now focused on risk assessments and risk management, terms which were absent in the Seebohm Report which might be seen as more about promoting welfare and well-being.

The Maria Colwell Inquiry

The Colwell Inquiry reported in 1974 [1]. The inquiry was established following the death in Brighton, East Sussex, of Maria Colwell, aged seven years, who was neglected, physically abused and killed following a violent assault by her stepfather. Maria had spent many years in foster care but was returned to her mother at her mother's request.

It is still something of a mystery why some child deaths attract considerable attention and others go unreported or only receive brief attention. In 1946 it was the death of Dennis O'Neil, a 12-year-old boy in foster care killed by the foster father, which led to the Monckton Inquiry [2] and with the Curtis Committee [3] then shaping the 1948 Children Act which strengthened the requirements about the residential and foster care of children. It was 25 years until another child's death captured significant media and hence public attention.

Olive Stevenson, in the early 1970s a reader in social work at Oxford University, states that she does not know why or how she came to be asked to be a member of the Colwell inquiry panel along with three others (a solicitor who chaired the inquiry, a doctor and a county councillor from outside East Sussex).

Stevenson's view is that Maria Colwell's death attracted so much interest for two reasons. First, it was the local paper which gave it much attention and this was then picked up by the national press, and as the inquiry which was then set up had its hearings in public, it fed a continuing press interest and, Stevenson noted, consequent 'onslaughts' on social workers [4]. Olive Stevenson commented:

> The Brighton Evening Argos, which was the local paper, gave an absolutely huge amount of coverage, which then spilled into the nationals. It was, of course, enhanced by the fact that unlike so many until Climbie the inquiry was held in public so it was just like a pseudo court. It was court rise when we walked in, that sort of stuff. And we had really unsavoury people in Brighton who would go to anything gruesome and they were there every day [along with] a nightclub owner who was looking to set a museum of mementos of Maria Colwell and we found him prowling around stealing our name plates afterwards. And the Evening Argos was taking pictures of the foster mother with a teddy bear at Maria's grave. The social worker I think was not got at home, but there was a lot of anxiety when she came to give evidence. [Olive Stevenson interview]

Roy Parker had a similar recollection:

> Well if you look at Maria Colwell, how did it get into the public arena at the very beginning? A local journalist. And I think you have to look at the development of what is now called investigative journalism. I think that really does date to some time in the 70s, and that spread not simply to the nationals, but I think to the locals, then with syndicated news, and also the changes in the nature of the tabloid press. I've still got the front page of The Mirror with Maria Colwell. [Roy Parker interview]

The threat and theatre of the inquiry are described evocatively by Butler and Drakeford:

> 'Diana Lees' [the local authority social worker's] cross-examination began with a warning aimed directly at her from Mr Mildon [counsel for the

Inquiry] that has resonated with a folk horror through social work: "What I am going to do is to suggest that Maria's death occurred because of the failure to seize an opportunity which occurred in April, 1972, and that you were primarily responsible" [5] ... At the Maria Colwell public inquiry in 1973 "lawyers routinely referred to [social workers and health visitors as] 'defendants' and even the chair referred to 'the defence'".

The social worker was the target of particular harassment:

Press photographers were already gathered to record [Diana Lees'] arrival, as they were to take photographs of her arriving and leaving from every session ... Then during the lunch interval, matters deteriorated further. The *Daily Mirror* (6 November 1973) reported that, 'Fury erupted at an inquiry yesterday over the heart-rending ordeal of tug-of-love girl Maria Colwell ... When 29 year old Miss Lees left during the lunch break, she was followed by thirty women who booed and chanted, "Liar' and 'Get out!". The police escorted her for 100 yards before the crowd broke up.' *The Sun* (6 November 1973), on the same day, told readers that, 'A crowd of booing, fist-waving people chased social worker Diana Lees along a street yesterday after she gave evidence at the Maria Colwell inquiry ... Even as Miss Lees gave her evidence, there were cries of abuse from the public gallery. At the end of the day, a crowd of 20 people, almost all women, was waiting again. Police surrounded Miss Lees as she hurried to a waiting taxi ...' The *Daily Express* (14 November 1973), among others, was bringing readers up to date with new details that verged on the surreal. Under the headline 'Maria social worker gets bodyguard', it reported: "Social worker Diana Lees, the woman at the centre of the storm over the death of seven-year old Maria Colwell, has been provided with a squad of bodyguards. The move follows harassment from the public, threats and vile letters". [6]

But it was not only, according to Olive Stevenson, the local press interest which was then picked up by the national press, which led to the Colwell Inquiry. There was also an increasing awareness of the physical abuse of children, the so-called battered baby syndrome [7]:

I've been thinking of this in relation to Climbie and 'Baby P' [discussed in a later chapter]. I think that one aspect of this is that the violent deaths of children at the hands of men invoke very powerful wide spread emotions in the general public … I mean we've had some horrible neglect cases and so on but they seem not to resonate in quite the same way that male violence of this kind seems to. But there were also much more subtle things, because just before [Maria Colwell's death and the inquiry] the Tunbridge Wells group as it was known of paediatricians were meeting to discuss the amazing findings from the States. Doctors were finding that children had been 'battered', quote unquote, and that the broken bones of babies showed up in x-rays and they couldn't at first believe for years that it *could* possibly have been intentional. And the more up and coming paediatricians in this country picked it up, so we had a growing awareness of violence to children. [Olive Stevenson interview]

Olive Stevenson wrote a minority report at the end of the Colwell Inquiry:

Lots of people who haven't read the report at all just hear that I did a minority report and have a tendency to think she would wouldn't she, she was just defending social workers. Absolutely not. I went with the general report in respect of the periods *after* Maria returned home because it simply wasn't adequately dealt with at all. It was the *run up* to it that was the difficulty [in the majority inquiry report] … As far as my reasons for doing the minority report were concerned it was basically a difference of opinion [with the other inquiry panel members] about the analysis [of how it was decided Maria should return home]. [Olive Stevenson interview]

Stevenson thought, however, that for those workers involved with Maria Colwell 'the interagency stuff was a shambles':

The positive side [of the inquiry] was that it set in train what are now regular policy reviews and statements about working together at government level … the idea of working together really took shape. But on the negative side of course it raised the anxiety levels of social services in particular, and set in motion the risk averse bureaucratic solutions to problems and bang in more procedures and we'll avoid [a child death]. We did not put in place the arrangements for reflective supervision which in my view are one of the ways which we know improve things. [Olive Stevenson interview]

Jean Renvoise, in her 1974 Penguin book on 'Children in Danger' which also reflected on the death of Maria Colwell, had a range of reflections and recommendations which anticipated what was to be implemented over the coming years, including the introduction of children's advocates (who were to become the court appointed guardian ad litems in care proceedings). Renvoise concluded:

> The Maria Colwell case has brought child abuse to the forefront of public attention. Questions are being asked in the House [of Commons], and changes in the law are suggested. But the danger is that once the public excitement has died down present pressure will be relaxed ... Between the millions of parents who sometimes feel exasperated and only just manage to refrain from striking their child, and the comparative few who batter to the point of death, there is an unbroken ladder. It is our job to learn how to pluck parents from that ladder before they have progressed very far up it. To do that we need knowledge, money to finance the acquisition of that knowledge, endless compassion and understanding. Is that too much to ask of a society like ours? [8]

Written in 1974, Renvoise message and question has a relevance almost 50 years later in 2020 amid the cuts in services to help families and to protect children, the demonisation of poor parents, and the targeting of social workers for blame and vilification.

The impact of the Colwell Inquiry, and the media coverage and comment it generated only two years after the formation of social services departments, was considerable and wide ranging:

> Well, I think it was very dramatic and sensational. I think it helped change dramatically the public view of social services and social workers. I think we were only able to get Seebohm through because those in power did see us as the goodies. There was no doubt we were disinterested, concerned about our clients, naive maybe and over-enthusiastic and not as objective in our thinking as we should have been, but generally we were seen as good chaps [although most were women]. But the press we got from The Mail, The Star and the rest began to get real negative feelings about people involved in the profession. [Tom White interview]

One of the consequences, in addition to the negativity generated about social services and social work, was the government's response:

Colwell was a very unpleasant shock at the time to us. One of the worst things about it for me was this then obsession on the part of central government with issuing detailed guidance and procedures about how child protection should be handled. I got very worked up about it and thought it was going to be the death of individual professional judgement. It was only afterwards when I got into a national position [as the head of the Department of Health and Social Security's Social Work Service] that I realised that the individual judgement could be pretty fallible at times and one did need a trade-off between procedures and professional judgement in something like child protection. [Bill Utting interview]

Writing in 2015 Terry Bamford recalled:

The [Colwell] committee of inquiry was critical of the lack of communication between the various agencies working with the family. It was concerned by the lack of specialist training for work in child protection. And these criticisms drew a prompt response from the Department for Social Security in terms of procedural actions in its circular *Non-accidental injury to children*.[1] This was designed to minimise risk in future by promoting inter-agency communication and collaboration. Actions included the establishment of area review committees [the forerunners of area child protection committees, which were later replaced by local safeguarding children boards which were ended in 2018] to coordinate procedures, a child protection register to identify those children at risk, a system of multi-agency case conferences to ensure communication of concerns and agree actions, and the designation of social services as the lead agency in the system. The framework still essentially governs practice today, although there have been many subsequent changes in administrative arrangements. [9]

---

[1] I carried the circular in my work bag along with a set of relevant legislation—the 1948 Children Act, 1963 Children Act, 1969 Children and Young Persons Act, 1948 National Assistance Act, 1959 Mental Health Act, Boarding Out Regulations and the Child Poverty Action Group's National Welfare Benefits Handbooks.

The proceduralisation which followed the Colwell Inquiry introduced and described in the 1974 circular was only seven pages long. Over the years, the statutory child protection guidance increased, often as a result of more recommendations and requirements following subsequent inquiries into the deaths of children. In 1988, the first 'Working Together' statutory guidance was issued. It was 70 pages long. By 2010, after several revisions and extensions during the preceding years, it was 390 pages long and much too heavy for anyone to carry around with them (the 1989 Children Act also had 10 thick volumes of practice guidance!). It had also become too complex for anyone to have fully assimilated all of the guidance. This increasing length, weight and complexity of the statutory guidance has been well tracked by Parton [10].

The Maria Colwell Inquiry heralded the start of a change in the role of social work and a move away from the 1960s focus on family social work and helping families in difficulty. As Rogwoski commented:

> From the 1960s and into the 1970s, child abuse was essentially seen as a medico-social problem, with the emphasis on diagnosing, curing and preventing the 'disease' or syndrome. Doctors and social workers were the ones who had the skills to prevent and cure the problem ... As a result of the Maria Colwell inquiry, case conferences and registers were established, with the involvement of doctors, health visitors and social workers considered crucial and the social services department, the statutory childcare agency, being pivotal. It was only in 1976 that the police's role was considered vital as up until then the medico-scientific model had remained dominant. This was to gradually change to a socio-legal model, with the emphasis on investigating, assessing and examining the evidence. [11]

Rogowski also noted:

> It was only after a number of child abuse tragedies, notably Maria Colwell, that the police's role began to become more significant ... It was a move which saw social workers move from working *therapeutically* to *protecting* children [emphasis in original text], with the law and order agencies of the police and courts taking an increased role. [12]

The Focus on 'Rescuing' Children

The impact of the Colwell Inquiry and its media coverage was wider, however, than the introduction of procedures to respond to child abuse. It also fanned a debate about children's welfare and children's social services values and philosophy, a debate which is still very current, as noted by Featherstone, White and Morris [13].

On one hand there were the 'rescuers' who argued more children should be removed, and removed more quickly, from neglectful and abusive parents, with adoption as the preferred route to alternative permanent care for these children.

On the other hand there were the 'rehabilitators' who saw deprivation as at the root of much poor child care, that the identity of a child was intrinsically linked with their birth parentage, and that parents could and should be assisted to parent well.

As noted by Jean Packman, the Colwell inquiry empowered the 'rescue' lobby:

> The tragedy of Maria Colwell, together with other recent instances of child abuse and death, added considerable impetus to the demand for new legislation, which was presaged by the Houghton Committee [on adoption reform]. Such scandals and well-publicised 'tug of love' cases in fostering, adoption and divorce and custody proceedings, have done much to engage the interest of the public at large ... Concern that children are suffering because bonds with parents are too tenaciously preserved and cannot be or are not broken often or soon enough led to the formation of pressure groups such as the Adoption and Guardianship Reform Organisation—AGRO-formed in 1973. [14]

The rescue lobby gained an ascendency which was reflected in the numbers of children in care, as noted in 1979 by Rachel Jenkins, who was director of child care for the Save the Children charity:

> In 1977 there were approximately 100,000 [children in care] compared with 69,000 in 1967. Even allowing for the fact that the 1977 figure includes children and young people who would formerly have been

counted separately as subject to approved school orders, the increase is still considerable. [15]

Jenkins commented on the impact of the 'condemnation' of social workers following the Maria Colwell Inquiry but also argued that the increase in numbers of children in care reflected the impact of the Seebohm reforms with 'a dispersal of the experienced and qualified staff of the former children's departments into senior management posts and training. This dispersal, together with the movement to generic social work training, has led to reduction in expertise at the field level in planning for children in care' [16].

There is a hint in the quotation above from the then contemporary 1975 text by Packman that it was not only—or even possibly primarily—the Colwell Inquiry which led to new adoption and child care legislation in 1975 and 1976. There was already a review underway of adoption legislation by the Houghton Committee, which had been initiated before the Colwell Inquiry. There was also new research which was seen and used to support the argument of the 'rescuers'. As at other key moments changing legislation for children's social services (1948, 1989, 2004) change was already underway with a 'scandal' covered by the media (the Inquiry into the death of Dennis O'Neil in 1946; and later the Cleveland Inquiry in 1988 and the Victoria Climbie Inquiry in 2003) becoming the symbol which badged the change already being shaped [17, 18].

The research which was used to feed the 'rescuers' argument in 1973 was what Roy Parker called the 'ground-breaking study' [19] by Rowe and Lambert [20] on drift in planning for children in care. Rowe and Lambert argued that there were 7000 children living in foster homes and children's homes who would benefit from a permanent substitute family. It has been argued that the study, evocatively titled *Children Who Wait*, was misinterpreted:

> The state had a duty to help parents to care for children as well as a duty to protect children from abuse. The 1975 (Adoption) Act backtracked. It was about child rescue, partly I think because the preventative services had not worked, not enough money was ever put into them and therefore [the work of] people like Jane Rowe was misinterpreted. She pointed out that

many children had not gone back home despite the 1963 Act and that many children were remaining long in care. Her argument was that more of them should go back home and should be helped to go back home, but she was interpreted as saying more of them ought to be adopted. Whatever the background of it, we returned very much to a child rescue philosophy in the mid-70s partly also because of Maria Colwell, of the abuse of children by their parents, and you got that swing back from the pro-family philosophy. [Presentation by June Thoburn at a seminar of the Social Work History Network and Making Research Count, 2009]

At the same 2009 seminar Jane Tunstill commented:

[In 1974] there was a huge amount of campaigning, which I am sure many people were involved in, about the fact that the 1975 Act was going backwards. BASW [the British Association of Social Workers] was really heavily involved in trying to prevent the stigmatisation of parents and the elevation of adoption as the best form of care that children could receive. [Presentation Jane Tunstill at a seminar of the Social Work History Network and Making Research Count, 2009]

One of the BASW activist at the time was Bob Holman, with a photograph in Community Care magazine in 1974 of him with others delivering a petition to the prime minister at 10, Downing Street, opposing the then draft adoption bill (at the time he was a social work lecturer at Birmingham University). Holman commented that:

By the 1970s there was a decline in preventative work within social services departments or it didn't take off the way we envisaged, and at the time it was also knocked back because of the rise of what we called the 'permanency movement'. Jane Rowe and Lydia Lambert, both of whom I knew, published a book, 'Children Who Wait', which had a tremendous impact, got leaders in The Guardian and so on. Basically what they were saying was that there were children in the care of local authorities who could be adopted or permanently fostered which was much more preferable to them staying at home with inadequate parents so-called, or being in the care of children's homes and local authority foster carers. And it was a very impressive book. I did have some criticisms about the research methods. If you look at the book, the number of children in their research whom they identified as being available for adoption from care was 35. In the Guardian editorials this became thousands, and the whole movement took off I think without a real accurate analysis of what was happening. Obviously some children do need to be permanently removed, but that should be balanced with prevention and enabling them to stay at home with their parents. This was really knocked out. [Bob Holman interview]

The 'rescue movement' was supported by the import of American Freudian writers such as Goldstein, Freud and Solnit [21]. In Britain, the Department of Health and Social Security commissioned a report by Dr Mia Kellmer Pringle, director of the National Children's Bureau, on the needs of children. Kellmer Pringle commented:

The myth of the blood tie should be replaced by the concept of responsible and informed parenthood. The ability and willingness to undertake its responsibilities are neither dependent, nor necessarily consequent upon, biological parenthood. Rather it is the unconditional desire to provide a caring home, together with the emotional maturity to do so, which are the hallmarks of good parenting. [22]

Kellmer Pringle also said that social workers:

by training and experience tend to be adult-centred; this tendency appears to have been further increased by a number of recent trends, including the Seebohm reorganisation of social services and the politically-fashionable emphasis on 'parental rights'. [23]

Sir Keith Joseph and the Cycle of Deprivation

In the foreword to Kellmer Pringle's book Sir Keith Joseph, the secretary of state for health and social services, wrote:

I have long been concerned that crippling social, material and emotional deprivations and miseries continue to be passed on from generation to generation. The problem has remained despite the continuing development of our health, education and social services and the devoted work of those who provide them. I suggested in a speech almost two years ago that a cyclical process might be at work, what I called 'the cycle of deprivation'... I know there are some who see the solution simply in terms of alleviating material deprivations—poverty and poor housing. I applaud and share their urgent desire to do this. But I am not shaken from my view that there is another dimension to the problem and that one of the ways of tackling it is likely to be by promoting wider understanding of the emotional needs of children and the importance from the earliest years of the quality of the relationships between a child and those who are responsible for his care. [24]

Someone soon to attain even more importance for social services, and for the nation, is referenced in Joseph's foreword:

Mrs Thatcher and I held meetings with a wide range of voluntary, professional and other organisations to discuss ways in which people might be better prepared for parenthood, and we received many very valuable suggestions ... We are now trying out in experimental projects some of the suggestions we received. [25]

In five years' time Mrs Thatcher, who was secretary of state for education, would become prime minister, with considerable implications for social services and other public services throughout the 1980s and beyond.

Alongside the review of the needs of children by Kellmer Pringle was another review. Michael Rutter and Nicola Madge, both at the University of London's Institute of Psychiatry, were commissioned by the Social Science Research Council to review the evidence relating to Sir Keith Joseph's concerns about a 'cycle of deprivation'. Their conclusions were measured and hardly overwhelmingly supportive of Joseph's concern.

Rutter and Madge noted the continued impact of poverty and deprivation in Britain and that 'despite changing levels of national prosperity, employment and income levels, there are strong and persistent patterns of regional inequalities. These suggest that local structural factors may be important influences upon both regional and individual poverty' [26]. They concluded:

Several qualifications have to be made concerning inter-generational continuities. In the first place, even with forms of disadvantage where they are strong, discontinuities are striking. At least half the children born into a disadvantaged home do not repeat the pattern of disadvantage in the next generation ... A second qualification is that continuities are much weaker over three generations than they are over two ... Thirdly, not only does the extent of continuity vary according to the type of disadvantage but it also varies considerably according to the *level* [emphasis is in the original text] of disadvantage. [27]

The overall conclusion was that there was some evidence to support Joseph's concern about intra-familial generated cycles of deprivation, but that the impact of structural, social and economic factors creating deprivation continued to be significant despite overall improvements in living standards.

There were also two particular conclusions that would be recognised as having immediate topical interest in social policy and social work discourses 50 years later. First, what now might be called 'resilience' [28] and which had been developed as a concept by Rutter [29]. In 1976, Rutter and Madge wrote:

It has been repeatedly emphasised that children raised in the most deplorable circumstances not infrequently develop into normal adults. It is true, of course, that many are seriously damaged by their experiences but, in our view, not enough attention has been paid to the fairly numerous exceptions. We are never likely to be in a position to remove all forms of 'bad' experiences or to enable all children to have an optimal upbringing, though we should strive to that end. More frequently, those in the helping professions have to do the best they can to assist people to cope with circumstances which fall far short of the ideal. Information on the factors which enable people to overcome an unpromising start to life or to take later stresses in their stride would be of enormous practical benefit. [30]

The second conclusion, still relevant in the 2000s [31, 32], was that inequality was significant even when overall living standards improved:

As indicated by Sir Keith Joseph in the original speech on a 'cycle of transmitted deprivation', the rise in national prosperity does not seem to have made much difference to most forms of disadvantage. But perhaps it is an inequality of incomes which leads to disadvantage rather than low incomes as such. [33]

In a paper presented at a Department of Health seminar attended by senior civil servants and others in Cambridge in 1977 Rutter succinctly stated:

> While we can scarcely hope to eliminate deprivation, we might be able to reduce its ill effects by building up protective factors or compensatory experiences. [34]

The End of the Party

As noted by Andy McSmith, Joseph was to become a strong supporter, indeed a persuader, of Margaret Thatcher and her drive while she was prime minister in the 1980s to cut public expenditure and to open up public services to the market place and private sector:

> After 1974, an anguished politician became a regular visitor to [the Institute of Economic Affairs—a right wing think tank] office in Lord North Street. This was Sir Keith Joseph. A man whose intense, almost tortured demeanour, earned him the nickname 'the Mad Monk'. He had served in Conservative cabinets since Harold Macmillan's time and was now renouncing his past as a high-spending secretary of state for social security in a Damascene conversion to monetarism. [35]

Joseph was a potential leader of the Conservatives to replace Edward Heath after the 1974 election defeat but:

> Joseph swiftly self-destructed. In yet another revisionist speech, at Edgbaston, he strayed beyond monetarism and advocated eugenics to restrain the immigrant population of Britain. The uproar was instantaneous and the tabloids dubbed him 'Sir Sheath'. With the media camped

outside his door he found the strain of exposure intolerable and decided he could not stand as leader. When he told Thatcher, she confessed herself despairing, though her reaction showed no hint of hesitation … The die was cast. She would challenge the party leader [Heath] for his job. [36]

It was Joseph who would be a leading advisor and prompt to Thatcher and her embrace of monetarism, with its corollaries of cutting public expenditure, privatising public services and creating a deregulated market. Sir Ian Gilmour, a member of Mrs Thatcher cabinets in the early 1980s commented:

> [Sir Keith Joseph] was the most distinguished of the new Conservative missionaries. He, who had sat in the Conservative cabinets of Harold Macmillan and Alec Douglas Home, as well as of Edward Heath, announced in between the two 1974 elections that it was only in 1974 that he had been converted to true Conservatism … belief in monetarism, it emerged, was now a prerequisite not only for controlling inflation but for being a real Conservative. [37]

Hugo Young noted that it was Joseph who introduced Thatcher 'to liberal economics' and monetarism [38]. This was despite, as commented by Dominic Sandbrook in his social history of the 1970s, Joseph 'as head of the DHSS [Department of Health and Social security] having presided over a steady expansion of the welfare state … he spent more money at a faster rate … than had ever happened under Labour'[2] [39].

For the personal social services Roy Parker noted that it was the Seebohm-recommended large departments which were able to gain a

---

[2] It is hard not to draw a comparison with Ian Duncan Smith in the Cameron governments elected in 2010 and 2015. Initially seen as caring and compassionate, visiting the FARE project (Family Action in Rogerfield and Easterhouse) he received the approval of Bob Holman: 'I always remember when Ian Duncan Smith first came up to Easterhouse. He came to FARE and saw it being run by what he called unmarried mothers and unemployed people. He said, and I have never quoted this, "These were the very people that Margaret [Thatcher] condemned running this project" and I was thinking that's just what I wanted to hear him say.' But Ian Duncan Smith, as secretary of state for work and pensions in Cameron's governments championed and introduced social security changes which were to make the poor much poorer, and Holman commented that 'I no longer recognise the Iain Duncan Smith with whom I have had a cross-party friendship for eight years' [Bob Holman interview].

growing budget within local authorities because of their size and voice within local government:

> The Conservative government [of 1970–1974] was prepared to allocate [growth], albeit from a low base, to social services, and social services did remarkably well, and that's partly central government but also local government [decisions] … one must remember that local government budgets were not ring-fenced [for social services] … and within the local government setting the bigger the department the more pull you had. (Roy Parker interview)

This latter point was reinforced by Tom White:

> Once you had a big department seen as important in local government it wasn't the minor politicians who were fighting for chairmanships, it was the big boys and the big boys demanded action and they wanted to see change. (Tom White interview)

What was also driving personal social services budget growth was the Conservative government's introduction in the early 1970s of ten year plans based on an expectation of growth:

> It was when we [local authorities] were expected to produce ten year plans with an assumption of 10% per annum growth, and so we were very growth orientated … The first 10 year plan we produced was about 1973 … It was about services for people with learning disabilities, older people, being more community-based and less residential … So we were actually aspiring to grow, and it was a period of significant growth … So it was an aspirational period and I don't remember it feeling over-constrained. (Anne Parker interview)

Tom White also recalled the significant budget growth and the opportunities it provided:

> You also had this remarkable phenomenon of Keith Joseph, [later] he was a Thatcherite right wing ideologue, saying '10% a year [growth] guaranteed gross'. It was astounding really, and very, very exciting … Well, it

continued for a while. There were so many different aspects. The community-based services that Seebohm wanted to see, that were pretty alien to local government generally. In Coventry, for example, city of 330,000 at the time, all the local authority services were based in the centre. But we had 21 district offices when I left—they didn't last all that long mind you. [Tom White interview]

The Economic Crisis of the 1970s

What led to Mrs Thatcher becoming Prime Minister in 1979 was largely a consequence of a series of national economic crisis during the 1970s. These were to lead to cuts in public spending and this was the second 1970s seismic shift for the personal social services. The promise of year-on-year growth ended abruptly. The social services ten year plans required from local authorities by the government, based on anticipated annual growth of 10%, were to be shelved.

The Heath government of 1970–1974 had to confront and respond to a financial crisis. Roy Jenkins had been a notably successful Labour chancellor of the exchequer [40] leaving a balance of payments surplus [41], but the term 'stagflation' had been coined to cover a combination of high inflation and low and slow national economic growth. Wage inflation was rampant and trade unions active. Strikes were frequent and costly, including across the public sector:

> More than any other event it was the council workers strike of October and November 1970 that demonstrated the weakness of Heath's modernising ambitions and set the tone for his unhappy premiership. By the middle of October more than 60,000 workers had walked out, with another 75,000 taking part in overtime bans, one-day strikes and unofficial stoppages. It was not a strike that did great damage to the economy, but it caused enormous and very visible inconvenience to millions of people, as parks and schools were closed for a lack of caretakers, as rubbish piled up in the streets, as raw sewerage poured into the nation's rivers … Even the Cabinet noted that 'there was a good deal of sympathy' with the striking workers since park-keepers, dustmen and sewerage workers were not well paid,

many people thought it was unfair to make them foot the bill for Heath's economic rigour. [42]

The power workers, then in the public sector of nationalised industries, sought a 25% pay increase to match that recently awarded in the private sector engineering works and car plants. They went on strike leaving much of the country and industry without electricity and in the dark.

In 1974 there were further industrial disputes and strikes, including by the miners. There was also an international oil crisis generated by the oil producing countries through their organisation, the Organisation of Petroleum Exporting Countries (OPEC), increasing the price and reducing the international availability of oil in opposition to American and other states support for Israel in a war with Egypt and Syria [43], leading to a three day week for much of industry because of power shortages [44]. The government was also having to tackle an intensification of sectarian violence in Northern Ireland and with Irish Republican Army (IRA) bombing brought to the British mainland. Heath called a general election asking the electorate 'who governs Britain' [45]. The response was 'not you' as it was Labour that was elected to form the new government.

But even within the context of 'crippling inflation, millions out of work, and a fight to the death between the government and unions' [46] public service funding had so far not only been protected but grown. The social security budget, for example, expanded from £3927m in 1970–1971 to £5723m in 1973–1974, and it continued its considerable growth throughout the 1970s under Labour governments reaching £16,490m in 1978–1979 [47]. Indeed, despite the intentions of the following 1980s Thatcher government's social security spend continued to grow, due to the increasing numbers of unemployed people receiving social security payments.

But the change in the political rhetoric and economic policy did not have to wait for the arrival of Margaret Thatcher as prime minister in 1979. The Wilson and Callaghan led Labour governments elected in 1974 and 1976 were confronted with a continuation of the issues which had led to the collapse of the 1970–1974 Heath Conservative government and the response to was to seek to cut public expenditure, as noted by Simon Jenkins:

Callaghan's three years as prime minister (1976–1979) sowed the seeds, but only the seeds, of the dismantling of the post-war consensus. In 1976 the nation faced the worst economic debacle since the Second World War. The Chancellor of the Exchequer, Denis Healey, had cut public spending by £1bn in the spring and promptly faced a seaman's strike, a run on sterling, interest rates at 15 per cent and a desperate and humiliating loan from the International Monetary Fund. This was granted only on condition of another £2.5 billion of spending cuts. [48]

In the context of little wriggle room in a tight corner closed in by the International Monetary Fund (IMF) the Labour government introduced cash limits on government spending [49]. It marked the start of the end of the anticipated continuing growth to fund the welfare state, including the personal social services.

But growth there had been, even in the mid-1970s after the rise in oil prices and in the midst of a national and international economic crisis. Nicholas Timmins commented:

[Healey as chancellor of the exchequer in the 1974–1976 Wilson Labour government] attempted to deal with the oil price rise by maintaining expenditure. He borrowed to meet the deficit … The result was that Labour put off for two years the action needed to deal with the oil shock. It did so partly because no one was to know until after the event how the price rise should be handled, but partly also because Labour was both a minority government which needed a rapid second general election, and one elected on a manifesto appreciably more left-wing than in 1964. [50]

But pre-1979, and before the advent of a Thatcher-led Conservative government, in the context of a struggling national economy the post-war welfare state consensus was beginning to tarnish, with Pierson arguing that 'the newly ideological Conservative party was able to tap into a growing (if inarticulate) strain of popular disenchantment (not least amongst skilled manual workers) about the state of welfare and thus to fashion the historic victory of May 1979'.[51] This was commented upon at the time in 1978 by David Donnison:

> Many of the traditional social democratic assumptions which inform polices in the social care field are being called into question. For a generation after the second world war most people assumed social policies would regulate and steer the nation's economic motor ... and redistribute the fruits of economic growth to compensate the losers at the expense of the gainers. But the motor itself could be relied upon to keep turning. Depression and the dramatic fall in birth rates mean that the economic motor and the demographic motor which helped to keep it turning have both lost their impetus. The collapse of confidence in the future has already eroded the social compassion which sustained the drive to create a more caring society. [52]

This was the context for the 1979 general election and what was to be the start of 17 years of Conservative governments which have left their own mark and brand on the personal social services in England.

But the 1970s were not only a stormy time for the personal social services because of changes in the economic wind. It was also a time of change and challenge about the profession of social work and the roles of the personal social services and social workers, as explored in the next chapter.

7

Norming and Storming: Social Work Debates and Developments in the 1970s

Along with the introduction of the early 1970s new local authority social services departments were changes in the profession of social work. These included the creation of a unified and integrated profession with one professional association spanning the UK. It also was a time of an expanding intake of graduates into social work.

Deviancy Theory and Its Impact on Social Work and Social Workers

The new entrants to social work in the 1970s were often social science graduates educated at the new 1960s universities (including Sussex, Lancaster, Bath, Keele and Brunel) and polytechnics (such as Middlesex, North London and Sheffield). Sociology was a core academic discipline linked to social work with the introduction four year combined degrees in sociology and social work. One of the core texts was Heraud's 'Sociology and Social Work' [1] with chapters, amongst others, on family and kinship, the analysis of community, the social functions of social work, and social deviance.

© The Author(s) 2020, corrected publication 2021
R. Jones, *A History of the Personal Social Services in England*,
https://doi.org/10.1007/978-3-030-46123-2_7

It was this focus on deviance which was to lead to a more radical sociological agenda about deviance as a social label which led to stigmatisation, segregation and membership of subcultures. It was argued to be a process which promoted a deviant identity and deviancy amplification with a spiral of further behaviour perceived and labelled as deviant. The proposed solution was to respond and react less to behaviours seen as deviant, including delinquency, as noted by Schur:

> In radical non-intervention delinquents are seen not as having special personal characteristics, nor even as being subject to socio-economic constraints, but rather as *suffering from contingencies.* Youthful 'misconduct', it is argued is extremely common; delinquents are those youths who, for a variety of reasons, drift into disapproved forms of behaviour and are caught and 'processed'. A great deal of the labelling of delinquents is socially unnecessary and counterproductive. [2]

With its roots in American sociology (Schur was head of the Department of Sociology at New York University) the focus on the 'underdog' as a response to the question 'Whose Side Are you On?' [3] was intellectually and politically attractive to the young UK sociologists, some of who like Stanley Cohen [4] and Geoffrey Pearson [5] had also worked as psychiatric social workers (then the status pinnacle of social workers).

Possibly rather surprisingly given that they had a close association with medicine and doctors, it was mental health social workers who were found in a survey in the early 1970s to be more focused on and in favour of social change than individual adjustment [6]. Mental health social workers as a category would have included mental welfare officers working in local authorities and psychiatric social workers (like Cohen and Pearson) working in NHS clinics and hospitals. The former had been largely professionally unqualified but were warranted under the 1959 Mental Health Act to take decisions, alongside doctors, to compulsorily admit and detain people in psychiatric hospitals.

The integration of the role of mental welfare officer as social worker in the new social services departments meant, however, that more recent recruits were often the new graduates who had been exposed to deviancy theories and the anti-psychiatry movement (see below). John Cypher, who was a lecturer in social administration and would later by an assistant general secretary of BASW, commented 'In our study support for [social] reform is spread throughout the age-range, but … greater support for conflict [as a means of achieving social reform] as opposed to consensus strategies is located amongst younger social workers' [7] and more recent entrants to social work have had 'a social science education enlarging on his [and her!] appreciation of various social structures and cultural forms and capacity to analyse social conditions' [8].

I recall as a young social worker with a degree in sociology who was working with adolescent boys appearing in juvenile courts that the social enquiry reports we prepared for the magistrates detailed the distress and disturbance the boys had often experienced within their homes. This fitted with the intention of the 1969 Act to see children and young people not as 'bad' but as 'sad', deprived rather than depraved. A primary role for social workers was to seek to divert the adolescents from further delinquency through activity programmes under the heading of 'intermediate treatment' (intermediate between meetings at home or in the office with a supervising social worker or probation officers and removing the young person from home and into care or custody) and to be wary of confirming the young person and others in a deviant identity through, for example, the interventions of the police and the courts [9, 10, 11].

But deviancy theory was not only applied to and about young people and delinquency. It also considered other types of what were defined as 'deviant behaviours'. This included, in particular, mental illness, which was increasingly now to be understood as a social definition as much as a medical diagnosis. Rather than 'mental illness' as aberrant behaviour it was presented as an understandable and indeed often rational response to confusing and conflicting relationships. It was a perspective and model that was developed and promoted in the USA by, in particular, Thomas Szasz, a psychiatrist [12, 13], and Thomas Scheff, a sociologist [14, 15], and taken forward in the UK by R.D. Laing and others [16, 17, 18, 19, 20]. It was reflected in the growth of group work and therapeutic communities where the focus was on democratisation, reflection, interpretation, and feedback on emotions and behaviours[1] [21].

Radical Social Work

The deviancy theorists in the UK met together within what was called the National Deviancy Conference. For many social science educated newly qualifying young social workers whom they had taught they were the intellectual—and cultural—role models. And social work had its own brand—radical social work—informed by, and to match, the deviancy theorists and Marxist sociologists.

The seminal text of the brand was 'Radical Social Work' [22], edited by two sociology lecturers who were members of the National Deviancy Conference. Chapters in the book were contributed by, amongst others, Stanley Cohen and Geoffrey Pearson. Other contributors included Peter Leonard, who in 1973 founded the social work course at Warwick University. He was previously a child care officer, then director of social work education at the National Institute for Social Work and was the youngest member of the Seebohm Committee.

Another contributor to the Bailey and Brake book was Crescy Cannan. She was a researcher in a social services department and a member of the editorial collective of 'Case Con, the revolutionary magazine for social workers' [23]. Case Con pre-dated the 'Radical Social Work' book. The latter was primarily a text written by academics whereas Case Con, as a magazine and as a collective promoting and spurring social action, was much more grassroots within the social work community of, in

---

[1] My placements as a social work student (1968–1972) and newly qualified social worker (1972) reflected the trends in social work in mental health services. My first placement was in a community team within a local authority mental health department, followed by a placement in the social work department of a large Victorian county asylum. I then had a placement in a therapeutic community Richmond Fellowship hostel. My final student placement was in a new social services department generic fieldwork team. On qualifying I received three certificates—the Certificate of Qualification in Social Work, the Home Office Letter of Recognition in Child Care, and membership of the Association of Psychiatric Social Workers. Within three months of being employed as a social services department social worker I was warranted as a mental welfare officer and was on the out-of-hours emergency service rota and out on my own as the sole social worker covering all the social services client groups for half of a large shire county for evenings, nights and weekends.

particular, the young sociology-educated social workers. Jeremy Weinstein was a member of the Case Con collective and worked as a social worker in Lambeth and Wandsworth. He was later to be a social work lecturer at London South Bank University. Comparing Case Con and Radical Social Work he noted that 'In Radical Social Work, of the nine contributors, six are listed as senior lecturers or professors and while there is an important place for intellectuals in working class movements, this does seem a significant shift in emphasis from activism to academia' [24]. But within Case Con as noted by Mike Simpkins, a member of the Case Con collective, 'the initial coalition around Case Con diminished as radicals divided between those who became drawn more and more into trade union rather than client-based activity, and those who focused mainly on community work, practised a permissive non-intervention or campaigned for welfare rights' [25].

So what was radical social work? Its focus spanned all who were marginalised and minimised by discrimination and disadvantage, including people who were poor but also including racial and cultural minorities, women, disabled people and those discriminated against because of their sexual orientation. It was an analysis and proscription based, amongst others, on the writings of Marx [26], Marcuse [27], Friere [28], Gramsci [29] and Reich [30]. Bailey and Brake stated that:

> Radical [social] work, we feel, is essentially understanding the position of the oppressed in the context of the social and economic structure they live in. A socialist perspective is, for us, the most human approach for social workers. Our aim is not, for example, to eliminate casework that supports ruling-class hegemony. To counteract the effects of oppression, the social workers needs to advocate a dual process, assisting people to understand their alienation in terms of their oppression, and building up their self-esteem. [31]

But what does this mean in terms of action and what social workers should do? Bailey and Brake argued that:

> A radical form of social work must be developed. Social workers themselves suffer from economic exploitation (though far less severely than, for

example, hospital workers), and development of a radical critique may mean their involvement in a programme of political action. They must distinguish their clients' material and personal needs, although for most of the working-class material deprivation lies behind many of their problems. However, a consideration of the personal must also remain—hating one's gender role, loving the same gender, hating one's occupation, disliking one's parents, spouse or children is not personal inadequacy. The danger of hegemony is that it may result in psychological damage to those who resist it. In this way casework may assist people to resist hegemony and develop pride instead of self-hatred.[2] [32]

So radical social work was partly seen as about consciousness raising but also about praxis—taking practical action based on an ideology of not accepting the power imbalances within society which left many stigmatised, marginalised and poor, and that this action should be taken alongside those with whom social workers worked who themselves were organising collectively. Bailey and Brake commented:

Social workers now have within their ranks an increasing group who are becoming critical of the contradictions of their profession. Pressure groups, such as Case Con for socialist social workers, and Child Poverty Action Group have made valuable contributions. The interests that militant groups have in community work (especially in Northern Ireland) suggests considerable dissatisfaction with traditional social work. Traditional approaches have wittingly or unwittingly clearly supported authority in local or national government. For the first time clients of social workers are taking

---

[2] In the late 1970s I was a (young) university lecturer in social work, and was a creature of my time! As a sociology and social work undergraduate in 1972 my final dissertation was titled 'Social Work, Politics, and Social Change'. When later a university lecturer in social work on Wednesday mornings I would sit in the reception area of the local social security office doing shifts for the Claimants Union, advising claimants about how best to make their claims, acting as an advocate beside them, and sometimes representing them at appeals tribunals. On Thursday evenings each week I led, as a volunteer, a group work programme for adolescents in trouble with the local courts as a part of diverting them from care and custody. During the university holidays I was a volunteer detached youth worker spending time on a large housing estate on a city outskirts working with young people and their families as part of a project set up by Bob Holman. He had been the professor of social work at the university where I worked as a lecturer and had resigned his post to set up a neighbourhood youth and family project on the estate where he with his family moved to live (Holman, B. (1981) Kids at the Door, London, Basil Blackwell; Holman, B. (2000) Kids at the Door Revisited, Lyme Regis, Russell House Publishing).

a radical stance and even challenging the very conceptual apparatus of the profession, for example the claimants' unions, the tenants' associations, single-parent family groups, the Mental Patients' Unions, the Women's Liberation Movement, the Gay and Lesbian Front and the Campaign for Homosexual Equality. [32]

Daphne Statham, a social worker who in the mid-1970s was a social work education advisor at the Central Council for the Education and Training of Social Workers (CCETSW) and who would later be the principal of the National Institute for Social Work, noted in 1977 that social workers as employees of their agency faced limitations in their potential to be radicals through their work. She argued, reinforcing the comment of Bailey and Brake above, that social workers needed to

'retain and develop links with movements in the wider society, because it is from these that the major impetus towards radical alternatives comes, [whilst] it is possible to utilise to some extent this experience within social work' [33] through, for example, 'trying to make links between the micro-experience of the family and macro-social issues, in addition to formulating recommendations for social policy changes and service provision' [34].

There were those who sought to span collective action and continuing casework. One was Bill Jordan. Whilst working as a probation officer, and then a psychiatric social worker, he was also secretary of the local claimants union [35]. Jordan was a prolific writer in the 1970s (and has remained so since) and his texts bring together the political and personal aspects of social work [36, 37, 38, 39, 40].

In 1975 at a British Association of Social Workers annual conference he delivered a paper titled 'Is the Client a Fellow Citizen?'. It both captured the mood of the time within radical social work, but also set an agenda for the future, of engaging humanely and non-hierarchically with clients. It introduced a new concept of professionals as working alongside and in partnership with service users as facilitators and enablers rather than the traditional definition and expectation of professionals as experts protected by social distance and status.

Social Work: Social Change or Social Control?

Issues about whether social work should primarily be about social control or social change [41], reform or revolution [42] and how to work with the personal and the political [43] drove debates and discourses throughout the 1970s [44]. Simpkin, writing in 1979, noted:

> In keeping with the trend towards making social work a central pillar of social policy, new entrants tended to be activists and community-orientated, with the belief that social work intervention could in some way be critical in promoting wider sider social change. But though some were starry-eyed, the majority were conscious of the limitations of social work, both in theory and as it was practised ... People who wanted to fight for change entered social work not so much because it was the ideal instrument, but because the increased availability of jobs was neatly geared to coincide with the glut of sociology graduates looking for ways of making a living which at worst would not involve too much compromise with their ideals and at best might enable their realisation. A generation already in revolt was to put its standards to the test; though some left in disappointment, others found their work experience radicalised them still further. [45]

Some of the roots of this debate were not totally new. Barbara Wootton, for example, had argued in 1959 that social work had become dominated by the American focus and fashion of psychoanalysis, psychiatry and counselling concentrating on personal failure and marginalising attention to the social and political causes of social problems which impinged on individuals and communities [46]. This was an argument also addressed by Peter Leonard and Paul Corrigan in 1978:

> At one level, resistance to welfare cuts is sometimes associated with political subversion and the debate moved from the substance of the cuts to the issue of seeking out those who are attempting to infiltrate the 'democratic processes'. At another level, the failure of crude models of individual pathology to explain continued poverty has led to the invention of an apparently more sophisticated response—the idea of 'transmitted deprivation'. As an explanation of the 'cycle of poverty', it performs an invaluable ideological function in directing attention towards those experiencing

poverty and away from broader structural questions which might be raised about the fundamental features and contradictions of an advanced capitalist economy. [47]

But there were other views about whether social workers through their work should have more concern than others about social issues and social problems than anyone else. Butrym argued that it was not key or core to their role:

> There are no grounds for social work to claim a sense of special over-all responsibility for such massive national social problems such as homelessness, poverty and unemployment. They are, by their very definition, problems of our society as a whole ...Their responsibilities carry a differential aspect in virtue of social workers' particular knowledge of, say, homelessness and its impact on individual and families, but are not necessarily greater than the responsibilities of other groups, for example doctors and teachers, who, also, in the course of their professional work, come face to face with these. [48]

Less sympathetically Patricia Morgan in 1978 questioned the legitimacy of social workers seeking to conduct 'revolution on the rates' [49] and Colin Brewer, a psychiatrist, and June Lait, who noted that she had trained in social work and was then a lecturer in social policy, wrote in 1980:

> One of the many causes of friction between doctors and social workers is the tendency of some of the latter, and many of their more vocal teachers and publicists, to see social work as politics. Doctors doubtless have overt political views as varied as those of any other occupational group, but they do not commonly regard their surgeries as convenient places to propagate them. [Social workers] without clearly defined jobs who are not very busy, tend to indulge in all sorts of extramural speculation, as it were intramurally, simply because they have time to do so. [50]

It also ought to be noted that whilst not champions for social workers as political activists and advocates Brewer and Lait were also scathing of psychotherapy and of its relevance for social work (they quite liked behaviourism). Indeed their overall view was to question whether there was a role for social work at all and to ask 'Can Social Work Survive?'.

Social Work as an Integrated Profession

The British Association of Social Workers had its roots in the Standing Conference of Organisations of Social Workers (SCOSW) which was formed in 1964. In 2010 Mark Ivory, a journalist with a lengthy career of reporting on social work, looked back 40 years to the formation of the British Association of Social Workers in 1970. He commented that in the 1960s 'social workers were a motley crew, divided by a multitude of professional allegiances into eight associations with profoundly contrasting histories and outlooks' [51]. It was these associations which together created SCOSW. Joan Baraclough, who was active in the Institute of Medical Social Workers and was to be an assistant general secretary of BASW, commented that SCOSW was formed 'because there was the feeling that if social work was really going to make an impact and influence government in terms of developing policies that met the needs of individuals then it needed to be bigger' [Joan Baraclough interview].

SCOSW was a significant step on the road to one professional association of social workers spanning the UK. But Baraclough noted that 'there was always the question of whether it should be a unified association or whether it should be a federal association. In the end it was decided it would be a unified association because then we would all speak with one voice and that was the way to influence government' [Joan Baraclough interview].

The issue of who could be members of BASW, however, quickly became contentious. Ivory noted:

> The newly formed social services departments posed a stark question for BASW in its infancy: should it be bound together by the social work qualification as a condition of full membership, which had always been its intention, or should it simply accept anyone employed by the new [social services] departments, qualified and unqualified. [52]

If membership of BASW was to be opened to all—qualified and unqualified—who might be employed as social workers, will it be a professional association with membership not restricted to those with a social work qualification, or will there be a middle-way of full membership for qualified social workers and associate membership for unqualified social workers? Ivory reported:

> According to Mr Bilton [who had been one of the general secretaries of the Association of Child Care Officers and was one of three assistant general secretaries of the new BASW], this question 'tore the association in two' right from the start: 'The trouble was that, although social services departments became widely seen as the home of social work, more social workers in them were unqualified compared to qualified. Some of us were opposed to full membership for unqualified social workers, but others thought it invidious and unacceptable that unqualified workers should be denied the same status as qualified ones'. [52]

In a presentation to the Social Work History Network in 2008 Bilton reflected:

> Open membership was never an issue during discussions which led to the formation of BASW. The commitment was to work towards the formation of a single association of qualified social workers, and the live issues were (i) the 'blanketing in' of unqualified members and associates of existing associations and (ii) whether unqualified practitioners should be wholly excluded from the new association or be allowed some form of associate status. The pressure from members for equality of membership rights for both qualified and unqualified practitioners arose unexpectedly quickly, and reflected the speed with which BASW found itself operating in a context significantly different from that in which it had been set up. Within a short period BASW was seen by many of its members much less as an association of people working in a variety of employment settings but sharing a common qualification and much more as an organisation primarily representing those who worked in Social Services and [in Scotland] Social Work Departments. [53]

This all came to a head at BASW's annual conference in 1973.[3] It was proposed that only those who were accredited with a recognised social worker qualification could become new full members of BASW and that unqualified social workers seeking to join BASW would be associate members. Following impassioned debate, this proposal was passed by a majority of only 3 out of the 500 people attending the 1973 annual conference. With such a narrow margin and the danger of a divisive debate continuing membership was opened to all who were employed as social workers. Baraclough commented that this was in the context that 'there was still a lot of feeling that we shouldn't be elitist and that we should be allowing everybody in' [Joan Baraclough interview].

So BASW from its inception was beset by controversy and conflict. But this was not only about membership. It was also about whether social work should be seen as a profession with a professional association. The new social science graduates qualifying in social work would have been taught about the 'ideal type' of professions [54] based on exclusive entry dependent on specific qualifications noting and claiming expertise and knowledge not held by others. This concept of a profession was seen as elitist and as creating a distance between social workers and those who used their service. It was an issue which was not unrelated to the debate about whether membership of BASW should be open to everyone employed as social workers or only to new entrants who were professionally qualified with Baraclough noting that there was the 'question of was BASW too elitist and that was why people weren't joining'. Indeed, BASW was, and has not been, successful in achieving membership by the majority of social workers. In the 1970s membership hovered around 10,000 to 12,000. In the late 2010s, there were around 20,000 BASW members but this was in the context of 125,000 registered social workers across the UK.

The concerns about professionalisation and professional elitism, however, clashed with the counter view that professionalisation of social work was a protection and insurance for clients, as argued by Butrym:

---

[3] BASW's annual conferences in the early and mid-1970s were big events. In 1975, for example, a train was specially chartered to take 900 BASW members from London to the annual conference in Edinburgh.

An important consideration with regard to the provision of any professional service is that of its quality. Whatever the nature and the degree of the expertise invested in a profession, one of its characteristics is the importance attached to public accountability in response to the public trust vested in it. [55]

Social Workers and Unionisation

Why did BASW in the 1970s fail to capture the membership of the majority of social workers? Terry Bamford, who was a BASW assistant general secretary at the time before becoming a social services director in Northern Ireland and then in London and chair of BASW, noted four reasons. First, BASW was felt by some members of the previous more specialists associations to be too generalist. Second, 'the turmoil in the new departments meant that organisational issues rather than professional concerns were paramount considerations for staff'. Third, 'BASW had no real influence on salaries and conditions of service', especially significant at a time of high inflation amid cuts in funding for public services. And, four, 'BASW itself was attacked as an elitist, professional closed-shop' [56].

Bill Utting noted that for many social workers being a trade union member was seen as more important and appropriate than being a member of a professional association:

BASW's problem was that in the 1970s most social workers saw themselves as unionised rather than professionalised. I mean they didn't actually see themselves as professional people because the majority of them frankly were not, so it was the union that they clung to, and there was the sort of febrile atmosphere of that period in relation to union politics and struggles with management—it was seen that the union was the arm that was going to rest more resources and more status and more money. [Bill Utting interview]

The trade union—BASW competition for members was heavily weighted in the early 1970s towards the unions being dominant. This, in part, reflected the then general strengths of trade unionism and within the radical social work movement 'the trade union movement [was seen] as an integral part of the struggle for a socialist welfare practice' [57].

The first significant trade union action by social workers was in 1971–1972 as social services departments were being formed. Simpkins noted that the nationwide withdrawal from out-of-hours services resulted from 'the refusal to allow any longer the extension of the intolerable conditions under which we were working, at nights and at weekends particularly, for no worthwhile remuneration'. This was at a time when instead of out-of-office-hours emergency duty teams social workers were on a rota to provide cover.

In 1979 in the context of the cuts in public expenditure and services by the Labour government under pressure from the International Monetary Fund there was in a national social workers strike [58]. It was a culmination of sporadic and scattered industrial action in many areas throughout the 1970s—as in most other employment sectors at the time.

The strike was not universal or that widely supported. It covered only 15 out of what were then 143 local authorities providing social services. It was focused on the terms and conditions of employment for field/community social workers, especially pay for out-of-hours night and weekend working. Other issues included the general pay grading for social workers (one outcome of the dispute was the initiation of a national career progression wage scheme for social workers) and the right for trade unions (primarily NALGO) to have local as well as national negotiating rights for social workers (and others). As well as not being widespread nationally the strike was not necessarily well supported or well regarded by other local authority workers. Bolger and his co-authors noted in 1981 that:

> In the end the union [NALGO] spent over £3m on strike pay for social workers: an expenditure and a commitment on this scale made it very difficult for, say clerks in the housing department or middle management in the treasurer's department to see it as a correct use of union funds to back up one small part of the membership. [59]

The strike was not well supported across the country and it generated considerable debate amongst social workers, as noted by McLaughlin

[60]. Bamford (who at the time was an assistant general secretary of BASW) looked back at the strike from a distance of 30 years and commented:

> The strike changed public perceptions of social work. First, social workers who hitherto had been generally regarded positively (although the Colwell case showed the level of anger that could be generated by perceived incompetence) had become just another group of public service workers using the same tactics as other groups. Second, by putting vulnerable people potentially at risk, they were viewed as betraying ethical responsibilities [albeit arrangements were in place with union consent to cover crisis and urgent work]. Third and most damaging of all was the lack of any visible impact from the strike, inevitably raising the issue of whether social workers fulfilled any useful function in society. [61]

Unlike the very visual consequences of bins not being emptied, and the slightly less visual but concerning experience of the dead not being buried or cremated, social workers' absence was unseen and unfelt (except by those who needed their assistance). This was acknowledged close to the time of the strike with Brake and Bailey commenting in 1980 that:

> The longest strike [during the 'winter of discontent'] of 1978/79 passed with little attention by the media and hence the appearance of little effect on the lives of most of 'the people'. After all, the real effect was on those who are in danger of being cast into the bracket of 'undeserving', and they are not in a position to influence either the media or public consciousness. The issue will be raised as to whether social workers are really necessary. [62]

There were further strikes within local authority social services, such as the residential workers strike of 1983 and social workers industrial action and work-to-rule in 1989. However, strike and similar action by social workers has been limited, infrequent and generally not well supported. With regard to BASW and trade unionism, in 2014 BASW spawned a separate and independent British Union of Social Workers (BUSW).

The Association of Directors of Social Services

Separately from BASW, the new directors of social services appointed in the early 1970s formed their own association, the Association of Directors of Social Services (ADSS). It had been proposed that the directors have their own sub-branch within BASW, but this was rejected by those establishing BASW as potentially disruptive as other occupational groups might each want their own sub-branches:

> There was Tom [White's] attempt to get a sort of constitutional provision with BASW for a special group for chief officers. It seemed a good idea … but unfortunately Tom introduced it just after the point where we'd gone through all the exhaustive and difficult negotiations about membership for the association, and the idea of having to revisit those and make a special exception for people who were paid lots of money was just not feasible. [Keith Bilton interview]

The outcome was that while some of the new cadre of directors of social services (who because it was a statutory requirement had social work qualifications—with only two or three exceptions which had to be agreed by the secretary of state) joined BASW, they all joined their own newly formed association, the Association of Directors of Social Services (ADSS).

Bilton commented that:

> ADSS had more focus than BASW. [There was] an over-democratic approach by BASW's senior staff. It was for the membership to say what they want … [and BASW] was quite weakened by all these differences within the association on just what sort of organisation it ought to be in terms of membership and status and so on. [Keith Bilton interview]

ADSS had more certainty. All directors of social services in England and Wales could be, and became, members (in Scotland the parallel organisation was the Association of Directors of Social Work). The focus was their roles as leaders and advocates for the new social services departments, and their senior status meant that they were often at the top table with government and other organisations. Tom White was an early president of ADSS. He commented that 'our most successful way of influencing the Health Department was through ADSS' [63].

Herbert Laming was also a former president of ADSS and in 1985 he became the social services chief inspector in the Department of Health. He recalled that:

> I arranged informal meetings where [directors of social services in ADSS] would come in and meet and have lunch with the secretary of state ... I used to worry like mad about how these meetings went. I used to try to make sure I'd briefed the [ADSS] president that, you know, 'You may find it helpful to raise this; if this comes up be wary of that', because I thought these meetings really, really mattered ... and frankly even if we had a strong BASW, which we should have had, they may not have been able to make those big picture points. [Herbert Laming interview]

Social Work Education

Those writing about and advocating a radical (left) social work not surprisingly had an interest in the education and training of social workers. Indeed, as noted above, some progressed to or were in the midst of university academic lectureships and professorships or were working within the social work education regulatory authority (CCETSW). And the discussion and debates about radical social work also increased the interest of employers in social work education, as noted by Steve Rogowski:

> The upsurge in radicalism saw employers question social work courses and the right of education institutions to determine the curriculum and ethos of social work education. The concern was that social work courses were turning out difficult employees, namely social workers who thought and acted as if they were autonomous professionals with obligations to improve, as they saw fit, the well-being of clients. [64]

Chris Jones argued there were two responses following the concerns about the radicalisation of social work students. First, 'CCETSW was to limit the role of the contributing social sciences and the non-professionally qualified social scientists who taught on courses' [65] and, second, 'the most decisive response to the issue of difficult and querulous social workers was the creation of the Certificate in Social Services in 1975 … For the first time a professional route into social work was removed from education and placed in the hands of the big state agencies' [66]. The CSS, however, was set as the qualification for those working in residential, day care and home care services and not for field social workers, but it did represent an increasing interest by agencies in the education of their potential employees.

One of the developments in social work education in the late 1970s was an import from the USA (replicating the import from the USA in to social work education of psychoanalytical models of practice in the 1940s and 1950s [67]). 'Integrated' or 'unitary methods' were seen to span the traditional social work education and practice triumvirate of casework [68, 69], group work [70, 71, 72] and community work [73, 74, 75, 76].

There was still the teaching of specific approaches [77, 78], such as psychosocial casework [79], behavioural approaches based on learning theory [80, 81, 82] and systemic family therapy [83, 84]. There were also texts on, for example, interviewing and communication in social work [85], the use of self in social work [86], mobilising support systems for clients [87] and task-centred and short-term contracts in social work [88, 89, 90, 91]. The latter was one of the more evidence-based imports from the USA which can be seen as the roots of the contemporary use of contracts in social work practice. But in the late 1970s the new kid on the block was 'unitary methods' which across social work education programmes rapidly became the new orthodoxy [92].

So what was the 'integrated model' of social work practice? Its roots were in the search, initially in the USA, for an overriding concept of social work and its practice. Writing in 1968 William Gordon, professor of research in the School of Social Work at Washington University, noted that it was:

> a conception that provides social work with a set of integrative and generative ideas—integrative in the sense of capturing the common elements across the varied practices of social work today without loss of historical

continuity, and generative in the sense of moving the profession's thinking forward in step with the future. [93]

Although developed in the USA in the 1960s, it was only in the 1970s that 'integrated social work methods' landed in the UK. It was in 1977 under the auspices of the National Institute for Social Work that 'Integrating Social Work Methods' [94] was published. It was an edited book with contributions by the many of the staff at the NISW plus contributions from the leading writers and advocates from the USA on the integrated methods model such as Howard Goldstein [92] and Allen Pincus and Anne Minahan [95, 96].

Anne Vickery, then a senior lecturer at NISW, noted that the use of the 'unitary model' was to provide 'a perspective on social work practice as a whole' and 'a vehicle for training workers to practise more than one method' [97]. For example, one of the key social work practice texts in use in social work education in the late 1970s was by Pincus and Minahan [95]. They conceptualised social work as having four essential systems:

- The 'change agent system': 'a change agent is a helper who is specifically employed for the purpose of creating planned change' [98] (such as a social worker). They give examples where the change may be focused on the client or in seeking to change agency or social policy.
- The 'client system': which is seen as 'the individual, family, group, community, organisation, or community that, in addition to being the expected beneficiary of service, is a system that asks for help and engages the services of a social worker as a change agent' [99].
- The 'target system': 'we call the people the "change agent" needs to change or influence in order to accomplish his goals the "target system" and "an important diagnostic task of the social worker, usually in collaboration with the client system", is to establish the goals for change and then determine the specific people—the targets—that will have to be changed if goals are to be reached' [100].
- The 'action system': 'The change agent does not work in isolation in his change efforts: he works with other people. We use the term "action system" to describe those with whom the social worker deals in his

efforts to accomplish the tasks and achieve the goals of the change effort' [101].

What this models allowed was the bringing together of what had been seen and taught as the separate trio of casework, group work and community work into one model of social work. It also allowed a breadth of ideological (and practice [102]) perspectives to be accommodated. For example, Peter Leonard commented:

> Those who wish to develop radical social work must formulate a model of practice which both includes a wide range of social-work activity and avoids the fragmentation that the traditional adherence to distinctive methods—casework, group work and community work—was bound to encourage. Just as we can use a revised systems approach to map out the variables within which social workers operate, so we can build an integrated model of radical social work on the basis of the current work being undertaken by non-radical social-work writers. [103]

There was an account of adopting the 'unitary model' in practice, albeit in a Family Services Unit (FSU) team rather than local authority social services, with the conclusion that 'the Unitary Approach has within it the potential to generate a conscious review of the of the value systems held by the agency, the worker, the client and other agencies' [104]. However, the popularity of teaching the American import of 'unitary' or 'integrated model' of social work waned and the focus was to be on the practice skills and competencies for practitioners (e.g. in interviewing or assessment) rather than overarching general models of practice or grand theory, albeit this may be seen as the roots of a later concern that social workers are becoming task-centred technocrats rather than reflective and value-driven professionals.

What may be noticeable from the accounts above about changes in the curriculum of social work education is that it is about the education of social workers and not others employed in the 1970s personal social services. This is not an omission in this text. It was an omission in practice. Little training was available for those working in non-social work qualified roles or in domiciliary, day or residential care. Social work was the higher status profession within the personal social services (although there were and are small numbers of occupational therapists within the personal social services who would also have claim to a higher professional status, and yet as late as 1989 occupational therapy was still being described as an 'emerging profession' even within health care [105]). Even with the introduction of the CSS most residential, day care and home care workers had little training, however the later introduction of National Vocational Qualifications promoted more on-the-job training and assessment.

Studies of the Perceptions and Views of Service Users

An exemplar of the changing concept of profession within social work was the interest newly being taken, ahead of many other professions, on how service users (clients) viewed the services they received. The 1970 book which was seen as seminal at the time, albeit of a very small study seeking the views of 61 clients of the voluntary Family Welfare Association social work services, was the 'The Client Speaks' by Mayer and Timms [106]. Timms followed this up in 1973 with an edited book of personal accounts of being on *The Receiving End* of social work, subtitled *Consumer Accounts of Social Help for Children* [107].

It is hard to imagine now just how unique it was asking service users about their views of the services they received as within the traditional concept of professionals as experts they were not to be questioned or challenged and would instruct others what to do based on the professionals' greater knowledge and status.

But following Mayer and Timms book there were further studies on, for example, the users' (and social worker's) views of long-term social work in a social services department, probation and a Family Service Unit [108], an overview of comparative client and social worker perceptions studies [109], and a study in a Scottish city of 90 people (and 38 social workers)| seeking help from a local authority social work department or a voluntary agency [110].

What were the key findings from these studies in the 1970s? In an overview of studies of service user perceptions Rees and Wallace concluded that:

> Three points stand out. Firstly, people value highly receiving personal interest and support at stressful times in their lives. Secondly, the prompt provision of material aid, in cash or kind, is highly regarded by clients. Thirdly, certain people appreciate initiatives on their behalf, as demonstrated by the social workers' willingness to use skills in advocacy and negotiations. [111]

This is not so different from what is known of service user views in the 2010s with, for example, a study of users' views of a 'troubled families' programme finding that it was the reliability, availability, personal demonstrations of commitment by workers, and their willingness to represent service users in their engagements and confrontations with other agencies which were especially valued [112].

The importance of listening to clients and actively seeking their views was emphasised by Robinson, a sociology lecturer and parent of a child with spina bifida:

> [It] is not to say that the client always knows everything about himself or that he is always right about himself. However, he knows, in a way no one else can, how he feels, how he sees his life as a whole, how his relationships with others are of importance to him, what he thinks about things and where he wants to go. Whether the professionals like it or not, all this will affect their relationship with him. It will affect whether he comes to them in the first place, whether he co-operates, in what ways and with what enthusiasm. It will affect whether he goes along with them when he is away from their gaze and how satisfactory the outcome is from his point of view. Professionals who will not listen and learn from their clients may well be less likely to be listened to, less likely to make sense and talk sense from the client's point of view and less likely to appear really helpful. [113]

In addition to direct research on the views of clients there was also the growth in the 1970s of studies based on the social science research disciplines of ethnography and phenomenology, with researchers observing and talking with service users, social workers and others in, for example, what were or had been approved schools [114, 115, 116], schools [117, 118], and young people and families in socio-economically deprived areas [119, 120, 121].

As Mike Fisher wrote in 1983 'it used to require a certain "frontier spirit" to ask clients what they thought about social work. Nowadays it is difficult to conduct respectable research without incorporating the clients' views' [122].

Anti-Discriminatory and Anti-Oppressive Practice

Not unrelated to the concerns about professionalism being viewed as elitist, and the growing interest in the perceptions of those who used the personal social services, was a growing commitment that social workers should confront and challenge discrimination, including within their own practice.

Daphne Statham, for example, writing in 1977 whilst working within the Central Council for Education and Training in Social Work, reflected on how the teaching and training of social workers needed to engage with the discussions about women's and gay liberation and the need for a 'major re-examination of the theories about masculinity, femininity and sexuality offered to social workers as a basis for their practice' [123].

This was reinforced by Elizabeth Wilson, a social work teacher at North London Polytechnic, who wrote in 1980 that 'Social workers do seem to be increasingly aware of the nature and extent of the problems faced by women. Feminists are demanding adult status for women and a life in which work and child care are not in such dire conflict. Social workers, in recognising and supporting feminists demands, are perhaps at last acting in the spirit of that "client self-determination" they were always claiming to espouse' [124].

Oppression was being understood as wider than class and economic oppression to include gender, sexual orientation, race and colour with, for example, books by Lisa Dominelli in 1997 on anti-racist social work

[125] and, in 1998, with Eileen McLeod on feminist social work [126] and with religious and cultural oppression becoming higher profile in the 2010s [127].

CCETSW in the 1980s and into the 1990s promoted a particular focus within social work education on anti-discriminatory and anti-oppressive practice but it was not without challenge and conflict. David Jones was working within CCETSW and he recalled:

> Virginia Bottomley [who was then a minister in the Department of Health] wrote to CCETSW on its anti-racist work and giving her personal support … but it was a major issue, constantly bubbling away, and it blew up and became so serious because of the political dimension and an intra-Conservative party battle. [David Jones interview]

He also commented 'what happened that made it blow up in CCETSW's face was partly resentment in some local authorities at the pressure we were putting on and the requirement to address these issues [of discrimination and oppression]'.

There was particular opposition to CCETSW when it argued that there was embedded discrimination in major institutions, as noted by Terry Bamford:

> CCETSW at the time came under fierce attack from the press and from politicians because to talk of endemic racism in society was regarded as a politically motivated critique of government. CCETSW, under heavy political pressure, was obliged to withdraw the section of its [1989 paper on the Rules and Requirements for the Diploma in Social Work] referring to endemic racism, yet now the concept is widely recognised (although not universally accepted). [128]

David Jones commented:

> I think subsequent history [such as the Macpherson inquiry into the Metropolitan Police] has proved that we were right, as often happens with social work. I think we should be prouder of this than we allow ourselves to be. [David Jones interview]

Social Workers' Use of Time

How did social workers spend their time? Several studies in the 1960s and the 1970s found that social workers spent between 20% and 30% of their time in direct contact with service users. This was so whether looking at child care officers in the pre-Seebohm children's departments [129] or at social workers working in the 1970s in social services area teams [108, 130]. The research was reviewed in 1987 by Jones [131]. Parsloe in her 1981 book on 'social services area teams' defended social workers who were spending a small proportion of their time in direct client contact:

> Studies of the way social workers use their time are occasionally used to suggest that they spend too little time in face-to-face contact with clients. Such critics may be taking too narrow a view of social work and comparing it, at least implicitly, with psychotherapy, where the only time of any importance is time spent with the client or patient. Vickery [132] points out that the needs of social work clients vary; one seen each week for counselling may require only the additional time required for making a brief note, whereas another, seen monthly, may need considerable between-contact work by the social worker to provide and co-ordinate a range of services. [133]

The amount of direct contact time between local authority social workers and service users remained similar in the 2010s. A study of multi-professional community health and social care teams [134] working with people with learning disabilities, working age and older adults with mental health difficulties, and younger and older adults with physical impairment found that social workers spent about 20% of their time in direct client contact. More time (75%) was spent in the office primarily on completing assessments (23%) recording/ report writing (29%) and on arranging services (12%). But this was not so different for other professionals such as occupational therapists, community matrons and dieticians who each spent about 30% of their time on report writing. But what was different was that community matrons and community nurses also spent about 30–35% of their time in direct patient contact.

The activities undertaken in non-client contact time may, however, have changed in terms of the nature and balance of activities since the 1970s. In the 1970s probably more time was spent on liaising with other agencies and on advocacy for service users whereas although these remain inevitable and important social work activities in the 2020s more time will now be spent on data inputting and reporting to feed performance management and service ratings.

The Barclay Report

At the start of the 1980s, and ten years into the life of social services departments, there was a review of the role of social work and social workers, most of whom were employed within social services departments. It was commissioned by the newly incoming Conservative government whose intentions for social work and local government personal social services were suspected to be, at best, equivocal and, at worse, antagonistic.

However, the review was to be chaired by Peter Barclay. From 1973 until 1985, he was chair and then president of the National Institute for Social Work and like Frederick Seebohm (who had also been president of NISW) he was a Quaker. He was hardly likely to be hostile to social work.

The Barclay Report starts with an account of the state of, and issues facing, social work in the early 1980s:

> Too much is generally expected of social workers. We load upon them unrealistic expectations and we then complain when they do not live up to them. Social work is a relatively young profession. It had grown rapidly as the flow of legislation has greatly increased the range and complexity of its work. In order to cope with demands which parliament has imposed on social services authorities, large departments have grown up in which social workers find it difficult to come to terms with the complex pressures which surround them. There is confusion about the direction in which they are going and unease about what they should be doing, and the way in which they are organised and deployed. When things go wrong the media have tended to blame because it is assumed that their job is to care for people so

as to prevent trouble arising. They operate uneasily on the frontier between what appears to be almost limitless needs on the one hand and an inadequate pool of resources to satisfy those needs on the other. Not surprisingly, for these and many other reasons, demands for an independent enquiry in to their work have grown increasingly insistent during the last few years. [135]

The Barclay review concluded with the championing of 'community social work':

The individual or family problems will of course remain the primary concern of social services agencies. The solution, easing or prevention of individual or family problems is and remains the reason for the existence of personal social services agencies. But the focus will be upon individuals in the communities or networks of which they are a part. There has been a tendency for social workers to see their own clients in sharp focus against a somewhat hazy background in which other people were somewhat less than life-sized. Community social work demands that the people who form a client's environment are seen for what they are or may be—an essential component of the client's welfare. [136]

Within a model of community social work the Barclay Report argued that (local authority) social workers had two tasks. The first was counselling, with its personal focus based on relationships, care and concern, and communication. It was what Bill Jordan writing in 1979 called 'helping':

It sounds simpleminded to talk of social work as 'helping people'; yet it is difficult to find a better way of describing what social workers try to do. To 'intervene' or 'monitor' may seem more professional, but after any amount of intervention and monitoring it is still reasonable to ask, 'Did it help?' Whether or not a social worker is helpful often appears to depend on a personal process of communication and influence. [137]

For the Barclay working party counselling was seen to cover:

A range of activities in which an attempt is made to understand the meaning of some event or state of being to an individual, family or group and to plan, with the person or people concerned, how to manage the emotional and practical realities which face them. [138]

The second task for social workers described in the Barclay Report was social care planning:

It is more than ever necessary that social services departments carry out a role in social care planning, which no other agency is expected to undertake. While the voluntary sector will have a vital role to play with particular families, groups and areas, only the local authority departments have a responsibility and coverage for coherent social care planning. They need to discover and bring into play the potential self-help, volunteer help, community organisations, voluntary and private facilities that exist. [139]

The Barclay Report can be seen as a reaffirmation of the underpinnings of the Seebohm Report with its focus on seeing people in context within their family and community context and harnessing community resources to assist people in difficulty.

There was not, however, unanimity within the Barclay working party about social work as counselling and social care planning. The dissenters went in two polar directions. Robert Pinker, who had worked in the probation service and in 1982 was Professor of Social Work Studies at the London School of Economics, argued that social work should be a selective rather than universal service and did not agree that it should be embedded within communities searching out need. He argued that there should be more focus on specialisation within a service which held on to its focus on social casework.

On the other hand, three of the working members in an appendix prepared by Roger Hadley, who had been a lecturer at the LSE and was professor of social administration at Lancaster University, argued for services to be organised within smaller neighbourhoods with social workers largely community-orientated and referring to more specialist social workers when necessary. It was a model which was introduced in several areas [140] but small generic patch teams working within neighbourhoods of about 10,000 population were always at risk of not being resilient and with the increasing specialisation which followed the children's and adults' social services legislation in 1989 and 1990 were not sustainable. Bamford commented:

> In practice, Barclay did not provide a national prescription for action. Some local authorities embraced the patch approach with enthusiasm, but the majority began to move towards greater specialisation as a means of improving quality in social work practice. [141]

The Debate About the Registration and Regulation of Social Workers

One disappointment for some with the Barclay Report's conclusions was that it did not support the call for the registration and regulation of social workers through a general social work council [142]. This had been advocated by the British Association of Social Workers which saw it as a means of protecting standards and the public and enhancing the perception of social work as a profession. It was opposed, however, by the National Association of Local Government Officers (NALGO), the trade union with the largest membership of social workers, which saw it as elitist and divisive for a workforce which still had a significant number of social workers who had no professional qualification.

The Barclay working party concluded:

> Not only are we divided in our views of the desirability of a General Council; those of us who think it is desirable are divided on the timing of its introduction. Most of us feel it to be unrealistic to set up a Council (assuming, which seems improbable, that there are available resources to do so) at a time when it has limited support among social workers and that there is no pressure for it from the public at large. Immediate moves to do so would, in our opinion, tend further to damage the public image of social work. The substantial opposition which could be expected to such a step would heighten the feelings of rejection which have been implanted in the minds of some social workers by the public enquiries and court cases arising from the non-accidental injury to children and the treatment sometimes accorded to them by the media. [143]

The Barclay Report's conclusion in 1982 was probably right and inevitable. It is highly unlikely that a recently elected and rampant Thatcher government would have accepted and agreed to a recommendation to set up and resource a General Council to register and regulate social workers. Its moment had not yet come.

It was not though an issue which would go away. Roy Parker prepared a report published in 1990 by the National Institute for Social Work which set out the arguments for a 'General Social Services Council' [144]. As with the Seebohm Committee's report an 'action group' [145] was established to push for the implementation of Parker's proposals, which were largely accepted by the Association of Directors of Social Services [146] and by the Labour Parliamentary Opposition, but not by the Conservative government now led by John Major. It was not until Labour formed the government in the late 1990s that the ground was fertile to reap the harvest of the General Council seeds which had already been sown.

8

Thatcher and Threat (1979–1989)

By the start of the 1980s the idea that the welfare state was a 'good idea' and a 'good thing' had come under challenge, not only because it was seen as costly but also because it was seen to have failed and to have become moribund. The 'welfare state consensus' [1], in which each national political party was signed up to its protection and growth, was undermined by views from the political right, and also to a lesser extent from the left, that it was failing to promote a general public good but instead was protecting its own vested interests. Writing in 1996, Chris Pierson, a professor of politics, argued:

> With the benefit of perfect hindsight, it has become the habit for some to write off the years between the end of the Second World War and the late 1970s as a rather shabby interlude in the continuing story of Britain's comparative economic decline. The welfare state, after its admittedly rather 'heroic' phase in the late 1940s, had settled into a routinized pattern of incremental growth and institutional torpor. It had become the object of official complacency and increasingly the feeding ground for a set of vested (and often well-organised) producer interests. [2]

© The Author(s) 2020, corrected publication 2021
R. Jones, *A History of the Personal Social Services in England*,
https://doi.org/10.1007/978-3-030-46123-2_8

The Aims and Ambitions of Margaret Thatcher

This was the context which Margaret Thatcher inherited, and indeed had helped to create, when she became prime minister in 1979, the start of 17 years uninterrupted Conservative governments. There were differences in what might be anticipated from Thatcher:

> I did hear Margaret Thatcher speak when she was Minister of Education [in the mid-1970s] and I thought 'My God, if she ever thinks to be a prime minister we're in for it'. She was scathing about public servants, she was scathing about public services, [she said] we were spending too much on all these kinds of things and what you needed was to encourage the private market and people's capacity to choose for themselves, spend their own money and reduce tax … I think it was at some kind of social work conference that she spoke. [Roy Parker interview]

> Actually in my early conversations with Mrs Thatcher, I thought she was certainly looking for an assurance that the most vulnerable people in the community were actually being properly supported and attended to. [Herbert Laming interview]

Whatever the first and early impressions of Mrs Thatcher she herself revelled in being called the 'iron lady' and that, in her own phrase, 'the lady's not for turning', with the acronym of TINA following the mantra that 'there is no alternative'[3] to the ideology and polices she was about to pursue with vigour.

Right from the start she got to work on turning the mantra into a mission:

> Whatever the short-term difficulties [in 1979], I was determined at least to begin work on long-term reforms of government itself. If we were to channel more of the nation's talent into wealth-creating private business, this would inevitably mean reducing employment in the public sector. [4]

She went on to note that:

> The proportion of the British workforce employed in the public sector crept inexorably upwards from 24 per cent in 1961 to almost reach 39 per cent by the time we came into office. By 1990 through privatisation and other measures we had brought it down again to a level below that of 1961. [4]

Alongside the privatisation of what had been publicly owned and publicly provided services, such as essential utilities like gas, electricity and water supplies, the other major means of reducing the public sector workforce was to cut public sector funding with the corollary of cuts in services and employment. Mrs Thatcher had inherited high rates of unemployment, and her government saw unemployment increase further both in the private and public sectors. This thwarted her intention to cut public sector expenditure overall as social security expenditure increased as a consequence of the growth in those receiving unemployment benefits.

Mrs Thatcher had two particular targets in her sights—the civil service and local authorities—and she quickly got to work on hitting both:

> At the first informal Cabinet meeting we began the painful but necessary process of shrinking down the public sector after years in which it was assumed that it should grow at the expense of the private sector. So we imposed an immediate freeze on all civil service recruitment, though this would later be modified and specific targets for reduction set. We started a review of the controls imposed by central on local government, though here, too, we would in due course be forced down the path of applying still tougher, financial controls, as the inability of local councils to run services efficiently became increasingly apparent. [5]

So the die was cast. The private sector was to be favoured over the public sector, and public sector services and workers, and especially local authorities and their employees, were cast as wasteful and inefficient. It was a narrative to continue beyond the Conservative governments of 1979–1997. It was repeated by Tony Blair as New Labour's prime minister and refreshed and revitalised with even more rampant vigour by Prime

Minister Cameron as head of the Conservative-led governments of the 2010s.

Thatcher's governments were to be the beneficiaries of two economic windfalls over its terms of office—North Sea oil revenue started to flow in the 1980s and receipts were received from selling off nationalised industries. Norman Barry, a professor of politics who saw benefits in competition for both individuals and the state, noted that:

> The suspicion must be that the prime aim of the privatisation programme is not to increase competition but to raise money. This suspicion is compounded by the fact that the major profitable public assets have been sold off as *private* monopolies. This obviously makes them more attractive to private buyers. [6]

A prudent prime minister might have banked these one-off gains (as the government did in Norway with its oil receipts) but instead in the UK the windfalls funded reductions in redistributive taxes at the same time as cutting public expenditure. Writing in 1989 Hugo Young noted:

> The most explicit electoral promise [in 1979] had been to cut tax and cut the public sector borrowing requirement (PSBR). The only way these could both be fulfilled was big cuts in public spending, few of which had been openly canvassed before the voters. However, much work had been done on them in secret ... The cabinet as a whole was committed to public spending cuts of 3 per cent, but these did not match the tax handouts ... The gap had to be bridged. It was done by the stunning expedient of almost doubling Value Added Tax (VAT), up to a single rate of 15 per cent [instantly increasing the rate of inflation]. [7]

This re-shaping of national taxation away from redistributive income tax, where the rich pay more, to an indirect tax placed on the price of goods, which hit those on the lowest incomes the hardest, is an inheritance which has been bequeathed by the Thatcher years and which is still embedded in taxation in the UK today.

Thatcherism and Turbulence

Mrs Thatcher's government in its early years was not popular. Inflation and unemployment, which might be expected to move in opposite directions, rose at the same time as a consequence of the government's economic policies. One Cabinet minister, Sir Ian Gilmour, noted a few years later that 'By the time of the 1981 Party Conference the Government was faced with an unprecedented combination of economic failure, social discontent and party disunity' [8].

The social discontent was reflected in riots in, amongst other urban areas, London, Liverpool, Leeds and Manchester, and with continuing strikes by civil servants and other public sector workers. In particular, the coal miners went on strike over pit closures, with recollections that it was industrial action by the miners in the early 1970s which was a significant contributor to the fall of the Heath government.

But in the context of rising unemployment and a general weariness and public dislike of the disruptions caused by strikes, union membership fell and the ground was prepared by the government to introduce legislation to curb the power of trade unions. It stocked pile coal in readiness for a major conflict with coal miners—the coal miners strikes of 1984–1985—where the police (who had been favoured by the government amongst public sector workers and protected from cuts) were mobilised to assist the government in breaking the miners' strike, most notoriously at Orgreave in South Yorkshire [9].

I was an assistant divisional director in South Wales and the South West for Barnardo's at the time and have vivid memories of long convoys of lorries moving imported coal along the M4 protected by escorts of police cars and police vans with the police in riot gear. It was a dramatic and an intimidating experience and in the valleys and coal fields of South Wales and elsewhere there was the intense poverty of the miners' families and communities who had no recourse to social security benefits.

These were turbulent times, not least for the Labour Party with a move to the left under the leadership of Michael Foot. This led to a break away movement with previous cabinet ministers—including David Owen, who had been Minister of State for Health and Social Security (and Social Services) in the 1974–1976 Wilson government and had taken a lead in introducing the 1975 Children Act—building an alliance with the Liberals (which later were to become the Liberal Democrats) and a new Social Democratic Party (the SDP). It was the divisions and turmoil within the opposition parties which left Mrs Thatcher in the early and mid-1980s with limited and little political challenge.

One of Mrs Thatcher's principle advisors and allies, indeed mentors, before and when she became prime minister was Sir Keith Joseph (who has featured in the previous chapter). Nigel Lawson, who was to be chancellor of the exchequer from 1983 until 1989, wrote that '[Joseph] had embraced monetarism with a fervour founded on the need (as he felt it) to atone for the sins of his inflationary past' [10] and that he had become an 'enthusiast for privatisation' [11].

Cutting back on regulation was seen as a means to encourage and promote a thriving private sector and to free up private enterprise from restrictions and the costs of bureaucracy. The intention was to incentivise individuals to compete within an open access unburdened market place. It was argued, as noted by Steadman Jones, that:

> In a free market system, the individual was paramount. Different individuals had different capacities, which would be valued differently in the marketplace ... Inequality did not matter because social mobility was possible, and for anyone who lost out, their own initiative would give them the opportunity to succeed through repeated attempts. If they were unable or unwilling to make such attempts, then it was not the role of government to treat individuals unequally by compensating for someone's lack of success. [12]

In particular, it was argued, it was important to avoid 'welfare dependency' where people chose and trapped themselves in a world and lifetime of relying on social security payments and public housing.

But there is a glaring flaw in the argument. There was no level playing field. It was not 'different capacities' which largely determined life's outcomes but different opportunities. Access to wealth from birth was skewed and access to resources such as well-funded education and housing, health and income were not remotely evenly distributed. Neither was access to networks of patronage [13].

Mrs Thatcher's ideology and policies were not, however, widely shared even within her own cabinet, as noted by Jonathan Aitken, who was a Conservative MP during the 1980s and a minister in the subsequent governments of John Major:

> Margaret Thatcher's determination to cure Britain's deep-rooted economic sickness came to be symbolised by her words at the Conservative Conference of October 1980: 'You turn if you want to—the lady's not for turning'. Although greeted with thunderous applause by the rank and file of the party, there were many in her cabinet who thought them foolhardy. For by this time unemployment had risen to 13 per cent and the recession was worsening. [14]

Those who disagreed with her included several government ministers, including Ian Gilmour:

> Up to 1974 [when the Heath government ended] the Conservative governments made efforts to maintain national cohesion, and nearly all of them saw that the best way of protecting the social fabric was to improve the conditions of the least well-off ... For [these governments] there were important areas of politics that could not be left to the market without unacceptable consequences, hence the government had to intervene for the good of society as a whole. The objective of the Conservative governments from 1979 to 1990 were altogether different ... [But] so far from market forces proving benign in social matters, citizenship was devalued and damaged. [15]

In her early years as Prime Minister Margaret Thatcher was also not popular with the public at large, as noted by Alan Clark, who was one of Mrs Thatcher's ministers in the mid- and late 1980s:

> Two years into her first Parliament, Margaret Thatcher was already cruelly beleaguered. Polls showed that she was more unpopular than any previous Prime Minister. Scarcely one person in her cabinet had a good word to say of her. [16]

And Nigel Lawson, who was to become Mrs Thatcher's chancellor of the exchequer, noted:

> Opposed to nationalisation, [the British public] were scared by privatisation. In advance of every significant privatisation, public opinion was invariably hostile to the idea. [17]

So how did Mrs Thatcher ride out the storms and unpopularity of her first years in government? Her success in getting re-elected as prime minister throughout the 1980s are argued to have been due to three factors. First, the popularity windfall she received as a consequence of the victory over Argentina in the 1982 Falklands War where her resolution was seen as sign of strength and determination. Secondly, and somewhat in the same vein, the government's breaking of the 1984–1985 miners strikes, albeit with the lasting destruction of former mining communities. And thirdly, the Parliamentary opposition was in some disarray, with former senior Labour ministers having left Labour to form the Social Democratic Party [18].

However, the intention of the Thatcher governments of the 1980s to roll back the state and reduce public expenditure was not quite as easy and straightforward as might have been imagined. There were three dynamics at work which made it difficult.

First, the outgoing Labour government under pressure from the IMF had already been cutting back public expenditure and public services and much of the low hanging, albeit prickly to pick, fruit was already in the basket of cuts. Second, the outgoing Labour government had agreed large pay awards for public sector workers in response to the strikes of the winter of 1978–1979 and these pay awards were inherited by the incoming Conservative government [19]. Third, the government's cutting back on expenditure and on investment itself created a demand and need for growing public expenditure as unemployment increased with the consequent effect that social security expenditure increased (up from 37.7% of public expenditure in 1974–1975 to 40% in the early 1980s and to 46.6%—almost half of all public expenditure—by 1985–1986 [20]). Increasing unemployment and economic recession also led to a reduction in tax receipts [21].

The government's response, as noted by Nicholas Timmins, was to raise the indirect tax of VAT (the top rate of income tax was actually reduced) and to cut the value of welfare benefits, both of which impinged disproportionately on those who were already poor [22]. However, even before these cuts social expenditure at the beginning of the 1980s was not high when compared with the other, at the time eighteen, members of the Organisation for Economic Co-operation and Development (OECD). Indeed the UK had slipped down the table of the proportion of GDP committed to social expenditure (which included spend on education, health services, welfare services and social security) [23].

What was it like in the latter years of the Conservative governments led by John Major? Timmins noted:

> Apart from the Citizen's Charter, which itself tended to reinforce the impact of the market approach to public services, Major proved to be a man of no new ideas. And so it came about that it was under Major rather than his predecessor that the Thatcherite revolution in public services began to run its full course: the tool-kit of contractorisation, privatisation, market testing and private finance turning from a means to an end into something close to dogma … Moreover, the £50 billion deficit was rapidly seized upon by the neo-Thatcherite right as the chance to do what Thatcher herself had largely failed to do—roll back the welfare state financially as well as managerially. With such a huge deficit, action to control spending was inevitable … The first government departments targeted were health, social security, education and the Home Office—the core of the welfare state. [24]

The Prospects for the Personal Social Services

The plans and promises in the early 1980s of Thatcher and her government hardly boded well for the personal social services. The denigration of the public sector and public sector professionals, along with the intention to cut public expenditure, set out the ground for a wide frontal assault on public services. The actual picture which emerged, however, was a little more complex.

The boom years of the early 1970s were over, but there was still limited growth. Between 1973–1974 and 1977–1978, the impact of the mid- and late 1970s IMF-demanded public sector cuts started to bite, but there had been year-on-year real terms growth for the personal social services averaging 7.6%. Between 1978–1979 and 1985–1986, when Thatcherism was in full swing, the average year-on-year growth had reduced to 2.4% [25]. It kept expenditure on the personal social services relatively stable at 3–4% of overall public expenditure [26], but should be seen alongside, for example, increasing numbers of older people who might need assistance and the progress being made on moving away from a dependence on care and confinement in large institutions largely falling to local authorities as an increasing community care responsibility and cost.

In reflecting on the funding experience for the personal social services in the early and mid-1980s Wendy Rose, who at the time was the assistant director for research, development and planning in Hammersmith and Fulham's social services department and was soon to move to the Department of Health with a policy lead role on children's services, commented:

> [The financial situation] led to pretty anguished strategic meetings. The management team were conscious that what we were trying to implement were, we would say, 'ideas that were born at a time of plenty' and we were trying to implement them in a time of famine … Were there areas that we had to preserve and continue to grow and were there areas where we could do things differently, and were there areas where we no longer should be providing services … It really was quite difficult to be able to match our ambitions and our vision of what we wanted with the resources that were going to be available so you were having to narrow down the whole time. [Wendy Rose interview]

On the other hand, as noted by Rose, 'we did have a chance to use [specific government grants] so long as we had a clear plan of what we wanted to do through that period when we were very much in limbo'. These specific grants had a strategic role for Mrs Thatcher's government. Amid the overall restraint on public spending they were one of the mechanisms to be used to develop services outside of the public sector and outside of local authorities. It was a time of opportunity for voluntary organisations, such as the big national children's charities, with strong relationships being built with local authorities [27], partly prompted by the joint interest in accessing the government's specific grants.

The Changing Role of Voluntary Children's Organisations

Specific government grants were available primarily for children's social services developed and provided by voluntary organisations. There had been a long tradition of charities providing children's homes. The big national children's charities established in the nineteenth century are still in operation, such as Action for Children (formerly the Methodist National Children's Homes), the Children's Society (formerly the Waifs and Strays Society which became the Church of England's Children's Society), Barnardo's (formerly Dr Barnardo's Homes), the Coram Foundation and, in Scotland, Quarriers.

They had largely been established to provide residential care for children who could not or were not being cared for by their families, especially amongst the poverty which went alongside increasing urbanisation and industrialisation. In the 1980s although these charities had started to diversify their range of services they still had a significant investment in large children's homes and even children's villages of cottage homes.

The move away from residential children's homes had been underway since the 1940s with foster care and assisting families to care for their children having become more mainstream. However, in the 1970s charities and local authorities were still major providers of residential care. But this was changing and the number of children in residential care reduced from 36,000 in 1977 to 14,300 in 1987 [28]. The reducing number of children in residential children's homes was both a cause and also a consequence of the big children's charities (and less so, initially, local authorities) closing children's homes.

The move away from residential care for children was not a change which was immediately grasped by the large children's charities. Roger Singleton had taught in approved schools, and in the early 1970s was a children's regional planning officer who focused on the change of approved schools to community homes with education before becoming deputy chief executive and then chief executive of Barnardo's. He commented:

> The voluntary [children's] societies were badly lagging. I don't think they ever until the late 1960s and indeed early 1970s really accepted that the role that they had done pre-war, namely in sort of warehousing large numbers of children in residential care, wouldn't somehow return. I think for NCH, Barnardo's and the Children's Society the 50s and 60s were the years of lost opportunity really and it took the 1969 Act to really make them think about where they should be going. [Roger Singleton interview]

It may be hard to recall or acknowledge that in the early 1970s there were still residential nurseries each accommodating 20 or 30-plus children aged under 5 years old. Singleton recalls Kenneth Brill, who had been a much respected Children's Officer in Devon and was the first general secretary of the British Association of Social Workers, saying 'if God had intended children to be brought up in residential nurseries babies would have been born in litters!'.

It has been argued that it took the spectre of financial cuts in the late 1970s to turn the tide of increasing numbers of children and young people being placed in community homes with educations (the former approved school for young offenders), as argued in 1981 by Bob Bessell who was director of social services in Warwickshire:

> The major activity in which all social services departments could make savings and improve the quality of service is by reducing the number of inappropriate admissions to residential institutions ... This tide was only stemmed when the economies enforced by the Labour Government in 1977 gave an impetus to social workers and social services directors to develop alternatives for those youngsters who had previously been sent away, not for any serious criminal behaviour but because they were a nuisance, with little regard for the corrupting influences to which they would

be exposed while they were away. However, it took the present government [of Mrs Thatcher], elected on a law and order ticket, to turn the withdrawal from the CHEs into a full-scale rout as social services departments were faced with a demand part way through the fiscal year in 1979, to make an immediate saving of three per cent across the board. [29]

In the 1980s, the children's charities repositioned themselves to provide more assistance for children and families in the community and also to develop specialist foster care and adoption services, which had first been piloted in Kent [30]. This was facilitated by the government's specific grants including the 'Under Fives Initiative' to develop services to support young children and their families and which funded, in particular, the emergence of family centres; the 'Opportunities for Volunteering' fund which supported the growth of volunteers working with social services charities; and the 'National Intermediate Treatment Fund' which was used by voluntary organisations to develop community alternatives to custody for children and young people.

At this time in the mid-1980s, I was an assistant divisional director for Wales and the South West with Barnardo's. My responsibilities and activities reflected the national policy to promote non-statutory services with the stimulus of specific grants which could only be claimed for services provided outside of the public sector. My brief within Barnardo's included developing and managing two family centres in Bristol and intermediate centres in Bristol and Newport, and managing the flagship Family Institute in Cardiff which was at the forefront of providing family therapy services. My role also included downsizing a large boarding school in Taunton for children with disabilities within the age range 4–18 years, with its partial replacement by an independent living house for disabled students aged 16–19 years. It was a time not only of voluntary sector expansion within children's services as, with funds through the All Wales Mental Handicap Strategy to close the large old mental handicap institutional hospitals, colleagues in Barnardo's were developing group homes and respite care services for children and adults with learning disabilities.

What was different from how services are purchased from voluntary (and increasingly private) providers in 2020 was the strategy taken within

Barnardo's in negotiating new developments and services with local authorities in the mid-1980s. The big children's charities were asset rich but less secure in the generation of revenue with day-to-day funding dependent on fluctuating and uncertain voluntary charitable donations. The charities were asset rich as they owned property and land of the former children's homes. As they sold these sites, they could bring to the negotiating table, therefore, the funds for the capital purchases of the buildings for new services, such as family centres. They were secure in the knowledge that they could recoup at least the capital costs in the future by selling on the land and buildings if the new services went beyond their fashionable sell-by-date and were closed.

In negotiations with local authorities, therefore, the big children's charities could bring forward the capital purchase and development funding for new services which was especially attractive to councils at a time the government had imposed tight restrictions on their capital borrowing and expenditure. I was also able to negotiate from the position of contributing 40% of the revenue running costs of the new services as well as access to the funding from specific grants.

What was not negotiable was that Barnardo's would not take on crucial statutory responsibilities such as statutory assessments and child protection investigations. Barnardo's, and the other voluntary organisations in the 1980s, saw their role as enhancing and supporting statutory public services, unlike the leadership of some of the big charities in the 2010s who were pitching to be providers of statutory children's services as they sought further expansion and growth.

Roger Singleton commented:

> I wouldn't say this was what completely drove [voluntary sector developments], but I think there was an element of opportunism [for voluntary organisations with the introduction of specific government grants] … We were [also] experiencing rampant inflation of over 20 per cent I think in 1978. That was having a catastrophic impact on the size of voluntary income because there wasn't any way that voluntary income would keep pace with inflation of that sort of proportion. That was increasingly driving us towards looking at the opportunities for statutory funding. [Roger Singleton interview]

Singleton was not, however, so persuaded that it was the voluntary sector which held the strengths on innovation:

> I think [innovation] was over-claimed. The voluntary sector generally over claims. I didn't like the arrogance that was implied in almost asserting that you've got the prerogative of fresh ideas and new ways of doing things. I remember meeting Fred Edwards [the director of social work for the Strathclyde region in Scotland] who said 'What I'm not prepared to do is to let the voluntary sector take all the plums in the cake leaving my staff with the stodge'. Now, I think that was fair. I really didn't like the superiority—a sort of turning your nose up at what colleagues in the statutory sector were doing when you had the privilege of being able to control your caseloads and workloads. So I was always a bit uncomfortable about this pioneering thing. [Roger Singleton interview]

The overall spirit of the 1980s, however, was largely one of respectful partnerships between the statutory and voluntary sectors, as noted by two interviewees who were both based within statutory local authority personal social services:

> It was a time when there were some very close relationships with the voluntary sector and so [specific grants only available for the development of services not provided by local authorities] was seen as positive. [Wendy Rose interview]

> [As we moved to a greater mixed economy of services] it wasn't such a huge battle ... We had a very strong set of partnerships in Berkshire with the voluntary sector. So that kind of approach in terms of the voluntary sector mixed economy was very well rooted in the department. [Anne Parker interview]

The Promised Green Paper

But there was also at the time an uncertainty about where Mrs Thatcher's Conservative governments of the early and mid-1980s might take the personal social services, including the uncertainty for Wendy Rose (who moved in the mid-1980s from being a local authority assistant director of social services to become assistant chief social services inspector in the Department of Health):

> There were all the external things going on. We were aware of the much more aggressive view about what we should be doing in terms of social welfare from the Conservative Government and which was going to lead to a green paper and so we knew that major change was on the way but of course the green paper then never appeared ... It was a period when we were rather in limbo in some ways but we still tried to hold together a sense of where we were trying to go. [Wendy Rose interview]

The government's green (consultative) paper on the future of the personal social services had been heralded in 1984 by Norman Fowler when he was Secretary of State for Social Services, a post he held from 1981 until 1987. Mike McCarthy, who was a former Assistant Secretary of BASW and was then a regional director with Retirement Security Limited, a private company set up by Bob Bessell to provide care villages for older people, wrote in 1989 about Fowler's promised but never-to-materialise green paper:

> The Secretary of State had reassessed Seebohm and found in it strong arguments for 'a wider conception of social services'. He saw the concept of 'enabling' as 'fundamental to the role of social services departments I want to promote'. In announcing his intentions for a review of the personal social services, Mr Fowler's view was that society must increasingly look away from the state for the provision of care and must tap instead what he and his colleagues believed to be 'a great reservoir of voluntary and private effort'. 'A wider conception of social services' offered the opportunity to reduce expenditure and shed responsibilities. [31]

David Jones was general secretary of BASW in the mid-1980s. He recalled:

> We had a discussion about the whole privatisation agenda and how we could position ourselves and took a pragmatic view that to be publicly and constantly opposed to it all the time would go against the grain of the way

that things were moving. We had to position the profession as being able to work across all of these agencies. Whilst it was important not to undermine public services we wouldn't voice constant opposition to the other sector developments … We recognised that social workers were going to be employed across a range of different agencies and that we wouldn't campaign against it, although we would constantly talk about the importance of the public sector. I think it possibly enabled us to keep talking with officials [in the civil service]. [David Jones interview]

Then, as now, however, the personal social services were a marginal and minor concern of central government. This was because personal social services were delivered by local authorities—unlike the health service or social security which are national services which have been in the direct remit of national government and secretaries of state—and partly because compared to health and social security expenditure the personal social services are small scale.

In Norman Fowler's *A Personal Memoir of the Thatcher Years*, published in 1991, in 372 pages there is no reference at all to the personal social services or to any allied aspect such as social work or the care of children, disabled and older people or even to voluntary organisations and charities [32]. Instead his focus was on the health service, and in particular, the disputes between the government and the trade unions representing doctors, nurses and other health workers, and on major reviews of the social security system and benefits and of pensions.

Thatcher's Levers to Favour and Promote the Market

Specific grants were one of the levers to develop and shape a market in what had been public services [33]. The process of moving services into the private for-profit and voluntary not-for-profit sectors was to be facilitated by making it financially beneficial to out-source personal social services.

Under the headings of seeking value for money (VFM) and promoting the three Es of economy, efficiency and effectiveness money was to be made available by the government but only if local authorities themselves did not provide and manage the services. At the same time, there was a reduction in the funding for publicly provided services and a restriction on capital borrowing and expenditure by local authorities.

There was a third—and even more dramatic—lever to be introduced and pulled. Compulsory competitive tendering (CCT) was largely championed by Sir Nicholas Ridley, as noted by Patrick Butler:

> [CCT] was introduced by the Conservative government in the early 1980s as a way to neuter strikes, downsize blue-collar council and NHS workforces, and cut costs. It was seen as a means of rolling back the "bureaucratic" state, and injecting into supposedly moribund services the competition that was needed to drive up quality and make them more responsive. The former Conservative environment secretary Nicholas Ridley led the free market charge on outsourcing. His 1988 pamphlet The Local Right, published by the Centre for Policy Studies, argued that local authorities should concentrate on enabling—rather than providing—services. [34]

Although the personal social services were not at the core or in the centre of the government's push on CCT and enforced outsourcing, unlike a wide range of blue collar public services, they too were captured in the managerial contract culture which was developed and promoted. This was not necessarily seen as totally negative as noted by Bob Holman when writing in 1993:

> It would be churlish to ignore the positive contribution of the New Right advocates. Their criticisms of the waste and bureaucracy within the government's civil service have been justified. Some of the reorganisation planned or being carried through may be beneficial. They have had the courage to attack the power of the legal and medical professions. [35]

Holman was certainly not an advocate for privatisation and the generation of private personal profit taken out of public funding. But his comment that the New Right Thatcherite ideology and policies had challenged, not always unhelpfully, the status quo was supported in 1994 by

Ann James, who was the Founder Director of the Social Services Management Unit at the University of Birmingham:

> Margaret Thatcher did Britain two favours. First, the scale, the speed and consistency with which she applied her policies in the public sector created the potential for nothing less than a paradigm shift in thinking about delivery of human services. Second, she ceased to be prime minister at a point at which the process of implementing that paradigm shift was incomplete and therefore both process and tomorrows were malleable. The challenge of the 1990s is one of using the space created by Thatcher's paradigm shift, at least to improve services and service delivery, at most to build healthy communities. [36]

The dilemmas in contracting personal social services outside of local authorities were noted by Leat, a member of the Policy Studies Institute, who was writing as the 1990 community care reforms were being implemented:

> The social services department which avoids risk in contracting may be damned by central government, and by disappointed private and voluntary sector suppliers for failing to promote competition, and damned by consumers for failing to allow choice. But the social services department which contracts with those it does not thoroughly know and trust, with those who do not have a long and unimpeachable track record, will, if anything goes wrong, be damned by the media, by consumers, by the taxpayer and by central government for taking risks and failing in its duties both to those in receipt of care and those who fund care. [37]

The Contract Culture and New Public Management

One consequence of the thrust to a culture of contracting out public services was a move to what has been called 'New Public Management' (NPM). It required those running public services to replicate the managerial methods and means of those running profit-driven private businesses. This was seen as positive by those who viewed the public sector as slow to change, inward looking, and thoughtless and careless in its use of resources, and who saw the welfare state as unaffordable and undesirable.

Julie Jones, who would later be Westminster council's director of social services and then chief executive of the Social Care Institute for Excellence, in the 1980s had a performance reporting role in the council. She recalled:

> The pressure to be more business-like and demonstrate value for money drives you to better information to argue your case. And in [places like] Westminster, what you learn early on is if you can't fight your battles on other people's terms, you don't win. We went through a phase with processes like the politically-led star chamber where budget setting is done and with very fierce competition for resources. You just have to get your act together and win the arguments on the evidence. It was no good getting your violin out, it just didn't work ... If we were really able to demonstrate what worked, how much it costs, and all of that then we could continue to be successful and grow the service to meet the needs that we knew were there. [Julie Jones interview]

However, as John Harris, a former social worker and social services manager and in 2003 a professor at Warwick University, noted:

> This critique of the welfare state predisposed Thatcher governments to take a sceptical view of social workers and local authority social services departments. Social work was a key component in the Conservatives' depiction of the social democratic welfare state's services in the business era as bureaucratic and insensitive to individual needs. [38]

What was required by the Thatcher governments was a major shift in the status and balance of power within public sector organisations away from the professional and other workers who directly provided services, such as doctors, teachers and social workers, to general managers and especially accountants who were the finance managers. Even for those professional managers who immediately managed frontline services interfacing with the public the focus was increasingly on the money and on expenditure in the context of devolved budgets becoming a major responsibility. As Norman Flynn noted in 1990:

Increasingly, managers have to operate within market mechanisms. For those people who are running facilities, such as residential or day care centres, the approach has become increasingly competitive and commercial. On the other hand, those people who are responsible for purchasing services on behalf of clients have had to become increasingly aware of budgets as they balance the quality and quantity of care available with the available cash. They also have to be aware of the options available in the market over a very wide range of suppliers. [39]

Norman Flynn was the Director of the Institute of Public Sector Management. Ann James, who has been quoted above, was Director of the Social Services Management Unit at the University of Birmingham. Both were at the forefront of preparing senior and middle managers for the new world immersed in a focus on value for money and the new contract culture.

The National Institute for Social Work (NISW) also had had a management component within its programmes from the 1970s onwards as did the research undertaken (replete with pages of structure charts of management hierarchies) by the Social Services Organisation Research Unit within the Brunel Institute of Organisation and Social Studies [40].

Much of the focus before the 1980s was on internal organisational management arrangements and requirements within the personal social services and local authorities. This was illustrated by the simulation exercise [41] provided within NISW and devised by Jimmy Algie and Tony Hall (who went on to head up CCETSW) which concentrated on negotiating funding and resource allocation between different local authority departments and on engaging with local community and voluntary groups.

There had also been a focus in the 1970s and initially in the early 1980s on managers concentrating on the work of social workers undertaking their professional task. This is illustrated in Terry Bamford's 1982 book on 'Managing Social Work' [42]. The index notes that 'contracts' are covered in two places in the book … the first is on contracts between social workers and clients and the second on contracts between supervisors and social workers. The attention to be given to the setting and management of commercial and service contracts had not yet arrived.

By the mid-1980s, however, the contract culture and the heavy focus on budget management had taken centre stage with the focus on controlling costs and contracting with external providers of services in what was termed a 'quasi-market' [43]? It is a term promoted, in particular, by Julian Le Grand, an academic economist who had been a professor of social policy at Bristol University and in the early 1990s moved to the London School of Economics. Le Grand's influence and impact on the personal social services within the 'New Labour' governments of Tony Blair and the Conservative-led governments of David Cameron are discussed in the following chapters. In 1993, Le Grand and Bartlett stated that:

> [Quasi-markets are] markets where the provision of a service is undertaken by competitive providers as in pure markets, but where the purchasers of the service are financed from resources provided by the state instead of from their own private resources. [44]

In 2011, Le Grand stressed that quasi-markets promoted choice:

> In quasi-markets the service is provided free or largely free at the point of use; unlike under most forms of state provision, in quasi-markets the user has a choice of providers and the providers themselves operate in a competitive market. [45]

However, in the personal social services, as in some other public services, 'choice' is a concept which may have limited applicability, as noted in 1989 by Martin Knapp, who was soon to be joined by Julian Le Grand at the London School of Economics. Knapp wrote:

> We must remember that governments often take responsibility in the first place because they are not happy to leave the service to market forces. In social policy contexts, the government takes responsibility partly because the users of services—school pupils, hospital patients, old people's home residents—might not be able to act with sufficient competence or power as consumers. They often cannot make their own views known and cannot easily move to another supplier. So on the one hand, the government wants to promote choice, but on the other hand it must recognise that the con-

sumer may find it difficult to exercise choice. It must regulate the quality of services. [46]

There were three concerns in the 1980s about the increasing marketi-sation of the personal social services. First, there was a concern, especially in the context of reductions in local authority funding and restrictions on expenditure, that the focus would be on costs not quality, as noted by Ascher:

Contracting out—the private provision of public services—has recently become a salient and controversial issue in British politics … While sup-porters of the Government's policy have forecast dramatic cuts in the cost of delivering public services, opponents have predicted a serious deteriora-tion in the standard of service provided to local citizens. [47]

This is a theme also noted by Knapp, who had an academic back-ground in economics, but with a rather more challenging view about the legitimacy of the argument:

I used to read 'Social Work Today' [which was then the BASW social work magazine] and Community Care [then a weekly print magazine] and I became adept at spotting either a £ sign or the word 'cost' on a page because they appeared so very rarely and you would find almost nothing on the economics of social care … If you suggested that you would look at the cost or cost-effectiveness of something they would say, "Oh, social care is about vulnerable, frail, people in difficult circumstances. Those people, those issues, are above and beyond money. We shouldn't be bringing money into the decision-making". [Martin Knapp interview]

There was also the challenge from Butt and Palmer, may be not sur-prisingly as they were within Price Waterhouse's Local Government Consultancy Services. Writing in 1985, they stated that 'contracting out has not always been geared towards financial savings—councils are also looking to improve the quality of services' and that 'the other trend is that the threat of contracting out has acted as a powerful catalyst for savings [within local authorities]' [48].

As much as anything else, this involvement of senior managers within Price Waterhouse in promoting the focus on Value for Money (VFM) within the public sector showed how in the mid-1980s (it has increased much further since) the consultancy companies, advising both public services on outsourcing and also private commercial companies on the business and commercial opportunities on taking on and gaining service contracts, were benefiting and growing from the marketisation of public services.

Rodney Brooke, who had been the chief executive in the Conservative flagship London Borough of Westminster council, in a 1989 book titled *Managing the Enabling Authority*, commented 'every consultant in the country is anxious to help' local authorities with advice on outsourcing [49]. Indeed, the concept of an 'enabling [local authority] shows how much progress was being made on progressing the marketisation journey as, in its final state, the "enabling authority"' would have contracted out all of its services and would remain only as a commissioner on behalf of its local community.

A second concern about the marketisation of services was that the outsourcing of the personal social services to other organisations where the contracting focuses on outputs (units of service delivered) may well undermine the professional value base of social workers which includes exposing, challenging and seeking to address inequality and poverty.

This was a concern noted by Beverley Hughes, a former probation officer who in the early 1990s was a university lecturer in social policy, and who went on to become an MP and a minister in the New Labour governments from 1999 until 2009, including as children's minister (she was interviewed for this book and is quoted in a later chapter). In 1993 she wrote that 'the language of community care [with the reforms of 1990 emphasising, as will be discussed later, a purchaser-provider separation and the introduction of 'care management'] reflects the new managerialism which obscures inequality and deprivation' [50].

Third, and reflecting the comment from Beverley Hughes, the emphasis on costs was seen to give more power to managers and less discretion to professional frontline workers. Bob Holman argued:

Management has begun to take over social welfare practice, to become its technique and philosophy. Its dominance is seen in the increasing centralisation of agencies with decision-making power concentrated, as in many private companies, in an elite of managers far removed from the individuals and teams at the grass-roots. It is seen in the new language which talks of packages of care, inputs and outputs, purchasers and providers, all of which sounds like a swarm of salesmen devoted to wringing the last penny out of customers than a social work policy which gives priority to meeting human needs. It is seen in the concept of a social service as, according to a senior consultant for Price Waterhouse, 'a sharp, well-informed business'. It is seen in the designation of staff responsible for the assessment of users' needs as 'case managers', not social workers. [51]

Within the quotes from Holman and from Brooke above are the references to consultants from the private sector accountancy companies being commissioned and contracted by local authority social services. The advent of management consultants was a 1980s trend (which has continued to blossom and expand) also noted by Roy Parker:

One of the things [about Mrs Thatcher] is that she dismantled the statistical service and the quality of statistical publications plummeted and she turned to management consultants, ignoring any academics and [saying] 'there's no such thing as society'. If you compare that with people like Crossman earlier or even Wilson [in the 1960s and 1970s] they were kind of on an academic circuit as well as their political one. She wasn't. She was on a business circuit and a management consultants' circuit … I think there was a lot of demoralisation both in the academic world and I think in social work as well. After all, if you're expected to do a good job you want to be valued and I think the legacy is that the devaluation begins to be accentuated with Thatcher. [Roy Parker interview]

The advent of New Public Management within the context of the marketisation of the personal social services had three particular dimensions, although the newness of what was happening in the 1980s can be overstated.

First, there was increased and closer scrutiny of the work of social workers, but there was already the supervision of social workers through discussions about their case assessments and plans and what actions they were taking. There were already caseload weighting and management tools and there was the requirement to keep records of work undertaken, partly to aid reflection within discussions with supervisors and partly as an accountability tool for the agency. There were also already procedures and procedure manuals. But there was a considerable heightening in the 1980s in the attention given to performance management and the collection of data.

Secondly, there was an increased focus on costs and expenditure with frontline managers becoming the holders of, and accountable for, team and service devolved budgets. This brought financial awareness and pressures to bear on frontline teams. It gave some opportunity to decide on the deployment and re-shaping of resources closer to the frontline but it also made frontline workers more accountable for the management of budgets and containing and curtailing expenditure.

Third, social workers were encouraged, indeed in services for adults, required to see themselves as managers with some authorities re-designating social workers as 'case managers' or 'care managers' who would arrange and 'manage' care for younger disabled and older people. But as budgets became more restricted and restrained social workers and others found themselves more the rationers as much as the arrangers of services and Hugman noted in 1991 that the 'political context must be grasped to understand the broad circumstances in which the case management model is being implemented' [52].

John Harris commented:

> The implications of these developments were increased control and oversight of the running of the business and decreased discretion for social workers. This control was to enable scarce resources to be directed at 'core business' and to increase efficiency. Much of this control is expressed in manuals, directions and guidelines that limit professional discretion and set up standardised and repetitive systems, tightly defined criteria and eligibility for services; standardised assessment tools; interventions which are often determined in advance from a limited list; minimisation of contact time; micro-case management and pressure for throughput. Key decisions are made by managers, rather than by social workers. [53]

There were, however, limitations to the organisational and managerial oversight and control of social workers as much of what they actually do is out-of-sight and unseen my managers and supervisors who are not present at home visits or in other encounters between service users and workers. Social workers were described by Michael Lipsky in 1980 as 'street-level bureaucrats' [54] who are employed to follow rules and regulations but actually have discretion in how they choose to implement— or even ignore—these requirements. This has been seen to give some scope to frontline social workers and others to act for service users rather than the organisation. This process was captured in a Guardian article in 2006 entitled 'The Rule Breakers' based on conversations with social workers and with some tolerance and acceptance by managers [55].

The tension was and is, however, that bureaucracy may overwhelm professionalism [56, 57]. Some social workers were, of course, employed outside of the local authority large social services departments and there was the continuation of big and small charities contributing to the provision of the personal social services. They had the potential attraction of less prescribed practice and greater professional freedom. But as, in particular, the large national charities expanded and became more dependent on contracts based on funding from central and local government they also came within the new requirements of demonstrating 'value for money' and the three Es of economy, efficiency and effectiveness.

It was not, however, only the managerial and marketisation revolutions which impacted on the personal social services and on social workers. More specifically, at the end of the 1980s, two Acts of Parliament had a major impact, taking services for children and services for adults in different directions and into different organisational structures.

Part III

New Laws and New Horizons

Part II

9

A Drama in Two Parts: Part I—The 1989 Children Act and Children's Social Services

There were two Acts focused on the personal social services which were enacted at the end of the 1980s. Each seemed to be unlikely products to emanate from a Thatcher-led Conservative government. The 1989 Children Act's underlying principle was that the best interest of the child would be promoted by stronger partnership working between parents and professionals. These were often the same parents who were demonised as feckless during the Thatcher years. The 1990s National Health Service (NHS) and Community Care Act gave additional responsibilities and resources to local authorities, yet local authorities had been a target of Thatcher's rhetoric about wasteful public services. How these two Acts came to be shaped is the subject of this and the following chapter.

The impact of the two Acts, which were implemented at the same time in the early 1990s, was to lead to a separation and specialisation within social services departments and for social workers between children's and adults' services, with the latter requiring a purchaser-provider management and organisational separation which was not required of children's social services.

© The Author(s) 2020, corrected publication 2021
R. Jones, *A History of the Personal Social Services in England*,
https://doi.org/10.1007/978-3-030-46123-2_9

The Impact of Inquiries

The 1989 Children Act set out to reposition statutory social work services with children and families. The distortions which the Act sought to correct were the move which had started in 1974 following the Maria Colwell Inquiry to focus social work with children and families on the protection of children. Child protection had become an overwhelming concern of local authority personal social services.

It was the repeated media—and therefore public and political—attention to the deaths of children following abuse or neglect which drove the skew towards social work practice giving increasing attention to the monitoring of families and the management of risk. It was never possible to anticipate when and which child's death might become a major media story but, following the precedent set by the Maria Colwell Inquiry in 1973, the government's response to major media coverage of a child's death was to initiate a public inquiry. Olive Otway, in a 1996 book chapter titled 'From child welfare to child protection', commented:

> Major criticisms of policy and practice and the competencies of social workers was called into question in the child abuse inquiries that followed the deaths of several children. It was the death of Maria Colwell that produced the first in a long line of inquiries. However, such inquiries gained a new level of intensity during the mid-1980s via inquiries into the deaths of Jasmine Beckford (London Borough of Brent, 1985), Tyra Henry (London Borough of Lambeth, 1987) and Kimberley Carlile (London Borough of Greenwich, 1987). It was public inquiries which provided the forum for political and professional debate concerning the response to child abuse. These inquiries took place in a very public way and received full media attention ... Up until the mid-1980s the thirty five inquiries had all been concerned with the deaths of children at the hands of their parents or caretakers. Many of the children had been in the care of the local authority but 'returned home on trial' or were under the legal supervision of social workers ... The child care professionals, particularly social workers, were seen to have failed to protect the children, with fatal repercussions. [1]

Writing in 1999 Nigel Parton noted the impact on social work practice and decision-making:

The emphasis in public inquiry recommendations was to encourage social workers to use their legal powers to intervene in families to protect children, and to improve practitioners' knowledge of the signs and symptoms of child abuse. [2]

The inquiry reports frequently concluded that there had been failures in policy and practice which led to a child being unprotected or inadequately protected. This portrayal was reinforced by the Department of Health and Social Security publishing its own study of reports of inquiries conducted between 1973 and 1981 [3], a precedent for the digests commissioned by the governments in the 2000s of the findings and learning from serious case reviews [4, 5, 6].

A major and repeated issue to emerge from inquiries were concerns about inter-agency and inter-professional communication and information sharing. There was also reflection and comment on the creation of generic social services departments and generic social workers working across client groups and the impact of reorganisations and restructuring:

Eight [out of 18 inquiry reports reviewed by the DHSS in 1982] mention the effects of major structural reorganisations on services ... Many of the problems of supervision, staffing, accommodation, etc ... were judged by the inquiries to have arisen out of reorganisations ... As social work became less specialised there was also a loss of expertise as those who had previous experience in particular fields were promoted to manage teams covering a wide range of work. [7]

The individual inquiry reports were lengthy and detailed. For example, the 1985 report of the inquiry chaired by Louis Blom-Cooper QC into the death of five-year-old Jasmine Beckford [8] in Brent was 304 pages long plus 140 pages of appendices; the 1987 report of the public inquiry chaired by Stephen Sedley QC into the death of 22-month-old Tyra Henry [9] in Lambeth was 176 pages; and the 1987 report of the inquiry, also chaired by Louis Blom-Cooper, following the death of 4-year-old Kimberley Carlile [10] in Greenwich was 292 pages long. These are substantial inquiries and significantly weighty publications and their frequency kept the issues and concerns about child deaths at the forefront of the attention of the press, politicians and professionals.

Eileen Munro commented on how selective media reporting of the inquiries into the non-accidental death of children targeted, in particular, social workers:

> Approximately 40 more inquiries [after the 1973–74 Maria Colwell Inquiry] were published up to 1990, providing a constant reminder to the public of the existence of child abuse and the apparent failure of professionals to protect children. A review of inquiry reports found that 25 per cent of the reports were not critical of any professional group and social workers escaped censure in 42 per cent. Media coverage, however, varied, with more attention being paid to inquiries that castigated professionals and less to the ones that exonerated them, fostering an image of all deaths being, in principle, preventable if only professionals acted competently. In this coverage, social workers were repeatedly singled out for blame even when other professional groups had played a major role. [11]

Munro continued by noting the impact of the inquiries and the media's selective and distorted reporting:

> The sustained impact of these public criticisms led professionals to place more and more priority on responding to allegations of child abuse. The increased public and professional awareness of abuse led to a rise in referrals to Social Services Departments. No national statistics were kept [unlike in the 2000s] on referral rates but some indication of the increase can be gauged from the numbers placed on the child protection register which rose from 11,844 in 1978 to 45,300 in 1991. The bulk of the extra work of responding to these referrals fell on social services teams, reducing their ability to meet their other responsibilities in relation to supporting families and looking after children in public care. [12]

It was not only, however, the increase in workloads which impacted on the work of social workers. The condemnation generated by inquiries and the distorted media coverage also skewed the focus of social work practice with children and families. Reflecting back on the impact of the 1980s inquiries Rogowski commented that:

> Eventually, as a result of overwhelming criticism of the processes that sought to transform 'dysfunctional' families into 'healthy' ones, the focus was to change from working therapeutically to protecting children.

Furthermore, the language used in this process changed, with terms such as 'investigation', 'assessment', 'dangerousness' and 'forensic evidence' now more reminiscent of law enforcement than a caring profession. [13]

The media and the public's attention given to the abuse of children within families, and the narrative of inaction and the gullibility of social workers, was turned on its head, however, by three particular controversies in the late 1980s, with social workers, but also other professionals, presented as over-enthusiastic and intruding unnecessarily and inappropriately into families and with children allegedly being taken into care without good reason.

The Cleveland Inquiry

The first controversy was in Cleveland in the north east of England. In 1987 in five months two paediatricians identified 121 children as being sexually abused. They relied heavily but not exclusively on a clinical test based on 'reflex relaxation and anal dilatation' as a sign of anal penetration. The increased child protection activity created considerable pressure for hospitals, the local authority and courts, with children made subject to emergency place of safety orders, held on hospital wards, and then placed with foster carers. Parents and children were not allowed access to each other as criminal investigations were initiated.

The diagnosis of the paediatricians were challenged by other doctors and the already strained relationships locally between the police and social services escalated as the social services managers largely accepted and acted upon the identification of sexual abuse by the paediatricians but with the police less accepting of the diagnosis of sexual abuse.

The local MP, Stuart Bell, became alerted to the concerns and distress of parents (he subsequently wrote a book titled *When Salem Came to the Boro: The True Story of the Cleveland Child Abuse Crisis*). He referred to it in Parliament and there was increasing media coverage of the crisis and controversy which was escalating. This led to the Secretary of State for Health and Social Services commissioning a Statutory Inquiry to be chaired by Lord Justice Butler-Sloss. She was assisted by the Inquiry panel of a professor of public health, a recently retired chief constable and a director of social services. The report of the Inquiry was published in June 1988 [14].

So what did the Inquiry conclude? There were comments and recommendations about multi-agency joint working and about how children and parents should be more actively and sensitively involved in child protection assessments and investigations. On the key concerns about the diagnosis of abuse by the paediatricians and whether children were unnecessarily removed from their parents and carers the Inquiry was less clear and committed:

> By reaching a firm conclusion on the basis of physical signs and acting as they would for non-accidental injury or physical abuse; by separating children from their parents and by admitting most of the children to hospital, [the paediatricians] compromised the work of the social workers and the Police. The medical diagnosis assumed a central and a determining role in the management of the child and the family ... It was entirely proper for the two paediatricians to play their part in the identification of sexual abuse in children referred to them. They were responsible for the care of their patients. Nonetheless they had a responsibility to examine their own actions; to consider whether their practice was always correct and whether it was in the best interest of the children and their patients. They are to be criticised for not doing so and the certainty and over-confidence with which they pursued the detection of sexual abuse in children referred to them. They were not solely nor indeed principally responsible for the subsequent management of the children concerned. However, the certainty of their findings in relation to children diagnosed by them without prior complaint, posed particular problems for the Police and Social Services. [15]

In essence, the two paediatricians were seen to have been too confident in identifying sexual abuse with the social services and, may be less so, the police (and the magistrates courts) accepting and acting on the basis of the medical diagnosis.

The Inquiry panel was, however, also cautious that they should not deter professionals from identifying and acting to address sexual abuse:

> It is however important to bear in mind that those who have a responsibility to protect children at risk, such as social workers, health visitors, police

and doctors have in the past been criticised for failure to act in sufficient time and to take adequate steps to protect children who are being damaged. In Cleveland the general criticism by the public has been of over-enthusiasm and zeal in the actions taken. It is difficult for professionals to balance the conflicting interests and needs in the enormously important and delicate field of child sexual abuse. We hope that professionals will not as result of the Cleveland experience stand back and hesitate to act to protect children. [16]

Particular attention was given in the Inquiry report to social workers:

In many Inquiries it is social workers who are under scrutiny for their failure to act in time. We are concerned that in advising a calm, measured and considered approach to the problem of child sexual abuse, we are not seen to imply either that there are never occasions when immediate action may need to be taken or that there is not a problem to be faced and children to be protected. It is a delicate and difficult line to tread between taking action too soon and not taking action soon enough. Social Services whilst putting the needs of the child first must respect the rights of the parents; they must also work if possible with the parents for the benefit of the children. These parents themselves are often in need of help. Inevitably a degree of conflict develops between these objectives. [16]

And the Inquiry report gave attention to media reporting:

We are also concerned about the extent of the misplaced adverse criticism social workers have received from the media and elsewhere. There is a danger that social workers, including those in Cleveland, will be demoralised. Some may hesitate to do what is right. Social workers need the support of the public to continue in the job the public needs them to do. It is time the public and the press gave it to them. [17]

The impact of the media was commented upon 30 years later by an editor of The Times:

When did it all go wrong between social workers and the media? You can do worse than to look back to 1987, exactly 30 years ago, to the Cleveland child abuse scandal. This was a profoundly disturbing case in which dozens of children were removed from their families on the basis of diagnoses given by two paediatricians. In the face of a public outcry the doctors were challenged and, eventually, many of the children were allowed to return home. By then, an entire community was traumatised and social workers, as well as paediatricians, had become demonised. Cleveland was far from being the first case of its kind, in which the competence of professionals tasked with child protection was questioned. But it came at a particularly sensitive moment, when the whole ethos of public service was being challenged by Margaret Thatcher's government. The case remained in the public consciousness well beyond Cleveland for several years, with a report by Elizabeth Butler-Sloss into the case, and implementation of the Children Act 1989. It weighed heavily on media coverage of cases that were investigated in the following years, such as the 'satanic abuse case in Rochdale in 1990 and the Orkney abuse scandal in 1991. Just as 24-hour rolling TV news was gaining traction, the public's appetite for details of each case appeared insatiable and social workers became big news. [18]

The selective and biased media coverage was commented upon by Sir Liam Donaldson, who at the time of the Cleveland Inquiry was the Regional Medical Officer and Regional Director of Public Health for the Northern Regional Health Authority, which included Cleveland. He later became Chief Medical Officer in the Department of Health:

The highest coverage of any single day of the Enquiry in both local and national newspapers occurred when Dr Marietta Higgs (one of the two principal paediatricians involved) made her first appearance. However, the highest interest was shown in evidence given by lawyers for the parents and the least in evidence given by public bodies. The evidence of witnesses was used very selectively by the press in emotive headlines ... This sustained several lines of reporting: criticism of the doctors and social workers, interprofessional conflicts, damage and wrong-doing to the families and the search for someone to blame... The Cleveland crisis occupied newspaper headlines in the United Kingdom for more than a year. Much of the newspaper coverage took an adversarial approach which sought to apportion blame and take sides. The press appeared to report negative issues which were newsworthy and did not give a balanced view. Broader policy issues, which formed an important part of the Enquiry report's influence on subsequent child protection legislation, were largely ignored. [19]

The conclusions and lessons to be drawn from Cleveland in 1987–1988 were [20, 21, 22] and have remained controversial. Here is a comment from the 2020 advanced publicity for a book by Bea Campbell:

> Three decades ago doctors in Cleveland, a county in the north-East of England, identified sexual abuse in 121 girls and boys. Their average age was eight. Official Secrets reveals that the enquiry that followed was a cover-up. Confidential documents and correspondence in the National Archive prove that the government knew that most diagnoses were believed to be correct, but ministers withheld the explosive evidence. Parliament and the people were led to believe that there had been a scandal and that scores of children had been wrongly seized from innocent parents. Doctors were discouraged and social workers disempowered—a legacy that leads all the way to the current Independent Inquiry into Child Sexual Abuse. The response to the Cleveland controversy defined an era of scepticism and blame, and not the protection of children. [23]

And here is a report from the Daily Mail in 2008 about two of the young children who had been removed from, and later returned, to their parents:

> Raised by a loving family, they were the first victims of the 1987 scandal when hundreds of parents in the North-East of England were wrongly accused of the worst crime imaginable: molesting their own children Lindsey and Paula Wise are speaking out today for the first time. [24]

Although there may be continuing controversy about what happened in Cleveland in 1987 there can be little debate that it had an impact on the child protection system in England and Wales. Even before the Inquiry was established, changes were being debated and demanded in Parliament, with Michael Meacher asking:

> Is the Minister aware that, while the Opposition in principle welcome any initiative that will cool the partisan sensationalism of the past few weeks, we are concerned that this does not turn into a narrow judgmental inquiry confined to one area when what is needed is to implement new agreed child care procedures throughout the country to safeguard the rights of

both parents and children alike? What specific evidence of a breakdown in medical and social procedures has been discovered which now justifies a full public inquiry? Will the Minister state the precise terms of reference for the inquiry, which, surprisingly, are left vague in his statement? Will this inquiry be in public or behind closed doors? Why is it that, after 12 years of mounting public anxiety over child abuse and 13 months of consultation, the Government still have not produced an advisory code of practice for handling such cases? Will he give a firm date when it will be produced? [25]

It was only in the 1980s that sexual abuse became a significant issue and focus within child protection. Indeed it is possible, as noted in the figure below, to track how the understandings of child abuse and the net of child protection has expanded over the past 50 years.

Fifty years of the expanding concerns about child abuse	
1960s	Battered babies
1970s	Physical abuse
1980s	Sexual abuse
	Abuse in institutions
1990s	Neglect
2000s	Emotional abuse
2010s	Networked sexual abuse
2020s	Thought abuse (radicalisation)?
	Trafficking?

Writing in 1999, Olive Stevenson (who had been a member of the Maria Colwell Inquiry in 1973) reflected on Cleveland:

As expectations of cooperative behaviour [between workers and agencies] became established, the dimensions of child abuse were widened to include, from the 1980s, sexual abuse. The powerful effects of this were to be illustrated in the second half of the 1980s by the Cleveland debacle ... As the Cleveland report showed, those events, challenged—some would say blew apart—the consensus which had begun to emerge about the basis of co-operative work. The spectacular rifts between police, paediatricians, police surgeons and social workers were only matched by the splits *within* some of those professions. For the first time, professionals other than social workers were under public and media scrutiny. The effects have been long-lasting, notably amongst individual paediatricians whose responses vary between powerful, dedicated commitment to child protection work and extreme reluctance to become involved.[1] [26]

Stevenson continued:

Leaving aside the debate at that time [and since] as to whether certain children had in fact been sexually abused and the medical disputes about physical symptoms, what this episode illustrated so powerfully was the uncertainty and ambivalence in society at large (including the professionals) about sexual abuse. What constituted sexual abuse, what was acceptable and unacceptable parental behaviour, what action to take if there were good grounds for suspicion but no actual proof—these issues were revealed as contested and raising passionate feelings in which the gender of the onlookers and professionals played a significant part [as noted also in Beatrix Campbell's book which was published in 1988 in the midst of the Cleveland events and debates [21]]. [27]

In 1988 the government did, as demanded by Michael Meacher, issue national guidance on tackling child abuse. 'Working Together' [28] has had several revisions and iterations and become much lengthier. It had 72 pages in 1988, 124 pages in 1991 and the 2010 version had 390 pages. It set out to address the concerns which arose through the Cleveland Inquiry, and other inquiries, about inter-agency cooperation to protect children.

The events in Cleveland in 1987 did not stand alone in raising concerns about the involvement—the intrusion—of doctors, police and, especially, social workers into families where there were allegations of child abuse, including in Rochdale in 1990 and in Orkney in 1991 (with a subsequent government—commissioned independent inquiry by Lord Clyde) [29] where there had been allegations of ritual satanic sexual abuse

---

[1] There was a similar reluctance of some paediatricians to take on work which might involve child protection after a community paediatrician was placed centre stage by the media when it shaped the 'Baby P' story 30 years after Cleveland in 2008 (Doctor's should not fear raising child abuse concerns, 10 July, https://www.bbc.co.uk/news/health-18773101), with it becoming more difficult to recruit paediatricians (Laming, Lord (2009) The Protection of Children in England, London, HMSO, p. 59).

and with children being removed from their families but later (largely) being returned to their parents by the courts [30].

The 1988 Cleveland Inquiry might be seen to have led to the 1989 Children Act, with its emphasis on partnership working with parents. Writing in 1996 Olive Otway, a lecturer in social work, noted that:

> It was during the mid-1980s that the parents' lobby achieved its most coherent voice, with the creation of Parents Against Injustice (PAIN). While its direct influence and lobbying upon the Children Act may be considered minimal, it did assist in drawing up and vocalising some of the chief concerns raised during the events in Cleveland and subsequently in Rochdale and Orkney ... Consequently the rights of parents and of children to remain at home, undisturbed by state intervention, were placed on the political and professional agendas. As a result state intervention, through the practices of health and welfare professionals, as well as parental violence, was recognised as being actively and potentially abusive. [31]

It may seem strange and shocking now, but in the 1980s local authorities could through an executive order 'assume the parental rights' of parents where, as stated in Section 3 of the 1980 Children Act, the parent has abandoned the child, suffers from some permanent disability rendering him [sic] incapable of caring for the child, suffers from a mental disorder which renders him unfit to have the care of the child, is of such habits or mode of life as to be unfit to have the care of the child, has so consistently failed without reasonable cause to discharge the obligations of a parent as to be unfit to have the care of the child, or that throughout the three years preceding the passing of the resolution the child has been in the voluntary care of a local authority [32].

What this meant was that without any reference to or hearing in a court a local authority could keep in care a child without a court order unless challenged by the parent. Once parental rights had been taken by the local authority without a challenge from the parent within one month of the local authority order, it was the parent who would have to initiate court proceedings if they wanted to remove their child from local authority care.

This power increasingly sat uncomfortably with the growing focus on working in partnership with parents and the Association of Directors of Social Services along with others actively campaigned for its removal. It does reflect, however, the imbalance of power and the disempowerment of parents which was addressed by the 1989 Act.

The Genesis of the 1989 Children Act

But although the Act followed the Cleveland Inquiry where parents had been found to have been excluded from the processes of decision-making about their children it was not the Cleveland scandal which primarily led to the Act. The build-up to the Act had a longer and broader trajectory, as noted by Rogowski:

> The 1989 Children Act aimed to address the wide-ranging disquiet about the practice of social workers and, to a less extent, other health and welfare professionals in relation to child abuse. However, it was also informed by research and a series of official reports which aimed to update and rationalise child care legislation. [33]

The antecedents of 1989 included the report by a House of Commons Select Committee, a review of child care law, research on social work with families and on children in care, reviews and media scandal following the killing of children by their parents and carers, and—latterly—the Cleveland Inquiry.

Along with these processes and events there were key figures who were central to the shaping and then the enacting of the legislation, especially a senior civil servant—Rupert Hughes—and a government minister for children—David Mellor. It was an act that was many years in its gestation throughout the mid- and late 1980s.

It was the Select Committee report of 1984 on children in care which was an early spur to the 1989 legislation. The committee was chaired by Labour MP Renee Short, and it identified several issues which the later legislation sought to tackle. Select Committees were at this time a recent innovation and had much more influence than might be the position in 2020:

Oh, they were regarded as a very big innovation and really quite a threatening one at the time. When we went along to give evidence some hands were trembling. They were introduced about 1980 … So the Renee Short recommendations were extremely important in getting the review of children's legislation underway. [Bill Utting interview][2]

There was a concern from the Committee that the attention and resources given to taking and keeping children in care was not matched by providing help to families to care for their children:

While there is a general acceptance that more could and should be done explicitly to prevent children entering long-term care, and some awareness of the courses of action that would make this possible, there is as yet regrettably little indication of any concerted strategy which could translate pious thought into action. There are many reasons for this. One must surely be the lack of any organisational commitment to prevention to parallel that to fostering and adoption. Few authorities if any have a similar commitment to prevention. If half the funds and intellectual effort which has gone towards developing strategies for finding alternative families had been put into what we can only lamely call preventive work, there would be unquestionable advantage to all concerned. [34]

The committee noted that in March 1982 there were 93,200 children in care in England and Wales. During the 1990s and 2000s this number reduced, in part as more attention was given to helping families in difficulty care for their children, but in the 2010s the numbers of children in care at any one time has increased. In 2008, for example, there were 63,975 children in care in England and Wales (England 59,400; Wales 4635) but by 2018 this had increased to over 80,000 (England 75,420; Wales 6405). In 1984, as in the 2010s, the link between care and (increasing) deprivation was noted by the Short Committee [35].

---

[2] I have given written and oral evidence to several select committees in the 2010s but their impact today seems much lessened. They prepare a report, it may or may not get one day of marginal media attention, and several months later the government provides a published response which gets little attention and which generally restates current government policy.

The Short Committee also commented that it wanted more involvement of parents, as well as more assistance for them, in decisions about the care of their children:

> We have considerable sympathy with the advocates of family rights. We would like to see the position of parents of children in care improved in a number of ways, most of all in receiving assistance in order to prevent break-up of a family. Families should be more involved in the process of care. [36]

The themes of more help for parents, and more involvement with them in decisions about the care of their children, were taken on board in the 1989 Act. The Committee also recommended that a working party on child care law be established [37], and in acting on this recommendation the government put in place a further building block for the 1989 Act.

The Act had many key players who were significant in its development, several of whom as will be seen below were interviewed for this book. One person in particular, a long-serving career civil servant was central to bringing the Act to fruition.

Rupert Hughes completed a degree in classics and philosophy at Oxford University in 1959 and then joined the civil service and was assigned to the Department of Health and by 1983 had become a senior civil servant, an Assistant Secretary. He commented that:

> I was a lay administrator working with professional colleagues throughout, and in 1983 someone said to me, and I think it was said on a Friday and I was there on the Monday, 'What about this job on children'. [Rupert Hughes interview]

This 'job on children' was to last until 1989 and beyond and he recalled that 'I took on responsibilities which were basically child protection, adoption, fostering and some other topics on children's social services' [Rupert Hughes interview]. His previous work in the Department of Health had been on health issues—'hospital topics, private medicine, transplantation, maternity, abortion, a whole range of different things that one does as a civil servant'. This was his first assignment on children's social services:

> One of the first things that happened was that the Social Services [Select Committee] in the Commons had being doing work on children in care and produced a report, Renee Short's report, and that came out fairly quickly after I arrived. Almost simultaneously, there was a Bill and then an Act in Parliament called the HASSASSA [the Health and Social Services and Social Security Adjudications Act] and Tony Newton was then the minister. I wouldn't say he was attacked but he had quite a hard time dealing with some of the questions on children's interests [in the Bill] and he then became interested in them and these two things together [the Short Report and the emerging interest of the minister] gave a sufficient push to get started on the review of the law in relation to children which the Select Committee said should be done in nine months and we actually didn't take much longer than that. We produced what was called the Yellow Peril [the yellow covered Review of Child Care Law [38]] in September 1985. [Rupert Hughes interview]

The HASSASSA was a jumble of unrelated topics ranging from local authority powers to charge disabled and older people for care services, to joint financing of new developments between area health services and local authorities, to the registration of care homes, to revising the powers, and the duties of Central Council for Education and Training in Social Work (CCETSW). In relation to children, the HASSASSA included the introduction of the opportunity for a parent or guardian to apply to a court to get an order requiring a local authority to give access to a child where the local authority had taken an executive decision to deny access, abolished the regional planning of children's homes, and a number of paragraphs clarifying or amending previous children's legislation. There was the added complication that some of the HASSASSA Act applied to England and Wales and some to Scotland. It might have been no surprise that the minister had some difficulty responding to questions in Parliament during debates on the Bill!

The coming together of a Select Committee report and a minister who through another route had his interest stimulated in children's legalisation was the sort of serendipitous occurrence which leads to reflection and change, a point reinforced in a paper in the Family Law journal published in 2006:

> Some of those involved [attributed] a significant part of the perceived success of the Bill [which led to the 1989 Act] to luck. They pointed to the coincidence of the government's response to the Short Committee Report with the arrival in the [Law] Commission of an expert in the field, Brenda Hoggett, and a Commission Secretary bent on finding a new role for the organisation. They pointed to the constant stream of official reports into the deaths and alleged abuse of children which gave the policy 'legs' and secured it a legislative slot despite the absence of any party-political imperative ... Finally, the interviewees instanced the chance but beneficial mix of individuals in the team and the continuity achieved through the return of Commission-based staff to jobs in Whitehall that kept them involved. [39]

Another contributor on the route to the passing of the 1989 Act was the findings of research [40] which had been commissioned by the Department for Health. The research highlighted the marginalisation of parents in decision-making about their children near the threshold or in care. The research—as with the Cleveland Inquiry—gave support to the changes underway through the Law Review but were not in themselves the stimulus for the changes:

> It is quite difficult to be specific actually [about the contribution of research]. I think it was much more about [influencing] general attitudes and approaches than about anything really specific ... [And] Cleveland was in 1987 and by that point we were already pretty well on to the main bits of the Bill. I remember showing a bit to Elizabeth Butler-Sloss [the judge who undertook the Cleveland inquiry] who may have discussed one or two points but we were doing it anyway I think. [Rupert Hughes interview]

In Rupert Hughes obituary in 2015 Malcolm Dean, who as a Guardian newspaper social services journalist would have tracked social services legislative changes, commented on the key role played by Rupert Hughes in chaperoning the Children Act through its gestation:

In a decade in which the government of Margaret Thatcher was seeking to curb state activities, Hughes managed to steer through the Act with cross-party support, and set a threshold for compulsory state intervention in family life that was both more precise and wider than existing law. [41]

Another significant key person in parenting the 1989 Act was Brenda Hoggett, who had been a law lecturer at Manchester University and professor of law in 1986 when she became a Law Commissioner (in 2017 as Lady Hale she became president of the Supreme Court). It should have been no surprise that with her role as a Law Commissioner reviewing children and family legislation the subsequent Bill and Act brought together the public and private law relating to children as this was what she covered in the content of her 1977 book 'Social Work and Law: Children and Families'[3] [42]. Adoption and juvenile justice, however, were left outside of the 1989 Act, the former to avoid widening debate and delaying the passage of the Act and the latter because it was within the territory of the Home Office.

Speaking at a (slightly belated) seminar in 2016 to mark the 25th anniversary of the 1989 Act Lady Hale commented:

> The Bill [leading into the 1989 Act] represented a scheme of extraordinary elegance which really has very rarely been seen in this sort of thing, the revolutionary idea that all the courts could be applying the same law, the same principles and the same procedures. [43]

She also reflected on the context in which the new legislation was being drafted and debated:

> The scandals of the early 1980s (and indeed 1970s) where children had not been rescued from abusive homes—Kimberley Carlile, Jasmine Beckford, Tyra Hindley and so on—were then balanced by the Cleveland scandal where perhaps too many children had been removed from non-abusive homes, and so the need to balance intervention and protection and rights

---

[3] Indeed, Brenda Hale was close to social work and in the 1990s took over from Sir Michael Rutter as the chair of the Nuffield Foundations children and families research grants committee (of which I was a member).

of children and rights of the parents became much clearer and Dame Elizabeth Butler-Sloss supported our recommendations to improve the parents' position in care proceedings. [43]

It was Wendy Rose, formerly an assistant director of social services in Hammersmith and Fulham and then an assistant chief inspector in the Department of Health's Social Services Inspectorate, who in the mid- and late 1980s had a policy lead in the Department of Health on children's social services and was involved in the drafting of the White Paper which heralded the 1989 Act.

'The Law on Child Care and Family Services' White Paper [44] sought to re-set the balance between the state, as represented by local authorities and the courts, and children and parents, with parents to be given more powers to be participants in court proceedings concerning their children and with local authorities to first of all be a resource to families to assist them in caring for their children:

> It is proposed to give local authorities a broad 'umbrella' *power* [italic here and below in this quote in original text] to provide services to promote the care and upbringing of children, and to help prevent the breakdown of family relationships which might eventually lead to a court order committing the child to the local authority's care. Within this power the local authority will be able to provide services to a child *at home*, for example a family aide to assist within the home; at a *day centre,* for example a day nursery for pre-school children, an after-school scheme for school age children or placement with a childminder, or *residential facilities* allowing a child to stay for short or long periods away from home, say with a foster family or in a children's home. The local authority will also be able to offer financial assistance in exceptional circumstances ... [the Act] should help to focus attention on the role of the local authority in supporting the family in various ways especially when parents are under stress. [45]

Whilst the White Paper also covered proposed changes in the law to protect children (such as shortening the period of emergency place of safety orders) a primacy was given in the White Paper to providing resources to help struggling families care for their children, including receptions in to care with the agreement of parents as a resource to share the care of children.

The White Paper and the subsequent 1989 Children Act with it focus on helping families in difficulty ran counter to the Thatcher mantra and attacks on welfare dependency and welfare provision. How did this happen? Wendy Rose's view was that it was a consequence of 'benign neglect' by Mrs Thatcher and 'senior politicians':

> Obviously it was not seen as of primary importance to the Thatcher government. I think the argument was pretty persuasive that one had all these different pieces of legislation scattered around, so the idea of streamlining it was absolutely incontrovertible, there was a need to make a more coherent body, but not necessarily reform … There was the serendipity of having key people who were enthusiastic and committed right across the board in the Lord Chancellor's Department and externally. John Rea Price and the directors of social services on the ADSS [Association of Directors of Social Services] Children's Committee were critically important, and there were fundamentally important people in the voluntary sector like Tom White [who was then chief executive of NCH Action for Children] and others who were of the same mind, including researchers like Roy [Parker] and others who were producing really powerful and compelling findings, so that it was all coming together. [Wendy Rose interview]

The lack of government and political interest in the 1989 Children Act and its preparation during the mid- and late 1980s was also noted by David Walden, who was also a senior civil servant in the Department of Health at the time:

> Not only weren't the politicians interested [in the 1989 Act] but the Department [of Health also] wasn't interested in its own legislation! It was very, very difficult to get the departmental board which was the main board for the Department of Health to focus on the Children Bill and the Children Act. It allowed [Rupert Hughes, Wendy Rose and David Mellor] to run their own sort of private army and do their own thing and there was a lot of that. And I mean it's incredible really that all that SSI [Social Services Inspectorate] guidance and so on followed the Children's Act. It was not on the political radar at the time … I think it was probably sold to politicians as a consolidation measure—my advice would be to be suspicious of consolidation measures! It's impossible to consolidate everything because 20 years or whatever has passed and things have changed so you can't just consolidate. [David Walden interview]

The 1989 Act may have progressed under the political and prime minister's radar but there were sympathetic ministers and cross-party engagement and support:

> There were political champions for it across the parties and, mercifully, there was no time within the House of Commons for the Bill to be heard so it started in the House of Lords with Lord Mackay [then Lord Chancellor] who was very committed to it and there were champions in every party. I think the success was that it never became controversial during its passage through Parliament because all the work was done behind the scenes and we were very lucky to have David Mellor as our minister. He was an exceedingly able barrister by background who was very good at grasping and taking a briefing. He was willing to go and negotiate and get things through and he knew when to compromise and when it's appropriate ... It was an extraordinary piece of revolutionary and reforming legislation that was got through by stealth. [Wendy Rose interview]

When David Mellor was moved to the Home Office in 1989 he was succeeded by Virginia Bottomley as minister at the Department of Health, and in 1992 she became secretary of state for health. Bottomley was a sociology graduate from Essex University, one of the new 1960s universities, and had worked as a researcher with the Child Poverty Action Group and as a psychiatric social worker (the mother of her husband Peter Bottomley—another government minister—had also been a social worker) before becoming a Conservative MP in 1984. At a seminar in 2016 reflecting on the 1989 Act she reiterated the importance of the Children's Bill having started its Parliamentary process in the House of Lords:

> I arrived (as minister) in the month in which the Act received Royal Assent, so I didn't take it through Parliament, but a lot had been squeezed into schedules, regulations and supplementary legislation so I had a lot of work to do in actually following up on a lot of the detail ... Why did it go so well? The classic thing for an important Bill is to start in the House of

Lords because in the House of Lords you have got sane people—mostly sane people—who are not trying to sort of audition for News at Ten or write or do something for their local newspaper. And, of course, [Lord] James Mackay was a deeply wonderful, very clever, very committed ethical man who did a wonderful job in the Lords and the debates were very good. [46]

The comment from Virginia Bottomley that although she was not the minister who took the Children's Bill through Parliament she still had much to do after the Bill was passed into legislation reflects the considerable attention that was paid to seeking to ensure the Act was implemented and had an impact, as noted by Wendy Rose:

> I was particularly keen [on implementation and impact] because of the inquiry on Shirley Woodcock [Shirley, aged 3, died following being abused in 1982 while placed with foster carers in Hammersmith and Fulham [47] where Wendy Rose was an assistant director of social services]. We asked all the practitioners and managers what had informed the basis of their practice and very few of them knew anything about the boarding out regulations and could produce them. There were these scrappy bits of paper the Department [of Health] issued and the Department and the government seemed to think that if you had a law and then produced these flimsy bits of paper with the regulations on that was sufficient. It was quite obvious we needed to approach [the implementation of the 1989 Act] in quite a different way if we were going to influence policy and practice locally. We therefore had a complete strategy across absolutely every aspect of communication, statistics, training, all sorts of things that we would need to do, so we had something called the Joint Action for Implementation Group which was set up as soon as we got Royal Assent … We decided to bring together the guidance with the regulations in ten volumes … We thought this was an important building block really for beginning to help people understand and bring about change which had then to be backed up by senior management committing locally and by training and supervision. [The ten volumes] weren't seen as something that could sit there on their own and make a difference, but they would be a resource to begin with. [Wendy Rose interview]

The Act and its Schedules were 218 pages long, the 'Introduction to the Act' published by HMSO was 90 pages long, and a separate publication on 'Principles and Practice in Regulations and Guidance' was 20 pages long. The ten volumes of themed guidance and regulations—such as Volume 1 on Court Orders; Volume 2 on Family Support; Day Care and Educational Provision for Young Children; Volume 3 on Family Placements; and so on ... totalled just under 1000 pages. No longer were social workers and their managers able to carry with them the key legislation and guidance as I had been able to do in the 1970s and early 1980s!

In addition to the published volumes of guidance, and the training to make social workers and others aware of the guidance, a programme of research was put in place by the Department of Health to track the Act's implementation and impact with the intention that the research itself should have impact. Wendy Rose wrote:

> Researchers and policy makers have recognised that completion of research studies is not the end of the story, and improvement in outcomes for children means that research findings need to be translated into changes in professional practice. This requires a strategy for making the findings accessible and relevant to a wide range of stakeholders. First, this has been achieved in England by researchers, policy makers and professionals working together to produce a series of overviews of related research studies, summarising the key findings, acknowledging the strengths and limitations of the research methodologies and discussing the implications of the findings for policy and practice. The overviews [more than ten since the first overview in 1985] have been distributed widely by government, supported by conferences and other dissemination events. Secondly, in association with the production of the overviews, practice tools and guidance have been developed for practitioners and managers, and they have been provided with, for example, training materials, self-audit materials, and 'true for us' exercises which can be tried out in local services to test the relevance of the findings to their situation. Inspections, audits and further research have subsequently been used to identify whether changes in practice are becoming embedded and what effect they are having on children's experiences, as part of the iterative process. [48]

The most significant of the research digests was 'The Children Act Now: Messages from Research' looking back, in 2001, over ten years since the implementation of the Act and reviewing 24 research studies. It concluded:

What is the overall verdict on the Children Act 1989? Basically, the Children Act as the overarching primary legislation is sound and has provided a working framework for the provision and delivery of services to children in need and their families. The principles of the Act—such as safeguarding and promoting children's welfare in all circumstances; promoting the upbringing of children by their families wherever possible; working with parents to enhance parental responsibilities; and providing a range of services for children in need and their families—have underpinned practice. Although there have been some flaws in practice, the principles of achieving a balance between voluntary and compulsory measurers have also had an impact. The participation of children and families in the process of service delivery has begun to improve but more needs to be done. Some parts of the Act have proved problematic, either because the Act's intentions were unclear or have been misinterpreted or because of sluggishness in changing old habits. There have also been considerable difficulties in meeting the requirements of the Act in a climate of intense competition for resources for public welfare services. [49]

The limitations in implementing the Act because government did not provide the funding needed by local authorities and by families was also noted by Professor Jane Tunstill. She had been involved with the Family Rights Group, the Child Poverty Action Group and others in advocating in the 1980s for more help and resources for families. Speaking in 2009 she concluded:

If I was to say what was the elephant in the room with the 1989 Act, it was the nature of the broader socioeconomic political backdrop, because on paper the 1989 Act, like motherhood and apple pie, you couldn't really be against most of it. But what screwed its chances of being implemented in the proactive and optimistic and ultimately productive way that the civil servants and politicians intended, was that it unfortunately coincided with all of these [ideologies and policies] coming on-stream, both across the 1980s under Thatcher, but also under New labour once it got into the 1990s. And most of all there was this disenchantment with collectivism, a bigger concern for cost-effectiveness but no real mechanism for relating money to individual outcomes for children. [There was] the madness of the new managerialist agenda [introducing] market principles into public policy and the positive preference for privately provided services ... At a stroke it fragments the integrated system [that one might have had]. [50]

The issue of limited resources hampering the implementation of the Act was also noted by Rose, but she also noted that continuing emphasis on child protection beyond 1989 also held back the Act's intention that more attention should be given to assisting parents to fulfil their parental responsibilities:

I think that the 1989 Act still provides an extraordinary framework within which to develop children's services. I think it was stunted as much as anything by the changing context, the financial pressures and the way in which child abuse and tragedies were shaped and pushed ... I always feel that we should never have had the Victoria Climbie Inquiry [discussed in a later chapter] because in a way it did untold damage to the way in which policy was then framed. [Wendy Rose interview]

Wendy Rose's reflection on the continuing focus on child protection was echoed by Rupert Hughes:

We certainly, I don't think, got the balance between the supportive and the hard end that we would have wanted ... We were hoping for a larger proportion of voluntary arrangements for children being looked after, as compared to compulsory, than we'd actually got. I mean [social workers] like to be able to have the authority of a court behind them sometimes I think, but we were hoping that the number of times when care proceedings were instituted would be the minimum. [Rupert Hughes interview]

Rupert Hughes' senior manager in the Department of Health when the Children Act was being implemented was Tom Luce. His exposure to the policy issues around children's social services led him to conclude:

One of my feelings about all of this area is that if you look across the whole functions of the public sector in Britain, there is probably no field in which the judgments are harder. I mean obviously there are some areas like brain surgery where the sort of technical aspects are very demanding, but the actual judgments may well be in my opinion harder in this area of public service than in any other. And when the press and politicians complain, you know after 'Baby P' [see chapter 11] and all these other dreadful cases, there is no recognition of that. It may be that they blame local authorities or they blame social workers, but there is no recognition of the enormous difficulty of the judgments that have to be made. [Tom Luce interview]

Children's Homes

There was another aspect of the 1989 Act which did not play out quite as intended and expected. This was the role of children's residential care (and foster care) as a resource for children and families. Two reports in in the early and late 1980s sought to project and promote residential care—for children and for adults—as a 'positive choice' rather than a last resort to be avoided if at all possible.

The first report, published in 1980, was prepared by a National Children's Bureau working group chaired by Roy Parker. It stated that:

> Community care has been regarded as the preferable alternative to residential care, although the term is sometimes used without making clear what is meant. Community-based residential care avoids these polarised options. By community-based residential care we mean making available reasonably small units which offer their facilities in a variety of ways to meet the needs of children and their families as they arise in reasonably local areas. Such centres would be part of the preventive *and* [italic in original text] more permanent care resources; provide short-term back-up and respite for families facing great stress or foster homes under pressure. [51]

The second review, published in 1988, was a report called 'Residential Care A Positive Choice' which was the report of an independent review of residential care for children and adults commissioned by Norman Fowler as Secretary of State for Health and Social Services. It was undertaken under the auspices of the National Institute for Social Work and chaired by Lady Gillian Wagner. It stated that:

> We believe it to be essential that a person entering a residential establishment should do so by positive choice, since the quality of life in a residential establishment will depend quite crucially on the consent and cooperation of those who share it ... Positive choosing does not end with the decision over admission. Whether a package of services is provided in their own home or in a residential setting, the process of having positive choices, of the consumer being in control as far as possible, and of negotiation in relation to the needs and wishes of others, must continue. [52]

The White Paper which preceded the 1989 Act did portray residential care as a positive resource for children and for families. It promoted a model of shared care in partnership with parents who retained parental responsibility, but with the child living short or long term in foster placements or care homes and with parents still actively involved in their children's lives and in decision-making about the children.

Writing in 1999 and looking back at the 1989 Act Roger Bullock, who was a member of the research team at Dartington Hall which undertook a number of studies of residential children's homes, noted that:

> The Children Act 1989 echoes previous attempts to shed the 'last resort' image of residential care and ensure that it is integral to children's services. It should be a 'positive choice' whenever needed … Of particular importance has been the preparedness of social workers to eschew a 'for' or 'against' view of residential care for one that perceives it in the wider context of the young person's needs and the services that are most appropriate. [53]

Children's Residential Care and Abuse

This was the concept promoted by the 1987 White Paper and enshrined in the 1989 Act. The Act also stressed that local authorities were to ensure safe care for children living away from home:

> Where the local authority are responsible for accommodating a child as a result of a voluntary arrangement or have been given the parental responsibilities by a court it is important for them to act as a good parent. This entails planning for the child's well-being, monitoring the outcome of the plan, and ensuring that any placement is satisfactory. [54]

This requirement enshrined in the 1989 Act had particular traction and relevance in the context of a flurry of inquiries into the abuse of children in residential care homes. Among others, there was the inquiry into 'Pindown' in Staffordshire's children's homes (1991) where children were subject to what was described as 'humiliating and degrading treatment' and confined in their bedrooms for long periods [55]; the inquiry chaired by Andrew Kirkwood into the physical and sexual abuse of children in Leicestershire's children's homes [56] (1993); and the inquiry commissioned in 1996 and chaired by Sir Ronald Waterhouse into the abuse in residential (and foster) homes of children in the care of Gwynedd and Clwyd county councils in Wales [57].

The plethora of inquiries into concerns about the care of children and adults is reflected in the 2004 book edited by Stanley and Manthorpe which they titled *The Age of Inquiry: Learning and Blaming in Health and Social Care* [58] and by Butler and Drakeford in their 2003 text 'Scandal, Social Policy and Social Welfare' [59]. That two books should be published at a similar time in the early 2000s reflects that the preceding two decades had indeed become the 'the age of inquiry'.

One dimension in several of the inquiries into abuse in children's homes was the concern about elected local authority councillors not keeping in touch and being aware of what was happening within the council's services, especially services for children in the care of the council. In some local authorities, councillors were found to have been uninformed about what was happening within the council's children's social services. In others, it was not disinterest but disruption which characterised councillors' behaviour.

Local Authorities and Local Politicians

In Islington, for example, there had been increasing concern about the abuse of children in the London borough's children's homes, as reflected upon in a 2003 report in 'The Guardian':

> Liz Davies [who was a social worker in Islington at the time and later was reader in child protection at London Metropolitan University] remembers the moment when she realised that she had a scandal on her hands. For several months she had been talking to groups of children she suspected were being abused. Then, one day, two young boys walked into her small council office in Islington. One of the boys looked afraid, but the other reassured him. 'It's all right,' he said 'She's not one of them.' It was those

chilling words that gave Davies her first hint that much of the horrible child abuse she was uncovering was happening within the care system of Islington Council—the very organisation meant to protect the borough's most vulnerable children. That was in April 1990. The scandal would eventually explode into the national consciousness two-and-a-half years later in a series of exposés in London's Evening Standard. They described a care system penetrated by paedophiles that had abysmally failed to care for scores of children. The council, then led by Margaret Hodge, appointed last month as the country's first Minister for Children, initially condemned the stories, for which Davies and several other social workers acted as anonymous whistle blowers.[60]

The concerns about abuse in Islington's children's homes led to an inquiry in 1994 conducted by Ian White, who was then the director of social service in Oxfordshire. He described Islington's social services as 'chaotic' without clear lines of management and accountability. It was a consequence of the radical redesign of the council's services which introduced neighbourhood teams combining all council services and where, for example, social workers might have an environmental health officer as their neighbourhood manager, as noted in report in The Independent in 1995, with difficulties in recruiting staff to work within social services:

Housing, social services and environmental health were decentralised to 24 neighbourhood offices. It was a recipe for loose management and Hodge now regrets it. "There are no easy answers, particularly in London. It was incredibly difficult to recruit social workers. Finding people to work in children's homes was impossible. We were dependent on agency staff". [61]

John Rea Price was the social services director at the time and recalls what he had inherited from the initial creation of social services at the beginning of the 1970s:

I arrived in February 1972 essentially to find the department hyper, completely manic. There were thirteen teams [within a total population of about 180,000 people this meant that each team served a neighbourhood of 15,000 people] in a borough which was about 3 miles wide at its widest. It was by far the most decentralised in London. Some of the thirteen teams were still based in headquarters and some were in quite inappropriate church halls and it all collided with a lot of community ferment with a lot of it around housing and squatters. There was a very significant squatters movement and I had only been in post for about a week when the commander of Islington police rang and he said "Have you seen the papers this morning?" and I said "It's about Belfast barricades". He said "Yes, it's barricades OK, but it's not Belfast. It's Islington and they've been built by your bloody social workers". [John Rea price interview]

Rea Price noted that:

In all my time in Islington I only managed to get about four or five [councillors] really interested in social services. Most members would be on [the council] as part of their strategy for establishing their national political career, and there was no way they wanted to be contaminated [by social services] ... In one year we had five changes of council. We were the firsts SDP [Social Democratic Party, which was founded in 1981] council, and it swung backwards and forwards, and I was supposed to run a department in the midst of all this. [John Rea Price interview]

Rea Price continued:

[A councillor] was the architect of 24 neighbourhood offices. He was also one of my social workers. There were going to be 24 neighbourhood offices and housing, social services, environmental health, building works and God knows what were all going to be deployed into them ... [The offices] were something between a Pizza Hut and an East German frontier station ... We had a rather unpleasant debate in the council chamber where the Federation of Tenants Associations had raised a concern that the social services clients were polluting these offices and they should have a side entrance ... And then there was the whole discussion about a 'boss in the office' which was that there should be one lead as a neighbourhood officer [who could be from any profession or service background]. [John Rea Price interview]

Margaret Hodge was the council leader. She was elected as an MP in 1994. From 2003 until 2005 she was minister of state for children in the Labour government led by Tony Blair. She was the minister of state when the 2004 Children Act led to the disaggregation of social services departments into separate children' services and adults' services. Social workers could indeed then find themselves with senior managers in children' services who had been teachers or education administrators and in adult services by housing or environmental health managers.

The confusion, conflict and chaos depicted by John Rea Price's comments above were somewhat exceptional and extreme but not unique. There were other councils where social workers were also (senior) councillors and committee chairs, either in their own council or in a neighbouring council, and where the links between trade union officials representing council workers and leading councillors were very close and undermined management responsibilities.

In Islington's neighbouring authority, Hackney, the 1980s and 1990s were also a time of council turmoil, as noted by Anthony Douglas (who was a senior manager there for part of the time and went on to become chief executive of the Children and Family Court Advisory and Support Service—CAFCASS) and Terry Philpott (who was the editor of Community Care magazine). Writing in 1998 they commented:

> Hackney had a reasonable reputation ... and in 1982 [Mary Sugden, its director of social services] crowned a distinguished career by moving on to be principal of the National Institute for Social Work before retiring. Some local Labour party activists were happy to see her go. Many of those activists were also staff in Hackney social services. Others were local councillors. This was the age before the Widdicombe proposals were introduced in 1988, which prevented senior local government managers also standing and serving as councillors ... In the mid-1980s the Chair of social services at the time, Patrick Kodikara [who was also at the same time assistant director of social services in Tower Hamlets [62]] became very involved in the direct running of the department and appointed a number of staff ... Kodikara felt that to hold a professional qualification was a form of contamination and signified an inability to understand the needs of local black people ... Managers of services had no say in the staff they were given, as personnel staff had been given complete responsibility for the redeployment process ... The saga of Hackney social services is not unique. Similar machinations can be found in many councils across the UK, although they represent the worse excesses rather than the general state of play. [63]

There is a link between the Islington and Hackney accounts above. Gordon Peters, who became Hackney's director of social services in 1983 had previously been a social worker in Islington:

I had been a social worker in the market team in Islington in the early 1970s which was an interesting time … and we were out on the streets quite a lot defending squatters. I was quite active in the trade unions as one of the ways in which the community struggled for better housing and that's how I got to know John Rea Price … It was an interesting time to be in Islington. I suppose we thought everything was possible post-Seebohm … at some point I got promoted as a research officer … and from there moved in to academia as a social work lecturer, from that jumping to become director of social services in Hackney. [Gordon Peter's interview]

Peters continued:

We were trying to do some good things [in Hackney], especially equalising in terms of population type policies like the race and ethnic minority developments and community participative politics. [There were] more and more trade union issues and cuts all coming together. There were all different trade unions so amongst other things I had to spend quite a lot of time taking them seriously because you couldn't ignore them, in order to allow some other people to get on with the good work they were trying to do in the borough … We pioneered same-race placements, which was never an absolute policy by the way … [and] we had gone from 70% of kids in residential care to 70% in foster and adoptive care during my time [1983–1990] as director … [and we also had the mental health [and learning disability] hospital closures. There was a lot going on in the last two or three years of my stay in Hackney. [Gordon Peter's interview]

Gordon Peters' commented that as well having had children placed outside the borough in Essex and the Home Counties they also had children placed in children's homes as far away as North Wales, which was the location of the homes which were the centre of the Waterhouse inquiry noted above.

Government Reviews of Children's Residential Care

It was the 1980s and early 1990s inquiries and scandals about abuse in children's homes which led to several government initiated reviews. In 1991 Bill Utting, who was soon to retire from his post as chief inspector in the Department of Health's Social Services Inspectorate, undertook a review of residential child care [64]. He noted that 70% of residential child care workers had no relevant qualification. He recommended that the heads of the homes should be professionally qualified as social workers, a third of children's homes workers should hold a relevant professional qualification, and other staff should have an appropriate National Vocational Qualification (NVQ). This led to the relatively short-lived Residential Child Care Training Initiative with the secondment of about 450 residential workers to undertake Diploma in Social Work programmes [65].

The 1991 Utting Review was followed in 1992 by a Committee of Inquiry commissioned by the Secretary of State for Health, to 'look into the selection, development and management of staff in children's homes' [66]. The Inquiry was chaired by Norman Warner, who had been a career civil servant before becoming director of social services in Kent. The Inquiry was initiated following the conviction of Frank Beck for sexual and other offences of abuse against children during the Pindown regime in Leicestershire.

Many of the Warner Committee's recommendations were about how staff in children's homes should be recruited, employed and managed, including tightening up on police checks about criminal records, the taking up of references, and supervision and performance appraisal. The recommendations and actions which followed were to be strengthened further 12 years later when the Bishard Inquiry Report [67], which followed the murders of two young girls by their school's caretaker in Soham in Cambridgeshire, led to a vetting and registration scheme for all who sought to work with children.

In 1997 in the midst of further revelations about past abuse in children's homes Utting was asked to undertake a further review, this time to look at the how the safeguards which had been introduced were being implemented and whether they were having an impact. In addition to children homes the review also included foster care, boarding schools, hospitals and penal settings. Utting calculated that about 200,000 of the 12 million children under the age of 18 in England and Wales (50,000 of whom were in the care of local authorities) were at any one time living away from their parent's home for at least 28 days. Utting concluded that:

> Safeguards are stronger than they were 10 years ago and of a higher order altogether than they were 10 years before that. This is due in large part to increased awareness and knowledge of what children away from home need to be protected against. This knowledge is widely, if unevenly, distributed among people with professional responsibilities to children. The work of voluntary organisations in particular, supplemented by press, radio and television, has raised awareness in the community. High levels of incomprehension and denial nevertheless remain. This is unsurprising: my contemporaries and I passed the first half of our professional careers in similar states of innocence and ignorance—less excusably, perhaps, than average members of the public today. [68]

Utting continued that 'Unreflecting trust, however, in adults who are presumed to be just like us in their concern for our children is itself a major danger'. This message had particular resonance in the 1990s, and should still resonate today, following two high profile and senior figures within social services and children's social care being separately and unrelatedly guilty of the sexual abuse of children

The first was Dr Rod Ryall. A former deputy headmaster of an Approved School and a Regional Planning Officer for children's residential care, he was an assistant director and then director of social services in Calderdale. In 1988 he was convicted of charges of indecent assault and buggery against two boys under the age of 16 years and was sentenced to six years imprisonment [69].

The second high profile person convicted of offences especially relevant to children was Peter Righton. He had worked in children's homes and had become Director of Education at the National Institute for Social Work, an advisor to the National Children's Bureau, and has been described as having been 'Britain's top expert on children's homes' [70].

The phrase hiding in plain sight could certainly be applied to Righton. He was a founding member of the Paedophile Resource Exchange and had written supporting sexual relationships between adults and children. In 1992, he was prosecuted and fined for importing pornography showing the abuse of children. His long-term partner was Richard Alston who in 2015 was found guilty of gross indecency with a child aged less than 14 years [71]. Alston had been headmaster of New Barnes residential school in Gloucestershire for emotionally disturbed children and Righton was a governor of the school. In the court case concerning Alston there was evidence that Righton was involved in the abuse of boys along with Alston. Righton died in 2007.[4]

---

[4]Although not employed in children's social services, others used their influence with children's social services to gain access to children who they then sexually abused. They include Cyril Smith, a high profile Liberal MP who had gained access to children in care while a councillor and mayor in Rochdale, and Jimmy Saville, a media personality famous in part for his 'Jim Will Fix It' children's television series.

10

A Drama in Two Parts: Part II—The 1990 NHS and Community Care Act and Adult Social Services and Social Work

One particular piece of legislation in many ways symbolises and is an exemplar of the ideology and policies of the Thatcher government's intentions and impact on the personal social services. It was the 1990 NHS and Community Care Act which fuelled up and energised the already expanding market in adult social care. It led not only to increased privatisation within the personal social services but also the start of the fragmentation of integrated social work services.

The Long Haul to 1990

Social services for younger and older disabled people had been framed by the 1948 National Assistance Act and the 1970 Chronically Sick and Disabled Persons Act. The 1948 Act gave a (mandatory) *duty* to local authorities 'to provide residential accommodation for persons who by reason of age, infirmity or any other circumstances are in need of care and attention' [1] and a (discretionary) *power* 'to make arrangements for promoting the welfare of [disabled and older] persons' [2]. The 1970 Act made it a local authority *duty* to 'meet the needs' of disabled people

© The Author(s) 2020, corrected publication 2021
R. Jones, *A History of the Personal Social Services in England*,
https://doi.org/10.1007/978-3-030-46123-2_10

through a range of help and services (see Chap. 5) and, more generally, the Act required the providers of premises open to the public to make the premises accessible 'in so far as it is in the circumstances both practicable and reasonable' [3].

It may now be taken for granted, although still not always delivered, that disabled people should be able to access and use everyday facilities such as shops, pubs, cinemas, parks, and so on. But in 1970 this was not assumed with many disabled people either living their lives totally in institutions or restricted and confined within their homes.

Debates ensued throughout the 1970s and into the 1980s and beyond about what was 'practicable and reasonable' in adapting and designing public access buildings. There was also debate about the feasibility of local authorities delivering on the duty that they assess and assist all disabled people in their area. This came to a head when Gloucestershire County Council was taken to the High Court after it introduced explicit eligibility and rationing criteria for who it would assist within the resources it had available.

The 'Gloucestershire judgement' in the Court of Appeal allowed local authorities to take into account the resources—the funding—they had available in determining to whom and to what extent assistance was to be provided. As one of the judges commented:

> The Secretary of State for Health is joined in the appeal. It is as well that he should be for it is the failure of central Government to supply the funds necessary to enable the Council to carry out what I regard as their statutory duty … By your Lordships' decision today the Council has escaped from the impossible position in which they, and other local authorities have been placed … The solution lies with the government. The passing of the Chronically Sick and Disabled Persons Act 1970 was a noble aspiration. Having willed the end, Parliament must be asked to provide the means. [4]

This judgement was issued on 20 March 1997 just weeks before the end of 17 years of Conservative governments and just before the election of Labour with Tony Blair as prime minister. It was a judgement which recognised that local authority budgets are finite and cash-limited, but it also reflected that the rights of disabled people to assistance from and through the state were very limited rights, unlike, for example, entitlement and eligibility to social security benefits which are not cash-limited budgets (albeit they are increasingly constrained by the legislation and benefit rates determined by the government).

Concerns About Local Authority Services

There was not only a concern about the availability and rationing of local authority services. There was also a concern about their responsiveness and standards. In this context, the key and expanded role given to local authorities for the social care of disabled people during the Thatcher period of government was perhaps surprising, especially as Mrs Thatcher did not view local authorities, or public services in general, as efficient and effective. So how and why did the remit of local authorities and their social services departments come to be expanded and enhanced?

The journey can be traced back to the pre-Thatcher mid-1970s. Bleddyn Davies, who in 1974 was the founder of the Personal Social Services Research Unit (PSSRU) at the LSE and expanded it to include the University of Kent and Manchester University, recalls the genesis of the concept of care management, which was to be crucial to the community care reforms:

> One of the directors [in the new social services departments] was Nicolas Stacey. He had been at Dartmouth as a naval cadet, was an ordained priest in the Church of England, an Olympic athlete [he participated in the 1952 Olympic Games where he was a semi-finalist in the 200 metres and a finalist in the 4 × 400 metres relay], been the vicar of Woolwich [where he developed an innovative church-based community project], and Deputy Director of Oxfam. He was a really radical chap. He arrived in Kent in 1974 [as director of social services, having been the first social services director for Ealing council from 1971 to 1974—a controversial appointment as he was not a social worker and had no local government experience] ... Nick gave a lecture and said "Right, I've got this home help service

that does exactly what it wants. Talk until the cows come home, there's nothing I can really do about it". I am paraphrasing pretty heavily here as you can understand, and he said "But if what we were to do was to assess [the older person] and give vouchers and the users could then hire somebody else they'd get it done in the way they want it. We'd monitor it, of course, but I'd only have to speak into the ear of the home help organisers and they would respond like magic to this market development". [Bleddyn Davies interview]

Martin Knapp, who was also within the PSSRU, recalls a similar conversation:

I remember talking to an assistant director [of social services] in a London borough at the time, who went on to be a director elsewhere and then to higher and greater things. I remember him saying that when that borough, which is a Tory-controlled borough, contracted out their care services to a private agency, for the first time in his 5 or 6 years career there he had control over homecare services. All the time they'd been within house he'd had no control. [Martin Knapp interview]

Knapp continued:

I think the strength of the unions was considerable at the time [mid- and late 1970s] and I don't think the quality of care and the responsiveness of care was particularly good. So the private sector initially offered things that the public sector had not been able to deliver. But there was still, underneath it, this concern about the profit motive and whether that might affect behaviour and, through that, quality of care and the quality of life for people experiencing services. [Martin Knapp interview]

Writing in 1988 Wally Harbert, a former welfare officer who was director of social services for Avon County Council, wrote about the management responsibility and decision-making powers held within local authority home help services:

In social services departments social workers represent only about 10% of the workforce but they have been very articulate and influential ... where the home help service has developed with a trained workforce, organisers [who often undertook management modules within the Certificate of Social Services] are a direct challenge to the status and authority of social workers since they command a large group of domiciliary staff and in most authorities can determine how it will be allocated. [5]

Case and Care Management

This was the context in which the Kent Community Care Project was developed. The model was described by David Challis and Bleddyn Davies, its leading researchers (and promoters):

> The Personal Social Services Research Unit (PSSRU) approach to community care decentralises to field workers the responsibility, authority and accountability for performing what we call 'the core tasks of case management', providing them with the opportunity, control over a budget, incentives and knowledge to mobilise and use resources to achieve more equitable and efficient outcomes for clients and carers. [6]

The assessing and arranging role of 'case managers' (who within a few years were re-termed 'care managers') in Kent was further developed to provide 'a community-based alternative to long-stay hospital care for physically frail elderly people', this time in Darlington through a 'geriatric multi-disciplinary team':

> The project developed enhanced home care for frail elderly people by combining the function of a home help, an auxiliary nurse and aides to various professional staff into the activities of one person: the home care assistant. According to the differing needs of the frail elderly clients, the home care assistants acted as aides to, and were instructed by, several different health and social services personnel. The aim was both to extend the range of services and to reduce the number of hands-on staff involved in providing care to individual elderly people. [7]

A succinct precis of the 'care management' model and its impact is given by Means, Richards and Smith writing in 1994:

> The approach of the Department of Health [in the 1980s and 1990s] to care management was heavily influenced by the research findings of the Personal Social Services Research Unit at the University of Kent in their evaluation of care management pilots in Thanet (Kent) and Gateshead. Both were aimed at frail elderly people at risk of entering residential or nursing home care. The emphasis was on giving social workers with considerable experience, and with smaller caseloads than usual, access to a decentralised budget ... The results were overwhelmingly positive. The probability of death within one year was halved and the probability of continuing to live at home was doubled. Informal carers felt less exploited and more supported, while perceptions of well-being on the part of the service users were improved. All of this was achieved at a lower cost than if residential care had been the main option. [8]

The care management concept took hold in Kent and was rolled out across the county by Norman Warner, a senior civil servant in the Department of Health when he replaced Nicolas Stacey as Kent's social services director. It was also taken up by the Department of Health as a concept to be promoted nationally and for all disabled people, including those leaving long-stay hospitals as a part of their closures [9].

The Audit Commission

It was not only the Department of Health which picked up and promoted the concept of care management. The Audit Commission was also an early enthusiast. The Audit Commission for Local Authorities in England and Wales focused on 'the economy, efficiency and effectiveness of local authorities' services' and as well as undertaking 'value for money projects' [10].

The Audit Commission published three influential reports between 1985 and 1992 on community care for older (and younger) disabled people. The first two reports, published in 1985 [11] and 1986 [12] provided a platform for the 1987 Griffiths Report which largely shaped the personal social services components of the 1990 legislation. The third Audit Commission report was published in 1992 and gave advice on the implementation of the new legislation [13].

There were three main arguments made by the Audit Commission. First, it would be more economic, and would improve the quality of life of many older people, if fewer were cared for in residential homes and instead were assisted to remain living in their own homes in the community [14, 15].

Secondly, more attention should be given to the unit costs of all forms of personal social services for older (and younger) disabled people with the potential to reduce expenditure on high cost services [16]. This focus on unit costs may now seem standard but, according to the Audit Commission, it was not so usual in the mid-1980s.

And, thirdly, the Audit Commission argued that there should be more targeting of services on those in greatest need of help:

[In some areas] community services [are] not directed to those who need them most [where] half or more of the expenditure on community services for the elderly was allocated to those who do not obviously need it [and where] provision for those most dependent on the support of the public sector was below average. [17]

The argument of the Audit Commission about targeting expenditure and services on those in greatest need for assistance, and the management scrutiny and gate-keeping of access to services, had a significant impact on home care services. Much of the home help service had been a household cleaning service. Greater targeting meant that the personal care needs of those being assisted became more pronounced and prevalent, reshaping the remit and work of what had changed to be called a home care service rather than home help service.

Social Security and the Funding of Residential Care

In addition to the three concerns noted above there were two contextual issues which were also made explicit by the Audit Commission. The first was how the care of older people had become skewed because in the late 1970s social security supplementary benefits could be claimed by those financially eligible to directly fund their care in private care homes. Timmins, writing in 1996, commented on this policy change with its now obvious but then unintended consequences:

> The full consequences of this decision [made by local supplementary benefit offices to make payments for residential care in voluntary and private care homes] were simply not realised at the time. Private and voluntary homes were soon to prove the single fastest growth area in public spending. Numbers and costs virtually doubled each year, the bill rising from £100 million in 1979 to £500 million by early 1986. In 1979, just 11,000 people were financed in such homes. By 1992, more than a quarter of a million were, and the bill had reached £2.5 billion. Unwittingly, the Conservatives had created a new state-financed, if privately run, industry. Yet as this corner of the social security bill rose almost exponentially, the local authorities, locked into an ever more vicious battle with central government over spending, found they had too little cash to provide much cheaper, and in some cases much better, care for people still living at home. [18]

For those who were receiving supplementary benefit to fund their residential care there was no requirement for an assessment to determine whether residential care was required by the older person. They could take this decision for themselves, maybe in discussion with relatives and family carers. The only assessment was a financial assessment to decide if the older person was entitled to supplementary benefit. The Audit Commission noted in 1986 that:

> Anybody fulfilling the Supplementary Benefit rules (irrespective of the extent of disabilities) who chooses to live in a residential home is entitled

to allowances meeting their full fees up to £125 or more per week ... In these circumstances the temptation must be strong for anyone trying to look after a relative at home to make use of the more generous, and far less stringent, payments for board and lodging, by placing them in residential care. [19]

The availability of public social security funds to pay the fees of private residential care homes was not only potentially attractive to older people and their relatives, but it also had some attractions for local authorities with care in a private home funded by central government through the social security budget rather than by a local authority through its social services budget.

Not surprisingly, the private care homes market expanded. Local builders, for example, adapted large properties (which was not too onerous as standards were not set for care homes for older people until 1984 [20]) with another family member taking on the role of manager of the home (albeit this was regulated through the 1984 Registered Care Homes Act which specified the registration requirements for managers of care homes). These 'owner driver' care homes, if successful, were then often sold on to bigger companies seeing a business opportunity by buying up existing private care homes and entering the growing market for care.

As the Audit Commission noted, it was an unrestricted and unrestrained call on public funds which, if the rules were not changed to reduce or stop the flow of Supplementary Benefits funding for private residential care, public expenditure would continue to increase and it would not be the best use of the funding [21].

The Cost to Local Authorities of Long-Term Hospital Closures

The second contextual issue identified by the Audit Commission was the relationship between the NHS and local authority personal social services. This also had what might be seen as another perverse incentive with the NHS pulling back from long-standing responsibilities to provide long-term care for people who were unable to care for themselves and instead now seeing this as a task for local authorities, albeit the funding was still historically held within the NHS budgets.

This was especially so as the NHS moved ahead with the closure of the large aging Victorian institutions such as the mental health asylums, hospitals for people who were 'mentally handicapped', and the geriatric wards in community hospitals. To the extent that any funding was transferred from the NHS to local authorities it was often time-limited and ring-fenced to fund the care of 'long-stay patients' who were having to move out of the closing institutions and now to be cared for in the community by local authorities or through services commissioned and paid for through local authorities.

The sting in the tale was that the funding was only for these discharged patients, many of who had increased impairment as a consequence of lives lived in large institutions isolated from the wider community. The funding did not, however, cover the costs of assisting others who would have come to have been placed in these long-stay hospitals and wards if they still existed. So additional services and costs now came to be within the remit of local authority personal social services at a time when the government was looking to reduce its funding to local authorities and also restricting the money councils could raise through local rates (what now would be the council tax) [22].

There were also the additional costs, as noted by the Audit Commission, of managing the change from long-stay hospitals to community care:

> The mismatch between finance and service requirements is further exacerbated by a shortage of funding to bridge the transition to a community-based service. As old hospitals run down, community services must be built up in parallel if the overall level of service is to be maintained. While the final cost of the community based service may be no more than the cost of the hospital based service, additional transition costs will be incurred during the period when both services are running in parallel. [23]

Although the closure of the decaying large institutions was good news the underfunding of replacement community care services goes some way to explain why care in the community for some was neglect within the community.

Sir Roy Griffiths and the Griffiths Report

In the midst of these escalating issues, the government commissioned a review of community care. The go-to person who the Thatcher governments of the mid-1980s had identified as the adviser on the NHS and also on the personal social services for disabled and older people was Sir Roy Griffiths. Griffiths had a background in retail shopping, and especially selling groceries. In one of his obituaries there is the comment that he was a grocer who advised the grocer's daughter (Margaret Thatcher) [24]. He had been the managing director and deputy chairman of Sainsburys, which at the time 'still ran shops with counters, not out-of-town supermarkets' [25].

In 1983 Griffiths was appointed by the government to produce a report on the management of the NHS. Two major themes in his report were the introduction of general management (rather than professional leadership supported by administrators) in the NHS and the devolution of budgets and decision-making on resource deployment to 'units' (i.e. the NHS' service delivery organisations such as hospitals and community health services).

This may not seem so radical now, but in the 1980s many hospitals, for example, did not have their own budgets and financial allocation but spent against an aggregate budget held by Regional and Area Health Authorities. The 1983 Griffiths report on NHS management did not recommend a purchaser-provider split within the NHS but the advent of general management, decentralised budgets, unit costing, and service and cost targets did put in place mechanisms on which the later NHS purchaser-provider separation would be built.

Sir Roy Griffiths was then asked by the government to report on the arrangements for community care. The primary reason for the review was the escalating supplementary benefit expenditure on residential care for older people in private care homes:

His interest—the need for his work—was stimulated very much by the out of control social security budget funding people in care homes, that was the kind of final straw that pushed him into doing his report, but there were many other things going on that needed a fundamental examination.

And, of course, he at the time got very interested in things like the care management experience, and the experiments that Bleddyn [Davies] and David [Challis] were then running in 4 or 5 parts of the country. He very rightly saw them as an opportunity to achieve the same outcomes or more outcomes with the same resources by reorganising services in a more sensible way. [Martin Knapp interview]

Bleddyn Davies recalls his close involvement with Roy Griffiths and his review team:

I wrote draft speeches and got very close to Griffiths. Griffiths got me to do two seminars for his team on care management and the related financing devices … [Griffiths] would be listening to an argument but also reading what lay behind the argument in terms of the motivations and the personalities of the people undertaking the argument. I always had the feeling that Griffiths had that ability [but] his [review] secretary seconded from the civil service, no doubt to keep tabs on him, whispered to me 'we've got no idea what he's thinking, no idea what he's going to do next. [Bleddyn Davies interview]

The review secretary seconded to Roy Griffiths from the civil services was David Walden, who had entered the civil service in the late 1970s as a management trainee and spent much of his civil service career in the Department of Health (and subsequently within the Commission for Social Care Inspection and then the Social Care Institute for Excellence). He recalls that 'local authority social services were probably the nearest thing to Siberia that was available to the [Department of Health] in the 1970s. It was a sort of slightly strange land about which we knew very little. [David Walden interview]

The Griffiths report contained a number of recommendations for the government which, in particular, would close off the open-ended availability of social security payments to fund residential care and also assist with the closure of long-stay hospitals. Griffiths also wanted to ensure that the private sector was fully involved in future arrangements for the provision of care

At the local level the role of social services should be reorientated towards ensuring that the needs of individuals within the specified groups are identified, packages of care are devised and services coordinated; and where appropriate a specific care manager is assigned. The type of services to be provided would be derived from analysis of the individual care needs: the responsibility of social services authorities is to ensure that these services are provided within the appropriate budgets by the public or private sector according to where they can be provided most economically and efficiently. The onus in all cases should be on the social services authorities to show that the private sector is being fully stimulated and encouraged and that competitive tenders or other means of testing the market are being taken. [26]

Griffiths concluded that local authority social services should assess the community care needs of their area, set local priorities, and develop local Community Care Plans in consultation with health authorities and others. They should then identify and assess individuals' needs, taking into account personal preferences and those of informal carers; design packages of care best suited to enabling the consumer to live as normal a life as possible; and arrange the delivery of packages of care to individuals. They were first to take into account the available contribution of informal carers and neighbourhood support, then the provision of domiciliary and day services and, if appropriate, residential care.

Griffiths argued that local authorities should 'act for these purposes as the designers, organisers and purchasers of non-health care services, and not primarily as direct providers, making the maximum use of voluntary and private sector bodies to widen consumer choice, stimulate innovation and encourage efficiency' [27].

Griffiths also had messages for national government which should publish 'a clear, short, statement of government's community care objectives and aims', review local authority plans, set up an 'adequate machinery for identifying the results of local authority activity', and make 'arrangements for the distribution of a specific grant … and ensuring necessary matching between policy objectives and resources provided to meet them' [27]. Griffiths commented in 1997 that:

Nothing could be more radical in the public sector than to spell out responsibilities, insist on performance and accountability and to evidence that action has been taken; and even more radical, to match policy with appropriate resources and agreed timescales. [28]

It may be hard to recollect and realise now how radical were the Griffith's community care proposals. Some were already embedded in understandings of good practice but the focus on consumer choice, an expanded mixed market of services, the role of local authorities as commissioners, and social workers and others as care managers assessing, arranging and purchasing care was largely new and novel. So too was the recommendation that the government make available a specific grant to local authorities as they took on the funding role which had emerged for social security over the past decade.[1]

The Response to the Griffiths Proposals

So how were the Griffiths' proposals received and responded to within the personal social services and by other interested parties? Peter Westland had been director of social services in Hammersmith and Fulham and when the Griffiths Report was published, he was the principle social services advisor within the Association of Metropolitan Authorities (AMA). Westland recalled:

---

[1] The radical nature of the Griffiths' proposals generated a flurry of activity. When the subsequent White Paper was published in 1998 on how the government intended to respond to and implement the proposals, I was deputy director of social services in Berkshire. Following the 1990 legislation providing the statutory framework for the implementation of the proposals I was, in 1992, director of social services in Wiltshire when the first 'Community Care Plan' for the county was being prepared and published. Much of the attention and action during 1988 to 1992 was focused on the implications and implementation of what Griffiths had proposed in 1987. Indeed, in 1990, my role and title within Berkshire County Council's social services department changed from deputy director of social services and director of operations to 'senior assistant director (purchasing)' within an organisation which introduced a purchaser-provider organisational separation within its social services. Ted Unsworth, who had a similar role change in another county, described himself as 'head of shopping'!

Taken together, the Audit Commission and the Griffiths' reports and subsequent White Paper laid the foundations for local authority responsibility for services, the disposal of local authority assets to the independent sector, rationing in the context of financial vagueness and local authority accountability for service failures. The implementation of the legislation, the 1990 NHS and Community Care Act, was deferred for one year because of issues associated with the Poll Tax. Guidance and Directions issued under the Act compelled local authorities to outsource provision of services for older people. In the aftermath of the Act and ensuing years funding for state provision has reduced even further, eligibility criteria have hardened, and regulation has been enfeebled by under-resourcing. [29]

The concern about not adequately funding the changes required by the new community care legislation was also reiterated by Bill Utting, who was the chief inspector for social services in the Department of Health at the time of the Griffiths Report and the subsequent White Paper and legislation:

> The great deficiency was the resources to implement these marvellous policies. We could just not dig [the resources] out before I retired [in 1991], and they certainly didn't come along afterwards and the implementation kept being put back. I mean they [the government] simply would not take on the consequences that if you are going to bring about change like this, you need to strengthen community services before you actually run down in any sense the residential ones. They had made that mistake over emptying the mental illness hospitals and they were still making that mistake in 1990, but that was simply on political grounds that there wasn't going to be the money. [Bill Utting interview]

Anne Parker was director of social services in Berkshire and the honorary secretary of ADSS. She recalled it was hard to anticipate what Griffiths would be recommending as he did not share his thinking. There were arguments being made that adult social care functions held by local authorities should be transferred to the NHS or to a new standalone national community care agency. When Griffiths reported his recommendations were welcomed by ADSS:

[The civil servant] [David Walden] who was secretary of the Griffith's review said that Griffiths wrote his report himself and that when colleagues in the Department of Health were saying 'Well, what's he going to say?' I said 'I really don't know!'. When the report was published ADSS and the local government community went with it, largely driven by the thought of getting their hands on the [social security] money, although conscious of the fact that it was a diminishing asset and it wasn't going to be the answer to everything. But I think it was seen as a strengthening of local government's position, and therefore to be welcomed in that sense. The elements of which people were thoughtful were about the market economy of course ... Everybody had got themselves so sure that this supermarket man was going to do the supermarket stuff, so that we were all [in advance] positioning ourselves around that. [Anne Parker interview]

The view of Anne Parker was shared by Herbert Laming, who was an advisor to Sir Roy Griffiths when he undertook his review and was director of social services in Hertfordshire before becoming chief inspector of social services in the Department of Health when Bill Utting retired in 1991:

I thought it was a period of great opportunity. I thought the 1990 Act opened up tremendous opportunities to change the value that we placed upon the quality of life and the independence of people with long-term disabilities of one kind or another and their opportunity to influence and control. In other words they should no longer be given no choice—'Take it or leave it, the State knows best'—to much more encouragement to working alongside, not doing things for people but doing things with people. [Herbert Laming interview]

The idea of giving service users—clients and consumers—choice would have been attractive within Margaret Thatcher's market philosophy but her antagonism and antipathy towards local government, and public services in general, required Griffiths to be persuasive in his contacts with the prime minister, but even then the community care reforms were delayed:

I have a great admiration for Roy Griffiths. I think he was a remarkable man and he was a great friend of local government and of the local delivery of social services and came up with absolutely the right recipe for community care, but it was one that caused considerable difficulty in government. As far as government was concerned [finding a way to contain the escalating social security spend] was the main driver and I don't think it would have bothered if it hadn't been for that … but it proved very difficult at senior levels because of the hostility to local government. And frankly I was surprised when the decision came through in favour of local government … I've always suspected that it might have been [Griffiths] direct access to [Margaret Thatcher], and the context of the NHS not really being in a position to take this on in the middle of a grand reorganisation, that meant that the Cabinet settled reluctantly perhaps for local government. [Bill Utting interview]

David Walden also commented on the tension, and then the acceptance, that additional community care responsibilities and funding should be allocated to local government:

As often is the case, by the time the Griffiths review was reported the Secretary of State had changed and the political climate had changed a bit because John Moore was then Secretary of State. Rightly or wrongly, he didn't want responsibilities handed to local government and thought Mrs Thatcher didn't either, although she was actually more pragmatic than she was often given credit for … Roy Griffiths had a heart attack and was in hospital at some crucial point in the story and, of course, John Moore fell out of favour. On the face of it I think John Moore was terrified of going to Thatcher and saying 'We have got this great report that I commissioned and it suggests giving a whole load of power and money to local government' … So it was a pretty brave thing in a way for Griffiths to recommend … And I think eventually Thatcher saw the logic of what he was saying and it was a way of capping costs. I think she might have thought that the NHS could absorb vast amounts of resource and be difficult to resist, whereas local government was easier to resist in subsequent years … Eventually she saw the point of it. [David Walden interview]

John Moore was in 1988 replaced by Ken Clarke as Secretary of State for Health. Tom Luce, who was at the time seconded from the Department of Health to the Treasury but who was to return to the Department of Health as the senior civil servant working on the implementation of the 1990 Act, commented:

> [Mrs Thatcher] wasn't the only minister who wasn't keen on giving extra things to local authorities. I mean Ken Clarke wasn't keen on it and when I actually arrived at the Community Services Division my predecessor had done an exercise, a sort of last-resort attempt to see if there were any actual alternatives to the transfer to local authorities. But it had been accepted by ministers generally that the real driver was to curb rising demand. Within social security it was an entitlement expenditure so they had no way of capping it and that was what basically enabled the government to cohere on the prospect of savings, long-term savings in social security, that was the key point. [Tom Luce interview]

Walden commented:

> Clarke was there at the crucial moment and he was the arch pragmatist probably and I think Virginia Bottomley [who as minister of state for health from 1989 until 1992, and then Secretary of State from 1992, was politically central and crucial to the implementation of the community care reforms] was pretty pragmatic and of course she was a social worker, so I think Clarke and Bottomley saw things fairly similarly and I think Kenneth Clarke saw the logic of it all … I mean John Moore was very ideologically driven. Kenneth Clarke, if anything, was left of centre of the Tory party and was a pragmatist. He was very dry economically so he would have been just keen to cap the runaway costs and understood the logic of how to do it. [David Walden interview]

There were three issues which Walden noted shaped Griffiths' thinking that it was local government rather than the NHS which should be given the additional community care responsibilities. Firstly, the NHS was not primarily organised to work with local communities:

> Griffiths was going around the country and I went on many of his visits. It was pretty obvious that actually community care and social care were so embedded in the fabric of what local communities did in a way that health-

care wasn't that actually giving social care to the Health Service, which was the other front runner, was never really a viable option. You could go to St Thomas's Hospital in the middle of a very deprived area and you could find this world-class hospital full of tertiary specialists and Nobel laureate doctors. It might have been anywhere in the world and connections to the local community were really pretty minimal, whereas social care was very much in the fabric of local communities and it couldn't work without interaction with the local voluntary sector and so on. So Griffiths came out with this proposition that actually you should give the responsibility and the resources to local government which was wholly counter-intuitive in those days. [David Walden interview]

Secondly, the NHS had not engaged so strongly with the review and had not organised to canvas for the additional community care responsibilities:

There was bit of clean slate and there were stronger lobby groups in social care—ADSS was quite influential and I think having children and adults services in one place gave them more clout than subsequent iterations have done—and the disability groups were beginning to gear up and were very much on the empowerment agenda and the personal choice agenda. [David Walden interview]

Thirdly, and related to the point above:

I don't think social workers saw themselves—unlike doctors and nurses— as the bringers of 'the professional skill that will sort out your problem, just leave it our tender mercy'. I think [those working within local authority social services] thought they had to work in partnership with the people they were trying to help or it wouldn't work basically so it wasn't just 'I'll tell you what to do, hopefully you'll be unconscious when I do it and you'll wake up feeling eternally grateful for all of that' and 'I don't really need to communicate with you or interact with you because that's not what I'm here for'. [David Walden interview]

A phrase used by Anne Parker at the time of the community care reforms was that it was a 'poisoned chalice' for local government. Local government was being given additional responsibilities but with the social security expenditure on residential care being transferred to local authorities then capped and gradually reduced over subsequent years. It was also in the context of central government restraining its funding of local government and limiting the money local councils could raise for themselves through rate capping, and with the difficulties local authorities had collecting what at the time was called the 'community charge' which had replaced local rates.[2]

Despite the difficulties, Parker commented:

> I think it was better to have the poisoned chalice than not to or for somebody else to have it. In other words, I think we [local government and directors of social services] always felt that we were best positioned to deliver what improvements could be achieved out of these changes, and we wouldn't have wanted somebody else to do it. [Anne Parker interview]

This is also a view expressed explicitly by ADSS in its formal written response to the Griffiths' report:

> 'Community Care: Agenda for Action' represents a challenge to local authorities. The ADSS considers that Social Services Departments will respond positively: many are already operating in the ways the report suggests. Sir Roy Griffiths has had his ear close to the ground and picked up the good practice and innovative schemes already operating up and down the country. Social Services managers and staff have demonstrated that they can work in the ways proposed in 'Agenda for Action'. They are doing this already because they know that the public benefits from services provided more in line with the consumers' needs and wishes and representing better value for public. [30]

There were three themes in the Griffiths' Report and the subsequent community care changes which were inter-related. First, greater choice was to be given to users of services about how their needs and wishes

---

[2] It was the regressive community charge, a flat rate local tax levied on all adults (hence the term 'poll tax') which impinged on poorer people while the rich paid less than before. The public dissent and demonstrations it generated were to lead to the downfall of Margaret Thatcher in 1990 and her replacement by her chancellor of the exchequer, John Major, as prime minister.

should be met.[3] Second, this was in part to be achieved by generating even more of a mixed economy with a wider range of providers of care services. Third, it would require cooperation and strong planning and partnerships across agencies—such as social services, health and housing—and across sectors—including private and voluntary organisations—with the focus on value for money. This had implications about how services and relationships were to be managed.

There were dangers and difficulties, as noted by Denise Platt in 1989 when she was director of social services in Hammersmith and Fulham and was speaking at a conference of the National Council for Voluntary Organisations:

> In an environment where much of the statutory sector is under financial pressure, contracts may go to those organisations which offer the cheapest rates. Better quality services will not be seen as financially viable. Where other kinds of existing public services have been privatised often private companies have made low bids, and then offered a low quality service ... Most voluntary groups have mixed feelings about contracts. They can see the advantages of formal but flexible arrangements. The drawback is that they are being introduced at a time when many local authorities are cutting back their own direct provision and by implication asking the voluntary sector to substitute for them. The voluntary sector faces the prospect of less autonomy in deciding how it works and further limitations on innovative and developmental work, which have traditionally been part of its role. [31]

What is noticeable, however, bearing in mind the statutory changes that were introduced within ten years of the Griffiths report, was that Sir Roy Griffiths did not argue or advocate for younger and older disabled people to be given control of the money so that they themselves could

---

[3] In 1985 a committee was commissioned by Norman Fowler, then secretary of state for health and social services, chaired by Gillian Wagner and administered by the National Institute for Social Work, to 'review the role of residential care ... and what changes, if any, are required to enable the residential care sector to respond effectively to changing social needs'. Their report (National Institute for Social Work (1988) Residential Care: A Positive Choice, London, HMSO) noted that although the national policy thrust was towards giving younger and older disabled people assistance to live at home residential care could and should still be an available positive option and choice.

decide and buy the assistance they needed and in the way they wanted provided, although he did trail this possibility:

> There is no reason why, on a controlled basis, social services authorities should not experiment with vouchers or credits for particular levels of community care, allowing individuals to spend them on particular forms of domiciliary care and to choose between particular suppliers as they wish. [32]

The 1990 Act and the Community Care Reforms

This was a theme picked up and promoted in 1990, as the new community care legislation was about to be implemented, in a 'code of practice for community care' published by the Centre for Policy on Ageing:

> [Local authorities have the role of] controlling the money in the public purse for community care. This might include grants to consumers/ proxy consumers [such as family carers acting for the service user] to shop around for the required services to restore independent living, or contracts to private or voluntary agencies. [33]

The Centre for Policy on Ageing's 'code of practice for community care' was one of the many guides to how the new legislation should be interpreted and implemented, including a guide produced by the National Institute for Social Work (NISW) [34] and a NISW report on 'Empowerment, Assessment, Care Management and the Skilled Worker' [35].

The government was itself active in publishing a 'brief guide' [36] to the Act and 'practice guidance' on, for example, care management and assessment [37], assessment systems and community care (on computerising records and assessments) [38], 'improving independent sector involvement in community care planning' [39] (written within the Department of Health in partnership with KPMG, who then as now were promoting market forces and privatisation within social care), 'purchasing services' [40], and on complaints procedures [41].

The government also published a research digest on the pilot studies it commissioned to inform the new legislation and its implementation [42], and in 1995 the NHS Executive and the Department of Health's Social Services Inspectorate circulated a report based on local authority self-monitoring and NHS surveys on the implementation of the community care reforms [43].

In the circular letter issued with the 1995 report it was stated that the monitoring 'suggests a steadily improving picture which reflects a great deal of credit on all the agencies concerned' but with issues identified about funding and rationing which would haunt community care into the future:

> Some local authorities seemed to be experiencing difficulty in coming to terms with providing services in such a way as to meet needs within available resources. In addition, while progress was reported, concerns about hospital discharge procedures and health and social services' responsibilities for long term care were also raised again, both by local authority and health respondents ... There was evidence of local authorities re-evaluating their priorities ... An example of this is care management where, initially, some local authorities reported they had not set eligibility criteria for this and were consequently experiencing an unnecessarily high workload. [44]

In 1994 Anne Parker retired as Berkshire's director of social services. She was later in 2002 to be appointed as the chair of the National Care Standards Commission (discussed in the next chapter). She too had concerns about how in some areas the community care changes were being implemented:

> I was very disappointed when I left Berkshire and started to go around the country. I saw how in so many places just lip-service was paid to [the community care reforms, care management and greater flexibility for service users] and that it had made no difference at all to the way people were shaping services. It was quite late on when I was at the NCSC that I found some people are only now just beginning get the idea. [Anne Parker interview]

In particular, Parker thought it ran against the grain of the community care reforms that local authorities were transferring their care homes for older people to for-profit and not-for-profit companies and entering into long-term contracts to buy placements in the homes:

> They let these enormous twenty five years contracts for all their old people's homes beds, which I thought was completely antithetical to the direction of travel which seemed to be ossifying the thing in a protectionist kind of way and not really running with the vision at all. [Anne Parker interview]

But Parker noted that what really undermined the potential of the community care reforms was inadequate funding from the government (as warned about by Griffiths):

> It was a huge boost to social services budgets but rapidly absorbed by the costs of the stuff offloaded from the health services—the learning disability costs, the mental illness costs [from long-stay hospital closures]—really absorbed huge chunks of it as we showed in Berkshire when we did our forward projections. It poisoned the chalice and it was not long before we got to the dregs where the poison was. [Anne Parker interview]

There was, however, initial relief within local government about the government's financial allocation for the community care changes:

> The STG [Special Transitional Grant] gave local authorities the equivalent amount [as the current social security spend] and built in demographics and demand. So when at the ADSS conference in 1992 Virginia Bottomley announced all of this. I think she got a standing ovation—she certainly got a strong round of applause. [David Walden interview]

There was a delay in implementing the 1990 Act while the government decided what funding should be allocated to local authorities which generated some ambivalence and uncertainty about the government's intentions [45], although the delay was seen as helpful in preparing for the community care changes:

It was delayed for two years from 1991 to 1993 partly to keep the community charge bills down when it was first introduced, the poll tax and all that, and partly I think because people were panicking about the implementation run-in, and those two years, although they may have been politically driven to a degree … gave people two years of implementation [preparation] so a [national] support force was set up chaired by Terry Butler [who was the director of social services in Hampshire] and Andrew Foster [who had been a director of social services and who in 1991 was a NHS regional general manager], and I think in those two years a huge amount was done to get councils in a position to be ready. [David Walden interview]

Mental Health and Learning Disability

At the same time the community care legislation was being shaped and then implemented there was a major programme of closing the old long-stay psychiatric and learning disability hospitals. As well as the focus on moving long-stay patients out of the hospitals there was also the intention to reduce the flow of people being admitted.

The 1983 Mental Health Act introduced the role of (mental health) approved social workers (ASWs) to replace the mental welfare officers (MWOs). The 1983 Act required that ASWs had a specialist post-qualifying training. The ASW role, later to be replaced by the Approved Mental Health Practitioner, was the only statutory social work role which required a specialist qualification. The 1983 Act emphasised that the ASW role was to seek to prevent compulsory admission and detention of people in hospital by, where possible, drawing on resources in the community [46, 47]. The Code of Practice which was issued alongside the 1983 Mental Health Act stressed that ASWs had an 'individual professional responsibility' and 'overall responsibility for co-ordinating the process of the assessment and, where he [sic] decides to make an application [for hospital admission], for implementing that decision' [48]. Not only, therefore, were ASWs unlike other social workers in that they had to have a post-qualifying CCETSW approved qualification, but they were the only social workers who held a personal professional responsibility—beyond an agency responsibility—for their work and decisions.

The move away from institutional care also applied to people with a learning disability. Within the 1983 Mental Health Act the terms 'mental impairment' and 'severe mental impairment' were introduced as 'the new terms used to distinguish the small minority of mentally handicapped people who need to be detained in hospital or received into guardianship, from the great majority who do not'[4] [49].

The move away from institutional care in the old, large, often geographically remote, long-stay hospitals had been trailed by two white papers in the 1970s—'Better Services for the Mentally Handicapped' in 1971 and 'Better Services for the Mentally Ill' in 1975. However, when the hospitals started to be closed it was a time of stringent public finance controls and cuts, starting with the demands of the IMF in the late 1970s and continuing under the Conservative governments of the 1980s, as noted by Bill Utting:

> Unfortunately the [White Paper on Services for the Mentally Ill] came out just as the money dried up ... David Ennals [the Labour minister] had worked for MIND [the mental health charity] and he had to work away on getting a new Act on the statute book without the resources to develop services side by side, but he did much of the spade work and provided much of the impetus for the [1983] Act. It was well on the way to completion by the time the government changed [in 1979] and the new government just carried on with the work. [Bill Utting interview]

---

[4] It may be surprising that in 1983 it was still necessary to make the point that 'a person may not be dealt with under the [Mental Health] Act as suffering from a mental disorder purely by reason of promiscuity, other immoral conduct, sexual deviance or dependence on alcohol or drugs'. When the large mental handicap hospital on the Berkshire/Oxfordshire border north of Reading was closed in the early 1990s I was then the deputy director of social services for Berkshire. I was passed the large leather-bound legers which recorded the admissions of patients to the hospital and for them to be held by the county council records office. They recorded that in the 1960s there were still young women aged 14–18 years of age admitted and detained at the hospital with the diagnosis of 'moral defective', that is they had what was termed as an 'illegitimate child' as they were not married. They became long-stay patients and 25 years later when the hospital was closed they had become totally institutionalised and as a consequence had come to have a significant mental impairment.

The closure of the long-stay hospitals in the 1980s and 1990s was a positive policy but one which was hampered and hindered by the lack of adequate investment in alternative community services. Community care as a consequence was seen as leaving many discharged patients, and those who might have become patients, stranded and without the help they might have needed. Some became a part of the 'revolving door' population with repeated short-term hospital admissions followed by speedy discharge back into the community but with no adequate services and little action until the next crisis arose and they were admitted to hospital again [50].

The Impact of the Disability Movement

Despite the hesitancy of Griffiths noted above to recommend that disabled people be allocated the cash to give them choice and control in deciding how the assistance they needed should be provided, some local authority social services departments acted to take the community care reforms beyond the proposals from Griffiths.

They were energised and encouraged to do so by disabled people for whom the Griffiths proposals did not go far enough. Indeed, the pace and significance of the beyond-Griffiths changes were not much recognised with, for example, a book published in 1996 on 'Social Care Markets: Progress and Prospects' [51] not referring at all to how cash might be transferred to disabled people so that they could decide on and purchase assistance.

The idea of making cash available to disabled people had its genesis in 1988 with the national Independent Living Fund (ILF). It had made payments to disabled people who had what were assessed as high support needs so that they could live in the community rather than in residential care. In essence, it topped up—using money transferred to the ILF from the social security budget—the amount which a local authority would have paid for a residential care home placement so that it met the additional cost of a disabled person receiving help to live more independently. There was also the precedent of attendance allowance, a social security payment which was introduced in 1970, to help meet the costs of someone who needed high levels of care or supervision and to avoid them having to move in to residential care.

For many disabled people, however, including younger adults, their significant care needs were only met by having to move in to residential care or by receiving pre-defined services—such as home care and day care. This was recognised by the Audit Commission in 1992 in the months just before the start of the transfer in April 1993 to local authorities of the money spent from within the social security budget on residential care:

> Major changes in attitude are needed ... The concept of user needs-led support for people in their own homes is widely accepted by local social services departments. But the consequences of this philosophy are less well accepted. If implementation of the 1990 Act and guidance from the Department of Health and Welsh Office is to be successful, traditional behaviour patterns in social services must be changed affecting council members, central management, local management and staff working directly with service users alike. [52]

Possibly not surprisingly, these comments from the Audit Commission about 'major changes in attitude' being needed from social workers and within social services departments were not well received by the Association of Directors of Social Services. Denise Platt, at the time director of social services in Hammersmith and Fulham and later to be the chief inspector of social services in the Department of Health, commented that 'I'm sure social workers would bridle at the suggestion that they don't have the needs of the service user in their sights all the time' and Terry Butler, the director in Hampshire, noted 'we have gone a long way in the last few years, from opening up the records of clients to engaging users and carers in helping us to design services. I could give dozens of examples in Hampshire, and dozens in other authorities' [53].

One person who was central to significant changes being introduced in Hampshire was John Evans. He described how he came to be in Leonard Cheshire's Le Court care home:

Well, the reason I found myself there was because there was nowhere else I could go and through no choice of my own. I had broken my neck three years prior [in 1975 when aged 25] and the two years after I finished my initial spinal cord rehabilitation I lived with a friend and a girlfriend and basically they took care of me, if you want to use that [19]70s terminology. I broke my neck when in the mountains in New Mexico, setting up at the time a community having just done a peace project in the Middle East to bring young Israelis and young Arabs together. I was very much involved in that type of work, direct action and change and looking at how people could have influence. I went to Le Court in 1978. As soon as I got there I immediately got right into the middle of things and got involved in the residents' committee and I was quite impressed—they had two or three representatives on the management committee of the home among the usual judges, ex-Army and RAF people, and middle-class go-gooders and all the other people that tend to be on these sorts of committees. [John Evans interview]

John Evans was in the Leonard Cheshire care home for five years until 1983. Here is how describes how he came to leave the home:

Project 81 was a scheme that was thought up by a few of us in Le Court Cheshire Home. It was a scheme that we felt was going to be our escape route. In other words we felt, as we were young disabled people at that time, we didn't particularly want to spend the rest of our lives in a home like that simply because we did not have family to support us and we didn't have the money to provide the support or to pay for the support we needed in the community ... The original idea was to have a house together and we decided Southampton would be the place to start—it was a toss up between Winchester and Southampton—because there were more students there and we thought that was a pool of potential personal assistants for the future and also the universities, the cultural life, it had things that appealed to us ... And somewhere along the line everybody started realising that we were all individuals and we weren't sure this was going to be the right thing with us all working and living together, and we decided we had to go individually. I managed to get [my flat—where he continues to live] through the local council. [John Evans interview]

And so the Independent Living Movement, started in the USA by disabled veterans of the Vietnam War, took off in the UK. It was at a time when disabled people started to combine to create a collective voice and to campaign together. Early successes included the 1986 Disabled Persons (Services, Consultation and Representation) Act which required local authorities to actively involve and take into account the views of disabled people.

The disability movement was also active in campaigning for disability anti-discrimination legislation to match and mirror the legislation already in place to tackle race and gender discrimination. This may not be seen as so ground breaking and radical today but when a Private Members Bill was introduced proposing the new legislation it was opposed by the Conservative government. It attracted much publicity when the government minister for disability (Nicholas Scott) was attacked by his daughter (Victoria):

> All day, Victoria Scott raced from one television studio to another, one radio interview to another, rubbishing the Government's conduct as the guiding hand in the collapse of a Bill to end discrimination against the disabled. As the co-ordinator of Rights Now, a coalition campaign group for the disabled, the 28-year-old former anti-apartheid worker has spent the past six months condemning the Government's underhand opposition. But yesterday, her first salvo before 3.5 million listeners to Radio 4's Today programme took on a special poignancy. Nicholas Scott, minister for the disabled, was already under intense pressure to resign over his admission that he misled the House of Commons over his officials' role in the collapse of the Bill last Friday. He happens also to be Miss Scott's father. Yet, throughout the day, she kept up her barrage of criticism, unwilling to soften her line on the basis that her professional duty demanded that she stood firm. [54]

Disabled people, and those such as Victoria Scott who were allies, were not only active in media studios and the press. They were also active on the streets within, for example, DAN (the Disability Action Network):

> In the 1990s hundreds of disabled people took to the streets in protest at the injustice they felt. Their efforts helped to bring about the Disability

Discrimination Act which is 20 years old this week. Disabled people chaining themselves to public transport, wheelchair users blocking streets, chanting loudly and being lifted from their chairs by police and laid down in the roads to stop them, protesters shouting out for civil rights—these were powerful images on the TV news in the early 90s, and a far cry from how disabled people were often represented (when they were represented at all), as passive and grateful recipients of charity. [55]

Jane Campbell was one of those who was active, and increasingly high profile, in the disability movement. She was a former chair of the British Council of Disabled People (BCODP) and in 1996 was the co-founder of the National Centre for Independent living (NCIL). She was subsequently a commissioner within the Disability Rights Commission, and in 2007 was made a life peer as Baroness Campbell of Surbiton. In a BBC radio programme of 2016 she recalls the civil disobedience as a part of the campaigning for the 1995 Disability Discrimination Act:

When I came across the disability movement and they explained to me the social model, I mean, it was so simple. It's basically saying that you are not the problem. My condition and my person is not the problem, it's the fact that society is not accessible, and unequal in its treatment towards disabled people. We had a very strong mantra which was, "Nothing about us without us." [Sue Murray—BBC presenter—"Jane Campbell, do you recall your first demo?"] Well, for instance, we would line Westminster Bridge. Normally it was the electric wheelchairs. Now, these wheelchairs, you cannot lift them; it takes five grown men. And there we would stay, and we would stop the traffic. That began to capture the attention of the public, for good or bad. [Sue Murray: "And did it attract the attention of the police as well?"] It certainly did. I remember once the police came, and they brought their vans along in order to bundle us in the back. Unfortunately you can't bundle an electric wheelchair in the back of a van, so they then walked us down to the local police station. But of course, they couldn't put us in any cells because they were downstairs, so in the end they would turn to us and say, "Oh, for god's sake, just go," and so we would go away, muttering, "It's our right to be arrested. [56]

Within the same BBC programme Mike Oliver, an activist and academic who was also a disabled person commented:

> All we were asking for was a decent education, the right to work, to be able to access the same kind of buildings and leisure as everybody else, the right to decide what time we got up in the morning, what time we went to bed at night, and the right to decide who we went to bed with.[5] [56]

Writing in 1996 about disability politics Campbell and Oliver stated:

> The decade of the 1980s saw a transformation in our understanding of disability ... At the heart of this was the rise in the number of organisations controlled and run by disabled people themselves. At the beginning of the decade there were very few such organisations, but by 1990 there was an international organisation known as Disabled People's International (DPI) and a national co-ordinating body, the British Council of Disabled People (BCODP) ... This growth was not merely a numerical phenomenon, but also reflected the individual and collective empowerment of disabled people through the organisations they were creating. This can be seen in a number of ways. It can be seen in the challenge to dominant social perceptions of disability as personal tragedy and the affirmation of positive images of disability through the development of the politics of personal identity. It can also be seen in the development and articulation of the social model of disability, which, by focusing on disabling environments rather than individual impairments, freed up disabled people's hearts and minds by offering an alternative conceptualisation of the problem. [57]

---

[5] In the 1990s and into the 2000s, I had frequent direct contacts with members of the disability movement. Locally, in Wiltshire, as director of social services I had professional contact, and increasing personal friendships, with disabled people who had combined together to form the Wiltshire Users Network, led by Clare Evans, a disabled person who was also a qualified social worker (https://www.theguardian.com/society/2018/dec/03/clare-evans-obituary) . Nationally, for the Association of Director of Social Services I had convened and chaired the ADSS Disabilities Network of social services senior disability services managers and policy officers. Through this role I met, and led on practice and policy negotiations, with NCIL and with DAN (the Disabilities Action Network). It was DAN who organised a demonstration of disabled people at an annual ADSS conference attracting much media coverage. I was also in the early 2000s the chief executive of the Social Care Institute for Excellence—Jane Campbell was the chair, and both Mike Oliver and John Evans were to be SCIE board members.

Jane Campbell recalled:

> It was at the same time that the women's movement was quite strong, and there were a lot developments around race and racism, so for me it was always bound up in a sense of equality, we were part of the move towards making a society fairer for everybody, for women, and for black people and for disabled people ... But of course disability is always going to be different because we had another layer of oppression which is around what we call the specificity of disability. So for the disabled people's movement transport and access was always going to be the first barrier that we wanted to overcome before we then started to deal with the more insidious attitudinal eugenic type of oppression ... I think we needed people who were quite intellectual to help us unpick our oppression ... The seeds of our emancipation came from three or four brilliant individuals who had the experience and the intellectual ability to conceptualise the oppression. There was Paul Hunt who was a genius. Vic Finkelstein was a very clever man. And then Mike Oliver joined that critical group. [Jane Campbell interview]

Independent Living Movement and Direct Payments

Alongside the concept of the social model of disability it was the independent living movement which energised and powered the increasingly strong and increasingly heard voices of disabled people. Jenny Morris was a champion within this movement and wrote in 1993:

> The concept of independent living is a broad one, embracing as it does the full range of human and civil rights. This means the right to have personal relationships, to be a parent,[6] the right to equal access to education, training, employment and leisure activities and the right to participate in the life of the community ... Control over the personal assistance that is

---

[6] The Disabled Parents Network, with leadership from Michele Wates, was active in emphasising that assisting disabled parents to undertake their parenting role was primarily a task for adult services not children's services [Morris, J. and Wates, M. (2006) SCIE Knowledge review 11: Supporting disabled parents and parents with additional support needs, London, Social Care Institute for Excellence].

required to go about daily life is crucial, therefore, to the concept of individual living. [58]

Key to choice and control to enable independent living for disabled people was having access to the money to pay for the assistance they might require. As experienced by John Evans and his colleagues as they worked to 'break out' of the Leonard Cheshire care home getting control of the cash which was being used to fund their residential care placement and to use it instead to fund assistance as they moved to live in the community was not easy or straightforward. It was not easy because at the time it was illegal.

Despite the Griffith's reports recommendations to give disabled people more choice of services he had stopped short of proposing that local authorities should transfer to disabled people the money to buy assistance—for Griffith's the focus was still on (more flexible) services rather than on giving disabled people the means, the cash, to organise and arrange their own assistance. However, as noted by Geoffrey Mercer:

> A key break with mainstream provision occurred in 1979 when disabled residents [including John Evans] at Le Court Cheshire Home in Hampshire persuaded the local authority to allow cash payments (equivalent to the cost of their residential 'care') to be paid to inmates [sic] through a third party, in this case the residential home. Disabled people used these funds to make accommodation accessible for their use and to employ their own personal assistants (PAs). Despite their dubious legality, such schemes attracted widening interest precisely because they enabled disabled people to assume more choice and control over their community living support— in stark contrast to Social Services Departments who relied on regimented 'care' regimes typified by day centres. [59]

The creative manoeuvre used by Hampshire County Council to give money to the Leonard Cheshire Foundation which then passed it on as cash to the disabled people leaving the care home was, however, fragile and tenuous, as noted by David Brindle in a 2008 Guardian profile of John Evans:

There was a wobble in 1986, when the county solicitor and county treasure got cold feet about the artifice. By a stroke of good fortune, at exactly the same time the Audit Commission published an influential report, *Making a Reality of Community Care*, that praised Hampshire's approach and questioned the legal objection to it. A second wobble came in 1992 when the Department of Health issued a circular instructing councils to stop all direct payments: many councils did so, but Hampshire held its nerve. [60]

In addition to Hampshire County Councils and its directors of social services (first, Arthur Hunt and then Terry Butler) there were some other councils in the early 1990s who used a third party organisation to transfer cash to disabled people through what were called, in the absence of legislation at the time to allow direct payments, indirect payment schemes. These councils included Kingston upon Thames were Roy Taylor was the social services director and Somerset where Chris Davis was the director.

Another was Wiltshire where I was the director. The Wiltshire scheme was described by Anthony Douglas and Terry Philpot in a book published in 1998:

A few third party organisations grew up during the 1990s to administer funds on behalf of disabled people, partly to circumvent the law which did not allow for direct payments until 1997. The Wiltshire Independent Living Fund (WILF) was established by Wiltshire County Council and is based upon each disabled person holding a bank account in WILF's name. The disabled person is then made the authorised signatory for cheque payments. A WILF panel [of disabled people, with social workers and occupational therapists attending as advisors] looks at [largely self-] assessments and allocates funds to individuals. WILF links strongly into a user network [which had a contract from the county council to give advice and support to those who received money from WILF]. The Somerset Self-Operated Care Scheme works in a similar way. Some local authorities are worried such a scheme would be hijacked by the most vocal disabled people who might not necessarily have the highest needs. This is a flawed argument. It is better to encourage vocal people to become involved, and to ensure the allocation of resources is controlled by carrying out good assessments of need. [61]

The Wiltshire experience, as elsewhere, was that disabled people were imaginative and creative but modest and measured in using money to meet their needs. Any concerns that money might be misspent were not realised … rather the opposite, with funds allocated to disabled people from WILF sometimes underspent as disabled people held back to create a reserve in case there was a rainy day ahead! WILF was initiated in 1993. By 1996 and the introduction of direct payments a total over £1m a year was being paid through WILF to disabled people, including people with physical and sensory impairment, learning disabilities and mental health difficulties.

It was the campaigning of disabled people and the success of the indirect payment schemes which led the Conservative government in 1996 to introduce the Community Care (Direct Payments) Act which gave local authorities the permissive power to make cash payments to disabled people. David Walden recalled:

> Virginia Bottomley [when Secretary of State for Health] in 1993/94 was lobbied quite hard by Tory MPs in particular, not surprisingly, saying we are on the side of these disability groups, we think disabled people should have the right to control their own resources, you know, it's part of the sort of choice and control agenda which can either be a left or a right wing agenda depending on how you play it. At that time it was about getting the money out of those dreadful local authorities and giving it to individuals and she resisted it for a couple of years on the grounds that the we had only just brought in the community care reforms and that it was a pretty fragile system and there might be problems … She finally after meeting one delegation said to officials I think they have got a strong case and I think we should do it but it had to done at no cost—that's the only way the Treasury would sign up to it, and we said slightly disingenuously 'Well it will be [at no additional cost] because the direct payment will be equivalent to the package [of care] you would have had anyway', stepping smartly aside from the admin costs etc. [David Walden interview]

Jane Campbell commented on the political acumen of those within the disability in campaigning for direct payments and how their strategy targeted differing political ideologies:

We played that very well because we sold it to the Tories under 'getting on your bike' [the phrase from Norman Tebbit when a Conservative minister that unemployed people should 'get on their bikes' to go out seeking employment] and we sold it to Labour as a human rights issue to be empowered to control our own situation. We were very political and very skilled. What people don't realise is disabled people at that time were the most skilled operators I've ever come across and I still find that in a lot of situations. [Jane Campbell interview]

Initially the 1996 legislation restricted direct payments to those aged 18–65 years but the 2000 Carers and Disabled Children Act extended direct payments to 16 and 17 year olds and to carers and the 2001 Health and Social Care Act placed a mandatory duty on local authorities to provide the option of direct payments to those who were 'willing and able' to receive and manage the payments, including those aged over 65 years.

An unpublished survey I undertook for the ADSS in 2000 into the discretionary implementation by local authorities of direct payments found regional differences which reflected political differences across councils. For example, 94% of councils in London and 93% in central England had introduced direct payment schemes, but only 70% in the north of England and 66% in Wales, reflecting in the Labour-controlled areas a concern that direct payments would undermine direct public service provision by local authorities. It was also found that 26 out of the 136 authorities which completed the survey had excluded people with learning disabilities and mental health difficulties from receiving direct payments, presumably on the basis that the local authority was not confident that they would be 'able' to manage a direct payment although 'willing' to do so.

But it was local authorities through indirect payment schemes and as allies alongside the campaigning of disabled people which had led to the 1996 and then the 2000 and 2001 legislation first allowing direct payments and then making them available for all disabled people. In essence the period from 1988 and the Griffiths Report and the 1996 direct payment legislation reflected and reinforced substantial change in how the personal social services for disabled people were focused and on the changing role of social workers. It was the platform on which the later personalisation agendas were to be built.

The Promotion of Privatisation

There was one further adult social care change which occurred in the 1980s and into the 1990s under Conservative governments. The 1990 Act had the intention of containing and indeed curtailing public expenditure on residential care by transferring capped and then reduced social security costs on care to local authorities. The rule that 85% of the transferred funding had to be spent on care purchased by councils from independent, largely private, sector-providers was to ensure that the market in private for-profit care homes was not destabilised, as noted by Tom Luce who was a senior civil servant leading on the changes:

> All or nearly all of the social security money was actually being spent in private residential care homes, not in local authority residential homes, so ministers, and indeed the Civil Service Department, were concerned that if it was suddenly switched away from the private sector there would be an overall serious shortage of provision ... The Treasury is always against earmarking local authority money, very strongly against, and I do remember going to have lunch with the deputy secretary in the Treasury, and explaining to him that if we couldn't earmark this money in this way the main losses would be in the private sector and I think that was the critical reason why there was a special grant and why it was focussed in this way. [Tom Luce interview]

Tom Luce also noted that:

> The structural consequences [of the 1990 Act] were certainly not only recognised but very strongly pressed [by central government] and I think this was partly because the Conservative government at that time was keen on purchaser-provider splits for obvious reasons. [Tom Luce interview]

The 'obvious reasons' were that the government wanted to promote an increased market place and space for private services. Within this market the intention was to promote and enable private sector ownership and provision and to reduce and run down [both in the sense of quantity but also reputation as a means of undermining public sector services] public services.

The interests and intentions went beyond the protection of the care market in the private sector which had developed through social security funding. The government introduced measure which made it very difficult for local authorities to continue to directly provide residential care homes. These measures included reducing recurrent revenue and one-off capital government funding to local authorities whilst at the same time restricting the funding local authorities could raise by increasing council tax. There were also strict controls to hinder local authorities from borrowing to spend on capital projects or even to use the proceeds of selling capital assets such as land and buildings to re-invest in new capital developments.

The consequence was that local authorities were not able to maintain and refurbish their own care homes, and were not able to adapt and upgrade the homes to meet increased registration requirements which were described and detailed in 'Home Life' and the subsequent requirements on standards set by the Social Services Inspectorate [62].

The cost to the local authorities of residents in their local authority care homes were also higher as there were still social security payments such as attendance allowance which could be claimed by residents and used to contribute to the paying for their care but not if they were in a local authority home. Local authority care home running costs were also often higher than the running costs of private care homes as terms and conditions of employment of care workers in local authority homes were often better than in private sector homes and with less investment in staff training and management in the private sector homes.

During the 1990s local authority homes were largely either closed or transferred to other providers through a process required by the government of competitive tendering. Some local authorities set up independent trusts to which their care homes were transferred but by the end of the 1990s it was the private sector which dominated the skewed care homes market with in many areas no remaining local authority care homes. This market has continued to consolidate with small providers taken over or squeezed out by big companies running large numbers of care homes and often owned by international venture capitalists with an overriding commitment to generate a profit but little or no concern for the residents in the homes [63].

Tom Luce noted that this change was driven by the Department of Environment (which determined central government funding to local government and local authority funding rules) and by the Treasury rather than by the Department of Health:

> The policy of rate capping and the controls on capital expenditure were not invented in the Department of Health. They were invented in the Treasury and the Department of Environment. We did not support them in any way. They were things we just had to live with. [Tom Luce interview]

He reinforced this point by commenting 'I mean there was certainly not in the 1990s in the Department of Health or on the part of its ministers an active privatisation policy for children's services'. The focus on the increased marketisation of the personal social services, however, was to continue, as noted in the following chapters.

Part IV

The Recent Reforms and Unravelling

11

New Labour: New Agendas (1997–2010)

When Labour formed the new government in 1997 its leadership had named it 'New Labour'. It was a symbolic term to mean that it was moving on from the past and its former commitments, for example, to the public ownership of key national services. A relatively young new leadership team was in place with Tony Blair as prime minister, Gordon Brown as chancellor of the exchequer, and Peter Mandelson, who had been Labour's campaign director, appointed as a minister in the Cabinet to coordinate government activity.

This latter appointment was a precursor of how New Labour was to act. It would not only determine policies to be enshrined in legislation. It would also pull the levers—some of which were to be newly created—to deliver the implementation of the policies, including those where the responsibility was held by local government. There was to be a re-shaping, but not an abandonment, of central government holding control and power over local government.

There was to be a focus on 'joined up' services with the joining up to be led by the Cabinet Office through, for example, the setting up of special units such as the Social Exclusion Unit to tackle disadvantage and discrimination and the Standards and Effectiveness Unit to tackle

© The Author(s) 2020, corrected publication 2021
R. Jones, *A History of the Personal Social Services in England*,
https://doi.org/10.1007/978-3-030-46123-2_11

what were deemed to be poorly performing schools and which was to be forerunner of Ofsted. It was Blair's ministers rather than Blair himself, however, who were to be more active in pushing for 'joined-up government' [1].

The commitment to improve school performance was emphasised by the mantra of 'education, education, education' as the government's top priority. Other mantras included 'tough on crime, tough on the causes of crime', which was intended to capture some of the 'law and order' territory traditionally held by the Conservatives.

New Labour sought to acquire what was also thought to be held by the Conservatives—a reputation for tight economic management. Brown as chancellor committed the incoming government to the budget plans of the outgoing Conservative government, and for the first three years from 1997 to 2000 there was continued restraint on public expenditure.

Derek Draper, who had been an advisor to Peter Mandelson, wrote in 1997 in a book about Blair's first 100 days as prime minister:

> As [the outgoing] Chancellor, Kenneth Clarke had already described the [Conservatives'] public expenditure plans for 1997–98 as 'eye-wateringly' tight, and Labour's steadfast commitment to financial rectitude has locked them into accepting Conservative constraints. At the same time, Labour has made public commitments to increase expenditure on education and health in real terms. Metaphors involving circles and squares spring to mind. [2]

The consequence amid overall financial frugality and fragility was that the Conservative government's constraints on local government budgets continued for the first three years under the New Labour government. It meant, for example, that the transfer of local authority care homes to other owners and providers still took place as the money to refurbish the homes and to adapt them to meet more stringent registration standards was not available while the homes remained managed by local councils.

There was a difference, which was to become a tension, in the attitudes and approach of the two men at the top of the Labour government, as described by Tony Blair in his political autobiography:

> When I was with a group of entrepreneurs, I felt at home. Gordon was completely different. He could analyse what a good business was and discuss the intricacies of this policy over that in order to promote it; but he never *felt* it [italics in original text] ... if I had chosen a different path, [I] would have liked running a business and making money ... Gordon was a public service guy who, if he had chosen a different path, would have been a bigger public service guy. [3]

Indeed, Blair seemed much more at home in the company of financiers than public servants. In a speech to the British Venture Capital Association in 1999 he spoke about the 'scars on his back' from trying to change the public sector and public sector workers and said 'They are more rooted in the concept that if "it's always been done this way, it must always be done this way" than any other group I have ever come across' [4]. What is noteworthy is not only Blair's sweeping and damning comments about the public sector but with whom he shared his comments— venture capitalists who during the previous Conservative governments had profited from the privatisation of public services and who would continue to benefit under New Labour.

There was a difference, however, between the explicit intentions of Thatcher, and later of Cameron, to drive services out of the public sector and into a commercial market place. The stated intention of New Labour was the *modernisation* not *marketisation* of public services, albeit that some of the modernisation measures which were introduced, such as the public finance initiative, academy schools, foundation hospitals, and 'social work practices' opened up public services to increasing colonisation and control by the private sector.

The concept of 'social work practices' [5] was created by Julian Le Grand, a professor of social policy at the LSE and an advisor to New Labour and subsequent Conservative-led governments. The Department for Education noted:

A [social work] practice would be an autonomous organisation, whether a voluntary or community sector organisation, a social enterprise or a private business—similar to a GP practice—registered with the Commission for Social Care Inspection and responsible for employing social workers. [6]

In essence, social work practices were to be a means of moving social work services outside of local authorities and were piloted in children's and adults' social services. They were not a success as it was found that they had to stay close to, and remained substantially dependent on, the local authorities which still retained the statutory responsibility and accountability for the services which were being contracted out [7, 8].

Social work practices reflected a view that services would be better provided outside the public sector. They also, may be somewhat strangely, were based on an assumption that taking services outside of local authorities and other public sector organisations would reduce bureaucracy and free-up workers. Why was this assumption strange? First, contracting out services and having to report back on services which have been contracted out generates more monitoring and reporting. Second, as noted by Chris Jones in 2001, it was New Labour which itself was generating increased bureaucracy within public services:

> [The New Labour proponents] might well talk about the necessities of accountability but audit and monitoring has been much more than this. It has been about challenging trust and is situated in a particularly negative view of state workers which initially flourished under Margaret Thatcher but continues under New Labour. [9]

Social work practices, along with a number of New Labour initiatives, were a part of the 'third way' blurring of the differences and distances between the public and private sectors [10, 11] with public-private partnerships promoted. This included the private finance initiative where private investment was used to fund major public works, such as the building of new hospitals and schools, but with a legacy for the future of high interest repayments for 20 or 30 years to the private investors [12].

This all left Labour in opposition after 2010 somewhat compromised in being able to challenge the more rampant privatisation promoted by

Cameron which was built on the embryonic private sector initiatives introduced by Blair and Brown's New Labour governments.

The continuities between the policies of the 1979–1997 Conservative governments led by Thatcher and Major and the policies of the New Labour government have been noted by Simon Jenkins who titled his account of the transition to the Blair-led governments *Thatcher and Sons*. Jenkins called Blair "a cuckoo in [Labour's] nest" and commented that:

> As early as 1995 he was calling [Thatcher] 'a radical, not a Tory'. By the time he took office their relationship was regarded by those around him as little short of a 'love affair'. The mutual admiration of Thatcher and Blair was crucial to the maturing of Thatcherism through the 1990s and into the new century … Far from putting Thatcherism into reverse after taking office in 1997, as many Labour supporters had assumed, they super-charged it. [13]

New Labour and Local Government

In particular, Jenkins reflected on the roots of Blair's aversion to local government:

> The Blairs first tangled with Labour politics when living in North London. No one who experienced Hackney socialism in the 1980s is likely to forget it. It was well cast to convince any newcomer that such a party, with its ideological feuds and late-night squabbles, would never win mass appeal. The Labour group on Hackney council [see chapter 9] was a running aversion therapy for old Labour and historians need look no further for an explanation of Blair's distaste for local government. He had experienced it at its worse. [14]

New Labour's approach to local government was no more trusting than was Thatcher's, with means and mechanisms introduced to by-pass local authorities. Toynbee and Walker noted that:

> If trust was Blair's big problem Labour hunted for an anti-dote in the 'new localism' to reconnect with the people … Ministers floated new ideas for ways to connect the people directly to the institutions that ran their lives …

A reason for seeking out exotic new democratic bases was to cut out local councils. [15]

The Toynbee and Walker's 2006 appraisal was of the first nine years of New Labour governments. By 2010 the movement of services away from local government had been pushed further with the advent of academy schools, social work practices, and the continuing demise of council housing and growth in private rented housing. Similarly, foundation hospitals moved health services away from the influence of local health authorities. Toynbee and Walker's 2010 comment was that:

> A watchword became 'partnership', bringing councils closer to the NHS, police and other services. But Labour's own decisions often flew in the face of joined-upness, notably concerning foundation trusts and part-privately run academies outside council control. On the one hand Labour liked tsars, edicts and targets; on the other, they talked of liberated communities, empowered with their own budgets [but by-passing local authorities]. [16]

It was New Labour which also introduced elected mayors with executive powers within cities, towns and metropolitan areas. Within local authorities New Labour replaced service committees, which had debated and taken decisions in public and with a membership from across the political parties elected to the council, by one-party cabinets which met and took decisions in private with little public transparency. This was intended to make local government more efficient and to speed up decision-making. But what it also meant was that the senior managers of services no longer gave their advice in public to all political parties but instead became primarily the agents implementing the decisions of one political group. It reduced public transparency and distorted the role of those who in part were employed to give professional advice to the council.

Beverley Hughes trained as a social worker and worked as a probation officer before becoming a social work and social policy lecturer. She had been leader of Trafford Council and had a number of ministerial posts in the Blair governments, including as minister for local government. From

2005 to 2009 she was minister for children. She commented on what was seen as the change needed in local government:

> Local government needed to think of itself as being much more accessible and much more accountable to local people, and hopefully to be the leaders in terms of service improvement. In order to do that it needed not to be ideologically driven about who provided the services, but to have a much more open mindset about partnerships with the voluntary or private sector. The guiding light should be 'how can we make this better for our people?' not 'it will only be good if it's delivered in house. [Beverley Hughes interview]

Reform and Modernisation

Reform and modernisation were the headlines of New Labour. What did this mean for the personal social services that were well immersed in the melting pot which was being stirred? The government gave early attention to the personal social services. Within nineteen months of coming into power it published a White Paper *Modernising Social Services* with a focus on 'promoting independence, improving protection and raising standards' [17].

In 1997 towards the end of the Conservative government its Secretary of State, Stephen Dorrell, in a letter to 'chairmen of all Social Services Committees in England' stated that they needed 'to check their efficiency and effectiveness and to search for improvements in value for money' [18]. In contrast, Frank Dobson, the new Labour Secretary of State, stated that the focus was now to be on standards and more money was to be provided:

> Despite the efforts of a lot of very dedicated staff many services are not provided sufficiently conveniently, promptly or to a good enough standard ... One big trouble social services have suffered from is that up to now no Government has spelled out exactly what people can expect or what staff are expected to do. Nor have any clear standards of performance been laid down. The Government is to change all that ... Doing things properly doesn't necessarily cost more than doing things badly. Sometimes it can be

even cheaper. But we recognise that extra funds are required and over the next three years nearly £3 billion extra will be found. £1.3 billion will form a Social Services Modernisation Fund to lead the major changes that are necessary across the whole social services programme. [19]

Tom Luce was a senior civil servant in the Department of Health in 1997. He commented that:

Frank Dobson wasn't particularly interested in privatisation and all that stuff. He would say he was kind of Labour rather than New Labour. I think his involvement in social services was mainly to try and work on the sort of inherited problem—making them work better and more safely—that's my surmise. [Tom Luce interview]

Denise Platt was the social services advisor to the Association of Metropolitan Authorities (AMA). She recalled:

I was working with a predominantly Labour-controlled metropolitan-focussed organisation that was trying to influence the incoming government ... There was an awful lot of to-ing and fro-ing with politicians who had local government connections because [David] Blunkett had chaired the social services committee of the AMA [and had been leader of Sheffield City Council], so had Tessa Jowell [who had been a social worker]. A lot of these discussions that had been going on in a [political] party context became task forces, working groups and those sort of things. [Denise Platt interview]

But she also recalled that 'Quite a lot of local authority councillors had become MPs in 1997 and who in those turbulent times arrived with their prejudices intact. Not helpful really' [Denise Platt interview].

Denise Platt became the chief inspector of social services in 1998. Herbert Laming was her immediate predecessor:

There had been seventeen years of Conservative governments and the Labour government wanted to bring about change and they decided to drive from the centre. They had to drive them from the centre because I suspect they did not have the confidence that local government would actually drive it itself. There had already been for financial reasons the centralisation of power in Whitehall—that was definitely financially driven—but I think they just kept that momentum going and began to set targets in a really, really rigorous way and that's carried on I think and I think we've paid a heavy price for it. [Herbert Laming interview]

Laming's view was that centralisation was not positive:

I think it's impossible for people in Whitehall to know what is best for people of Torbay, or what is best in the city of Hull. I think what has happened is that it has created uniformity, it's created a tick-box mentality, it's directed people's attention around certain things that are measurable and that the centre can relate to, and I think what it has done is to weaken the confidence of local people to actually influence their local communities. [Herbert Laming interview]

What were the levers to be pulled centrally by New Labour to impact on the local delivery of the personal social services? Some were structural, some were about process, and many were about performance monitoring and reporting. Together they have had an impact—and set a tone of central-local government relationships—which still continues and has become accepted. It is now hard to recall how different it was in the 1970s and through the 1980s when in essence Parliament set the legislative framework, the courts determined the interpretation of the legislation, and implementation was then largely left to local authorities to get on with it.

As a part of its modernisation agenda the government created a new personal social services national infrastructure. It also through the 2000 Care Standards Act for the first time across the UK made 'social worker' a protected titled that could only be used by those who held a graduate professional qualification in social work and who were registered as social workers. This marked what might be seen as the coming of age of the social work profession in the UK, mirroring and matching what was already in place for doctors, allied health professions, lawyers and others.

Reflecting on social work across the UK becoming a graduate profession David Jones commented on the opposition from Margaret Thatcher and what later led to the change:

> [I was at a meeting with Margaret Thatcher when she said] "one of the worse decisions I ever made was to make nursing a graduate profession. I will never do it for social work. It takes people away from contact with real people" … Perhaps the strongest influence [leading to social work becoming a graduate profession] was Europe in that a Mutual Recognition of Diplomas Directive meant that member states had to recognise qualifications of people in their different countries so they could move across borders and one of the conditions was that [social work] was a graduate profession. [David Jones interview]

He also noted:

> There was a view which began to emerge, particularly with the Labour government which was committed to public service, but also within the Conservatives with people like Tim Loughton, that social workers needed to be well qualified, needed to have analytic skills, and that meant they had to be graduates and well trained, which was different from the narrative before that if you are a graduate and are trained you are unable to engage with the hoi polloi because you are by definition at a big remove from them … there was also the general issue that 50 per cent of the population were becoming graduates so why would social work not be? [David Jones interview]

The new national personal social services infrastructure included three new bodies—a General Social Care Council (GSCC), a National Care Standards Commission (NCSC), and the Social Care Institute for Excellence (SCIE).

Registration and the GSCC

The GSCC was to 'replace the Central Council for Education and Training in Social Work [CCETSW] in regulating the training of social workers, set conduct and practice standards for all social services staff, and register those in the most sensitive areas' [20]. The GSCC did not go on to develop in England quite as initially imagined as the prospect of taking on a role and responsibility for all working within the personal social services—including the large numbers of residential and home carers—was daunting and overwhelming and the focus of the GSCC stayed on social workers (unlike, for example, in Northern Ireland with the equivalent body regulating and registering a wider all-be-it smaller social care workforce).

As noted in an earlier chapter, there had been campaigning over many years that there should be a process and body for regulating and registering social workers. Terry Bamford, who was a founder member of the GSCC when it was established in 2002, noted:

> As early as 1975, the BASW annual general meeting passed a resolution calling for the accreditation of social workers based on competence in practice and qualification. [Then in 1981] in its evidence to the Barclay Committee, BASW argued for the setting up of a new body with associated accreditation machinery to maintain, develop and enforce standards of training and professional behaviour in social work. [21]

In 1990 a General Social Services Council Action Group had been set up following Roy Parker's report, published by NISW, on 'Safeguarding Standards' [22] and in 1992 the National Institute for Social Work (NISW) published a Consultation Paper proposing a General Social Services Council [23]. It had concluded that all social services social care staff should be subject to regulation and registration. This was accepted by the Association of Directors of Social Services [24].

However, as noted above, the GSCC restricted its attention to the regulation and registration of social workers and of their education. Even that was found to be a mammoth task and by 2012 there were over 105,000 social workers in England who were registered [25]. But the GSCC's funding was constrained by government and to stay within budget the GSCC delayed undertaking conduct hearings and a backlog built up [26]. This was used by the incoming Conservative government in 2010, amidst its cull of quangos, to abolish the GSCC and to transfer its responsibilities to the Health and Care Professions Council (HCPC), only then in 2017 through the Children and Social Work Act to change its mind and to legislate for a dedicated social work regulator for England. This inconsistency and swapping and changing by the Conservative government hardly was an exemplar of economy, efficiency or effectiveness. It wasted time and money and generated uncertainty and disruption.

Inspection and the NCSC and CSCI

The inconsistency of government was demonstrated much sooner by the New Labour government. Within a few years of establishing the National Care Standards Commission it was to be ended and replaced by a Commission for Social Care Inspection.

The 1998 Modernising Social Services White Paper summarised the confusion, complexity and incomplete nature of the then inspection landscape:

> The existing arrangements for regulating care services have developed in a piecemeal fashion. Responsibilities for regulating the various services for adults and children are divided between local authorities, health authorities and the Department of Health centrally. Other services—notably councils' own care homes, small children's homes and domiciliary care agencies (care given to people in their own homes)—are not subject to any regulation. This situation leads to a number of problems. [There is a] lack of independence—local and health authorities have to combine purchasing, providing and regulating care services. As well as the conflict of interest that this causes, this means that people in local authority care homes do not benefit from independent regulation ... Standards vary from one area to another, creating uncertainty for both providers and service users ... The Social Services Inspectorate has done valuable work in assessing local authorities' regulatory work, but a clear national approach has been lacking. [27]

This is a clear summary of the situation and circumstances of inspection of the personal social services in 1998. It was fragmented, incomplete, inconsistent and patchy. However, the changes canvassed in the White Paper were to take the inspection process in a direction where the journey had already started several years before with a focus on judging and rating rather than development and improvement.

In the Department of Health there had already been change in what had been the Social Work Service [SWS] led by a chief social work services officer. The SWS had been established at the time of the creation of local authority social services departments following the 1970 Local Authority Social Services Act. Joan Cooper was the first director of the SWS and Bill Utting took over from Joan Cooper when she retired in 1976. He recalled that 'merely to mention inspection brought on a fit of the vapours' and that rather than undertaking inspections 'Joan and the SWS presented interpretation and advice about the mass of new legislation that assaulted departments' [28].

Tom Luce was a senior civil servant in the Department of Health at the time:

In mental handicap there was a thing called the Mental Handicap Development Group or something like that, that was supposed to be going around advising on standards. But there seemed to be some kind of ethical or quasi-ethical holding back in the sense that I think quite a lot of the professionals in the Department felt that their role was to help the external services to improve, not just to judge them. In the Social Work Service I remember that sort of debate going on a bit, and when Bill Utting was chief inspector he changed the title for the Social Work Service to the Social Services Inspectorate, but actually it didn't really do inspection until Herbert Laming came along and changed it somewhat. [Tom Luce interview]

Bill Utting's view was that:

[The SWS] was largely an advisory service to local authorities and a source of information for the department through its regional organisation. The inspection side was virtually moribund ... because of the professional ethos of the DHSS at the time when inspection was sort of a dirty word as far as health services were concerned. And there was also I think more justifiably the view that these were large new local authority social services departments which were well resourced and you could confidently leave it to local authorities to run these with the minimum of interference. [Bill Utting interview]

So how did inspection start to become more central to the Department of Health? Bill Utting commented that it was tied up with the focus in the 1980s on value for money:

The thing I was able to latch on to in the Conservative manifesto was their value for money approach because they woke up to the fact that they were dishing out large sums of money ... That was one of the reasons we started pushing the inspectorial role more so that there would be evidence coming through in structured reviews of services and were they actually achieving some of the objectives they were intended to achieve. [Bill Utting interview]

Hence the move towards the inspection of services rather than advice and guidance had started in the mid-1980s. It had been ratcheted up by the Conservative government with the introduction within local authorities of inspection units in 1991 to regulate, inspect and register the increasing number of independent sector providers of residential and home care services (but not local authorities directly provided services). A review of social services inspection was then commissioned by the Conservative government in 1996. The review was undertaken by an 'independent assessor', Tom Burgner, a retired Treasury civil servant.

Burgner recommended greater national consistency in the standards to be met for registration, more children and adult social services to be required to be inspected and registered, and for this to include services directly provided by local authorities. Burgner did not, however, make a clear recommendation on how inspection services should be organised and managed.

An early response was to make local authority social services inspection units accountable to the local authority's chief executive rather than the director of social services. It was assumed this would reduce the conflict of interest when the inspectors were inspecting services provided or purchased from within the social services department. This seemed somewhat strange as local authority chief executives were as much, and probably more, concerned about the profile and reputation of their council but without the knowledge, and may be the value-base, to take on and tackle poor care. At the same time it removed from social services directors intelligence available from the inspection unit about the state of personal social services across the providers in their area.

David Walden was the senior civil servant tasked to advise the government on the shaping of inspection:

> I said "Actually you need to bring all this together because consistency and clarity of the regulatory approach is very important to providers, particularly now you have got big corporate chains moving in. It seemed to me a no-brainer, although maybe people would wish that I hadn't. So anyway, that became the National Care Standards Commission [NCSC]." [David Walden interview]

Walden also commented that:

> I think it was also partly that we [the government] were starting to give [local authorities] lots of money, even though relative to the Health Service it wasn't as much but it was more than they had under Thatcher, because Labour did start to loosen the purse strings a bit, and [there was] a sense of 'What are we getting for this, can we guarantee the outputs and the outcomes?' and I am not entirely sure we trust these people to deliver what we want coupled with a sense of the postcode lottery thing that was starting to build up and 'You should be able to expect a standard level of service wherever you are'. [David Walden interview]

When in December 1999 the New Labour government published its Care Standards Bill it stated its intention to establish a National Care Standards Commission (NCSC) and with ministers to set national minimum standards for services and these would be enforced by the NCSC. The push towards a national social care inspectorate was powered by the view that local authority directly provided services should be independently regulated and inspected alongside independent sector provision, and that the workloads of inspectorates were increasing as independent—and especially private—sector provision was growing. There was also the issue that although there was some standardisation of service requirements between councils this needed to be strengthened along with more consistency in inspection processes, especially with the growth of larger social care companies in the private sector providing services across many local authority areas.

Anne Parker was the first chair of the National Care Standards Commission from 2001 when it was founded until 2004 when it was disbanded and replaced by CSCI. She commented:

> My perception was that independence in inspection and [along] with the government's minimum standards, with metrics and measurement of performance and service, started to produce an impact ... The combination of independence and minimum standards, and nationally a more or less [inspection] level playing field [across provider sectors] was a very powerful instrument. [Anne Parker interview]

What the subsequent 2000 Care Standards Act did not do, however, was to lead to the demise of the Social Services Inspectorate in the Department of Health. It still initially retained its role in providing professional advice to ministers. Indeed it had been given an enhanced role in inspecting local authority social services through a programme of Joint Reviews conducted between the SSI and the Audit Commission, of which more below.

Evidence and SCIE

The third leg on New Labour's social services modernisation stool was the Social Care Institute for Excellence (SCIE).[1] SCIE was not within the plans sketched out in the 1998 White Paper nor in the 2000 Care Standards Act. It did not require legislation for it to be established as, unlike the NCSC and GSCC which were created as statutory non-governmental public bodies, it was set up as a charity and company limited by guarantee. This had a major significance as its could not be caught in the future Labour and then Conservative governments cull of quangos, although it was heavily dependent of government grants and its work

---

[1] In 2002 I was appointed as the founding first chief executive of SCIE, with Jane Campbell as SCIE's first chair.

programme was largely negotiated—certainly in its early years—with civil servants.

Its remit was to review and disseminate the knowledge-base for the personal social services. This was reflective of the increasing interest and commitment to promote what was called evidence-based policy and practice. It is now more sensibly known as evidence-informed policy and practice as there are other variables which have influence, such as political ideologies and agency roles and remits along with the inherent wisdom built through experience by practitioners and service users.

One of the early commissions by SCIE was a review of the types of knowledge relevant to the personal social services. Then [29, 30] as now [31] there was a push that randomised controlled trials (RCTs) were the evidence gold standard, but then as now this was contested as the nature and complexity of personal and social issues are multi-factorial and controlling all the variables is not practical or feasible. Indeed, it is often difficult to define and measure the components of person-to-person human interactions which have been found by user-perception studies from the 1970s onwards, as noted in an earlier chapter, to determine user views of the quality of the personal social services and of the social work interactions they have experienced.

The 2003 SCIE commissioned review of types and quality of knowledge in social care concluded that 'when conducting a systematic review in social care the following five sources of knowledge should be used [from] organisations, practitioners, the policy community (that is, knowledge gained from the wider policy context), research (gathered systematically with a planned design), and service users and carers' [32].

SCIE's programme included undertaking and commissioning knowledge reviews, producing practice guidance based on the reviews, and with a commitment throughout to have user involvement in the process of shaping its work and products, now reflected in its commitment to promote the co-production of services between service users, carers and service providers.

SCIE was not, however, alone in its promotion of evidence-informed practice. The Association of Directors of Social Services with the Dartington Hall Trust had already spawned Research in Practice for children (RiP) and then Research in Practice for Adults (RiPfA), the

Department of Health with social services directors in south west England created the Centre for Evidence-Based Social Services (CEBBS) at Exeter University,[2] and a number of local authorities were paying partners with Making Research Count (MRC) which was coordinated from King's College, London.

All of these organisations, and the focus on evidence-informed policy and practice, were to be subject to disparaging criticism in a 2009 book by Gray, Plath and Webb [33]. The different perspectives on the emergence of attention given to research and other evidence are exemplified by two quotes. The first is from advocates at CEBSS for this new trend:

> The problem was that the results from the first social work experiments were almost wholly nil-nil draws [finding no discernible impact], or worse [a negative impact]. Indeed, these brave, early studies should have taught us long ago something that all the helping professions (including medicine) have only recently begun seriously to acknowledge, namely that it is perfectly possible for good-hearted, well-meaning, reasonably clever, appropriately qualified, hard-working staff, employing the most promising contemporary approaches available to them, to make no difference at all to (or even on occasion to worsen) the condition of those whom they seek to assist. [34]

In essence, it was argued that there is a moral and professional necessity to check on the impact and outcomes of the actions and interventions of those working in the personal social services and to frame future actions on the evidence which is generated.

But this was countered by a reminder about the messiness and complexity of the lives of people who might be engaged by the personal social services:

> Evidence-based practice, while applying a sliding scale of 'factuality' to decisions, imagines a move for social work from messy realities and more tightly framed around performance. This is a far cry from the harsh realities of street-level poverty, survival tactics, drugs and narcotics, family violence and abuse, and so on, that are ever-present in the difficult and often stress-

---

[2] I had been the chair of RiP, RiPfa, and CEBSS in the 1990s.

ful judgements of social workers in how best to intervene. Evidence-based practice offers no challenge at all to these conditions. [35]

This points to the real world of the personal social services, especially to the limits of making a difference and having an impact where the interventions of social workers and others will be marginal and minuscule compared to the much bigger impact of social conditions—such as poverty, poor housing and truncated and limited life opportunities—which require a broader social policy response. The reality is that social work may be a still necessary sellotape trying to hold lives together in the absence of the super glue needed to bond together a broken society.

Social workers with others should be personally and professionally active in challenging disadvantage, deprivation and discrimination. It is also important, however, to know if, for example, placing children within kinship networks rather than with unrelated foster carers is likely to create more stability for a child whilst providing reasonable care, or if multi-professional care teams are more likely to assist older people to live their lives as they want as compared to contact with an array of workers who are separately managed and located. These are important questions to address in planning services and shaping practice.

Training and TOPSS

The revamping of the personal social services national infrastructure also included a national training organisation for the social care workforce across all sectors and providers. The Training Organisation for Personal Social Services (TOPSS) was created and a Training Support Grant was provided by the government as a part of its Social Services Modernisation Fund. TOPSS was subsequently immersed in Skills for Care which was also created in the early 2000s to lead on workforce development for social care. A separate Children's Workforce Development Council was established by the Labour government in 2005 as a part of the 'Every Child Matters' agenda but was abolished by the Conservative government in 2012 amid its 'bonfire of the quangos' [36].

Change and Churn Within the National Infrastructure

Many of the personal social services organisations created in the early 2000s will not now be known or recognised. Only SCIE continues, albeit with parts of its work programme commissioned and funded by the National Institute for Health and Care Evidence (NICE—which was also founded by the government in the early 2000s as the National Centre for Clinical Evidence before having its remit expended into social care), and with its brief to help create, capture and cascade the knowledge-base for children's social services now within the remit of the government-funded What Works Centre for Children's Social Care [37]. The GSCC had its role for the registration, regulation and education of social workers subsumed with the Health and Care Professions Council (HCPC), but that too is now being rewound with the setting up of a new social worker regulator Social Work England. The NCSC was replaced by the Commission for Social Care Inspections (CSCI) but this was then ended and its inspection responsibilities were divided between Ofsted (for children's services inspections) and the Care Quality Commission (CQC) which was created out of the merger of the adult social care responsibilities of CSCI and what had been the Healthcare Commission and Mental Health Act Commission. TOPSS was replaced by Skills for Care.

David Behan was appointed in 2003 as the first chief executive of CSCI and commented 'People knew we were on the side of social care, people knew we were on the side of people that use social care, and in a sense people could say we were technocrats, but there was a vision and a purpose … we occupied a space which championed high quality services which promoted people's independence' [David Behan interview].

The turmoil and turbulence within the national infrastructure arrangements for the personal social services in England—which has been costly and disruptive—has not been replicated across the UK, where the bodies created and arrangements put in place in the early 2000s are still largely intact 20 years later, allowing attention to remain on their core functions rather than the flux of frequent organisational change.

Fair Access to Care Services

As a part of its ambitions to create more consistency across England in the personal social services the government introduced in 2002 a national framework for Fair Access to Care for disabled and older people. It set the requirement that each council with social services responsibilities produce its own FACS policy and statement to consider "risk to independence and other consequences if needs are not addressed" [38] and with the local authority policies based on a national framework which set eligibility criteria across four bands—critical, substantial, moderate and low. This became more of a framework for rationing assistance and excluding people from help than promoting consistency in eligibility as judgments and assessments were still framed within the resources differentially available to each council.

'Best Value Reviews' and the Social Services Inspectorate and Audit Commission Joint Reviews

The drive from central government to oversee and generate improvement and consistent standards also underpinned the Audit Commission and the Department of Health's Social Services Inspectorate's Joint Reviews. Joint Reviews were a major programme of inspections of all 172 local authorities in England and Wales which had responsibilities for personal social services. They were undertaken at the same time that a Social Services Performance Assessment Framework was created and also as local authorities were required to subject all of their services to 'Best Value Reviews' [39].

The 1998 'Modernising Local Government' White Paper noted that 'Best Value Reviews' would be expected to *'challenge* why the particular service(s) are needed at all, *compare* performance with others taking into account the views of both service users and potential suppliers, *consult* with local taxpayers, service users and the wider business community in the setting of new performance targets, and *compete* in the sense of demonstrating that the preferred means of delivering the service(s) has been—and will be—arrived at through a competitive process' [40]. The output of each Best Value review was to include 'the setting of improved performance targets in respect of economy, efficiency and effectiveness' [41]. It was made explicit that this was a replacement of the compulsory competitive tendering (CCT) required by the previous Conservative governments as:

> Under CCT service quality has often been neglected, and efficiency gains have been uneven and uncertain, and it has proved inflexible in practice ... All too often the process of competition has become an end in itself. In short, CCT has provided a poor deal for employees, employers, and local people. CCT will therefore be abolished. [42]

John Bolton was immersed in the focus on reviews and inspections. As a social services senior manager in Camden in the late 1990s he developed a quality framework and a performance management framework for social care as well as chairing the corporate performance management group. He had much earlier been influenced by management-by-objectives models while doing courses at the National Institute for Social Work. In the late 1990s he joined the Audit Commission and SSI Joint Review team, and then became its director, later to be a director of social services and then the social care director of strategic finance in the Department of Health focused on value for money and service outcomes. Bolton recalled that:

> I actually think that the Joint Review Team's methodology around case files, the engagement with service users, that early first fortnight of field-work [in local authorities] was probably much more powerful and its use of data ... I think it created a methodology and an approach to service delivery which was generally sound. And its third dimension was its interest in council governance being critical to the delivery of social care, and so it raised social care up the political agenda because councillors were being, probably for the first time, held to account. [John Bolton interview]

He also, however, noted:

I don't think regulators—and I still think this today—understood their power and how if that power was misused, it was really damaging … I can think of four or five directors losing their jobs after a joint review … but I always said it's about the whole systems capacity, what are you doing as chief executive to support your director … But the desire for the institution to have a scapegoat for anything that's critical was very hard to break down. [John Bolton interview]

The Demise of the Social Services Inspectorate

The Department of Health's Social Services Inspectorate along with the Audit Commission delivered the programme of Joint Reviews across all the local authorities in England and Wales which had social services responsibilities. The Social Services Inspectorate's (SSI) role in inspections was, however, about to end. Indeed the SSI itself was about to be abolished, with its inspection functions allocated the newly created Commission for Social Care Inspections but leaving a void and vacuum on how professionally informed policy advice on the personal social services was to be provided within the civil service to the government.

Through its long history, dating back to the unification of the personal social services in the 1970s, first as the Department of Health's Social Work Service and then as the SSI it had three functions—advising ministers on issues, policies and legislation concerning the personal social services, advising local authorities and others on the development of services and including the implementation of new legislation, and—increasingly—inspecting and reporting on local authority social services performance.

Herbert Laming became chief inspector in the SSI in 1991 and on day one the Prime Minister, John Major, announced there was to be a review of the government's inspectorates, starting with the SSI:

He was talking about how we're going to change not only the face of public services to make them more sensitive to people, to make them more aware of their customers, but he then went on to say 'And the government inspectorates have got to be in the lead to bring about this change, and the first inspectorate that needs to change is the SSI … What was clear was that the government wanted to make the SSI an external agency, to get the SSI out of the Department [of Health]. I thought that would be a disaster for a variety of reasons, but not least because I saw my job as not just controlling the inspectorate but of being a policy adviser—not just to government ministers in the Department of Health but the government as a whole. If we were going to change the kind of things that I thought we ought to change, I wanted to have influence upon social security payments, I wanted to have influence upon the Home Office, upon the Department for Education and Science, and indeed one of the early things that landed on my desk was about the Ministry of Defence and the way in which they treated military families and children. So I thought it was terribly important that I kept right at the heart of Whitehall. [Herbert Laming interview]

Laming's response was to change the internal arrangements for the SSI:

I thought the only way we can deal with this issue is to split the SSI into two, to have two deputy chief inspectors, to make one whole division nothing else but inspections, and the other division to be the links with the local authorities to drive forward the results of the inspection programme, but also to be my eyes and ears about what was happening in 100-odd local authorities. [Herbert Laming interview]

Wendy Rose was leading on children's services policy in the SSI at the time:

Increasingly as children's services and the government context was much more about performance targets, so the name changed and the SSI liaison inspectors [with local authorities] became business managers and I get the impression that it became a much more arms-length relationships. I feel that what could be achieved in terms of development was hugely limited by that and the confidence and trust between the centre and the local authorities also became more difficult and of course in that period we moved [as a consequence of Local Government Reorganisation] from 108 local authorities to 150, so the scale changed enormously and the size of the local authorities changed to the very small unitaries with their own sets of problems and circumstances and the big counties that had suddenly lost their key cities. [Wendy Rose interview]

The SSI thrust towards inspection and performance monitoring rather than development and policy work included the Annual Performance Assessment (APAs) for each local authority which were based on the annual service data returns from each council. These were then collated and generated a published annual 'Performance Ratings for Social Services in England' report [43]. This graded councils on whether they were judged to be "serving people well" and their "prospects for improvement", graded separately for children's and adults' services and then with an overall zero to three star rating.

Naming and Shaming

This all became a shock and controversy when in October 2001, with no warning or prior announcement, at the annual National Social Services Conference held in Newcastle the process of performance monitoring and reporting became a process of naming and shaming. Alan Milburn was the Secretary of State for Health and to the astonishment and anger of the councillors, social services directors and others at the conference he used his conference platform to list 14 councils who were described as the worst performing. The Guardian reported that:

> Health secretary Alan Milburn has named and shamed the 14 worst per-forming social services departments in England and warned that new man-agement could be brought in if they fail to make "significant improvements" by next year. From 2002, the government will rank England's 150 social services departments in a new performance league table using the star rat-ing system already in place in the NHS, Mr Milburn told the national social services conference today. He said managers from the top three-star grade performers could take over services in the poorest no-star depart-ments. The private and voluntary sector may also be brought in to turn around persistent poor performers. [44]

Milburn's naming and shaming was all the more unexpected, as noted in Community Care, as his speech was launching a recruitment cam-paign for social workers:

The Local Government Association and the Association of Directors of Social Services said the announcement reinforced an "unjust negative image" at a time when social services were "already beleaguered" and the majority of departments were improving. Public sector union Unison immediately accused Milburn of missing a "golden opportunity" to boost the image and reputation of social services and warned that social services needed support, "not threatening with a big stick." [45]

David Walden recalled:

Denise [Platt as chief inspector in the SSI] and I [head of social care policy] tried to stop it [Milburn's naming and shaming], mainly because it wasn't well founded really and I think some of the ten who were put in the best category thought 'Oh God, I hope nobody is going to look too closely at this', and vice versa, and I can remember ADSS colleagues being absolutely hopping mad about all of that, but he was determined to make a political point ... [But it did have an impact with] the sector now taking responsibility for its own improvements which I think is a good thing. [David Walden interview]

Speaking more generally about the impact of performance monitoring and reporting, Denise Platt made a similar comment to David Walden:

I think it promoted directors to really scrutinise what they were doing. Some of the best self-assessment processes that we introduced were some of the best because of the discussions that directors had before we arrived to do the performance discussion had probably put rigour into it ... People not only understand the performance information but they understand how to cluster them to actually describe what's going on in their service. [Denise Platt interview]

Herbert Laming also reflected on changes in inspection processes:

I feel very sad that we have lost the developmental function. I have never seen inspection as a one-off snapshot. I've always been very aware of the limitations of inspection. It would be not only arrogant, it would be stupid to think that you can parachute a team of people in from outside, that they can see everything, know everything, and evaluate everything, and make recommendations that are far-seeing, and then disappear and the world is going to change. So I felt that it was terribly important that inspection was informed by the people who knew a lot about local services, not only about the local authority, but knew about what the local authority was up against with the health service, with the police service, whatever it may be. [Herbert Laming interview]

When in 2004 the government abolished the SSI and also the NCSC (which it had only established in 2001) their inspection responsibilities were now grouped together in a new Commission for Social Care Inspection, with Denise Platt as its first chair. At the same time central government responsibility for children's social services was transferred to the Department for Education. Platt recalled:

We [CSCI] took 300 people out of the Department [of Health] with us, and [the Department for Education] took all the children's social care branches ... When [CSCI] was created [the Department of Health was left] with a few lone voices that sort of struggled. [Denise Platt interview]

Annual Reports on the State of the Personal Social Services

David Behan was appointed as CSCI's first chief executive. Like Platt, he was a former director of social services and a past president of the Association of Directors of Social Services. He noted that:

The government of the day introduced the legislation [to establish CSCI] but it was Parliament that said 'This is what we want you to do?' and therefore our functions were derived from that ... It said you would account to Parliament on an annual basis through laying your report before Parliament and that was a powerful, powerful mandate. [David Behan interview]

The publication of an annual report on the state of the personal social services was not a novel idea. The Chief Inspector of Social Services had been producing and publishing annual reports since the beginning of the

1990s. In the final 2001–2002 chief inspector's report before she became founding chair of CSCI Platt wrote:

> The agenda for social services is to promote independence and life chances, to improve the protection of vulnerable people, and to raise the standards of social care. And there is evidence all around the country of improvements that are being made in local services ... Councils now need to make the innovative and new schemes the normal experience for people seeking assistance. [46]

It was only seven years later, in January 2009, that Denise Platt was the co-author of CSCI's final annual report [47] as the government had decided, in part to reduce the number of quangos, to merge CSCI with the Healthcare Commission (and the Mental Health Act Commission) into a Care Quality Commission (CQC) and CSCI having already in 2007 had its children's social services inspection responsibilities transferred to Ofsted.

Health and Social Care Integration

The merger of CSCI and the Healthcare Commission into the CQC reflected, in addition to its intentions to reduce the number of quangos, the government's ambitions to bring health and social care closer together. The reality for some time had been that social care had been seen as a means and a tool to help alleviate and ameliorate pressures in the NHS rather than being seen as a valuable and valid service in its own right and that the NHS would always be given the attention, priority and funding rather than social services. Platt commented:

> My experience was that people always thought health first and then how can social care support health. And the health and social care integration argument was at its fiercest around dealing with winter crisis [in the NHS] and delayed [hospital] discharges. [Denise Platt interview]

This is a view shared by David Walden:

We tried to get Wanless [when he was reviewing the NHS for New Labour] to look at health and social care as a single system and failed. I think that was because Gordon Brown who was the Chancellor and who basically ran domestic policy also shared the sort of 'not sure about local government, do we want to give them lots of money?' and just didn't see the interconnectedness. I think this was a seriously missed opportunity that we are still living with now because of the relative growth of health versus the relative lack of growth in social care. [David Walden interview]

In September 1998, just over a year after being elected, the government issued guidance on priorities for health and social services. It noted that "the Government recognises the complex causes of ill health and the part that economic and social factors have to play", that "tackling them involves a range of linked programmes across government" and "improvement in health will require the engagement of Local Authorities acting corporately across all their functions". Particular attention was given to "bringing together health, social services, and local government more widely, as well as integrating services" [48].

At the same time a circular was issued to Health Services and Local Authorities. Its first paragraph emphasised "the interdependence of health and social care" and that "Health Authorities and Social Services Authorities will need to agree … local targets representing the contribution they will make to the national objectives and targets" set by the government, with local authorities given the lead responsibility for promoting "inter-agency working" [49]. Here was another attempt to bridge the gap and bring together health and social care which had started in the 1970s.

To give an impetus to joined-up working between health and social care the 1999 Health Act promoted three means through which the NHS and local authorities might work together—pooled budgets, lead commissioning, and integrated providers of health and social care services.

Unhelpfully, however, the 1999 Act also heralded another NHS reorganisation with Health Authorities to be replaced by Primary Care Trusts, adding complexity and fragmentation within health services, and with variation in the coterminosity which it achieved between PCTs as health service commissioners and local authorities. Some PCTS were too small to have the capacity to undertake the commissioning role, including commissioning district hospital services, and combined across PCTs or bought in the big management accountancy companies to do the commissioning.

Julie Jones was the social services director in Westminster. She recalled:

> What was happening around us was enormous upheaval. We went during my time as director from a health authority in the early days which we shared with Kensington and Chelsea to the three primary care groups [PCGs] that crossed both boroughs to two PCGs to, having to fight off that the PCT should be both boroughs, to a PCT that was then coterminous … but we were luckier than many during that [period] of NHS upheaval … it was a really horribly difficult time. [Julie Jones]

In addition to the introduction of the 1999 Health Act flexibilities Alan Milburn, secretary of state for health, and John Hutton, the minister for social care in the Department of Health, proposed and pushed forward the concept of care trusts. These were to be NHS health organisations which would have delegated and devolved responsibilities from local authorities to also provide social care services which were the statutory responsibility of the local authority. For a brief period at the beginning of the 2000s it looked as though this was the government's direction of travel.

It had its greatest impetus and impact in mental health services with local authorities transferring or seconding their mental health social workers to NHS Mental Health Trusts. In only one area, Torbay, was a long-lasting arrangement made with the establishment an integrated NHS health and social care trust which included hospital and community health services and the adult social care responsibilities and capacity of the local authority.

Other areas introduced different means of bringing health and social care services closer together, such as the appointment of a joint PCT and local authority chief executive in Herefordshire and the development of the integrated management of adult community health and social services teams in Wiltshire but with joint accountability to separate PCT and local authority senior managers.

Apart from the continuing arrangement in Torbay other initiatives were short-lived reflecting the fragility of arrangements which were undermined by the differing governance and financial arrangements for the NHS and local authorities. The more loosely structured virtual arrangements for children's trusts focused on shared strategic planning of health and social services for children were no less fragile and vulnerable to frequent NHS organisational changes and changes of local NHS leadership.

In the mid-2000s when Patricia Hewitt was the secretary of state for health the decree and demand from the government was that within one year all NHS organisations should achieve financial balance, an impossibility when the deficits and budget overspends of PCTs and community and hospitals trusts were extensive and historic. A consequence, however, was NHS retrenchment from integrated and joint arrangements and with evidence of cost-shunting to local authorities. The divide between health and social services had been described as a 'Berlin wall'. David Walden noted when interviewed that he 'used to say at conferences in the 2000s at least the Berlin wall got dismantled whereas ours didn't!'.

Delayed Hospital Discharge

Nowhere was the divide and tensions between health and social services more marked and immediate than where hospitals reduced the number of in-patient beds, shut down wards and closed whole community hospitals. This placed intense and increasing pressure on the remaining hospital beds and generated a fearsome focus on discharging patients quickly to free up the remaining beds.

Local authority hospital social workers who had had the role of being beside patients and their families at times of crisis generated by illness and helping with emotional and practical needs, now found their role skewed to focus on making hastily and often too-rushed arrangements for someone being discharged home alone or to their family carers. They were also having to seek placements in residential and nursing homes with patients given little or no time to make major life-changing decisions about where and with whom they were now to live.

Glasby noted in 2007:

> As hospital lengths of stay have reduced and as acute care has become more focused on those with the most complex needs, many older people are discharged from hospital quicker and sicker—that is, with greater health needs than once would have been the case. With fewer beds and more rapid throughput of patients, the safe and timely discharge of older people has become a key policy issue, promoting significant amounts of government guidance and creating substantial inter-agency tensions. [50]

The thrust to keeping older (and other) people out of hospital and if they were admitted to get them discharged quickly was a coherent script developed over several years from the late 1990s onwards and which was captured and contained in a stream of government statements and Green and White Papers [51, 52, 53]. It was a script based on a broader public health and well-being agenda to sustain and enhance the quality of life of an aging population [54, 55] with services to be more responsive and enabling [56] and assisting and promoting independence. Attention was also given to supporting carers with a cross-government policy statement issued in 2008 [57].

The script was delivered with some success, supported by increased funding for, in particular, the NHS. National Service Frameworks (NSFs) sketched out the route to be followed with government-defined priorities for service developments. Nationally determined performance targets were set and with performance of health and social services organisations separately monitored and reported. This, however, generated tensions as hitting a target for one organisation—such as shorter hospital stays—might shift the pressure to social services to get more people out of hospital more quickly.

There was also pressure to develop services which were alternatives to hospital admissions. As noted in the 2001 National Service Framework for older people:

> Older people will have access to a new range of intermediate care services at home or in designated care settings, to promote their independence by providing enhanced services from the NHS and councils to prevent

unnecessary hospital admission and effective rehabilitation services to enable early discharge from hospital and to prevent premature or unnecessary admission to long-term care. [58]

The push on reablement and intermediate care were positive initiatives. In the NHS and local authority personal social services it allowed occupational therapists, for example, to regain and re-shape their role to undertake direct work with younger and older disabled people to rebuild confidence and capacity rather than overwhelmingly and sometimes exclusively assessing and ordering aids for daily living equipment and redesigning living space. But in the absence of adequate funding to develop and sustain the new services which the government was demanding the government's agenda generated local tensions and sometimes conflict.

Personalisation

The continued and enhanced focus on the personalisation of health and social services was also potentially positive in allowing younger and older disabled more choice and control over how they lived their lives and how they wanted assistance to be provided. The personal social services were, as in the mid-1990s, at the forefront of this agenda.

The progress of personalisation was promoted by introducing the concept of 'individual' and 'personal' budgets. Disabled people (and carers) would have an explicit cash sum allocated to them which they could either take as a direct cash payment or it would be held as a nominal allocation by the local authority but with the disabled person able to direct how it was to be used. This latter opportunity tackled the issue of disabled people maybe not wanting the role and responsibilities of themselves having to arrange and purchase the assistance they needed but still having a say on how assistance and services were to be provided on their behalf. For people with a learning disability there was a particular initiative—'In Control'—which encouraged and enabled them to have more choice and control within their lives.

But all was not positive in pushing the personalisation agenda forward. There were two particular and related concerns. The first was that the process of determining the amount of money to be allocated to someone as a personal budget became increasingly proceduralised and bureaucratised. New systems were introduced, such as Resource Allocation Systems, to calculate how much money should be allocated (awarded) to someone based on the range of needs noted and captured in their assessment by a care manager [59]. As funding became more restricted, especially after 2010 and the politically chosen austerity policies of the Conservative and Liberal Democrat coalition government (discussed further in the next chapter), rationing of help and assistance became even higher profile [60], with Resource Allocation Panels of senior managers established in local authorities to seek to contain expenditure.

Secondly, for disabled people, such as those in receipt of direct payments, it meant that they became the rationer of the assistance and help they needed with personal budgets salami-sliced year-on-year as council budgets were reduced. Unlike, however, the closer of a day centre or care home the cuts to care through direct payments and personal budgets were not obvious and seen by the public-at-large. User-controlled organisations and centres for independent living, led and managed by disabled people, sought to expose the impact of the cuts but their voice was diminished, and in some areas silenced, as the funding they received from local authorities was also cut and curtailed.

Personalisation, however, was and is not only about money and funding. It was also about challenging and changing paternalistic and patronising attitudes towards disabled people and re-shaping the understanding of social workers and others who might have paid roles in working with disabled people [61]. The focus was to be on facilitating, enabling and being an ally, working in partnership with disabled people—what became termed 'co-production'—to enhance assistance and help rather than the provision of what could be disempowering and stifling care.

Funding Tensions Between Health and Social Services

The role of the personal social services, however, often seemed to be as much, indeed more, about assisting the NHS with its pressures than with helping disabled people and people with long-term illnesses. Indeed, there was research which demonstrated that as well as enhancing the life experiences of older people targeted investment of £1 in local partnerships including adult social services would save £1.20 in hospital and health service costs [62]. It was not a finding, however, which attracted much traction in gaining funding for adult social services.

Some of the NHS pressures were self-inflicted as a consequence of seeking to make savings by closing too many hospital beds, with too few beds planned and provided in new hospitals, and with poor workforce planning leading to staffing shortages. Other pressures were the consequence of continuing changing demography with many more (much) older people and younger people with severe impairments and chronic conditions. But when additional funding was made available for adult care within the personal social services it was often routed through local NHS organisations rather than direct to local authorities, and with the requirement that it ameliorated the pressures on hospitals.

Year-on-year, with no sensible long-term planning, 'winter pressures' funding would be announced in the late autumn as a response to escalating concerns about hospital accident and emergency departments and in-patient wards being full and overwhelmed, with fingers crossed that there would not be a major influenza epidemic. Slightly more sensibly than ad hoc 'winter pressures' funding, 'whole systems (additional) funding' was provided to be allocated and used to deliver joint local health and social services plans but again, in part, to tackle NHS pressures.

Much less sensibly, a power was given to hospitals to levy 'fines' (reimbursements) on local authorities for each day someone's discharge from hospital was seen to be due to lack of personal social services action and capacity. Platt noted:

> When the government got the reimbursement policy in place it felt it had sorted it. Well, of course, it's still there … People not being discharged from hospital was never one-sided as it's quite a lot about continuing health care and continuing health care funding. [Denise Platt interview]

But there was also a lack of local authority funding, for example, to purchase more care and nursing home places. Fining local authorities only made the situation worse by reducing further the social services money which was available to provide assistance—albeit the money paid in fines to hospitals could be and was used to reduce the hospital's bottom-line overspend. It was also not a sensible way forward as the process of collecting and reporting data on delayed discharges (which was also termed 'bed blocking') locally and nationally every week was complex and itself costly.

Herbert Laming noted:

> One of the things that I used to say ad nauseum to ministers and to health service managers is that you will never achieve your objectives for the health service without effective social care. At first I think that was not taken seriously until bed-blocking became a real big issue. But unfortunately their response was to blame social care, social care is not doing its job etc etc. It took a long time for people to understand that it is only through effective teamwork and proper planning and a more flexible use of budgets that you can actually do this. And actually the scape-goating of social care just created a defensiveness that meant it is worse not better. I think there was a lot of ground lost at that time of scape-goating. [Herbert Laming interview]

Adult Abuse and Safeguarding

The focus on delayed discharge skewed the work of hospital and other adult care social workers where, as noted earlier, the priority was on quick and rushed discharge planning and action. Another skew during the 2000s was the increasing attention given to adult abuse with the requirement and reality that for social workers, such as those within community teams for people with learning disabilities, more and more time was spent on risk assessments and risk management, mirroring as noted below similar trends in children's social services.

In June 1999 Mencap reported [63] that nearly nine out of ten people with a learning disability had been bullied in the past year. This was followed in 2000 by government guidance on developing multi-agency policies and procedures to protect vulnerable adults from abuse [64]. This was the start of a journey for adult safeguarding which reflected the 30 year development of child protection policies, procedures and practice.

In 2008 the Commission for Social Care Inspection noted that there was 'uneven progress in the development of effective arrangements by councils' and that 'actions to help prevent abuse and support better outcomes for people who have experienced abuse are variable within and across council areas and within individual care services' [65]. In the absence of a statutory adult safeguarding framework the Association of Directors of Social Services (ADSS) took the lead in developing 'A National Framework of Standards' for adult protection work, with the standards including that every local authority establish a multi-agency partnership, policy and procedures as well as each agency having its own internal guidelines [66].

There was a perceived tension [67, 68] between adult safeguarding and the thrust that disabled people should have more choice and control in their lives which included being able to live independently and to take decisions for themselves. This created some concern for social workers, social services managers and others who might be the target of blame if they had not taken action to protect someone from risky decision-making. As Manthorpe noted in 2014, drawing on the argument of Carr [69], 'person-centred working would also have to take on board one of the tenets of risk enablement—that things will indeed go wrong at times (otherwise it is not a risk but a certainty)'! [70].

The tensions within safeguarding and personalisation were reflected in the relationship between the right to choose and what might be termed the right to be protected. For example, in the 2001 'really useful guide' to the government's strategy paper 'Valuing People' it is stated that people with a learning disability 'have the same rights ... as everyone else' to 'having a relationship with friends or a partner, marrying, voting, having a flat or home, and living with the people you choose' [71]. On the other hand, CSCI in their 2008 study of the adult safeguarding arrangements had as one the main points that 'more must be done to ensure people who direct their own support on a daily basis are also able to benefit from appropriate and individually tailored safeguards' [65].

Much of the concern about adult abuse had been—and is—about the abuse of disabled younger adults and older people in care and nursing homes and hospitals. For example, in 1998 there was an inquiry into the abuse of residents in two private care homes in Buckinghamshire run by Longcare Ltd [72], and in 2006 there were reports of abuse in supported housing and hospital services run by Cornwall NHS Partnership Trust [73]. The focus on institutional abuse has continued with undercover reporters exposing abuse in, amongst others, Winterbourne View, a private learning disability hospital in South Gloucestershire [74], and private care homes for older people in Essex and South London [75].

Every so often, if rarely, there is national media coverage of the abuse of a disabled adult living independently in the community or within their family. Two such events attracted media coverage in the mid-2000s. The first was about the killing in 2006 of Steven Hoskins, who had a learning disability, in St Austell in Cornwall [76]. The other was about the death of James Hughes, a young man with profound learning difficulties, and the suicide of his mother, Heather Wardle, in 2008 in Redditch, Worcestershire [77]. Both raised questions about the actions of, and the capacity and resources available to, local authority personal social services.[3]

It was the issue of personal 'capacity' which led to the 2005 Mental Capacity Act and its implementation in 2007. There had been a review of the law triggered in part by a legal case about whether someone who it was deemed could not make a judgement for herself could and should be sterilised. In the period between the passing of the Act and its implementation, the Act was amended to take on board the implications of the 'Bournewood Judgement' concerning a 49-year-old man with autism who was being prevented by a NHS Trust from leaving Bournewood House, a part of St Peter's Hospital in Chertsey, Surrey.

---

[3] I had roles in relation to inquiries following the deaths of Steven Hoskins and of James Hughes and Heather Wardle. I undertook a 3 month long independent management inquiry for Cornwall County Council following the killing of Steven Hoskins. I was appointed by West Mercia Police to work with them over a period of six months during their inquiries into the deaths of James Hughes and Heather Wardle and submitted a report to the Coroner.

Deprivation of Liberty Safeguards

The 2007 Mental Health Act amended the 2005 Act by introducing the statutory requirement that 'deprivation of liberty safeguard' assessments (DOLS) were to be undertaken to ascertain if someone had capacity to take decisions for themselves or whether someone (a Best Interest Assessor) should determine whether restricting their liberty is necessary and in their best interest. This was extended in 2014 following the Supreme Court judgement in relation to an older person in residential care in the area of Cheshire West Council, with its Deputy President, Baroness Hale,[4] concluding:

> Because of the extreme vulnerability of people [such as those considered in this case] I believe that we should err on the side of caution in deciding what constitutes a deprivation of liberty in their case. They need a periodic independent check on whether the arrangements made for them are in their best interests. [78]

At a stroke the Mental Capacity Act and DOLS workloads of local authority adult social services Best Interest Assessors were dramatically increased, as will be shown in the next chapter. Older people living in care and nursing homes with, for example, dementia became the subjects of DOLS and Best Interest Assessments to determine if they could decide for themselves where they should live and whether the care arrangements were in their best interest.

Mental Health Risk and Reform

Inquiries and concerns in the 1990s and 2000s about people with mental health difficulties [79, 80], however, tended to move the personal social services and the work of social workers in a different direction. The focus

---

[4] Baroness Hale was to become the first female President of the Supreme Court. As Brenda Hoggett in the 1980s, when a law lecturer and barrister and a member of the Law Commission's review of public and private law related to children, she was influential in shaping the 1989 Children Act (see Chap. 9).

was not on safeguarding the person with a mental disorder but protecting the community from the potential threatening and dangerous behaviours of the person with the disorder. More powers and services were created to monitor and manage people with a mental disorder in the community. This included the introduction of compulsory community treatment orders, supervised discharge orders, and more intensive assertive outreach services.

The 2007 Mental Health Act was the culmination of many attempts by the government to reform mental health legislation for England and Wales, and in particular to tackle concerns about risks to the public posed by people with a serious mental disorder living in the community. As noted by the King's Fund, the process started in 1998 within the first year of the New Labour government:

> First indications of a reform of legislation came on 1 January 1998 with the publication of the government's Mental Health Policy: Safe, sound and supportive (Department of Health 1998). In this, Secretary of State for Health, Frank Dobson, wrote, 'care in community has failed' because 'it left far too many walking the streets, often at risk to themselves and a nuisance to others'. The law was to be updated to ensure that patients who were considered a danger to themselves or others could not refuse to comply with treatment and to permit the detention of people with dangerous, untreatable psychiatric disorders. [81]

It was another nine years, however, before new legislation passed into statute in July 2007, and only after a consultative Green Paper in 1999, a White Paper in 2000 with firm reform proposals, a draft Mental Health Bill in 2002, a revised Mental Health Bill in 2004, a critical House of Commons and House of Lords report on the draft Bill in 2005, and the final Bill which was introduced in 2006 and was passed into statute in July 2007 [81]. The rebalancing of rights and risks within mental health legislation was contentious.

The new legislation led to a re-patterning of mental health services. Although the numbers of mental health in-patients in England and Wales reduced from 32,100 on 31 March 2001 to 22,700 in 2011, the numbers who were compulsorily admitted during the year increased during this period from 23,100 to 31,800. In addition, in England (the figures were not recorded for Wales) at the end of March 2011 there were 4500 people outside of hospitals subject to compulsory treatment orders [82].

A further change introduced by the 2007 Mental Health Act could also be seen to be related to the management of risk. It was social workers who had held statutory responsibilities to both safeguard the rights of people with a mental disorder and to take decisions and actions to tackle risks they might pose to themselves or others. Under the 1959 Mental Health Act, they were called mental welfare officers and the 1983 Mental Health Act re-badged them as Approved Social Workers (ASWs). The 2007 Act, however, replaced ASWs with Approved Mental Health Practitioners (AMHPs) and opened up this role to others such as nurses and psychologists, although in practice it is mental health social workers who largely undertake the AMHP role [83, 84]. In part this is because the role is still within the legal remit of local authorities but also it might be suspected and expected that other professionals are not rushing to take on the potentially high profile, and high blame, role of risk assessment and risk management.

New Labour and Children's Personal Social Services

It was the handling of risk, and the response to press, public and political responses when there was media coverage of the deaths of children following neglect and abuse, which came to shape much of New Labour's attention to children's social services. Initially, however, the government included children' services within its reforming zeal and showed determination to improve the well-being of all children.

The direction of travel for children's services was similar to New Labour's policies for other public services. First, there was the intention to be hands-on and to drive change from central government. Second, there was to be a focus on addressing social exclusion through the input and impact of universal as well as selective targeted services. Third, this was to be assisted by joining-up and integrating services. Fourth, there was to be increased funding and investment. Fifth, there was monitoring and reporting by central government of the impact of the better resourced public services, and actions to be taken by central government if performance was not improving. Sixth, it was this latter concern about performance and standards which led New Labour to continue the movement of the previous Conservative governments to allow public services to be placed in a market place which included the potential privatisation of children's services.

Quality Protects

An early New Labour initiative was 'Quality Protects'. Launched in 1998, it had its roots in the concerns which arose from the inquiries into the abuse of children in care homes and boarding schools such as the North Wales inquiry, the Staffordshire 'pindown inquiry', and the inquiry into abuse in children's homes in Leicestershire by Frank Beck and others (see Chap. 9). These led to the 1997 review by Bill Utting, the former social services chief inspector in the Department of Health, into the safeguards for children living in children's homes, foster care and boarding schools [85].

Initially planned for three year the Quality Protects programme was extended to five years. It was focused on improving the public care system for children requiring support and help from the personal social services, and especially the care provided for children looked after by local authorities [86]. It was funded through a £885 million Children's Services Special Grant which, among other initiatives, paid for regional development officers, training for residential child care workers, and post-qualifying education and training for social workers. This was also promoted by the creation of regional post-qualifying (PQ) consortia of social work employers and social work education providers within each region. It spawned and supported, for example, the PQ1 training for newly qualified social workers and specialist advanced awards in in social work for those working in children's and in adults services.

The 'Quality Protects' programme also included the development of key indicators for children in care, such as the number of placement changes in a year, and promoted the focus on quality of life and outcomes for children, such as educational attainment and health reviews as well as their safety. In particular, it introduced the concept of local authorities as 'corporate parents' where it was not only the responsibility of the social services department to care for and enhance opportunities for children looked after but that this should also be within the scope and remit of the council overall. Casting the responsibility more widely within local authorities for improving the life chances for looked after children was prompted by the 1998 experience that 75% of looked after children left school with no academic qualifications and over half of young people leaving care after age 16 were unemployed [87].

These issues along with others were the focus of the 2000 Children (Care Leavers) Act. It was an Act which gave local authority social services the responsibility to prepare pathways plans with young people leaving care, to provide personal advisors to help young people who were leaving or had left care, and to continue to be in touch with and to assist the young person until the age of 21 (later extended to up to 24 years). Particular aspects to be addressed were to include education, training and employment, and accommodation, with financial assistance to be within the menu of help which could and should be provided.

The 2000 Act was influenced by the research and writings of, especially, Mike Stein, a professor of social work at York University [88, 89]. It was an Act which followed the canvassing and campaigning by young people through initiatives such as the Who Cares magazine and trust, created in the mid-1980s by Tory Laughland, a social worker in the London Borough of Westminster [90]. It is now known as Become [91]. It was pre-dated by a charity, Voice for the Child in Care, started in 1975 by Gwen James, another social worker, and which is now Coram Voice [92].

Child and Family Poverty

The New Labour focus on the welfare and well-being of children was not confined, however, to children in local authority care. For example, between 1997 and 2010 there was demonstrable success, as noted by the Institute for Fiscal Studies, in reducing child and family poverty and poverty for older people:

> Labour had very clear objectives to reduce poverty amongst families with children and pensioners, and accorded these objectives high priority. Tony Blair made a famous commitment to end child poverty within a generation, and Gordon Brown promised to 'to end pensioner poverty in our country' ... Both absolute and relative measures of income poverty fell markedly among children and pensioners. [93]

Particular attention was given by New Labour to help for families with young children through, for example, the introduction in the UK in 2007 of Family Nurse Partnerships with regular contact by specially trained nurses with mothers aged under 24 until their children were 2 years old [94]. This was an evidence-informed policy initiative with Family Nurse Partnerships having been well researched in the USA [95].

Sure Start

Another, and larger, earlier evidenced-informed New Labour import from the USA was Sure Start. It was launched in the UK in 1998 by Tessa Jowell, who was then minister for public health in the Department of Health. She was a former social worker who had worked as a child care officer and psychiatric social worker before becoming assistant director of MIND, the mental health charity. When Sure Start was introduced in the UK it was seen as a public health initiative which crossed the responsibilities of government departments and with the aim of reducing early childhood inequalities.

Naomi Eisenstadt was the national director of Sure Start. She had worked in children's day nurseries and been the chief executive of Family Service Units. She and Norman Glass—a senior Treasury civil servant—were the champions who shaped and promoted Sure Start.

The development and expansion of Sure Start moved through several phases. It was initially a joined-up programme of help and assistance for families with young children in the poorest areas:

> It was working with children and parents and [as such] was two dimensional. It was persistent and multi-layered in terms of working across health, social care, education and the community, housing and employment. It was flexible at the point of delivery and one of the key features was that the local programme boards had to engage local parents and have parents on the board. And we were very outcome driven and had our own Public Service Agreement [with government]. So a key feature was a tight-loose kind of management where everyone is working to the same set of outcomes but given the diversity of provision in any particular neighbourhood the way in which you reached those outcomes had to be different … The whole point was about joining together what was already there and building on it so no area would have the same set. And it was an area-based initiative for all children in the area. [Naomi Eisenstadt interview]

As Sure Start was seen as a success it was rolled out to other areas with high rates of poverty and when in 2004 the government published a Ten Year Strategy for Child Care it included the policy to roll out Sure Start to all 3500 communities in England. This had implications for the management of Sure Start.

When first introduced Sure Start Local Programmes (SSLPs) received their funding direct from central government and their management and accountability was through a local Partnership Board which would report to the Sure Start national unit. Naomi Eisenstadt noted:

> The Board would have representation from all key statutory services, as well as any voluntary-sector providers in the area and, most importantly, local parents. The Board would identify a 'lead body' to be the key contact organisation for all partners and an 'accountable body' to handle the finance for the development of the programme. From the very beginning,

David Blunkett held the view that the lead body should not be the local authority. Ministers were very keen that the lead body role should be played by voluntary-sector organisations. In the event ... the vast majority were local authorities. [96]

Local authorities took on the role of "accountable bodies" primarily because they could use existing back office services and it reduced the administrative overhead costs of the SSLPs, and as Sure Start was expanded to many more areas after 2004 local authorities increasingly became responsible for its local delivery, albeit not as a directly managed local authority service.

But why were ministers not wanting local authorities to have the lead role in managing Sure Start? Eisenstadt recalled:

[Ministers] were absolutely enchanted with the voluntary sector ... They were very hostile to local government and to social work. It was perceived to be based on a deficit model and much more about family dysfunction and not about systems reform, and one of the things that was very prominent in the modernising agenda was this notion of [and concern about] 'provider capture' and professional ideology that was driven by the profession and not by users. All of those features I think were very key and made ministers hostile to social work. [Naomi Eisenstadt interview]

Hilton Dawson was a Labour MP at the time. He was formerly a social worker and social work manager and would later be chief executive of BASW. He noted:

My utter, utter frustration was that from Tony [Blair] down ministers completely undervalued social work, did not see it as important, and often saw it as a hindrance and a nuisance. I think in some ways they saw social work as something which presented challenges which apparently the government didn't at the time welcome and was seen as irrelevant to a really strong focus on outcomes. [Hilton Dawson interview]

At least five the interviewees for this book who were in key roles in the early 2000s separately commented that New Labour was hostile to, or at least not convinced about the effectiveness of, social work. In particular,

Margaret Hodge (who was minster for children), Paul Boateng (who was the Treasury minister who coordinated the preparation of the Every Child Matters policy paper) and David Blunkett (who was Home Secretary with the Home Office leading on Sure Start) were all seen as antagonistic to social work and kept it on the margins of developments.

Sure Start itself was much broader than social work and even broader than the responsibilities of the Department for Education. Naomi Eisenstadt commented that in its initial conception "it was very much an anti-poverty programme … It was the sort of girls' version of regeneration. Re-generation was always about roads and industry and all that, and the girls version was all about children". This in part explains why Sure Starts ministerial responsibility was initially located as a public health responsibility in the Department of Health rather than an early years child care responsibility in the Department for Education.

A similar point about the broader children's remit that was needed was made by Beverley Hughes:

> When I was both Minister for Children and Minister for the North West I started to have round table meetings with local authority chief executives to say, "Look, you need a link in what you are trying to do for children and young people squarely into your macro-economic regeneration strategies because otherwise you'll end up being able to show some headline improvements but actually your're not touching the children that need it most." [Beverley Hughes interview]

Every Child Matters

Sure Start was an example of seeking to provide less stigmatising and more accessible and acceptable universal services available to all young children and their parents, and which would then also benefit children where families were in difficulty or might be struggling to parent well. This was also the ethos of the Every Child Matters (ECM) Green Paper [97].

Its development was initially led by Beverley Hughes as the communities minister in the Home Office as "much more needed to be done to see children and families in a holistic way … with a much stronger integration of services … and a much stronger focus on prevention as well as early intervention" [Beverley Hughes interview].

The Green Paper was then taken forward in 2003 by Margaret Hodge when she was appointed to the new post of children's minister established in the Department for Education. As the leader of Islington Council in the 1980s she had driven the development of cross-service and multi-professional neighbourhood teams each with a general neighbourhood manager (see Chap. 9), and this joined-up approach was evident within the ECM agenda.

The ECM agenda had a focus on five outcomes for children … be healthy, stay safe, enjoy and achieve, make a positive contribution, and achieve economic well-being. Eisenstadt commented that 'some of the Sure Start principles were taken on board by ECM, and some of the new ECM principles would solve some of the big problems Sure Start was having' [Naomi Eisenstadt interview] such as getting agencies to share information and the introduction of the Common Assessment Framework later critiqued by Sue White and colleagues as 'top-down governance of practice' [98].

The Green Paper stated that 'to support local integration, the Government has created a new Minister for Children, Young People and Families in the Department for Education and Skills to co-ordinate policies across Government' [99]. It also heralded the creation of the statutory post of director of children's services in every local authority in England, a lead councillor for children, and Area Child Protection Committees were to be replaced with Local Safeguarding Children's Board with a wider remit beyond, but to include, child protection.

Hilton Dawson recalled:

> There was an inspirational agenda around issues such as ending child poverty and ending social exclusion. There was a huge, huge concern for putting a very clear focus on children and on integrating children's services. This accorded so much with my experience as a social worker and social work manager of often having to fight with the education department even within your own local authority and certainly fight with health for a proper resource and proper focus and emphasis on children. [Hilton Dawson interview]

Victoria Climbie Inquiry

In the midst of the development of the Every Child Matters agenda there was a particular media story which was to have especial traction and impact for local authority children's social workers and council's personal social services.

In February 2000 in Haringey in north London eight-year-old Victoria Climbie died as a consequence of sustained and intense neglect and abuse whilst in the care of an aunt and the aunt's boyfriend. In January 2001 both were found guilty of her murder. The Inquiry into Victoria's death, to be chaired by Lord Laming, a former director of social services in Hertfordshire and chief social services inspector in the Department of Health, was announced in April 2000 and started in May 2001.

The Climbie Inquiry [100] found significant failings in practice, in communication, and in management and leadership across and between all agencies, including the top management of the council's social services department. It concluded with 108 recommendations. None recommended the demise and disaggregation of local authority social services departments and directors of social services. Indeed, twenty four of the Inquiry's recommendations were specifically and explicitly addressed to directors of social services. These were largely about clarifying and confirming the clear accountability of the directors for the services for which they had responsibility. There was also the recommendation for a named lead councillor to have political accountability for statutory children's social services within the local authority.

2004 Children Act

The Laming Report, however, was erroneously seen as the primary generator of the 2004 Children Act. The statutory changes it introduced flowed from the Every Child Matters agenda which were already in train before the Climbie Inquiry reported. Hilton Dawson commented that '[The Climbie Report] helped to develop threads which were already there and which were developing in any case' [Hilton Dawson interview] and Beverley Hughes noted:

The [ECM] Green Paper, the Children Act legislation which followed, and the restructuring [within local government] very much reflected a direction of travel that had started a long time before ... I certainly feel that the work that Herbert [Laming] did both accelerated and clarified the need for further change but the journey in thinking had started before. [Beverley Hughes interview]

This was also commented upon by Paul Ennals.[5] He had a background in residential child care and working with disabled children and their families, and in the early 2000s was chief executive of the National Children's Bureau with a brief to work collaboratively across sectors and organisations on behalf of children. Ennals commented:

It is a mistake to think that 'Every Child Matters' was entirely driven by the Victoria Climbie Inquiry. It was driven by the failures in the child protection system at the time but it simply chimed with what was already happening in other parts of children's services, recognising the lack of join up. [Paul Ennals interview]

He noted that that the joined-up agenda had already been moving ahead in services for disabled children, and he commented that there was a particular champion in the civil service, Tom Jeffery, for joining up services for children.

The 2004 Children Act required local authorities to create the statutory post of director of children's services and to bring together local authority responsibilities for schools and education with its responsibilities for children's social services. The consequence in most local authorities was the creation of a department of children's services and a separate department of adult social services.

Paul Ennals viewed the creation of local authority children's services as constructive and positive but he reflected:

The restructuring process in local government was, on balance, too fast and didn't allow some changes to emerge in alignment with local needs ... and

---

[5] Paul Ennals was the son of David Ennals who between 1976 and 1979 was Labour's Secretary of State for Health and Social Services.

there wasn't sufficient focus on building up the skills set of the new joined up directors to cover those areas in which they didn't have experience. [Paul Ennals, interview]

David Behan, who was in the future to hold the posts of chief executive of CSCI and of the Care Quality Commission and to be director general of social care in the Department of Health, was president of ADSS in 2002–2003. He commented that 'I was of the view at the time that it was the right thing to do to create a separate children's service … and to search for coherence around all children's services' but:

Structural change by itself will not change attitudes and behaviours, and the real change that is going to be secured in children's services is by professionals working together in a different way than they have done to date. [David Behan interview]

With two existing chief officers to be found roles in the new arrangement the default position was that the director of education (with a background in teaching or education administration) became the director of children's services (DCS) and the director of social services became the director of adult social services (DASS). In most local authorities in England (devolution meant that the 2004 Act did not apply in Wales) by 2006 children's personal social services were no longer led by someone with experience and qualification grounded in the personal social services and in social work. Some local authorities appointed a joint director of children's and adults' services and maintained one adults and children's department which now also included responsibilities for schools and education, and over time more and more local authorities came to appoint DCSs who were social workers but, in essence, the 2004 Act signalled the end of social services departments in English local authorities (there are still social services departments in Wales and social work departments in Scotland). This was not the intention of Lord Laming and his 2003 report:

I can't claim any credit for the separation of adult services from children's services. That was a step beyond me and that was a government initiative. Whether that will prove a good thing in the long term I don't know …

There was nothing in the Victoria Climbie report that was a stimulus to that, so that came from elsewhere … It wasn't driven in consultation with me. I was not part of that. [Herbert Laming interview]

He continued:

And I'll tell you what my concern is about it, which is that about 80 per cent of the budget for children's services is hypothecated [to schools]. If you have only about 20 per cent which is free to play with and that happens to be the 20 per cent which deals with the social care of children and you're required to produce 3 per cent efficiency savings each year, I feel extremely worried about it. [Herbert Laming interview]

In 2009 Roger Singleton was appointed by the government as its children's safeguarding advisor and to oversee what was established as the National Safeguarding Delivery Unit. But after a change of government in 2010 the Unit was disbanded and Singleton resigned and his post too was abolished. He commented:

I don't know whether children are better protected as a result of the 2004 Act. My guess is probably not … In terms of improving practice at the front line I'm dubious about changing structures … and I do think some of what I would call wisdom and competence of knowing about the front line and being close to it has been lost in some places. If you were a director of education you weren't close to your front line because it was the head teachers who were on your front line. [Roger Singleton interview]

The abolition of social services departments and of directors of social services was not an obvious response to the Climbie Inquiry findings and recommendations. It was, however, a direction of travel flagged by the ECM agenda of joined up public services for children. Three reflections on this major step change of separating children's and adult's social services.

First, it was a change introduced by the government which was also initiating a process which was to lead to the removal of schools from any local management or influence. It was New Labour which introduced the concept of 'academy schools' which would be outside of local government's education remit. The initial intention was that this would be a means of improving schools that were judged to be performing poorly by Ofsted, the national schools inspectorate. They would be given independence from local authorities and would receive funding direct from the Department for Education. They were to be adopted and controlled by commercial and charitable organisations who would provide expertise and resources intended to lead to the academy schools' improvement. A threshold was crossed by New Labour. No longer would schools necessarily be a local authority responsibility and provision, reflecting the view at the centre of the New Labour government that public sector professionals and public sector provision and management were not efficient or effective compared to a commercial and private sector market place.

Secondly, although the provision and support of schools was to be a declining local authority responsibility, local authorities still prioritised education—at least initially—when deciding on the senior management of children's services. Local authority councillors had schools within their electoral wards, all (or at least most) children went to their local schools so it was a major interest to their electorate, and many councillors had had experience as school governors. By contrast, the work of the personal social services with children and families was largely unseen and unrecognised and not seen as a major local political concern or community interest. The profile of the personal social services for children and families diminished, at least for a time, with the abolition of social services departments.

Thirdly, it largely went unacknowledged that the local authority leadership requirement and role for children's social services was different from that which had been required for schools. Schools were actually within the leadership of head teachers accountable not to the local authority but to the school's governing body. Leadership from the local authority was through earned influence with head teachers, strategic planning and delivery of the overall school provision within a local authority area, and through advice and development services to schools. But even this latter local authority engagement with schools was to diminish as local authorities could no longer retain funding for school advisory and support services. Schools could chose to use their funding as they wished with no requirement that they would pay for any services from the local authority.

Naomi Eisenstadt commented on the different leaderships required from within local authorities for education and children's social services:

> The way it was described to me by a senior civil servant was that the skills you need to be a chief education officer are about a helicopter view and hiring really great head teachers and letting them get on with it. The skills you need to be a director of social services are about detail, detail, detail, and knowing the name of every child in care in your authority. And you don't get the same skills set in the same person. [Naomi Eisenstadt interview]

Fourthly, it did not require the breaking up of the personal social services to create more joined up and integrated local services for children. Indeed there is no evidence that this has been achieved. There are, however, long-lasting examples of inter-agency and multi-professional services for children and families. They have not been the consequence of major organisational structural change. Instead family intervention projects [101] targeted to tackle anti-social behaviour and which were to be extended as the Troubled Families programme by the next Conservative-led coalition government [102], youth offending teams (YOTS), child and adolescent mental health services (CAMHS), and integrated early years services, and more recently multi-agency safeguarding hubs (MASH), have been created by separate agencies seconding staff to joint teams with an agreed common service manager.

A consequence of the 2004 Children Act has not only been the fragmentation of the personal social services. It also created the opportunity which was taken by 2010 Conservative and Liberal Democrat coalition government to fragment social work. Naomi Eisenstadt in 2010 anticipated but did not welcome this development:

> I would be *very* upset about a split in the [social work] profession between children and adults. There was a debate about it … if they are trained and are doing their best for the children they have to understand the adults. It has to be both, it can't be one or the other. [Naomi Eisenstadt interview]

One consequence of the creation of local authority children's services largely led by former directors of education was how risk to children came to be managed differently. Social workers who had become directors of social services would have had career-spanning experience in reflecting on and managing risk to children (and adults) without necessarily escalating actions to remove children from their families. But there was already a prime ministerial agenda to have more children adopted [103], with the publication in 2000 of a White Paper [104] and an Adoption Task Force to speed up adoptions.

The Story of 'Baby P' and Its Impact

It was, however, the media's coverage and response to the death of another child in Haringey which changed dramatically the response to risk to children. Peter Connelly was 17 months old when he died in August 2007 following abuse and neglect by the adults in his household. His mother, her boyfriend, and the boyfriend's brother in November 2008 were each found guilty of 'causing or allowing' Peter's death. In the initial reporting of the trial and its outcome Peter was called 'Baby P'.

The BBC and *The Sun* newspaper had been preparing their coverage of the case and were ready to launch the coverage as soon as there was the finding of guilt at the November 2008 criminal trial. The coverage targeted the social worker and her managers, along with a community paediatrician, with a front page headline in The Sun of 'Blood on Their Hands'. One person in particular, Sharon Shoesmith, Haringey's director of children's services, was the focus of media-generated vilification and threat with the very danger of violence to her and her family. This was also the experience of others named and with their photographs published by *The Sun*.

Within weeks Ed Balls, the secretary of state in what had been re-badged from the Department for Education to the Department for Children, Schools and Families (symbolic of the government's joined-up agenda for children), removed Sharon Shoesmith from her post as director of children's services in Haringey. It is now known that he was under considerable personal pressure from Rebekah Brooks, the editor of *The*

Sun, and other journalists to take this action [105], and also that his action was subsequently judged to have been inappropriate by the High Court which concluded Sharon Shoesmith had been scapegoated [106].

It was not only Mr Balls who might be seen to have caved in and crumbled under the media pressure. Mr Balls rejected the first serious case review, essentially because it did not allocate blame to workers in any agency for Peter's death. A second rushed SCR delivered what was being demanded by the press and politicians and airbrushed out reflections on the role and limitations of the police and health services and concluded that it was Haringey council and its children's services managers and workers who had performed poorly. Ofsted also quickly reversed its previous positive rating of children's services in Haringey, with it now known that Christine Gilbert, Ofsted's chief inspector, was closely engaged with senior civil servants at the time Ofsted u-turned on its Haringey rating. Haringey council itself within months dismissed its director of children's social services, head of children's social care, child protection policy lead officer, and the team manager and social worker for the Connelly family.

It was a purge under pressure from right wing tabloids such as *The Sun* and *The Mail,* and opposition politicians, including Mr Cameron who was leader of the Conservative opposition at the time, who sought to make political capital out of attacking a Labour local council and the Labour government. Tim Loughton was the Conservative shadow children's minister and he noted:

> David Cameron latched on to it for political reasons and bashed Gordon Brown. Ed Balls was secretary of state and I don't think the Education Department handled it very well ... Politics being politics it became rather more political so my job was really to say 'Look, we need to look beneath the headlines as to how the system allowed this sort of thing to happen' not 'Right, who is going to be the scapegoat, who are we going to blame?'. [Tim Loughton interview]

It is now known from a 2014 BBC TV documentary [107] based in part on a book I authored which tracked the 'Baby P' story and its impact [108], a book by Sharon Shoesmith [109], the High Court appeal into Sharon Shoesmith's sacking [106], and the Leveson Inquiry [110] into phone hacking and other misdemeanours by press reporters and their editors, that it was the symbiotic relationship between the police, press and politicians which could be seen to have led to the 'Baby P' story being skewed in its telling to attack social workers [111]. But whatever its genesis and motivations the impact of the 'Baby P' story on the child protection system across England was immediate and intense.

Within weeks applications for care proceedings by local authorities to seek the removal of children from their families had a step change [112]. Right through the child protection sequence of investigations, case conferences, child protection plans, care proceedings and children in the care (looked after by) local authorities rates of activity quickly increased. And as with the continuing telling and referencing by the press and other media of the 'Baby P' story over subsequent years (it is still referred to in coverage more than ten years later when other children are killed) the trends set under way by the media's shaping and telling of the 'Baby P' story have continued (as will be discussed further in the next chapter).

Social Work Task Force

One potentially positive consequence of the 'Baby P' story was the setting up by the government of a Social Work Task Force to review and advise on the recruitment, training, quality and status of social workers. It was chaired by Moira Gibb, a social worker by professional background, a former chair of BASW's children's and families committee, who had been director of social services in Kensington and Chelsea, and was now chief executive of Camden Council. Controversially, the government appointed *The Sun*'s 'agony aunt' columnist as a member of the Task Force [113], possibly reflecting the political imperative to keep the tabloids, and especially *The Sun* and its editor, on-side rather than undermining and attacking from the side-lines.

The Task Force engaged widely across the social work profession and beyond and its final report was produced within less than 12 months. The Task Force's recommendations included increasing the entry requirements to become a social work student, improving the quality and consistency of initial qualifying social work education and a national

framework for continuing professional development, a dedicated programme to train and support frontline managers, mapping what should
be expected and required of social workers with a process of licensing
based on acquiring and requiring specialist expertise, and standards for
employers to improve the working conditions of social workers.
Importantly, the Task Force concluded that the social work profession
should take control of its own standards, supported by a College of Social
Work which would also assist in improving the public understanding of
social work [114].

To follow through and implement the Task Force's recommendations,
which were accepted by the government, Moira Gibb was asked to chair
a Social Work Reform Board. It was to continue its work despite the
2010 change of government, as noted in the next chapter.

12

Coalition and Conservatives: Austerity and Hostility (2010–2020)

The 2010 general election resulted in a hung Parliament. The Conservatives had the largest number of MPs and after days of negotiation and uncertainty formed a coalition government with the Liberal Democrats. It was also open for the Liberal Democrats to have formed a coalition government with Labour but that was not the choice made by Nick Clegg and his Liberal Democrat MPs. Gordon Brown resigned as leader of the Labour Party and was replaced by Ed Miliband. David Cameron was the new prime minister with George Osborne as the chancellor of the exchequer and Nick Clegg as deputy prime minister.

The 2008 Banking Crisis

The General Election had been fought, in part, on the economic record of the New Labour government. It was a record which had been tarnished by the national and international banking crisis of 2008. It was a

© The Author(s) 2020, corrected publication 2021
R. Jones, *A History of the Personal Social Services in England*,
https://doi.org/10.1007/978-3-030-46123-2_12

crisis which started in the USA where subprime mortgages, which were above the actual value of properties amid falling property values, led to the collapse of two big mortgage lenders. It was a crisis which was further fuelled when it became known that investment instruments had been created where bad debt, including the mortgage debts, were bundled into investment packages and sold on between banks. In effect, the bankers had been recklessly gambling with the investments they held to drive big profits, big salaries and big bonuses [1, 2].

The investment vehicles which had been created were so multi-layered and complex that no one understood or knew about the real value of what was being traded between banks. When the scale of bank debt was realised and exposed the whole pack of cards quickly collapsed. Some banks closed and banks stopped trading with each other. Investors recognised their investments were at risk and there was a run on the funds held by banks as investors sought to quickly retrieve their vulnerable financial assets. Governments had to print money ('quantitative easing') and loan money to the banks to avoid further financial collapse and implosion.

This was not, however, how the story was told in the campaigning at the 2010, and indeed the 2015 and 2017, General Elections. Instead the Conservative campaign blamed the New Labour government's public service spending during the 2000s as having created what was an increasing national debt [3, 4].

Labour did indeed have some partial responsibility for the 2008 banking crisis. But it was not the public spending of the New Labour government which created the economic crisis. Rather it was New Labour's deregulation of the banks and of banking, and not stemming a bonus culture that enhanced the reckless behaviour of bankers [5, 6, 7]. New Labour's neoliberal deregulation activities had, in essence, continued the Thatcherite journey of the 1980s and 1990s, and it was to be continued by the Conservative and Liberal Democrat coalition government after 2010.

It was, however, Gordon Brown as the New Labour Prime Minister in 2008 and 2009 who led the international and national action to contain and then stem the banking crisis [8, 9] and David Sainsbury, who was chairman of Sainsbury, the grocery retailer, wrote in 2013:

The financial crisis of 2008 clearly raised very serious doubts about the economic theories underlying neo-liberalism. Also, after some thirty five years in which it has been the dominant political economy in the world, the time has come to evaluate the impact of neo-liberalism in terms of economic growth, inequality and financial stability. No one who lived through the 1980s will doubt that neo-liberalism has provided some valuable insights into how a complex modern economy should be managed, but in comparison with the period 1945 to 1975 [what had been termed the period of welfare state consensus] it has not performed well. [10]

And writing in 2009 in the midst of the banking crisis Paul Mason noted:

We have lived through an event most of us thought we would never see. Global capitalism, on the precipice of collapse, has been rescued by the state … Basically, neoliberalism is over: as an ideology, as an economic model. Get used to it and move on … It seems likely to me that social justice campaigners—again, probably against their inclinations—will now have to focus more on the state; that some form of big picture narrative will emerge that describes how the state intervenes to deliver social justice. [11]

This was not, however, how David Cameron and George Osborne with their Liberal Democrat coalition government colleagues represented and responded to the economic crisis caused by the bankers. Instead of seeking to deliver social justice they quickly moved to introduce a budget which targeted poor children, their families and working age adults (whilst largely protecting welfare benefits and pensions for older people). They set off on the journey which was maintained under the Conservative-led governments of Cameron, May and Johnson[1] throughout the next ten years of cutting funding for public services and, in particular, services provided by local authorities including personal social services. Alongside the cuts there was also a renewed and reinvigorated thrust to open up public services and public funding to a market place which favoured the

---

[1] It was particularly noteworthy that Boris Johnson as prime minister in 2019 appointed Sajid Javid as chancellor of the exchequer. Johnson was challenged about the appointment as it is alleged that as a senior investment banker with Deutsche Bank Javid had a key role in selling collateralised debt obligations (CDOs), one of the products central in creating the 2008 banking crash. He was now leading on the continuing cuts in public services and social security benefits.

profit-driven private sector. This too, as will be discussed below, has had its impact on the personal social services and social work.

Cuts in Welfare Benefits

The cuts in social security payments to the poorest children and families were made almost immediately following the 2010 general election:

> The newspapers make their predictions about the [leaked] budget. 'The most draconian in thirty years' is the view of the Daily Telegraph. 'The most brutal Budget in an generation' predicts the Financial Times … Welfare is highlighted in the Budget as it will be cut particularly heavily, by £11 billion—largely through changing the measure of inflation used for welfare payments from the retail price index (RPI) to the consumer price index (CPI)—a hugely significant change. [12]

Cuts in public expenditure were to make up 80% of the budget actions to reduce the government's deficit. But even where there was to be an increase in taxation it was by raising the rate of value-added tax (VAT) from 17.5% to 20%. VAT is a regressive tax which disproportionately hits and hurts the poor compared to, for example, progressive taxes on income and wealth.

This was only the start of changes in social security benefits and taxation which would target the poor whilst benefitting the rich. For example, the 2012 Welfare Reform Act introduced a benefits cap, the 'bedroom tax' which reduced housing benefit if there was a spare room in the property, and personal independence payments for disabled people. Each reduced the financial support available through welfare benefits, as well as passing to local authorities—where government funding was also being cut—the need to cut and ration council tax benefits and the Social Fund to make emergency payments to people who were destitute.

Even more perniciously, these cuts were followed by the introduction of Universal Credit, which merged a number of separate benefits. It was beset by administrative problems in its roll-out as well as the fundamental issue that it was not paid for the first six weeks of any claim, instantly throwing people into debt and difficulty. There was also the cap on payments to families with children with no increase in benefits payment if there were more than two children in the family. This was bound to increase and intensify family poverty as an obvious and anticipated consequence of the coalition government's policies [13].

The breadth and depth of the cuts in social security were supported by Liberal Democrat ministers and MPs, including Jo Swinson who was to become leader of the Liberal Democrats. It was reported that in the 2019 General Election campaign:

> During an interview with the BBC's Andrew Neil, Ms Swinson said she had been "wrong" to back the bedroom tax, which penalised welfare recipients with a spare room ... Ms Swinson said she believed that "too much was cut" as a result of the Coalition's austerity programme, adding: "Some cuts were necessary but the shape of those cuts and certainly the balance between cuts and tax rises I don't think was the right balance. I think we should have been raising more from taxation." [14]

The Funding of Adult Social Care

The cuts in social security which increased and intensified poverty were not the only economic policy which impacted on the personal social services. One issue in urgent need of attention but which remained unaddressed was the funding of social care for older (and younger) disabled people. The community care reforms of the early 1990s were, twenty years later, creating considerable difficulty and causing much distress.

As discussed in a previous chapter, the Griffiths Report on social care and the subsequent 1990 NHS and Community Care Act turned off the flow of social security payments for residential care and gave local authority social services the responsibility to assess and arrange care for those who were unable to pay for the care themselves. However, unlike the rights-based social security budget social services budgets were cash-limited and discretionary decision making was used to keep expenditure within the funding available. As central government cut its grant to local councils, whilst at the same time constraining them from raising council tax, rationing became more intense.

The King's Fund and Nuffield Trust in 2016 reported that between 2009/2010 (the last year of the New Labour government) and 2014/2015 (the years of the Conservative-Liberal Democrat coalition government) there had been a 37% reduction in central government funding to local authorities. Local authority gross expenditure on personal social services for older people fell by 9%, and the number of older people receiving assistance from local councils reduced by over a quarter. The largest reduction was in the number of older people receiving help while living at home—a fall of 30% between 2009/2010 and 2014/2015. There were similar, but not quite so large, cuts in help to disabled adults aged 18–65 years. The King's Fund and Nuffield Trust Report noted that:

> The social care system in its current form is struggling to meet the needs of older people. Six consecutive years of cuts to local authority budgets have seen 26 per cent fewer people get help. No one has a full picture of what has happened to older people who are no longer entitled to publicly funded care: the human and financial costs to them and those who care for them are mounting. [15]

The cuts in funding were not only an increasing problem for older and younger disabled people and family carers but were also creating significant difficulties for social care providers who, since the 1990s, had been mainly private companies

> Many social care providers are surviving by relying increasingly on people who can fund their own care, but those dependent on local authority contracts are in difficulty. Home care services face particularly acute workforce shortages and are now in a critical condition everywhere, threatening to undermine policies to support people at home. The possibility of large-scale provider failures is no longer of question of 'if' but 'when' and such a failure would jeopardise continuity of the care on which older people depend. [15]

The King's Fund and Nuffield Trust report concluded that:

Access to care depends increasingly on what people can afford—and where they live—rather than on what they need. This favours the relatively well off and well informed at the expense of the poorest people, who are reliant on an increasingly threadbare local authority safety net—especially if they live in areas where local authorities have been least able to sustain spending levels—and who are at a higher risk of declining quality and provider failure. [15]

'Provider failure' was not limited to the smaller private social care providers. After several years of asset stripping and big payments and profits to its owners, which included American private equity company Blackstone, Southern Cross in 2011 was unable to pay its creditors.

Southern Cross had grown from 70 care homes for older people to 750 care homes with 37,000 residents by 2011. There was a very real danger of the homes closing and alternative care having to be arranged quickly. This task would fall to local authority adult social services, although they would not have had knowledge of the self-funders who were the majority of Southern Crosses residents. What then happened was that the Southern Cross homes were sold on to other companies, including HC-One, itself a subsidiary of debt-laden NHP, which hardly made the future of the care homes more secure and safe [16]. In 2016–2017 the Southern Cross story of older people being left potentially stranded and vulnerable by a large private care home company was replicated by Four Seasons, another company with a dubious high risk financial and business model based on high levels of debt [17].

It was not only, however, the vulnerability of older people to the business failure of private care homes companies which was causing concern as there was also an increasing concern for those who were financially assessed as having the money to pay for the care they needed. Anyone in 2010 with £23,250 in assets was deemed able to pay their own full care costs. As the cost of residential and nursing home care increased this could significantly erode the savings and capital of someone who was a self-funder.

This was not a new or novel issue. As the population of older people increased, and with the greatest proportional increase for people aged over 80 years, it had been a demographic issue which was impacting during the years of New Labour governments and was projected as an increasing concern for the future.

There had been several attempts to tackle the issue, including in 1999 a Royal Commission on Long-Term Care chaired by Professor Sir Stewart Sutherland [18]. It recommended that personal care costs should be paid by the state and that housing and general living costs should be met by the person needing care, albeit subject to a means-test with £60,000 of capital being disregarded (the figure at the time for capital disregard was £16,000). But even within the Royal Commission there was dissent, with two commissioners taking the view that making personal care free would be too costly for the tax payer.

When the government responded a few months later it referred to the National Service Framework (NSF) for the care of older people and to its 'modernising social services' agenda but it did not accept or agree to the Commission's recommendation that personal care costs should be met by the state [19]. It subsequently decided that nursing care in residential and nursing homes should be funded by the state but not personal care. In 2003 the Royal Commissioners reviewed and reflected on the government's stance:

> There are still widespread concerns about the state of long-term care and its funding. By far the most important are the huge ethical, conceptual and practical difficulties in distinguishing between the 'nursing' and 'personal' care of ill and disabled people for funding purposes. The message of the Commission's Report was that attempting to do this would be full of pitfalls. [20]

This heralded, for example, the need to decide between whether assisting someone to bathe was a social bath or a health bath, and was the forerunner of local debates about the definition of continuing health care, which would be funded by the NHS, and social care, where the recipient would be means-tested to pay for the care.

Devolution across the UK's administrations also led to differences with in Scotland residential and nursing home care, and personal care provided within someone's home, being funded through taxation by the government [21], unlike in England, Wales and Northern Ireland, where mean-tests continued to be applied. It was, however, an issue which was seen politically as too-hot-to-handle as it would require increasing government revenue through some form of taxation, national insurance, or continuing and may be higher contributions from those receiving care.

Gordon Brown as prime minister attempted to tackle the issue at the 2010 general election with the proposal that there be deferred payments for care by self-funders which would be collected from their estate after their death. The Conservative's called this a 'death tax' and it was one of the political attacks on New Labour during the election campaign.

When the Conservative and Liberal Democrat coalition government came into office they initiated another review of how best to fund care and support for adults in England. The Commission on Funding Care and Support, was chaired by Andrew Dilnot, a former director of the Institute for Fiscal Studies. Alongside Andrew Dilnot as the other two members of the commission were two former directors of social services—Lord Norman Warner and Jo Williams.

The Dilnot Report was published in July 2011. It recommended that:

> Individuals' lifetime contributions towards their social care costs—which are currently potentially unlimited—should be capped. After the cap is reached, individuals would be eligible for full state support. This cap should be between £25,000 and £50,000. We consider that £35,000 is the most appropriate and fair figure. The means-tested threshold, above which people are liable for their full care costs, should be increased from £23,250 to £100,000. National eligibility criteria and portable assessments should be introduced to ensure greater consistency. [22]

The 'full state support' would be for the social care someone was assessed as needing. They would still be expected to pay their own living expenses—as with everyone else—which were anticipated to be between £7000 and £11,000 a year. But overall there would be a cap, a ceiling, on how much anyone had to pay for social assistance and support, protecting savings (and inheritance).

It was calculated that the annual cost to the state of these proposals would be £1.7 billion. The Commission was not specific as how this should be funded but it did conclude:

[The government] may decide to introduce a specific tax increase and, if it did so, it would make sense for this to be paid at least in part by those who are benefitting directly from the reforms. In particular, it would seem sensible for at least a part of the burden to fall on those over state pension age. If the Government decides to raise additional revenue, we believe it would be sensible to do so through an existing tax, rather than creating a new tax. [23]

Writing five years after the publication of the Dilnot Report Nick Taylor, who was a researcher with yet another Commission on Care, this time one established by the Political Studies Association, noted that:

Dilnot himself suggested that pensioners could start paying national insurance to meet the £2bn a year costs to the state—the first policy to earn the title of "granny tax". Liberal Democrat Paul Burstow, Minister of State for Care Services from 2010–2012, recommended in 2013 that the lifetime cap be raised to £60,000 and government costs be paid for by cuts to Winter Fuel Payments for wealthier pensioners and establishing a capital gains tax at death. Labour's Andy Burnham repeatedly proposed an estates tax of 10–15%, which was branded a "death tax" each time it was considered. [24]

Proposals which sought to share risk by raising funding from increasingly asset rich older people were anathema to each of the political parties who wanted the votes of an increasing older population, but with the population of older people not recognising or facing the reality that although it was a lottery whether they might avoid the need for assistance, many would require costly assistance:

The average person will need social care worth about £20,000 during their lifetime, with slightly more than a fifth of the population dying before they require any support. But for 10% of the population care costs are high: a couple with arthritis requiring residential care for the last 20 years of their lives will need care costing over £1m. [25]

In 2017 Theresa May when Conservative prime minister brought forward proposals at the general election that everyone receiving care and support with assets greater than £100,000 should be required to pay the full care costs whether in residential care or in their own home. The payment would be collected from their estate after their death and would include the value of their home, with £100,000 set as the 'floor' which would remain and not be taken into account in paying for the care they had received. This was quickly termed a 'dementia tax' by the Labour opposition and others. Within days there was a u-turn and the proposed policy was abandoned [26]. The grass into which the issue had been kicked was growing longer and longer and all the time the crisis in care was intensifying with NHS managers noting that it was the inadequate funding of social care which was now their major concern [27].

At the 2019 general election the Conservative and Liberal Democrat parties separately promised that if they formed the next government they would initiate a further review of the funding of care. Labour had a firmer proposal that, funded from general taxation, older people would not be charged for 'personal care' and that there would be an (unspecified) lifetime cap on the amount they would have to pay for the living costs element of residential care [28]. But in an election dominated by the Conservative slogan of 'Get Brexit Done', and lost amid a plethora of Labour manifesto policy proposals, the issue of funding care received little attention or traction.

Health and Social Care Divide

Alongside the continuing crisis in care funding was the still unresolved perennial concern about the separation and divide between health and social care services. The 2012 Health and Social Care Act claimed to 'liberate' the NHS but it promoted increased competition and private sector incursions into health services which were to add further complications in seeking to build local NHS and local authority partnerships [29]. It also sought to distance ministers and government from accountability for the NHS by creating NHS England as the NHS's leadership board.

In 2016 NHS England promoted 'sustainability and transformation partnerships (STPs)' some of which were later called 'integrated care systems' [30]. And there was a 'Better Care Fund' [31] to prompt shared planning, pooled budgets and integrated provision between NHS clinical commissioning groups, NHS health trusts and other health care providers. It looked remarkably like the attempts to bring health and social care together in the 1970s and 1980s through joint planning and joint finance, and in the 1990s and 2000s through 'winter pressures' and 'whole systems' funding. But as with the previous manoeuvres and mechanisms to narrow and span the health and social care divide it was marginal and minimal compared to the mainstream core concerns of local NHS organisations and local authority social services, and especially for local authorities in the context of significant reductions in government grant.

Terry Bamford, a former director of social services and chair of a NHS primary care group, noted in 2015 that the Better Care Fund 'is likely to be used where spending on social care will deliver improved outcomes for the NHS in terms of shorter bed stays for older people or enhanced community support preventing hospital admissions' [32]. He was right as evidenced by the 2019 NHS Plan Long Term Plan [33]. It once again subsumed discussions about the future for social care in a policy and guidance statement which was almost exclusively about the NHS and health care. Yet again, social care was only receiving attention as a solution to pressures within the NHS. And while the examples of health and social care integration using the Better Care Fund showed ingenuity and innovation they were hardly integral to the major and main workloads of either the NHS or social services [34].

England was not alone in using specific but limited pots of money to seek to stimulate local health and social care integration. Wales had its Health and Social Services Transformation Fund, which had the benefit of being more whole systems focused within Welsh regions than the isolated smaller scale initiatives scattered across England [35]. In Northern Ireland a 'Transformation Fund' has sought to deliver change through initiatives which covered the whole of the province [36]. In Scotland a rather different approach was been tried through establishing local NHS and local authority Integration Joint Boards rather than a separate fund to stimulate health and social services integration [37]. However, each country still has not found the magic potion which would bring together health and social services which were legislated for separately and differently as a part of the creation of the welfare state in the 1940s.

The 2010 Vision for Adult Social Care

The wider ambition being set for the personal social services was largely under the heading of 'well-being' agendas. In England in 2010 the then still new coalition government published its vision for adult social care. It was noted that:

> Frederick Seebohm, in his landmark 1968 report, said that social care should enable 'the greatest possible number of individuals to act reciprocally, giving and receiving service for the well-being of the whole community'. We need a return to these foundations. Care must again be about reinforcing personal and community resilience, reciprocity and responsibility, to prevent and postpone dependency and promote greater independence and choice. This vision cannot be achieved by Government alone. We need a social movement to form around these values, with different organisations and communities coming together to develop new ways of caring for people. All of us want a culture of dignity, respect and compassion deeply rooted in our communities. By working together towards this vision, we can make it happen. [38]

Here, however, was a vision for adult social care which was out of line with the Seebohm Report's recommendations for enhanced state-provided personal social services to assist and strengthen communities. But it was in line with Prime Minister Cameron's message about the 'Big Society', where it was to be individuals and communities rather than the state which should take on and shoulder responsibilities for what since the 1940s had largely been seen as within the remit of the state to shape and, at least in part, provide. In Mr Cameron's scenario it was for voluntary and charitable organisations and looser community networks to provide assistance without state funding.

Here was the ideological and political commitment which was to lead to the advent and expansion of food banks, baby clothing banks and volunteers running meals clubs for hungry children during school holidays—a modern day version of insecure and stigmatising alms for the poor. It has seen the emergence of 'holiday hunger' for children [39] and the overall average life expectancy of people, especially in more deprived areas, bucking the increasing longevity trends of the previous century and shortening [40].

For adult social care the vision was of a mix of personal, family and community commitment to provide care and support within the context of a shrinking and smaller state. The vision was based on six 'Ps': prevention ('empowered people and strong communities will work together to maintain independence'), personalisation ('individuals not institutions take control of their care'), partnership ('care and support delivered in a partnership between individuals, communities, the voluntary and private sectors, the NHS and councils'), plurality ('the variety of people's needs is matched by diverse service provision, with a broad market of high quality service providers'), protection ('sensible safeguards against the risk of abuse or neglect'), productivity ('improvements and innovation to deliver higher productivity and high quality care and support services') and people ('a workforce who can provide care and support with skill, compassion and imagination') [41].

The 2010 adult social care vision statement was followed in 2011 by the government launching a consultation on reforming care and support for disabled and older people [42] and then in 2012 by a White Paper 'Caring for Our Future: Reforming Care and Support'. The government stated that:

> Our vision is one that promotes people's independence and wellbeing by enabling them to prevent or postpone the need for care and support. We will also transform the system to put people's needs, goals and aspirations at the centre of care and support, supporting people to make their own decisions, to realise their potential, and to pursue life opportunities. [43]

Amongst the proposals were the extension of the right to a personal budget for those assessed as eligible for local authority assistance, a national minimum eligibility threshold so that people could transfer and transport their assessment across local authority boundaries, an increased right for assessments by disabled and older people and carers (based on the 2010 Carers Strategy [44]), more advice and information, and a capital fund of £200 million over five years to build more specialised housing for disabled and older people [45].

2014 Care Act

The 2014 Care Act was underpinned by the 'well-being principle' with a focus on prevention, early help and assistance in the community. It was generally well-received within the social work profession [46]. There were, however, concerns that there would not be the funding or the workforce to undertake an anticipated 500,000 increase in assessments [47] nor to meet the needs then identified. In many ways, however, the 2014 Act was legislatively catching up with developments in practice, especially in relation to personalisation and more responsive, flexible and adaptive help within communities [48].

The 2014 Act was passed into legislation with all party support and despite 'Labour leaders [believing] the reforms fall well short of a solution to the care crisis, they opted not to force the issue' [49]. In particular, there are two concerns about the Act and its implications and implementation.

First, it was stated in the Act that from 2016 people would have to pay the full costs of their care but only until their assets fell to £100,000. This section of the legislation has never been implemented. Secondly, there was a general concern that the government was not making additional funding available to councils to undertake and fulfil the new duties created within the Act. Indeed the Act came into force at the same time, as noted by Toynbee and Walker, that council funding was being cut:

> Council spending was disproportionately hit, cut by 29.1 per cent between 2010 and 2015 ... Despite an ageing, increasing population, and more people in hardship, by 2015 councils will be spending the same in cash terms as they did nine years ago, in 2006 ... visits to frail old people in their homes by underpaid care workers lasting only 15 minutes became notorious. [50]

The 2014 Care Act in England, underpinned by a general well-being principle and its promotion of personalisation and self-directed support, was matched and indeed proceeded by the 2013 Social Care (Self-directed Support) (Scotland) Act and the 2014 Social Services and Wellbeing (Wales) Act 2014. In Wales and Scotland the focus was on co-production and citizen-directed support unlike the focus on consumerism within personalisation in England. It was proposed that there should be a revision and updating of adult social care legislation in Northern Ireland [51, 52] but this was not taken forward as the Northern Ireland Assembly was suspended as a consequence of disagreements between its power-sharing leadership.

One aspect of the 2014 Act in England which was radical but received relatively little attention was that it empowered and enabled local authorities to delegate the social work functions of assessment and care planning and decisions about the provision and allocation of resources (but not adult safeguarding functions) [53]. Why was this radical? It meant that a local authority could now contract with NHS, for-profit and not-for-profit providers to undertake statutory adult social work tasks. It paved the way, for example, for Virgin Care and others to receive local authority contracts to provide statutory adult social work services in Bath and North East Somerset and elsewhere [54].

The concerns about funding the implementation and delivery of the intentions and ambitions of the Care Act in England led Peter Beresford to conclude in 2014 that 'the act looks less like a new beginning than a continuation by other means of social care's marginalisation' [55]. This prophesy by Beresford has proven to be accurate. The Care Act's rights, personalisation and broader well-being focus have been somewhat stymied by the reality of rationing and risk overwhelmingly dominating local authority adult social services.

Rationing and Risk

By 2019, with cuts continuing, the situation had worsened further, as noted by the Association of Directors of Adult Social Services (ADASS):

Alongside the £7bn reduction in adult social care funding since 2010, resulting in less spending on those with all levels of care needs and on services that prevent further care need, there has been a reduction in the levels of primary and community health care and the prevention of ill health, with fewer GPs, a 45% reduction in district nurses since 2010 and a 10%

reduction in the Government grant for public health since 2015/16. This has resulted in a vicious spiral for social care. Significant increases in hospital attendances and admissions, leading to increased need for social care on discharge, have been experienced by 87% of councils as a pressure. 71% of directors report that these pressures have been further exacerbated by insufficient capacity in primary care, community health care or mental health services. [56]

Based on the ADASS report Patrick Butler commented:

The government's failure to get to grips with the escalating financial crisis in social care has put tens of thousands of older and disabled people at risk of being denied basic support such as help with washing and dressing, care chiefs have warned. In a withering assessment, ADASS said social care in England was adrift in a "sea of inertia" caused by years of budget cuts and Brexit-related Whitehall policy paralysis. "The system is not only failing financially, it is failing people," it concluded. There were already signs that some fragile local care markets were imploding under the strain—almost half of councils had witnessed the closure of domestic home care providers in their area in the past year, and a third had seen residential care homes shut down, collectively affecting more than 8000 clients and residents. [57]

It was not, however, only the reduction in funding and the increased requirement to ration help which were impacting on adult social services. Local authorities also had to manage rapidly increasing adult protection and safeguarding workloads.

There were two aspects to the safeguarding workload increase. First, there was the continuing impact of the Deprivation of Liberty Safeguard Assessments (DOLS) which had been initiated by an amendment in 2007 to the 2005 Mental Capacity Act (see Chap. 11). DOLS had escalated following a Supreme Court judgement against Cheshire West Council which brought within the DOLS net, for example, older people with dementia in care and nursing homes who would meet the DOLS criteria of being subject to continuous supervision and control and not being free to decide to leave the care home.

In 2009/2010 there were 7157 DOLS applications to local authorities. In 2013/2014 this had increased to 13,000 (an increase of 82%). But in 2014/2015 this had jumped to 137,540 following the Cheshire West judgement, and it had increased further to 240,455 DOLS applications to local authorities in the 2018/2019 year (an increase of 3260% since 2009/2010 and averaging in 2019 every day of the year 660 new DOLS applications) [58].

In addition to this staggering increase in local authority DOLS workloads there was also a substantial increase in adult protection concerns reported to local authorities. In 2016–2017 there were 364,605 adult safeguarding concerns notified to local authorities. By 2018/2019 this had increased to 415,050, an average of over 1100 every day of the year. Adult protection enquiries conducted by local authorities under section 42 of the 2014 Care Act had increased from 102,970 in 2015–2016 to 143,050 in 2018–2019, an increase of almost 40%, with 400 new enquiries on average being started every day of the year by local authority adult social services in England [59].

Children's Social Services and the Focus on Risk

It was not only, however, adult social services and social workers who had been caught in the concentration on risk in the midst of tighter rationing of assistance. The same trends and tensions were to be found in children's social services during the 2010s, and as with adult services the pressures were escalating. The work of social workers was being skewed away from building relationships with children and adults in need, and deploying their own and other resources to provide help, to a focus instead on monitoring and surveillance as a part of managing risk within a context of shrinking services, and with the pressure to close cases down quickly so that the increasing number of incoming assessments could be taken on.

As discussed in the previous chapter, the focus on child protection rather than social work to provide assistance to families had a step change in November 2008. It followed the media's creation and telling of the 'Baby P story' which targeted social workers and their managers for vilification and threat. But the overwhelming focus of children's social services on child protection did not reduce and return to a more modest and measured level as might have been expected as the 'Baby P story' faded from the public's attention. This was in part because the story did not fade as the media's telling and referencing of the story continued not just for months but for years [60].

The scale of the increase in child protection activity was astounding. Between 2009–2010 and 2018–2019 the annual rate of child protection investigations (Section 47, 1989 Children Act) increased from 89,300 to 201,170 (+125%); initial child protection case conference were up from 49,300 to 77,400 (+76%); child protection plans in place on the 31 March each year increased from 29,200 to 52,620 (+80%), and court care proceedings initiated within the year by local authorities escalated from 6323 in 2007–2008 to 14,221 in 2018–2019 (+125%). These are staggering increases in child protection activity and workloads not only for local authority children's services social workers but also for other professionals and workers involved in child protection processes and procedures—police officers, teachers, doctors and other health professionals, early years and youth workers and others.

Children's Services Funding Crisis

The focus on child protection activity was not only driving higher and skewed workloads for social workers and others. It is also creating higher costs for local authorities as it was fuelling the increase in the number of children in care. On 31 March 2009 there were 60,000 children looked after by local authorities in England. On 31 March 2019 this had increased to 78,150 (+30%). A greater proportion (82% in 2019 compared to 68% in 2009) of children looked after are now in care compulsorily because of court orders [61].

It has been stated that the average cost of a child in care in England in 2017–2018 was £56,000 [62]. If that is multiplied by the 18,150 children looked after by councils at any one time compared to ten years ago it gives an increased cost to local authorities of £1,016,400,000. If that increased cost was divided equally across 152 local authorities in England with social services responsibilities (which of course it is not, as some are much larger than others) it would give an annual additional financial cost over £6.6 million for each council. Looked at in the context of the overall gross spend on children's services in 2017–2018 of £8.84 billion, the increased spend on the increased number of looked after children is 11.5%.

This helps explain the pressure on children's social services budgets in the late 2010s, but it is not the total explanation. Despite cuts in government grant local authorities had sought—indeed had been required through statutory duties—to maintain and even increase their spend on children's social services, albeit that this meant reducing funding more dramatically for other services and also using reserves.

However, as noted by the Institute of Local Government, while council spend on statutory children's social services had increased during the 2010s overall local authority spend on services for children had decreased:

> While local authorities have increased spending on children's social care, the picture has been challenging for children's services as a whole. Overall spending on children's services has fallen over the past decade: spending on Sure Start children's centres, services for young people and youth justice was slashed by 56% between 2009/10 and 2017/18. The biggest victim of the cuts—in both relative and absolute terms—has been Sure Start children's centres. Local authorities' spending on these centres fell from £1.5bn in 2009/10 to less than £0.7bn in 2017/18, a real-terms fall of 62%. [63]

Between 2009–2010 and 2016–2017 the total local authority spending on children's services reduced by 11%. While the spend on looked-after children has increased in real terms, and spend on safeguarding has been protected, 'early intervention' and 'preventative' services have had big cuts. This picture was summarised in a report from the Institute of Fiscal Studies for England's Children's Commissioner:

> These trends in spending are almost certainly driven by the increase in numbers of Looked After Children, which followed the Baby P case in 2007 … There has been a significant reorientation of spending on children's services. This change is noteworthy as the areas where spending has

increased (Looked After Children and Safeguarding) are generally high-cost, responsive and statutory duties, whilst areas that have seen falls in spending are those that are discretionary and more likely to be preventative. Given the overall squeeze on budgets, local authorities may have had little choice but to cut funding on non-statutory services. However, this could also store up problems for the future. Existing evidence already suggests that children with the most complex needs tend to come into care at a later age, and subsequently have the most costly care pathways whilst many preventative services tend to be lower cost in the long run. Thus, the reduction in spending on programmes such as Sure Start and young people's services could push up costs in the long run. [64]

The funding crisis in children's social services attracted the attention of Parliament. In 2018 the All Party Parliamentary Group (APPG) for Children concluded that children and families have to reach crisis before they receive any help [65] and it was reported that:

A former Tory children's minister has blamed the Government's "woeful underfunding" of local authorities for a crisis in child protection that is putting the safety of vulnerable young people at risk. The MP Tim Loughton, who served as children's minister in David Cameron's coalition government, said pressure on safeguarding services in some areas was so severe that often the only way to guarantee safety for children was to take them into care ... "In some places, the pressure on children's services is so acute it is leaving social workers feeling that the only tool available to them to keep a child safe is to remove them from their family," said Loughton, who is the co-chair of the all-party parliamentary group (APPG) for children. "As a result, families may look at these skilled and caring professionals with mistrust. But this is wrong. It is the woeful underfunding by government of a proper breadth of social care interventions that is to blame." In many areas, spending cuts had led to the erosion of early-support services for families, and made it harder for them to access help, the report said. There was "compelling evidence" that thresholds for accessing services were rising, to the point that social work was now "effectively crisis management". This meant safeguarding interventions were becoming more invasive, rather than supportive, leading to families being broken up unnecessarily, the report said. [66]

In 2019 the cross-party House of Commons Housing, Communities and Local Government Select Committee held an inquiry into the funding of children's social care. It concluded that 'additional core funding is urgently required to ensure that local authorities can meet increasing demand, provide high quality services and, ultimately, adequately safeguard children' [67].

As with adult social care, the government did not address the core concern about the crisis in funding children's social care. As with adult social care the issue was kicked into yet another patch of long grass. But unlike social care funding for adults, where the long grass approach was to promise another review, for children's social services the delay in addressing the issue was to be presented by ministers as still requiring evidence that more money was required. It was a delaying and denying view publicly supported by the chief social worker for children and by her close personal friend the director and sole owner of Morning Lane Associates [68], a private consultancy company which had received significant government funding from the Department for Education.

The Impact of Deprivation

There was evidence of a strong link between local authority funding, deprivation and child protection. Analysis of children's services annual statistical returns to the government and the data on deprivation in local authority areas showed clear correlations between higher rates of child protection activity, higher rates of deprivation, and lower and variable levels of funding between local authorities [69, 70, 71, 72]. This latter point was commented upon by Paul Bywaters:

> "The combination of cuts plus rising demand from families is having a major impact on services, so overall there has been a cut in spend-per-child since 2010 of 16% and the most deprived local authorities have taken a larger hit," says Professor Bywaters. "So the most deprived 20 per cent of authorities have cut their spending on children's services by a quarter, whereas the least deprived 20 per cent have cut only by four or five per cent". [73]

The link between deprivation and children and families being enmeshed in child protection procedures and children looked after (LAC) by local authorities was well established with Rick Hood and colleagues concluding that 'deprivation levels continue to be the key driver of referrals [to local authority children's services] and other categories of demand, and are strongly associated with variations in service response, particularly in the initial stages of referral and assessment' [74].

The research of Hood, Bywaters, Bilson and others referenced above showed that deprivation was a major contributor to the child protection and care workloads of local authority children's social services. This in its own right would be a part of the explanation for the increase in child protection and care activity during the 2010s amid more widespread, and more intense, child and family poverty. The cuts in help to families who were starting to struggle amid the stress, strain and stain of deepening deprivation would also have been pushing more children and families towards more intrusive and more threatening social work interventions.

The public at large probably thought that child protection was mainly about responding to and tackling the physical and sexual abuse of children and young people. The latter was high profile in the 2010s when the nature and extent of sexual exploitation of children and young people in Rotherham [75], Rochdale [76], Oxford [77], Telford and Wrekin [78], Bristol [79] and elsewhere became known.

It was networked abuse perpetrated in part by men of Pakistani heritage, and in Bristol of Somali heritage, and with the concern that the abuse had not been tackled by the police, councils and others because of a fear of damaging community relations and inflaming racism and because the young people themselves were blamed and seen as accountable for having made themselves vulnerable to violation. It led to the Independent Inquiry into Child Sexual Exploitation [80] chaired by Alexis Jay, who had led the inquiry into sexual exploitation and abuse in Rotherham. She was a social worker who had been chief social work adviser to the Scottish government and a former president of the Association of Directors of Social Work.

It was not, however, physical or sexual abuse which dominated child protection activity. On 31 March 2019, for example, 48% of child protection plans in England were due to concerns about neglect and 38%

were because of concerns about emotional abuse. Different local authorities and child protection systems had differing biases in allocating child protection concerns between these two categories of concern but taken together it means that 86% of child protection plans were because of concerns about emotional abuse and neglect whereas only 7% of plans were due to physical abuse and only 4% because of sexual abuse.

Neglect and emotional abuse are chronic experiences which have a cumulative impact over time. Unlike physical and sexual abuse they are not characterised by events and incidents for which there might be evidence such as radial fractures, burn marks or bruising or accounts and signs of sexual assault. It is more difficult to determine when and how seriously to intervene. They are also likely to be a reflection of parental stress and strain amongst increasing deprivation and poverty or of poor parenting competence and capacity. As such, they might well have been responded to in the past as families needing help and support whereas instead they were being escalated to child protection concerns in the absence of the time and services which might previously have been available to provide help.

This was all symbolised with changes in terminology and structures within local authority children's social services. Social workers called themselves child protection social workers rather than children's or family social workers and there was the creation of child protection teams and care and court proceedings teams rather than children and families teams. One consequence was that there was disruption in relationships with children and families and a loss of knowledge of their history and circumstances as they were passed across the thresholds between increasingly specialised and fragmented workers, teams and services. Threat replaced trust as a characteristic of families' views of social workers [81].

No Blame Game?

There was another issue which has remained consistent during the 2010s which was also likely to be a pervasive factor in escalating concerns about struggling families into child protection processes and care proceedings.

In the previous chapter there was discussion of the impact of the media's shaping and telling of the 'Baby P story'. There was, however, a glimmer of hope that the naming, blaming and shaming promoted by the press and politicians, and which had contributed to defensive practice and low thresholds of risk tolerance, would not continue.

In October 2007 the then Conservative opposition published a report of a commission on social workers [82]. The commission had been established by Tim Loughton, the shadow children's minister. The report was titled 'No More Blame Game' and in the Foreword to the report David Cameron, at that time the leader of the Conservative opposition, wrote:

> Social workers, particularly those dealing with child protection cases, are often dealing with very difficult and damaged families. They have a key role to play in early intervention to keep families together wherever possible, and in meeting the needs of vulnerable children who are taken into care when their safety is put at risk. Their importance in meeting the challenges we face as a society is no less than that of the teachers, police officers or doctors. Indeed, their involvement can often prevent any need for the latter two professions to be involved. Yet the perception of social workers held by the rest of society rarely matches the sensitivity and importance of their work and the skills they need to employ. Quite simply they are often identified as part of the problem rather than an integral and helpful part of the solution. This situation has not been helped by the relative lack of attention given to their professional development by the Government compared to front line doctors and teachers, and the willingness of some parts of the media to point a finger of blame when high profile cases go wrong. This blame game cannot benefit the vulnerable families who need the involvement of social workers, let alone the professional social workers themselves. [83]

The recommendations of the Commission included the importance of keeping initial social work education generic, resourcing post-qualifying learning and development, having a national high profile advertising campaign to promote social work, and creating a post of chief social worker within government who would be a public champion for social work. It also argued against performance indicators which favoured getting more children adopted and adopted more quickly, recognising that this was a perverse incentive which undermined work with families and had the potential consequence of children being inappropriately and unnecessarily removed permanently from their families.

All looked promising until rather hypocritically Mr Cameron rode on the media bandwagon only twelve months later when social workers were named, blamed and shamed (and harassed and threatened) following the death of Peter Connelly, 'Baby P'.

However, when the Conservatives led the coalition government after the 2010 election there was still hope. Tim Loughton was appointed children's minister. He was respected and appreciated across the social work community. He engaged widely with social workers and with children and families across England, and he was recognised as a champion within government for social work and for children's social services.

Munro Review of Child Protection

He would also have been instrumental in June 2010 in getting Michael Gove, the then new secretary of state for education (the Department for Children, Schools and Families was retitled by Mr Gove as the Department for Education—symbolic of the abandonment of the Every Child Matters agenda and the overwhelming focus now to be given to academic attainment school league tables) to commission Eileen Munro, a professor at the London School of Economics (LSE), to undertake a review of child protection in England.

The choice of Eileen Munro to undertake the review followed, as noted in earlier chapters, a long history of the London School of Economics providing social policy and social work advisors to government and political parties. What may be a little more surprising in the choice of Eileen Munro to undertake the child protection review was that her views on child protection and responding to risk, no doubt in part influenced by her practice experience as a social worker, were already well known. She had nailed her flag to the mast of not overly identifying and not overly responding to risk. For example, in 2004 Munro wrote:

There are persuasive arguments for re-focusing to make a broader assessment of children's needs beyond the need for protection but, despite persistent political directives, change is slow to materialise. This, it is argued, is because there is insufficient additional funding to finance support services *in addition to* [italics in original text] protection services. Since the majority of referrals are not substantiated or not considered serious enough for professional intervention, one option for saving money is to classify cases more accurately at the time of initial referral, thus reducing the time and resources spent on rigorous investigations. One obstacle lies in the intellectual difficulties in classifying referrals accurately on the limited knowledge available in the initial referral. Another obstacle comes from the defensive culture now prevalent in child protection agencies. The increasingly punitive attitude of society to mistakes, illustrated by public inquiries, encourages practitioners to err on the side of caution. The blame culture is also implicated in the shift towards creating more and more formal procedures. [84]

Eileen Munro's final of three reports was published in July 2011. Amongst its conclusions was the statement:

Practitioners and their managers told the review that statutory guidance, targets and local rules have become so extensive that they limit their ability to stay child-centred. The demands of bureaucracy have reduced their capacity to work directly with children, young people and families. Services have become so standardised that they do not provide the required range of responses to the variety of need that is presented. This review recommends a radical reduction in the amount of central prescription to help professionals move from a compliance culture to a learning culture, where they have more freedom to use their expertise in assessing need. [85]

The big message in Munro's report was the need to 'move from a compliance culture to a learning culture' and also to acknowledge that child protection was like 'trying to spot a needle in a haystack, and it gets harder if you make the haystack larger' [86], which had been an unintended and unwelcomed implication of the 'Every Child Matters' agenda of net widening the range of concerns about children who then got drawn in to the safeguarding children net.

In 2017 Munro was quoted as saying:

"The broader public sector was gripped by new public management at the time and the idea that top down control was the way to do it. It was called the 'targets and terror' approach. When you apply that to the child protection field, which has enough terror anyway because of the horror of a child dying, then it really was quite damaging," she says. "I was really quite disturbed by how many social workers talked about families they were working with in a very bureaucratic, rather than a human way. Somebody was a 'section 47' rather than a woman who is living with four children in an appalling house who is trying her hardest but making a bit of a mess of it. "If you don't make that human contact with a person then you can't help solve their problems. At least, to me, that's what social work is about. But social work had become about processing and referring-on, not helping." [87]

The 2011 Munro report was published six months after the December 2010 report of the Social Work Reform Board. The Munro recommendations reinforced those of the Reform Board, in particular through strengthening the education, and especially the post-qualifying education, of social workers and enhancing the public's perception and understanding of social work.

Tim Loughton recalls that 'an overriding message' of the 'No Blame Game' commission which he chaired and of subsequent reviews was 'not to separate academically children and adult social workers and the way we train people, although effectively that is what is now happening' [Tim Loughton interview].

Loughton was very engaged in driving forward the Reform Board and the Munro recommendations. He energetically drove the creation of the College of Social Workers (TCSW) and the appointment of a chief social worker. Both, however, were to be short-lived and undermined.

Not One but Two Chief Social Workers

The College of Social Work was weakened even before it was established by the fiasco of in-fighting between the parties within the profession and the civil service who should have been central to its constructive creation [88]. It was also doomed by a too ambitious and unrealistic business and financial plan which left the College too dependent on government funding [89]. This came to haunt it in part as a consequence of what happened after the process of appointing a chief social worker.

Following a full civil service appointment process the preferred candidate for the chief social worker post was not accepted by the secretaries of state for education and health. The government then decided to appoint two separate chief social workers in the Department for Education and the Department for Health:

> I had left the Department [for Education] and subsequently after a lot of vacillation it was decided to split the roles and subsequently two new people became respectively adult and children's social workers … It was never the original intention, but I think the bigger issue is the redefinition of what the chief social workers role was … The chief social workers role was to be the equivalent of the chief medical officer in terms of being the public face of social work, so when something goes wrong (and hopefully only occasionally) you've got the chief social worker saying 'This is what has happened,' so it's an independent respected voice explaining complex issues around child abuse or whatever … and to advise government on changes in social work and the state of the social work profession … and certainly to be a confidante and champion for the social work profession … you've got a problem when nobody knows who the chief social worker is because they have no media presence … and the chief social worker seems to have identified herself as just another civil servant in the Department for Education and that was never the intention … When you are for all extents and purposes being the minister's spokesperson it completely changes the dynamics of that position … it would be a disaster if we were to lose the chief social worker role or it were to be diluted because it's become something it was never intended to be. [Tim Loughton interview]

It was not difficult to speculate that it was the Department of Education, with Mr Gove was secretary of state, which was most instrumental in abandoning the intention of having one chief social worker with the seniority to advise government and the status to represent social work to the public. The government's actions which fragmented social work also included, led in the Department for Education, the funding of a fore-shortened education programme for children's social workers separate from all other social workers.

The Demise of the College of Social Work

It was stated that a significant factor leading to the closure of TCSW was the decision taken within the Department for Education to award a joint contract for the development of a national accreditation programme for local authority children's services social workers (which undermined the Professional Capabilities Framework developed by social workers through the work of the Social Work Reform Board) to KPMG, the international accountancy company, and to Morning Lane Associates (MLA), a company which the chief social worker had formed with partners prior to becoming the chief children's social worker. TCSW had looked to receive this substantial contract which would have assisted in strengthening its financial base, but it was reported it had lost the confidence and support of the Department for Education and the department's chief social worker who is quoted as stating that it was 'not tenable' for the government to keep 'ploughing in' money to the College [90].

The Privatisation of Children's Social Services and Social Work

The awarding to KPMG and MLA of the contract to develop a government initiated and controlled accreditation programme for children's social workers was in line with, and symbolic of, a wider process of the privatisation of children's services being driven by the coalition and subsequent Conservative governments.

As noted in a previous chapter New Labour in 2006, following recommendations from Julian Le Grand, introduced 'social work practices' in children's and adults' social services. Social work practices allowed, and indeed encouraged, local authorities to contract out statutory social work services to other organisations, including private for-profit companies.

The pilot social work practices were short-lived and largely unsuccessful, demonstrating that out-sourcing social work services was not economic, efficient or effective. The coalition government, however, was eager to take the privatisation of statutory social work with children and families much further and to move it out of local authorities and the public sector [91].

In 2013 Mr Gove ordered that Doncaster Council transfer its children's services to an independent trust. This followed damning Ofsted and Audit Commission reports about many years of poor political governance and corporate management within the council, including its children's services. Doncaster had embraced the New Labour changes within local government and had an elected executive mayor. It had disastrous consequences with council services imploding and children left unprotected among the chaos of badly designed and badly managed change [92].

In the same year Richmond and Kingston upon Thames councils decided voluntarily to jointly transfer their children's services to a new community interest company (CIC). This followed an Ofsted judgement that children's social services provided by the London Borough of Kingston were 'inadequate'. Joining with Richmond's services through a CIC was seen as a way of sharing senior management expertise and costs. It was also in line with the ideological thrust that councils should be strategic planners and not service providers. 'Lean councils' were in fashion.

The actions taken in Doncaster and in Kingston and Richmond abandoned the principle that statutory children's social work services should be provided as a public service by accountable and transparent democratic local authorities. The assessment of children, child protection investigations, the setting and management of children in need and child protection plans, decisions to initiate care proceedings to seek to have children removed from their families, and then deciding with whom the child should then live, were now to be contracted out by local authorities to independent organisations.

To make this acceptable and allowable within the law the government in 2014 introduced a change to statutory regulations. It explicitly allowed local authorities to transfer these statutory children's services activities to other organisations, including specifically to for-profit private companies (albeit these companies would have to set up a not-for-profit subsidiary through which the parent company could still make a profit from the charges it levied on its subsidiary for the services provided by the parent company).

This was all in line with the political messages from Prime Minister Cameron and Secretary of State Gove, as the quotes below show:

> Michael Gove has said that more struggling children's services departments in England could be taken over by independent providers. The Education Secretary also said he was considering opening up well performing departments to private and voluntary organisations so they could innovate and improve their services. [93]

This report in November 2013 of Mr Gove's ambitions and intentions was followed in 2015 by Mr Cameron saying:

> What energises markets are new insurgent companies, who break monopolies and bring in new ways of doing things. We should apply this thinking to government. So many of our country's efforts to extend opportunity have been undermined by a sort of tolerance of state failure: children in care and prisons being two absolutely stand out areas. In June I made the case for reform of social services and child protection. [94]

The 'case for reform' ignored the big cuts being made in children's services as a direct consequence of government reductions in funding. It ignored the blame culture to which Mr Cameron had himself contributed and which was driving a continuing escalation in child protection activity. And with its focus on the increasing marketisation and privatisation of social work and children's services it ignored the increasing track record of the failings within out-sourced public services [95].

While the politicians were speaking the civil servants were acting to deliver on the political messages and instruction they were being given. In Autumn 2014 meetings were convened by the Department of Education to encourage a market place of providers who would take on and deliver statutory children's social services. G4S, Serco, Amey and Mouchel—big out-sourcing companies with no experience in delivering statutory children's services—attended the meetings to explore the opportunity to gain contracts [96].

At the same time the DfE commissioned LaingBuisson, a market analysis company, to prepare a report on how to develop market capacity—what had been called 'Newcos' (new companies) in the DfE—to take over children's social services [97]. There was considerable delay in publishing the report. Amid the increasing media coverage of the failures in out-sourced public services, including the privatised probation service, the report's recommendations, which noted a market appetite for outsourcing children's services, had become toxic. The government distanced itself from the report when it was belatedly published [98].

But privatisation had already taken a strong hold in the provision of social care for children, just as since the 1990s it was the private sector which had come to dominate the provision of social care for older (and younger) disabled people. By 2018 three quarters of children's homes in England were provided by for-profit private companies. Almost a third of local authorities no longer directly provided any children's residential care. On 31 March 2018, 6990 children were placed by local authorities in private children's homes and 16,200 children (39% of all children in foster children in England) were in foster placements arranged through for-profit foster care agencies. In local authorities in England 15% of social workers working in children's social services were employed through private for-profit employment agencies [99].

Privatisation had also, rather incongruously, been promoted by local authorities having to down-size their own development capacity in response to government funding cuts and then having to buy in consultants from the private management accountancy companies and others when additional capacity was required.

It was not only, however, the big international management accountancy firms which benefited and profited. For example, Morning Lane Associates (MLA), the private company established by the chief social worker for children with two former colleagues from the London Borough of Hackney before she was appointed to her civil service post, received many millions of pounds of funding from central government and local authorities. When MLA was 'dissolved' in 2019 its most recent Company House accounts showed that the company had assets of just under £2.2 million and that it then had one sole shareholder who had been reported to have a 'close and personal' relationship with the children's chief social worker [100].

It was been calculated in 2019 that in England at least £220 million a year was being taken out of children's social services as profits by private companies [99]. And by 2019 seven local authorities had or were being forced or coerced by government to move their children's social services outside of their direct management to a range of trusts and companies.

The 2014 Care Act, like the 2014 children's services statutory regulation changes, also made it clear that statutory adult social work services, such as undertaking assessments and deciding what and how much help might be provided, could be out-sourced by local authorities (see above). However, unlike the statutory regulation changes for children's services which allowed the contracting out of child protection investigation and other child protection tasks, adult protection and safeguarding activities were still to remain directly within the control and provision of local authorities. It was difficult to understand why there was this difference beyond it being that those that those who were advising the DfE and government about children services may have been more accepting and agreeable to the private sector being awarded and paid for child protection and safeguarding roles [101] than were those advising the Department of Health and government about safeguarding adults.

The Political Control of Social Work and Social Workers

Alongside the thrust to increase the marketisation and privatisation of social services for children and adults was the government's intentions and plans to have more control over the social work profession and social workers. It was exemplified by the undermining of the work and recommendations of the Social Work Task Force and Reform Board.

First, as noted above, the government played a crucial role leading to the closure of the College of Social Work. The College had been one of the key recommendations of the Reform Board. Other developments and arguments shaped and championed by the Social Work Task and Reform Board which were undermined and marginalised by government actions included the introduction of two separate departmental chief social workers rather than one cross-government chief social worker.

The government's undermining of the Reform Board also included the introduction of specialist training for children's social workers through the government funded and favoured non-university Frontline programme led by a former teacher. It was mirrored in adult services by Think Ahead as an initial training for mental health social workers. Both were counter to the recommendation of the Reform Board that the initial qualifying university-based social work degree should be generic to be followed by specialists post-qualifying continuous professional development.

The Social Work Reform Board had developed a Professional Capabilities Framework [102] which had levels of required competencies which spanned the social work profession and social workers' careers. It too was undermined by actions within the Department for Education which contracted with KPMG to develop a government-owned Knowledge and Skills Statement (KSS) for children and families social workers [103]. It was to provide the platform for a government determined and controlled National Assessment and Accreditation System (NAAS) [104] for children's social workers. The Department of Health subsequently published a Knowledge and Skills Statement for Social Workers in Adult Services.

There were significant concerns from the British Association of Social Workers, the Association of Directors of Children's Services, the Association of Directors of Adult Social Services, and the House of Commons Education Select Committee, that as well as being costly the NAAS would destabilise an already fragile children's social work workforce and demote and demoralise those working in adult services [105, 106, 107, 108, 109].

Interviewed for a book by Carl Purcell on children's services reform between 1997 and 2020 Moira Gibb, who had chaired the Social Work Task Force and the Social Work Reform Board, commented on the government moving away from and undermining the developments promoted by the Social Work Reform Board saying "I am disappointed that the Reform Board's work has not had the continued attention from DfE in particular that it needed. It wasn't a quick win but a 10-year programme. New things are pursued instead" [110].

Social Work Education

In the face of these widespread concerns what was driving these actions and activity from within the Department for Education? Firstly, there had been a report by Sir Martin Narey on children's social workers and social work education. Rather bizarrely and wastefully the government had commissioned two reports at the same time on social work education, indicating either a lack of coordination across government departments or competition and conflict between government departments.

The Narey Report was commissioned by the Secretary of State for Education [111]. It recommended that 'universities should be encouraged to develop [specialist] degrees for those intending to work in children's social work'. Narey also argued for the current requirement that all registered social workers must have a degree in social work to be scrapped. Child protection, he argued, should become a two tier profession made up of graduates and a new cadre of "social work assistants" [112]. In contrast, the report commissioned by the Department for Health from David Croisedale-Appleby, concluded that the initial social work degree should be generic and be followed by specialist education and training and continuous professional development [113].

It was the Croisdale-Appleby Report which was viewed within the social work profession as more thorough and thoughtful and to have greater credibility than the much shorter and poorly evidenced Narey Report [114]. It was the anecdotal Narey Report, however, with its catalogue of criticisms of social work education and of social workers which was to be given weight and credibility in the DfE, including its recommendation that the DfE's chief social worker should prepare a definition of children's social work and that she should define the skills which children's social workers should be able to demonstrate.

The second motivator for the Department for Education driving ahead with its NAAS proposals might have been the views taken and expressed by the DfE's Chief Social Worker. She is reported as saying in 2015 that social worker's still needed to earn the trust of the public [115]. She also argued it was essential that the regulation of social workers should be controlled by the government [116].

A third driver for the DfE moving ahead with NAAS may have been the view taken by Sir Alan Wood. He had been the children's chief social worker's senior manager when they worked in Hackney. While she was the chief social worker for children he became what was called in the media the government's 'go to fixer' on child protection and children's social services [117]. He was blunt and bruising in his generalised view that newly qualified social workers were 'crap'.[2]

Children and Social Work Bill

The government's ambitions for the political control of social work and of children's social services went further, however, than social work education. Its intentions were presented in the Children and Social Work Bill with Edward Timpson, the children's minister, leading for the government in the House of Commons debates on the Bill.

Among the controversial clauses within the Bill were the proposal that a new social work regulator should be established within the Department for Education with its accountability to the Secretary of State for Education. The regulator would have the role of not only determining who could be registered and who could practice as a social worker but it would also control the education of social workers and the content of their education.

This proposal had particular and powerful implications as Mr Gove when Secretary of State for Education had stated that social workers were too concerned about deprivation and disadvantage and were too ready to explain and excuse, for example, poor parenting:

> In too many cases, social work training involves idealistic students being told that the individuals with whom they will work have been disempowered by society. They will be encouraged to see these individuals as victims of social injustice whose fate is overwhelmingly decreed by the economic forces and inherent inequalities which scar our society. [118]

---

[2] Sir Martin Narey, Isabelle Trowler and Sir Alan Wood were also each supportive of the government's intention to open up statutory children's social services to the private sector (see Jones, R. (2019) In Whose Interest? The Privatisation of Child Protection and Social Work, Bristol, Policy Press, chapter three).

It was also reported that Mr Gove wanted more children to be taken into care more quickly [119], that social work education needed to be reformed because 'it was too dominated by dogma and theories of society' [120], and that 'many social workers were not up to the job' [121]. The social work profession was not slow in challenging and rebutting Mr Gove's assertions that it was not for social workers to understand the impact of poverty (which was increasing as a direct consequence of government's policies) and his enveloping view that social work education was not fit for purpose [122, 123, 124].

The range and stridency, however, of the views of the Secretary of State about repositioning social work as a tool of social engineering rightly raised alarm bells about giving control of social work education and who could be a social worker to the Secretary of State for Education. How pervasive and pernicious this could be was illustrated by the first draft of the Department for Education's Key Skills Statement for children's social workers prepared by the children's chief social worker. It stated that social workers should 'demonstrate positive relationships and attitudes towards politicians' [125]. It was a draft requirement for social workers regardless of the policies and actions of politicians which might undermine social work profession's principles and value base, including confronting and challenging discrimination and disadvantage. It was a controversial proposal which quickly disappeared.

There was also concern when a proposal was inserted into the Children and Social Work Bill that power be given to the Secretary of State for Education to set aside the rights and responsibilities to protect and promote the welfare of children which had been set in statute by Parliament. It was argued by the government that this would remove hindrances to innovation within local authorities and other providers of children's social care.

It was, however, successfully opposed by a wide-ranging coalition of children's rights organisations and children's charities, along with professional associations of those who worked to assist and care for children [126]. It was a campaign led by Carolyne Willow [127], the director of Article 37, a children's rights campaigning charity, and within Parliament by Lord Watson in the House of Lords [128] and by Emma Lewell-Buck, the Labour shadow children's minister. She was a social worker who had worked in local authority children's social services.

The concern was that the so-called exemption clauses in the Children and Social Work Bill had the potential to give executive power to the Secretary of State to abandon statutory rights for children, and to remove the responsibilities of local authorities and other social care organisations to provide services and safeguards for children. There was also the suspicion that reducing statutory requirements might be intended to be attractive to private companies looking to expand within the children's social services market place the government was creating [129].

When the Children and Social Work Bill was legislated in 2017 as the Children and Social Work Act it did not included the 'exemption powers' proposed for the Secretary of State for Education and the new social work regulator, Social Work England, was not to be embedded in the Department for Education and accountable to the Secretary of State—although the Secretary of State would still decide on the chair of the regulator and still had to approve proposals regarding social work education. When the first chair and chief executive of Social Work England were appointed there was relief that they had both been social workers, although dismay that none of the board members were or had been social workers [130].

The Children and Social Work Act had positive clauses to enhance, for example, services for care leavers and the education of children in care, but the government's thwarted intentions to have more direct political control of the social work profession in England had been concerning and alarming, especially in the context of the government's continuing politically chosen austerity targeting public services and poor children, families and disabled adults and older people.

So many of the government's intentions for social work were shaped and led from within the Department for Education. Its ministers, civil servants and advisors publicly promoted a view of social work as not good enough and needing more political control. The stance taken, however, from within the Department of Health was much more about giving recognition to social workers and ensuring that they had a crucial and central role in assisting disabled and older people. This was illustrated within the Department of Health's 2016 strategic statement for social work:

> Social work should be a well understood and highly respected profession, but this is often not the case. The public know what a doctor, a nurse or a police officer is and what they do—they are valued and respected as professionals. They know the hard choices they can face on a day to day basis and that those choices can have an irreversible impact on people's lives. We want this to be the case for social workers … We aim to raise awareness and understanding of the invaluable role that social workers play in adult social care and health, recognising that it is often overshadowed by child and family statutory social work. Increasing public engagement, promoting the professional role of social workers and the wider social services sector, encouraging the sector to be more confident in promoting what it does well and the contribution it makes across a wide range of services and partnerships, are all vital to our vision of creating and sustaining a skilled, educated and confident profession, able to rise to the challenge of modern social work and the integration of health and social care. [131]

Significantly, and countering the developments from within the Department for Education, the Department of Health's vision specifically highlighted 'a commitment to social work as a single profession, with common values, skills and knowledge'. Two government departments, two chief social workers, two differing views and aspirations for social work.

Mental Health

There was little other relevant legislative activity by the Conservative governments led by Mrs May between 2016 and 2019, or subsequently in 2019 by the government led by Mr Johnson. Instead Parliament, political parties and public debate were dominated by Brexit following the 2016 referendum outcome that the UK was to leave the European Union.

Even the legislation which had been promised failed to materialise. In December 2018 there was the publication of a government-commissioned review of mental health legislation for England and Wales (in 2019 under its devolved powers the Scottish government [132] commissioned a separate review. There were no promises of a review for Northern Ireland with its legislature not meeting as a consequence of the continuing power sharing dispute).

Chaired by Sir Simon Wessely, a professor of psychiatry at King's College, London, the England and Wales review report was titled 'Modernising the Mental Health Act: increasing choice, reducing compulsion'. It sought to re-set and rebalance mental health services away from an overwhelming focus on risk which had led to an escalation in compulsory detention and treatment (see previous chapter).

Wessely noted that:

> Some of this can be traced to the reasons which lay behind the introduction of the 2007 Act, a process that began nearly ten years earlier. Reading the newspapers, speeches, discussion papers and documents from the time, the risk posed to the public by those with mental illness, and the failings of the mental health care system to adequately manage those risks, was the major driver of the perceived need for reform. And one can understand why. The killing of Jonathan Zito by Christopher Clunis had shocked everyone, as did the crimes committed by Michael Stone. Sadly looking back we can see that some of the decisions taken by government leading up to the 2007 Act were an overreaction. [133]

Wessely also noted that:

> Those of black African or Caribbean heritage are over eight times more likely to be subjected to Community Treatment Orders than those of white heritage. In other words, too often and in too many areas the experiences of those of black African and Caribbean heritage is one of either being excluded or detained. [134]

The review recommended four principles which ought to be enshrined in a new mental health act and which should underlie mental health services—choice and autonomy (ensuring service users' views and choices are respected); least restriction (ensuring the Act's powers are used in the least restrictive way); therapeutic benefit (ensuring patients are supported to get better); and the person as an individual (ensuring patients are viewed and treated as rounded individuals) [135].

As soon as the review report was published the government led by Mrs May promised new legislation to implement the review's recommendations [136]. A year later there had been no further action, although in October 2019 Mr Johnson, the then new prime minister, also promised new mental health legislation [137].

Here was another example, as with the funding of social care for older people and younger adults, discussed above, which was still waiting on political commitment and action. For adult social care there had been a promise of a Green Paper but as noted in a report for the House of Commons Library 'the publication of a social care Green Paper has been delayed several times: it was originally due to published in "summer 2017". The latest position, stated in September 2019, is that it will be published "in due course"' [138].

The 2019 General Election and Brexit

The December 2019 general election was fought largely on two slogans. The Conservative's campaign led with the message 'Get Brexit Done'. Labour's campaign message was 'For the Many Not the Few'. Labour's manifesto [139] promised reinvestment in public services to be funded by higher taxes on the most wealthy and on corporations, the re-funding of Sure Start, and the renationalisation of national utilities. The outcome? The Conservatives, with Mr Johnson as prime minister, were re-elected with a large Parliamentary majority and with the commitment to withdraw the UK from the European Union within a year.

The new government promised more funding for the police, health services and schools, albeit only going part way to reverse the cuts of the previous ten years. But there was no commitment to reverse or end the cuts to welfare benefits or to local government [140]. Indeed there were more cuts already planned which were still to be implemented. As Simon Jenkins noted 'Austerity will linger on but it will be hidden … Local government in all its guises remains Cinderella in the scullery' [141].

Brexit itself had implications for the personal social services and social work which were rarely made explicit. As well as a general concern about the potential damaging impact on the UK's economy, which would likely have a knock-on effect on public finances and public expenditure, there were specific concerns about restricting workers entering the UK from Europe and elsewhere. This presented a threat to the already under strength and over stretched workforce in health care, social care and social work. There were also concerns about the UK becoming more dependent on a trade agreement with the USA, with the anticipation of more public services being opened up and exposed to privatisation with American and other venture capitalists as the likely beneficiaries. This possibility seemed even more likely when one of the first acts of the December 2019 Conservative government was to allow the sale to a US private equity company of a key component of the UK's national defence [142].

So what are the prospects for the personal social services and social work in England? The final chapter looks back over the major messages from the past fifty years and looks forward to the future.

Part V

Reflecting and Re-routing

13

The Personal Social Services Today and Tomorrow

The previous chapters have traced a path for the personal social services in England from the feast of funding in the early 1970s to the financial famine since 2010. This final Postscript reflects on this 50-year journey and looks forward to the future.

Unlike the rest of the book it is rather more free flow and free form, focusing on my perceptions rather than—as in previous chapters—an account largely informed by the recollections and interpretations of those who had key roles as events were unfolding.

What to Celebrate

One of the features of the past half century of the personal social services is how social workers have been in, or close to, the vanguard in driving positive and constructive change. They have often played this role in alliance with others. Here are five examples:

© The Author(s) 2020, corrected publication 2021
R. Jones, *A History of the Personal Social Services in England*,
https://doi.org/10.1007/978-3-030-46123-2_13

1. It was social workers within the personal social services who were central to the closure of the large institutions. In the 1970s and 1980s it included the move away from residential nurseries for young children, the large approved schools for adolescents, and the big children's homes and children's cottage villages. In the 1980s and 1990s it included the closure and re-provisioning of services previously located in the large isolated county asylums, mental handicap hospitals, and the long-stay geriatric wards.

2. It was social workers who, with encouragement and campaigning from disabled people, moved away from a concept of the professional as distant patronising expert with closely protected knowledge to the professional social worker as an ally and enabler, recognising the strengths, capacity, competence and potential of others.

3. Before personalisation became a mainstream term and policy it was local authority social services who worked around restrictive legislation to make (in)direct cash payments available to disabled people, assisting them to have more choice and control.

4. It was social work, especially through its teachers and educators, which was aligned alongside others in the 1970s and 1980s in opening up the debate about discrimination and oppression in its varied forms.

5. The development within social work of strength-based models of practice and the commitment to exploring and reporting on their impact has re-shaped and strengthened social work. Strength-based models of practice do not remove the need for social workers to be intrigued and imaginative in their assessments and action planning, but they have the potential to promote and improve communication, engagement and partnership working with children and adults. There is a need, however, to avoid the danger that using the tools and techniques provided within the models becomes the goal rather than a means.

What to Recall and Remember

There are also traditions within social work which ought to be treasured and maintained, such as:

1. The importance of teams and team work and of reflective supervision. It is difficult to identify other professions which from the 1970s and before had team work and reflective supervision so ingrained in their structures and practice.

2. The need to be political as well as person-focused as a part of social workers' professional role. This has been challenged throughout the past 50 years, and especially by ministers and their advisors during the 2010s, but social work is about seeing people in their broader context. This includes recognising and challenging how discrimination, disadvantage and deprivation damages and distorts lives, and collectively exposing its impact and campaigning for it to be addressed.

3. Social work is often on the margins of attention and is a minor concern of the public, press and politicians (except when it becomes the focus of blame for a tragedy). On its own it is not likely to have much leverage and impact in creating agendas and generating change. Alliances and partnerships have been a part of social workers' approach to delivering on the professional responsibility to be clear about answering Howard Becker's question 'Whose Side Are We On?'

4. Social work is intellectually as well as emotionally demanding. It requires the capability to make judgements and to plan action based on complex but always incomplete information. It is why social workers need to have critical appraisal skills and to be intelligent and imaginative. This should be supported by social work being a graduate profession with entry standards and qualifying courses which prioritise intelligence and academic ability as well as valuing life experience and the value-base of its entrants.

What to Mourn

1. How risk and rationing have come to trump relationships and rights as key components of social workers' practice. It has skewed how social workers spend their time and how they might be viewed by others, including those they might seek to help. Their work and time is often

now more focused on monitoring and surveillance rather than being a resource to people at a time of crisis and creating and mobilising community resources.

2. How there is now an imbalance between professional space and discretion and proceduralised and bureaucratised practice. This is not an argument for unregulated and unseen practice with variations in competency and performance little recognised or addressed. It is an argument for recognising professional competence and creativity and having the confidence to let it blossom, and prioritising celebration and recognition over mistrust and monitoring.

3. How organisational structures and employment patterns of social workers have undermined the building of caring and trusting relationships with people, young and old, who are often in the midst of psychosocial crisis as a consequence of changing life circumstances because of illness, disability, relationship breakdown or abuse. Customer call centres and hand-overs between teams and social workers because of too much task specialisation is disruptive of relationships with service users. It also undermines knowing service users' history. In children's services, for example, work is moved between initial assessment, children in need, child protection, court proceedings, care and leaving care teams and workers, creating fragmentation and frustration. The pressure to close down work quickly to take on new work also challenges the opportunity to build knowledge of, and positive relationships with, those who social workers might seek to assist. None of this is helped by the relatively recent emergence of short-term agency social workers and managers.

4. The busyness which is squeezing out time for meaningful contact rather than monitoring between social workers and service users, and is also creating a less stable and less experienced workforce.

5. Divisive and too early specialisation within social worker's initial professional education. It restricts the breadth and blinkers the knowledge of social workers, which then limits assessment and understanding of complex lives and personal histories. The focus on creating too early specialisation and foreshortened education—now provided outside of universities and higher education and with funding from investment bankers—also restricts future life-long career choices and movement

for social workers. It has taken the focus away from developing post-qualifying education, training and qualifications which is where specialisation should be developed and given recognition.

6. The blame culture which promotes defensive and bureaucratised practice and creates less confident organisations, managers and practitioners, and leads to low morale and workforce turnover and instability.

7. Hit-and-run inspectorates, and hit-and-run inquiries and reviews, where judgements are based on standards of near perfection and with all the benefits of hindsight. They take little account of the realities and complexities of social work which are not reduced by more procedures and more monitoring and auditing. They often choose to ignore and fail to comment on the limitations of resources and the impact of negative organisational cultures. They are experienced as brutal and bullying and generate threat and fear. They distort attention, and protecting from criticism from inspectors becomes for some agencies the organisation's overriding goal.

8. The increasing attempts to politically control and reposition social work from governments which are creating division within communities, promoting discrimination through their rhetoric and policies, and generating greater inequality and more extensive and intensive deprivation.

9. The priority given to privatising the personal social services with pursuit of profit trumping a commitment to public service. It adds costs, complexity and opaque accountability through the processes of setting, letting and monitoring contracts, with distant ownership, and it drives down standards in the search to reduce costs to generate profits.

What to Expect

1. Circumstances and communities will continue to change. Climate and political changes are likely to lead to more, not less, population movement. In the context of increasing nationalism and state isolationism the vilification and targeting of migrating and asylum-seeking

people may intensify with intensifying punitive policies such as 'no access to public funds' and the continuing incarceration of asylum-seekers. An increasing child and adult protection concern and category is likely to be trafficking, and the state itself may be complicit in abusing children by the response it gives to asylum-seeking families.

2. More government monitoring and oversight with dissent demonised. This is already happening with anti-terrorists activities and the Respect and Prevent agendas and procedures now capturing within the net those who are active with their concerns about the environment, nuclear weapons and animal welfare [1]. There is the danger that 'thought abuse' [2] becomes another child and vulnerable adults abuse category for children, young people and others engaged and active in expressing concerns, for example, about the environment.

3. A widening gap between rich and poor is a continuing frightful prospect after ten years of politically chosen austerity already having increased inequality and, even more damning, reduced the life expectancy and quality of life for poor children and adults [3, 4, 5].

4. The opportunities of technology. As yet unpredictable whether what might be promised on the tin gets delivered, but the opportunities for technology to enhance independent living, quality of life, and smart working are still largely untapped, as are the advances in genome medicine with the possibility of extending life-spans but also, importantly, years of healthy and independent living.

5. A focus on housing, transport, communications and community infrastructures which enable people to live independently and when help is needed for this to be provided within inter-dependent communities rather than by separate, specialist and segregated services. This does not negate the role of social workers. It reinforces their community and resource development role. John Bolton—who had a professional background as a social worker which included community development—recalled when director of social services in Coventry:

> CSCI sent me a letter saying 'This is your improvement agenda for the next year. I sent the letter back saying 'Thank you for your improvement agenda, this is mine'. And I said 'I'm not going to do some of these things'. I was not going to help more people to live at home'. Every year

this upset CSCI. I said 'I'm going to help fewer people to live at home every year because I'm actually going to promote their independence'. It really annoyed them, but staff loved it because we had clarity about what we were doing and we were slightly putting a V sign up to the system which social workers liked. [John Bolton interview]

And two personal anecdotes from my time as social services director in Wiltshire. When a well past-its-sell-by-date local Leonard Cheshire care home out in the countryside was closing there were twelve residents who wanted to remain in our local area. There was district council owned sheltered accommodation in a town centre which was under-used. It was modernised and converted into housing where the care home residents could choose to move to as tenants and maintain their friendships but with independence. We thought we should attach a communal centre to the development, but instead the new tenants wanted the money spent under their direction to improve access to every-day universal facilities in the town—shops, cinema, swimming pool, sports ground, leisure centre and pubs—and with direct payments to assist them in using these community resources.

The second example was about the once or twice weekly luncheon clubs in village halls which the council's social services funded through grants which paid for the hire of the hall, payment of the cook, and taxi fares to bring older people to the luncheon clubs. Those attending paid about £5 per day. Attendance tailed off when the village pubs introduced on a couple of lunchtimes each week two course luncheons for people aged over 65 years for a similar price as the luncheon club meals. Older people chose the pub meals and ambience over the village hall luncheon clubs. It was a win-win for the older people and the community, which benefited from a pub which was more viable and vibrant throughout the week. The grants paid for the luncheon clubs were now made available as direct payments to cover the transport costs to the pubs.

What to Seek to Shape for the Future

1. A return to a focus on relationships as a key component of social work, with continuity of contact with service users, and with space and time to engage with service users as was and is still being achieved, for example, in family centres and mental health resource centres. As Brid Featherstone, Sue White and Kate Morris argued in 2014:

   > We need change because, over the past few decades, a transactional form of welfare developed. This model is rooted in market reforms with their embrace of centralised bureaucracy, targets and timescales, and emphasises efficiency and a particular limited form of accountability. Yet, time and time again, what service users value and indeed what the research tells us is needed for a good society is something more human, caring and time rich … We need change because we have lost sight of what is needed in a good society for its families to flourish. [6]

2. A focus on communities as a lived experience, and potential resource for service users, and with knowledge of communities as a part of understanding the context of people's lives. Locating and embedding the personal social services and social workers within communities is likely to increase their accessibility and acceptability and also their relevance as a local resource.
3. Promoting organisational and workforce continuity and stability over churn and change. Too frequent, too rapid, and too expansive change leads to disruption and disjunction and is also distracting. It also often is never allowed to bed in and fails to deliver what was intended. Churn and change not only disrupts the workforce and relationships with service users, but it also undermines partnership working and trust with other agencies and workers.
4. An understanding that terrible events and tragedies will happen and that these are not necessarily the consequence of 'failings' by workers or organisations. It is not possible to predict or have perfect control over the future. Judgements have to be made at the time in the context of workloads and work pressures, based on incomplete and changing

information, and without a perfect crystal ball. Learning cultures recognise and accept terrible events as an opportunity to reflect and learn. Blame cultures look to allocate accountability which is seen as equivalent to guilt. It is destructive and undermining of learning and development and measured judgements.

5. Professional commitment and strength to champion social work and its contribution and to build alliances with others to confront and challenge discrimination and oppression. As the personal social services in England and across the UK are largely shaped by statute and delivered as a state responsibility individual opportunity and capacity to challenge is inevitably limited by being an agency employee. All the more important for social workers and others to create collective voices locally, regionally and nationally so that they are not isolated and vulnerable. Use those collective voices through local and national media to challenge the narratives about poverty being the consequence of personal fecklessness and recklessness, impairment and illness as personal failings and weakness, and public services and public servants as sluggish and self-interested.

And what of the Seebohm Committee and its aspirations 50 years ago? David Behan reflected:

Seebohm was a solution to those issues which were identified by that first generation after the Second World War. My personal view is that we never saw the Seebohm departments delivered. [What we saw] was Seebohm without prevention. I began my career in 1974 and the investment in the 1970s got close to the preventative element of Seebohm, but when the economics began to bite in the 1980s I think that effectively finished the delivery of the vision that was Seebohm. My judgement of the underpinning philosophy of Seebohm was that it was absolutely first class and excellent, but the issue was to support the ambition of the idea through to delivery ... the economics, the social philosophy, the politics and the morality at the time was needed and you don't always get those alignments. [David Behan interview]

And what about social work and its future? David Jones commented:

I have never ever bought into the view that social work is as vulnerable as some people like to make it because it is such an essential service, and when it hits the fan people need social workers. I have always felt reasonably confident about that. I don't buy into "we are going to be wiped out." [David Jones interview]

Recent years have shown how uncertain and unpredictable what 'hits the fan' can be, from man-made disasters (such as the 2008 banking crisis and wars with displaced populations) and natural disasters (such earthquakes, volcanic eruptions and tsunamis) to disasters which are a culmination of human and natural activity (such as the climate change consequences of droughts, famines and widespread fires).

Most recently the coronavirus pandemic has not only shown the varying competence of governments but also brought to the fore who are the real 'key workers' when there is a crisis across communities—they are largely public sector workers and those in the private sector in the low-paid insecure gig economy. Alongside health workers, those working in social care and social workers have, rather belatedly, received public and then political recognition for the crucial work they undertake, but alongside the terrible cost of older people in care homes left stranded when they might have received treatment in hospitals when critically ill and vulnerable children and others left largely unseen at home. The danger is that it will be back to 'business as usual' once the pandemic is under control and the economy, growth and increasing affluence for a minority once again become the priority and the c-virus key workers are returned to their low and marginalised status.

There will, however, always be people needing help in the midst of personal and community crisis. There will always be major life-changing traumas and events where others can help to create space, safety and calm amongst chaos and turmoil and to help see and think through a way forward. There will be those who are vulnerable and victimised needing allies and advocates. And there is continuing social change to be shaped which would benefit from the values, knowledge and commitment of social workers.

Appendix: A Brief Note on Some of the Key Roles Held by the Interviewees

THE NUFFIELD FOUNDATION AWARDED A GRANT TOWARDS COVERING THE COSTS IN UNDERTAKING AND TRANSCRIBING THE INTERVIEWS

Mark Allen

Residential child care officer; journalist; founding editor Community Care magazine; publisher.

Joan Baraclough

Medical social worker; deputy head of hospital social work department; assistant general secretary BASW; lead on post-qualifying studies Central Council for Education and Training in Social Work; assistant chief inspector of social services and head of physical disability and mental health SSI policy group Department of Health.

© The Author(s) 2020
R. Jones, *A History of the Personal Social Services in England*,
https://doi.org/10.1007/978-3-030-46123-2

David Behan

Social worker; director of social services; president Association of Director of Social Services; chief executive Commission for Social Care Inspection; director general social care, local government and care partnerships Department of Health; chief executive Care Quality Commission.

Keith Bilton

Child care officer; general secretary of the Association of Child Care Officers; secretary of the Seebohm Implementation Action Group; assistant general secretary of the British Association of Social Workers; controller of social services Harrow.

John Bolton

Social worker; assistant director of social services; assistant director joint reviews Social Services Inspectorate and Audit Commission; director of social services; strategic finance director Department of Health.

Jane Campbell

Director of training London Boroughs Disability Resource Team; co-director National Centre for Independent Living; executive chair Social Care Institute for Excellence; commissioner Disability Rights Commission; member of the House of Lords.

Bleddyn Davies

Economist and researcher; professor of social policy; founder and director of Personal Social Services Research Unit.

Hilton Dawson

Social worker and social services manager; member of Parliament; founder All Parliamentary Group for Children and Young People in Care; chief executive British Association of Social Workers.

David Donnison

Lecturer, researcher and professor of social administration; chair Supplementary Benefits Commission and numerous government commissions and reviews.

Naomi Eisenstadt

Children's centre manager; chief executive Family Service Units; director Sure Start and Extended Schools Department for Education and Science; chief advisor on children's services to Secretary of State for Children, Schools and Families; director Cabinet Office Social Exclusion Task Force.

Paul Ennals

Children's residential care officer; director of services Sense; director of education and employment Royal National Institute for the Blind; chair of Council for Disabled Children; chief executive National Children's Bureau.

John Evans

National and international disability activist; early founder of independent living scheme; co-founder of the National Centre for Independent Living.

Bob Holman

Child care officer; lecturer and professor of social administrator; community worker.

Beverley Hughes

Probation officer; lecturer and head of university department of social policy and social work; council leader; member of Parliament; minister of state Home Office; minister for children Department of Children, Schools and Families; member of the House of Lords.

Rupert Hughes

Civil servant; assistant secretary children's division Department of Health and Social Security; lead civil servant on the 1989 Children Act.

David Jones

Social worker; NSPCC manager; general secretary of British Association of Social Workers; director of operations Central Council for Education and training in Social Work; joint reviewer Social Services Inspectorate and Audit Commission; policy development Department for Education, Schools and Families; president International Federation of Social Workers.

Julie Jones

Policy officer and deputy head of council policy unit; social services principal research officer; deputy director and director of social services; president Association of Directors of Social Services; chief executive Social Care Institute for Excellence.

Martin Knapp

Research economist; professor of health and care policy; director Personal Social Services Research Unit; director National Institute of Health Research School for Social Care Research.

Herbert Laming

Probation officer; assistant chief probation officer; deputy director and director of social services; president of Association of Directors of Social Services; chief inspector for social services Department of Health; chair Victoria Climbie Inquiry; member of the House of Lords.

Tim Loughton

Member of Parliament; shadow children's minister; children's minister; co-chair of the All Party Parliamentary Group for Children (APPG).

Tom Luce

Senior civil servant Department of Health and the Treasury; head of social care policy Department of Health.

Anne Parker

Health service manager; assistant county welfare officer; assistant director and director of social services; honorary secretary Association of Directors of Social Services; chair National Care Standards Commission; chair Carers National Association.

Roy Parker

Child care officer and residential child care officer; lecturer and professor of social policy; member of Seebohm Committee.

Gordon Peters

Social worker; member of Case Con; social services research officer; social
work lecturer; co-founder of Critical Social Policy journal; director of
social services.

Denise Platt

Medical social worker; principal hospital social worker; director of social
services; president Association of Directors of Social Services; under-
secretary for social services Association of Metropolitan Authorities;
head of social services Local Government Association; chair National
Institute for Social Work; chief inspector of social services Department
of Health; chair Commission for Social Care Inspection.

John Rea Price

Probation officer; senior child care officer; Southwark Community
Project; Home Office children's service inspector; director of social services; director National Children's Bureau.

Wendy Rose

Medical social worker; deputy principal medical social worker; development officer for health and social services; assistant director of social
services research, development and planning; assistant director (children's Services) Social Services Inspectorate, Department for Health
and Social Security.

Roger Singleton

Teacher and deputy head in approved schools; professional advisor to
regional children's planning committee; deputy director and then chief

executive Barnardo's; chief advisor to government on safety of children; chair Independent Safeguarding Authority.

Olive Stevenson

Child care officer; lecturer and professor of social policy and social work; member of Maria Colwell Inquiry panel; social work advisor to Supplementary Benefits Commission.

Bill Utting

Probation officer; principal probation officer; lecturer in applied social studies; director of social services; chief social work services officer/chief inspector of social services in the Department of Health.

David Walden

Senior civil servant Department of Health; secretary to Sir Roy Griffiths inquiry on adult social care; head of community care division Department for Health; director Anchor Housing Trust; director of strategy Commission for Social Care Inspection; head of adult social care Social Care Institute for Excellence.

Peter Westland

Probation officer; probation service inspector; deputy children's officer; director of social services; under-secretary for social services at the Association of Metropolitan Authorities.

Tom White

Child care officer; area and deputy children's officer; president of Association of Child Care officers; chair of Seebohm Implementation

Action Group; director of social services; president Association of Directors of Social Services, chief executive NCH Action for Children.

Presentations at seminars of the Social Work History Network were also recorded and transcribed:

1989 Children Act 25th anniversary seminar:

James Blewett, June Thorburn, Jane Tunstill, Brenda Hale, Virginia Bottomley

History of Council of Education and Training for Social Workers' seminar:

Hugh Barr, David Lane, Mary Braginsky, Jenny Weinstein, Simon Biggs

Bibliography

Chapter 1

1. Havel, V. (1993) Summer Meditations, London, Vintage, p. 121.
2. Harris, J. (2007) Principles, Poor Laws and Welfare States, in Hills, J., Le Grand, J. and Piachud, D. (eds) Making Social Policy Work, Bristol, Policy Press, pp. 13–34.
3. Triggle, N. (2012) Sharp rise in social care fees a stealth tax, BBC News, 30 December, www.bbc.co.uk/news/health-16353807.
4. Press Association (2011) Elderly people face rising cost of council care services, The Guardian, 30 December, www.guardian.co.uk/society/2011/dec/30/elderly-rising-cost-council-services.
5. Tett, G. (2009) Fool's Gold: How Unrestrained Greed Corrupted a Dream, Shattered Global Markets and Unleashed a Catastrophe, London, Little Brown.
6. Attlee, C. (1920) The Social Worker, London, Bell.
7. Holmes, R. (2008) The Age of Wonder: How the Romantic Generation Discovered The Beauty and Terror of Science, London, Harper Press, p. 93.

© The Author(s) 2020
R. Jones, *A History of the Personal Social Services in England*,
https://doi.org/10.1007/978-3-030-46123-2

8. Dewey, J., discussed in Wright Mills, C. (1966) The Sociology and Pragmatism, New York, Oxford University Press, pp. 356–446.
9. Quoted by Simms. B. (2004) in a review of Reynolds, D. In Command of History: Churchill Fighting and Writing the Second World War, The Sunday Times Culture Supplement, 31 October, p. 46.
10. Martines, L. (2003) April Blood: Florence and the Plot against the Medici, London, Pimlico, p. 254.
11. Orwell, G. (1989) Homage to Catalonia, London, Penguin, p. 186.

Chapter 2

1. Donnison, D. (1974) The Development of Casework in a Children's Department, in Donnison, D., Chapman, V., Meacher, M., Sears, A., and Unwin, K. (eds) Social Policy and Administration Revisited, London, George Allen and Unwin, pp. 103–132.
2. Packman, J. (1975) The Child's Generation: Child Care Policy from Curtis to Houghton, Oxford and London, Basil Blackwell and Martin Robertson, p. 155.
3. Titmuss (1965) Social Work and Social Service: A Challenge for Local Government, Lecture delivered to the Social Workers Conference at the Health Congress, Eastbourne, April 1965, reprinted in Titmuss, R.M. (1968) Commitment to Welfare, London, George Allen and Unwin, pp. 85–86.
4. Brill, M. (1972) The Local Authority Social Worker, in Jones, K. (ed.) The Year Book of Social Policy in Britain 1971, London, Routledge and Kegan Paul, p. 81.
5. Webb, A. and Wistow, G. (1987) Social Work, Social Care and Social Planning: The Personal Social Services Since Seebohm, Harlow, Longman, p. 50.
6. Forder, A, and Kay, S. (1973) Social Work, in Cooper, M.H. (ed.) Social Policy: A Survey of Recent Developments, Oxford, Basil Blackwood, p. 22.
7. Cooper, J. (1983) The Creation of the British Personal Social Services 1962–1974, London, Heinemann Educational Books, p. 31.

8. Seebohm Report (1968) Report of the Committee on Local Authority and Allied Personal Social Services, Appendix L, Cmnd 3703, London, HMSO, p. 329.

9. Seebohm Report (1968) Report of the Committee on Local Authority and Allied Personal Social Services, Appendix F, London, HMSO, p. 267.

10. Seebohm Report (1968) Report of the Committee on Local Authority and Allied Personal Social Services, Appendix F, London, HMSO, p. 296.

11. Seebohm Report (1968) Report of the Committee on Local Authority and Allied Personal Social Services, Appendix F, London, HMSO, p. 302.

12. Francis, M. (2013) Harold Wilson's 'white heat of technology' speech 50 years on, https://www.theguardian.com/science/political-science/2013/sep/19/harold-wilson-white-heat-technology-speech.

13. Evans, M. (2010) Harold Macmillan's 'never had it so good' speech followed the 1950s boom, https://www.telegraph.co.uk/news/politics/8145390/Harold-Macmillans-never-had-it-so-good-speech-followed-the-1950s-boom.html.

14. Abel-Smith, B. and Townsend, P. (1965) The Poor and the Poorest, London, Bell.

15. Townsend, P. (1962) The Last Refuge: A survey of residential institutions and homes for the aged in England and Wales, London, Routledge and Kegan Paul.

16. Robb, B. (1967) Sans Everything: A Case to Answer, London, Nelson.

17. Butler, I. and Drakeford, M. (2003) Scandal, Social Policy and Social Welfare, Bristol, Policy Press.

18. Goffman, E. (1962) Asylums, Harmondsworth, Penguin Books.

19. Packman, J. (1975) The Child's Generation: Child Care Policy from Curtis to Houghton, Oxford and London, Basil Blackwell and Martin Robertson, p. 158.

20. Maslow, A.H. (1954) Motivation and Personality, New York, Harper and Row.

21. McGregor, D. (1960) The Human Side of Enterprise, Sydney, McGraw-Hill Australia.

22. Titmuss (1965) Social Work and Social Service: A Challenge for Local Government, Lecture delivered to the Social Workers Conference at the Health Congress, Eastbourne, April 1965, reprinted in Titmuss, R.M. (1968) Commitment to Welfare, London, George Allen and Unwin, p. 87.
23. Social Work Task Force (2009) Building a safe, confident future— The final report of the Social Work Task Force, London, Department for Children, Schools and Families.
24. Munro, E. (2011) The Munro Review of Child Protection: Final Report, CM 6802, London, Department for Education.
25. Seebohm Report (1968) Report of the Committee on Local Authority and Allied Personal Social Services, Appendix F, London, HMSO, p. 276.
26. Hall, P. (1976) Reforming the Welfare: The politics of change in the personal social services, London, Heinemann, p. 21.
27. Holman, B. (1998) Child Care Revisited: The Children's Departments 1948–1971, London, Institute of Childcare and Social Education, p. 27.
28. Cooper, J. (1983) The Creation of the British Personal Social Services 1962–1974, London, Heinemann Educational Books, p. 56.
29. Hall, P. (1976) Reforming the Welfare: The politics of change in the personal social services, London, Heinemann, p. 25.
30. Hiddleston, V. (2006) The Social Work (Scotland) Act 1968, paper given at Edinburgh University, 3 November.
31. Hall, P. (1976) Reforming the Welfare: The politics of change in the personal social services, London, Heinemann, p. 26.
32. Donnison, D. (1974) Taking Decisions in a University, in Donnison, D., Chapman, V., Meacher, M., Sears, A., and Unwin, K. (eds) Social Policy and Administration Revisited, London, George Allen and Unwin, pp. 253–285.
33. Oakley, A. (2014) Father and Daughter: Patriarchy, Gender and Social Science, Bristol, Policy Press, p. 168.
34. Reisman, D.A. (1977) Richard Titmuss: Welfare and Society, London, Heinemann Educational Books.
35. Reisman, D.A. (1977) Richard Titmuss: Welfare and Society, London, Heinemann Educational Books, p. 5.

36. Report of the Working Party on Social Workers in the Local Authority Health and Welfare Services (1959) London, HMSO.
37. White, T. (2010) The Surprise of My Life, personal publication, p. 176.
38. Cooper, J. (1983) The Creation of the British Personal Social Services 1962–1974, London, Heinemann Educational Books, p. 66.
39. Webb, A. and Wistow, G. (1987) Social Work, Social Care and Social Planning: The Personal Social Services Since Seebohm, Harlow, Longman, p. 48.
40. Titmuss (1965) Social Work and Social Service: A Challenge for Local Government, Lecture delivered to the Social Workers Conference at the Health Congress, Eastbourne, April 1965, reprinted in Titmuss, R.M. (1968) Commitment to Welfare, London, George Allen and Unwin, pp. 88–89.
41. Cooper, J. (1983) The Creation of the British Personal Social Services 1962–1974, London, Heinemann Educational Books, p. 63.
42. Hall, P. (1976) Reforming the Welfare: The politics of change in the personal social services, London, Heinemann, p. 24.
43. Seebohm Report (1968) Report of the Committee on Local Authority and Allied Personal Social Services, Appendix L, Cmnd 3703, London, HMSO, p. 11.
44. Cooper, J. (1983) The Creation of the British Personal Social Services 1962–1974, London, Heinemann Educational Books, pp. 65–66.
45. Hall, P. (1976) Reforming the Welfare: The politics of change in the personal social services, London, Heinemann, p. 29.
46. Mayer, J. and Timms, N. (1970) The Client Speaks, London, Routledge and Kegan Paul.
47. Packman, J. (1968) Child Care Needs and Numbers, London, Allen and Unwin.
48. Raynor, P. and Vanstone, M. (2016) Moving Away from Social Work and Half Way Back Again: New Research on Skills in Probation, British Journal of Social Work, June, 46.4, pp. 131–147.
49. Cooper, J. (1983) The Creation of the British Personal Social Services 1962–1974, London, Heinemann Educational Books, pp. 46–47.
50. Cooper, J. (1983) The Creation of the British Personal Social Services 1962–1974, London, Heinemann Educational Books, p. 80.

51. Hall, P. (1976) Reforming the Welfare: The politics of change in the personal social services, London, Heinemann, p. 54.
52. Holman, B. (1998) Child Care Revisited: The Children's Departments 1948–1971, London, Institute of Childcare and Social Education UK, p. 31.

Chapter 3

1. Report of the Committee on Local Authority and Allied Personal Social Services (1968) Cmnd 3703, London, HMSO, p. 3.
2. Cooper, J. (1983) The Creation of the British Personal Social Services 1962–1974, London, Heinemann Educational Books, p. 90.
3. Glasby, J. (2007) Understanding Health and Social Care, Bristol, Policy Press.
4. Cooper, J. (1983) The Creation of the British Personal Social Services 1962–1974, London, Heinemann Educational Books, p. 87.
5. Cooper, J. (1983) The Creation of the British Personal Social Services 1962–1974, London, Heinemann Educational Books, p. 94.
6. Cooper, J. (1983) The Creation of the British Personal Social Services 1962–1974, London, Heinemann Educational Books, p. 96.
7. Cooper, J. (1983) The Creation of the British Personal Social Services 1962–1974, London, Heinemann Educational Books, p. 93.
8. Report of the Committee on Local Authority and Allied Personal Social Services (1968) Cmnd 3703, London, HMSO, p. 142.
9. Report of the Committee on Local Authority and Allied Personal Social Services (1968) Cmnd 3703, London, HMSO, p. 144.
10. Cooper, J. (1983) The Creation of the British Personal Social Services 1962–1974, London, Heinemann Educational Books, p. 89.
11. Young, M. and Willmott, P. (1957) Family and Kinship in East London, Harmondsworth, London.
12. Willmott, P. and Young, M. (1967) Family and Class in a London Suburb, London, The New English Library.
13. Frankenberg, R. (1966) Communities in Britain: Social Life in Town and Country, Harmondsworth, Penguin.

14. Rex, J. and Moore, R. (1967) Race, Community and Conflict: a study of Sparkbrook, Oxford, Oxford University Press.
15. Hall, P. (1976) Reforming the Welfare: The politics of change in the personal social services, London, Heinemann, p. 66.
16. Department for Education (2019) Characteristics of Children in Need, https://www.gov.uk/government/statistics/characteristics-of-children-in-need-2018-to-2019.
17. Public Health England (2019) Death in people aged 75 and older in England in 2017, https://www.gov.uk/government/publications/death-in-people-aged-75-years-and-older-in-england-in-2017/death-in-people-aged-75-years-and-older-in-england-in-2017.
18. Hall, P. (1976) Reforming the Welfare: The politics of change in the personal social services, London, Heinemann, p. 70.
19. Hall, P. (1976) Reforming the Welfare: The politics of change in the personal social services, London, Heinemann, pp. 87–88.
20. Hall, P. (1976) Reforming the Welfare: The politics of change in the personal social services, London, Heinemann, p. 68.
21. Hall, P. (1976) Reforming the Welfare: The politics of change in the personal social services, London, Heinemann, p. 69.

Chapter 4

1. The Plowden Report (1967) Children and their Primary Schools: A Report of the Central Advisory Council for Education (England), London, HMSO.
2. Ministry of Health (1968) The Administrative structure of the medical and related services in England and Wales, London, Ministry of Health.
3. Report of the Royal Commission on Local Government in England 1966–1969 (1969), London, HMSO.
4. The Skeffington Report (1969) People and Planning: Report of the Committee on Public Participation in Planning, London, HMSO.
5. Howard, A. (ed.) (1979) The Crossman Diaries: Selections from the Diaries of a Cabinet Minister 1964–1970, London, Methuen.

6. Howard, A. (ed.) (1979) The Crossman Diaries: Selections from the Diaries of a Cabinet Minister 1964–1970, London, Methuen, pp. 514–516.
7. Townsend, P. (1970) The Objectives of the New Local Social Service, in Townsend, P. (ed) The Fifth Social Service: A Critical Analysis of the Seebohm Proposals, London, Fabian Society.
8. Townsend, P. (1970) The Objectives of the New Local Social Service, in Townsend, P. (ed) The Fifth Social Service: A Critical Analysis of the Seebohm Proposals, London, Fabian Society, p. 11.
9. Townsend, P. (1970) The Objectives of the New Local Social Service, in Townsend, P. (ed) The Fifth Social Service: A Critical Analysis of the Seebohm Proposals, London, Fabian Society, p. 22.
10. Brooke, R. (1969) Civil Rights and Social Services, The Political Quarterly, 40.1, January–March.
11. Wistrich, E. The Committee on Local Authority and Allied Personal Social Services, The Political Quaterly, 40.1, January–March, pp. 112–116.
12. Sinfield, A. (1970) Which Way for Social Work, in Townsend, P. (ed) The Fifth Social Service: A Critical Analysis of the Seebohm Proposals, London, Fabian Society, p. 28.
13. Holman, B. (2001) Champions for Children, Bristol, Policy Press, p. 119.
14. Butrym, Z. (1977) Book review of 'Reforming the Welfare', 16 March, Community Care.
15. Packman, J. (1975) The Child's Generation: Child Care Policy from Curtis to Houghton, p. 162.
16. White, T. (2010) The Surprise of My Life, self-published, p. 117.
17. Hall, P. (1976) Reforming the Welfare: The politics of change in the personal social services, London, Heinemann, p. 87.
18. White, T. (2010) The Surprise of My Life, self-published, p. 179.
19. Hall, P. (1976) Reforming the Welfare: The politics of change in the personal social services, London, Heinemann, p. 91.
20. White, T. (2010) The Surprise of My Life, self-published, p. 178.
21. Bilton, K. (2008) The Unification of Social Work Services and of Organisations of Social Workers, 1963–1971, unpublished paper to Social Work History Network, 8 March.

22. Niechcial, J. (2010) Lucy Faithful: Mother to hundreds, self-published, p. 90.

23. Niechcial, J. (2010) Lucy Faithful: Mother to hundreds, self-published, p. 146.

24. Hall, P. (1976) Reforming the Welfare: The politics of change in the personal social services, London, Heinemann, p. 97.

25. Hall, P. (1976) Reforming the Welfare: The politics of change in the personal social services, London, Heinemann, pp. 109–110.

26. Hall, P. (1976) Reforming the Welfare: The politics of change in the personal social services, London, Heinemann, p. 84.

27. Hall, P. (1976) Reforming the Welfare: The politics of change in the personal social services, London, Heinemann, p. 83.

28. Hall, P. (1976) Reforming the Welfare: The politics of change in the personal social services, London, Heinemann, p. 92.

29. Cooper, J. (1983) The Creation of the British Personal Social Services 1962–1974, London, Heinemann Educational Books, p. 117.

30. Hall, P. (1976) Reforming the Welfare: The politics of change in the personal social services, London, Heinemann, p. 107.

31. White, T. (2010) The Surprise of My Life, self-published, p. 180.

32. Cooper, J. (1983) The Creation of the British Personal Social Services 1962–1974, London, Heinemann Educational Books, p. 110.

33. Cooper, J. (1983) The Creation of the British Personal Social Services 1962–1974, London, Heinemann Educational Books, p. 111.

34. Bilton, K. (2008) The Unification of Social Work Services and of Organisations of Social Workers, 1963–1971, unpublished paper to Social Work History Network, 8 March, p. 7.

35. Hall, P. (1976) Reforming the Welfare: The politics of change in the personal social services, London, Heinemann, p. 104.

36. Cooper, J. (1983) The Creation of the British Personal Social Services 1962–1974, London, Heinemann Educational Books, p. 112.

37. Hall, P. (1976) Reforming the Welfare: The politics of change in the personal social services, London, Heinemann, p. 103.

38. Cooper, J. (1983) The Creation of the British Personal Social Services 1962–1974, London, Heinemann Educational Books, p. 116.

39. Hall, P. (1976) Reforming the Welfare: The politics of change in the personal social services, London, Heinemann, p. 147.

40. Hall, P. (1976) Reforming the Welfare: The politics of change in the personal social services, London, Heinemann, p. 111.
41. Cooper, J. (1983) The Creation of the British Personal Social Services 1962–1974, London, Heinemann Educational Books, p. 119.

Chapter 5

1. White, T. (2010) The Surprise of My Life, self-published, p. 180.
2. Smith, J. (1972) Top Jobs in the Social Services, in Jones, K. (ed) The Year Book of Social Policy in Britain 1971, London, Routledge and Kegan Paul, p. 18.
3. Sandbrook, D. (2010) State of Emergency: The Way We Were in Britain: 1970–1974, p. 68.
4. Marwick, P. (1996) British Society Since 1945, Third Edition, London, Penguin, p. 224.
5. White, T. (2010) The Surprise of My Life, self-published, pp. 181–182.
6. Niechcial, J. (2010) Lucy Faithful: Mother to hundreds, self-published, p. 100.
7. Niechcial, J. (2010) Lucy Faithful: Mother to hundreds, self-published, p. 101.
8. Smith, J. (1972) Top Jobs in the Social Services, in Jones, K. (ed) The Year Book of Social Policy 1971, London, Routledge and Kegan Paul, p. 24.
9. Foren, R. and Brown, M. (1971) Planning for Service: An examination of the organisation and administration of Local Authority Social Services Departments, London, Charles Knight, p. 10.
10. Topliss, E. and Gould, B. (1981) A Charter for the Disabled, Oxford and London, Basil Blackwell and Martin Robertson.
11. Topliss, E. and Gould, B. (1981) A Charter for the Disabled, Oxford and London, Basil Blackwell and Martin Robertson, p. 136.
12. BBC (2010) Forty years of the Chronically Sick and Disabled Persons Act, http://news.bbc.co.uk/local/lancashire/hi/people_and_places/newsid_8697000/8697441.stm.

13. Phelan, P. (1979) Social Services for Physically Handicapped People, in Cypher, J. (ed) Seebohm Across Three Decades, Birmingham, BASW Publications, p. 54.

14. Bucke, M. (1972) Promoting the welfare of old people, in Jones, K. (ed) The Year Book of Social Policy in Britain 1971, London, Routledge and Kegan Paul, p. 150.

15. Topliss, E. (1975) Provision for the Disabled, Oxford and London, Basil Blackwell and Martin Robertson, p. 147.

16. Report of the Committee on Children and Young Persons (1960) Cmnd 1191, London, HMSO.

17. Longford, Lord (1964) Crime—A Challenge to Us All, June, London, Labour Party.

18. The Child, the Family and the Young Offender (1965), Cmnd 2742, London, HMSO.

19. Children in Trouble (1968), Cmnd 3601, London, HMSO.

20. Packman, J. (1975) The Child's Generation: Child Care Policy from Curtis to Houghton, Oxford and London, Basil Blackwell and Martin Robertson, pp. 113–114.

21. Department of Health and Social Security (1971) Intermediate Treatment: A guide for the Regional Planning of new forms of treatment for children in trouble, London, HMSO.

22. Paley, J. and Thorpe, D. (1974) Children: Handle with Care, Leicester, National Youth Bureau.

23. Jones, R. and Kerslake, A. (1979) Intermediate Treatment and Social Work, London, Heinemann.

24. Packman, J. (1975) The Child's Generation: Child Care Policy from Curtis to Houghton, Oxford and London, Basil Blackwell and Martin Robertson, p. 121.

25. Parker, H., Casburn, M. and Turnbull, D. (1981) Receiving Juvenile Justice, Oxford, Basil Blackwell, p. 3.

26. Packman, J. (1975) The Child's Generation: Child Care Policy from Curtis to Houghton, Oxford and London, Basil Blackwell and Martin Robertson, p. 124.

27. Berlins, M. and Wansell, G. (1974) Caught in the Act: Children, Society and the Law, Harmondsworth, Penguin, p. 78.

28. Berlins, M. and Wansell, G. (1974) Caught in the Act: Children, Society and the Law, Harmondsworth, Penguin, p. 85.
29. Taylor, I., Walton, P. and Young, J. (1973) The New Criminology: For a social theory of deviance, London, Routledge and Kegan Paul.
30. Schur, E. (1973) Radical Non-Intervention: Rethinking the Delinquency Problem, New York, Prentice Hall.
31. Berlins, M. and Wansell, G. (1974) Caught in the Act: Children, Society and the Law, Harmondsworth, Penguin, p. 87.
32. Berlins, M. and Wansell, G. (1974) Caught in the Act: Children, Society and the Law, Harmondsworth, Penguin, p. 88.
33. Thorpe, D., Smith, D., Green, C.J. and Paley, J.H. (1980) Out of Care: The Community Support of Juvenile Offenders, London, George Allen and Unwin.
34. Thorpe, D., Smith, D., Green, C.J. and Paley, J.H. (1980) Out of Care: The Community Support of Juvenile Offenders, London, George Allen and Unwin, p. 13.
35. Dunlop, A. (1974) The Approved School Experience: A Home Office Research Report, London, Her Majesty's Stationary Office.
36. Gill, O. (1974) Whitegate: An Approved School in Transition, Liverpool, Liverpool University Press.
37. Cornish, D. and Clarke, R. (1975) Residential Treatment and Its Effects on Delinquency, Home Office Research Study Number 32, London, Her Majesty's Stationary Office.
38. Tutt, N. (1994) Care or Custody: Community Homes and the Treatment of Delinquency, London, Darton, Longman and Todd.
39. Foren, R. and Brown, M. (1971) Planning for Service: An examination of the organisation and administration of Local Authority Social Services Departments, London, Charles Knight, p. 11.
40. Rowbottom, R., Hey, A. and Billis, D. (1974) Social Services Departments: Developing Patterns of Work and Organisation, London, Heinemann.
41. Billis, D., Bromley, G., Hey, A. and Rowbottom, R. (1980) Organising Social Services Departments, London, Heinemann.
42. Holman, B. (1998) Child Care Revisited: The Children's Departments 1848–1971, London, Institute of Child Care and Education, p. 125.

43. Leonard, P. (1970) Comment: A New Social Service?, Social Work, 15.6, pp. 3–6.
44. White, T. (2010) The Surprise of My Life, self-published, p. 185.
45. Hall, P. (1976) Reforming the Welfare: The politics of change in the personal social services, London, Heinemann, p. 129.
46. Stevenson, O. (1981) Specialisation in Social Service Teams, London, George Allen and Unwin.
47. Marshall, T.H. (1969) The Role of the Personal Social Services, The Political Quarterly, January–March, 40.1, p. 11.
48. Timmins, N. (1996) The Five Giants: A Biography of the Welfare State, London, Fontana Press, pp. 292–293.
49. Hey, A. (1979) Specialisation in Social Work, in Cypher, J. (ed) Seebohm Across Three Decades, Birmingham, BASW, p. 165.
50. White, T. (1981) Recent Developments and the Response of Social Services Departments, in Goldberg, E.M. and Hatch, S. (eds) A New Look at the Personal Social Services, London, Policy Studies Institute Paper Number 4, p. 5.
51. Biffen, J. (1994) Keith Joseph: Power behind the throne, https://www.theguardian.com/politics/1994/dec/12/obituaries.
52. Laurence, J. (2006) Keith Joseph, the father of Thatcherism, 'was autistic' claims professor, 12 July, https://www.independent.co.uk/life-style/health-and-families/health-news/keith-joseph-the-father-of-thatcherism-was-autistic-claims-professor-407600.html.
53. White, T. (2010) The Surprise of My Life, self-published, p. 186.

Chapter 6

1. Committee of Inquiry into the Care and Supervision Provided in Relation to Maria Colwell (1974) Report of the Committee of Inquiry into the Care and Supervision provided by local authorities and other agencies in Relation to Maria Colwell and the co-ordination between them, London, Her Majesty's Stationery Office.
2. Home Office (1945) Report by Sir William Monckton KCMG KCVO MC KC on the circumstances which led to the boarding out of Dennis and Terence O'Neill at Bank Farm, Minsterly and the

steps taken to supervise their welfare, Cmnd 6636, London, Home Office.

3. Care of Children Committee (1946) Report of the Care of Children Committee, Cmnd 6922 London, His Majesty's Stationery Office.

4. Stevenson, O. (1999) Child Welfare in the United Kingdom, Oxford, Blackwell, p. 105.

5. Butler, I. and Drakeford, M. (2011) Social Work on Trial: The Colwell Inquiry and the State of Welfare, Bristol, Policy Press, p. 123.

6. Butler, I. and Drakeford, M. (2011) Social Work on Trial: The Colwell Inquiry and the State of Welfare, Bristol, Policy Press, p. 113.

7. Kempe, C.H. and Helfer, R. E (1968), editors: The Battered Child, Chicago: Chicago University Press.

8. Renvoise, J. (1974) Children in Danger, Harmondsworth, Penguin.

9. Bamford, T. (2015) A Contemporary History of Social Work, Bristol, Policy Press, p. 41.

10. Parton, N. (2011) The increasing length and complexity of central government guidance about child abuse in England: 1974–2010. Discussion Paper. University of Huddersfield, Huddersfield (Unpublished).

11. Rogowski, S. (2010) Social Work: The Rise and Fall of a Profession?, Bristol, Policy Press, p. 73.

12. Rogowski, S. (2013) Critical Social Work with Children and Families: Theory, Context and Practice, Bristol, Policy Press, p. 54.

13. Featherstone, B, White, S. and Morris, K. (2014) Re-imagining child protection: Towards humane social work with families, Policy Press, Bristol.

14. Packman, J. (1975) The Child's Generation: Child Care Policy from Curtis to Houghton, Oxford and London, Basil Blackwell and Martin Robertson, p. 179.

15. Jenkins, R. (1979) Social Services for Children, in Cypher, J. (ed) Seebohm Across Three Decades, Birmingham, BASW, p. 28.

16. Jenkins, R. (1979) Social Services for Children, in Cypher, J. (ed) Seebohm Across Three Decades, Birmingham, BASW, p. 27.

17. Jones, R. (2009) Children's acts 1948–2008: the drivers for legislative change in England over 60 years. Journal of Children's Services, 4(4), pp. 39–52.

18. Jones, R. (2020) The Impact of Scandals and Inquiries on Social Work and the Personal Social Services, in Bamford, T. and Bilton, K. (eds) Social Work: Past, Present and Future, Bristol, Policy Press.

19. Parker, R. (2005) Then and Now: 40 Years of Social Research in the UK, in Axford, N., Berry, V., Little, M. and Morpeth, L. (eds.) Forty Years of Research, Policy and Practice, Chichester, Wiley, p. 25.

20. Rowe, J. and Lambert, L. (1973) Children Who Wait, Association of British Adoption Agencies, London.

21. Goldstein, J., Freud, A. and Solnit, A. (1973) Beyond the Best Interests of the Child, New York, The Free Press.

22. Kellmer Pringle, M. (1975) The Needs of Children, London, Hutchinson, p. 157.

23. Kellmer Pringle, M. (1975) The Needs of Children, London, Hutchinson, p. 139.

24. Joseph, K. (1975) Foreword, in Kellmer Pringle, M. (1975) The Needs of Children, London, Hutchinson, p. 9.

25. Joseph, K. (1975) Foreword, in Kellmer Pringle, M. (1975) The Needs of Children, London, Hutchinson, pp. 9–10.

26. Rutter, M. and Madge, N. (1976) Cycles of Disadvantage, London, Heinemann Educational Books, p. 27.

27. Rutter, M. and Madge, N. (1976) Cycles of Disadvantage, London, Heinemann Educational Books, pp. 303–304.

28. Newman, T. (2004) What Works in Building Resilience, Ilford, Barnardo's.

29. Rutter, M. (2008). Developing concepts in developmental psychopathology, pp. 3–22 in J.J. Hudziak (ed.), Developmental psychopathology and wellness: Genetic and environmental influences. Washington, DC: American Psychiatric Publishing.

30. Rutter, M. and Madge, N. (1976) Cycles of Disadvantage, London, Heinemann Educational Books, p. 325.

31. Wilkinson, R. and Pickett, K. (2010) The Spirit Level: Why Equality is Better for Everyone, London, Penguin Books.

32. Dorling, D. (2011) Injustice: Why Social Inequality Persists, Bristol, Policy Press.

33. Rutter, M. and Madge, N. (1976) Cycles of Disadvantage, London, Heinemann Educational Books, p. 327.

34. Rutter. M. (1977) Research into Prevention of Psychosocial Disorders in Childhood, in Barnes, J. and Connelly, N. (eds) Social Care Research, London, Bedford Square Press, p. 109.
35. McSmith, A. (2011) No Such Thing As Society: A History of Britain in the 1980s, London, Constable, p. 18.
36. Jenkins, S. (2007) Thatcher and Sons: A Revolution in Three Acts, London, Penguin Books, p. 44.
37. Gilmour, I. (1992) Dancing with Dogma: Britain under Thatcherism, London, Simon and Schuster, p. 2.
38. Young, H. (1989) One of Us: A Biography of Margaret Thatcher, London, Macmillan, p. 86.
39. Sandbrook, D. (2010) State of Emergency: The Way We Were in Britain: 1970–1974, p. 71.
40. Campbell, R. (2014) Roy Jenkins: A Well-Rounded Life, London, Jonathan Cape.
41. Sandbrook, D. (2010) State of Emergency: The Way We Were in Britain: 1970–1974, p. 72.
42. Sandbrook, D. (2010) State of Emergency: The Way We Were in Britain: 1970–1974, pp. 74–75.
43. Gilmour, I. and Garnett, M. (1998) Whatever Happened To The Tories: The Conservatives Since 1945, London, Fourth Estate, pp. 281–282.
44. Marwick, A. (1982) British Society Since 1945, London, Pelican Books, p. 186.
45. Jenkins, S. (2007) Thatcher and Sons: A Revolution in Three Acts, London, Penguin Books, p. 34.
46. Sandbrook, D. (2010) State of Emergency: The Way We Were in Britain: 1970–1974, p. 593.
47. Marwick, A. (1982) British Society Since 1945, London, Pelican Books, pp. 228–229.
48. Jenkins, S. (2007) Thatcher and Sons: A Revolution in Three Acts, London, Penguin Books, p. 35.
49. Steadman Jones, D. (2012) Masters of the Universe: Hayek, Friedman, and the Birth of Neoliberal Politics, Princeton, Princeton University Press, p. 242.

50. Timmins, N. (1996) The Five Giants: A Biography of the Welfare State, London, Fontana, p. 316.
51. Pierson, C. (1996) Social Policy, in Marquand, D. and Seldon, A. (1996) The Ideas that Shaped Post-War Britain, London, Fontana Press, p. 152.
52. Donnison, D. (1978) The Economic and Political Context, in Barnes, J. and Connelly, N. (eds) Social Care Research, London, Bedford Square Press, p. 70.

Chapter 7

1. Heraud, B. (1970) Sociology and Social Work: Perspectives and Problems, Oxford, Pergamon Press.
2. Schur, E. (1973) Radical Non-Intervention: Rethinking the Delinquency Problem, New York, Prentice-Hall, p. 23.
3. Becker. H. (1967) Whose Side Are We On? Social Problems, 14.3, pp. 239–247.
4. Cohen, S. (1973) Folk Devils and Moral Panics: The Creation of the Mods and Rockers, St Albans, Paladin.
5. Pearson, G. (1975) The Deviant Imagination: Psychiatry, Social Work and Social Change, London and Basingstoke, Macmillan.
6. Cypher, J. (1975) Social Work and Social Reform, in Jones, H. (ed) Towards a New Social Work, London, Routledge and Kegan Paul, p. 11.
7. Cypher, J. (1975) Social Work and Social Reform, in Jones, H. (ed) Towards a New Social Work, London, Routledge and Kegan Paul, p. 19.
8. Cypher, J. (1975) Social Work and Social Reform, in Jones, H. (ed) Towards a New Social Work, London, Routledge and Kegan Paul, p. 21.
9. Cohen, S. (1971) (ed) Images of Deviance, Harmondsworth, Penguin.
10. Taylor, I., Walton, P. and Young, J. (1973) The New Criminology: For A Social Theory of Deviance, London, Routledge and Kegan Paul.
11. Rock, P. (1973) Deviant Behaviour, London, Hutchinson.

12. Szasz, T. (1961) The Myth of Mental Illness, New York, Harper.
13. Szasz, T. (1970) The Manufacture of Madness: A Comparative Study of the Inquisition and the Mental Health Movement. New York, Syracuse University Press.
14. Scheff, Thomas J. (1967) Mental illness and social processes, New York, Harper & Row.
15. Scheff, Thomas J. (1970) Being Mentally Ill: A Sociological Theory, New Jersey, Transaction Publishers.
16. Laing, R.D. (1965) The Divided Self: An Existential Study in Sanity and Madness, Harmondsworth, Penguin Books.
17. Laing, R.D. (1969) Self and Others, Harmondsworth, Penguin Books.
18. Laing, R.D. & Esterson, A. (1964) Sanity, Madness, and the Family: Families of Schizophrenics, Harmondsworth, Penguin Books.
19. Cooper, D. (1967) (ed.) Psychiatry and Anti-Psychiatry, London, Paladin.
20. Cooper, D. (1974) The Death of the Family, Harmondsworth, Penguin Books.
21. Orford, J. (1976) The Social Psychology of Mental Disorder, Harmondsworth, Penguin Education, pp. 218–219.
22. Bailey, R. and Brake, M. (1975) (eds.) Radical Social Work, London, Edward Arnold.
23. Bailey, R. and Brake, M. (1975) (eds.) Radical Social Work, London, Edward Arnold, p. 198.
24. Weinstein, J. (2011) *Case Con* and radical social work in the 1970s: the impatient revolutionaries, in Lavalette, M. (ed.) Radical Social Work Today: Social Work at the Crossroads, Bristol, Policy Press, p. 21.
25. Simpkin, M. (1979) Trapped Within Welfare Surviving Social Work, London, Macmillan Press, p. 24.
26. Marx, K. and Engels, F. (1970) Selected Works, London, Lawrence and Wishart.
27. Marcuse, H. (1941) Reason and Revolution, Oxford, Oxford University Press.

28. Friere, P. (1972) Pedagogy and the Oppressed, Harmondsworth, Penguin.

29. Gramsci, A. (1971) Prison Notebooks, London, Lawrence and Wishart.

30. Reich, W. (1970) The Sexual Revolution, London, Vision Press.

31. Bailey, R. and Brake, M. (1975) (eds.) Radical Social Work, London, Edward Arnold, p. 9.

32. Bailey, R. and Brake, M. (1975) (eds.) Radical Social Work, London, Edward Arnold, p. 10.

33. Statham, D. (1978) Radicals in Social Work, London, Routledge and Kegan Paul, p. 98.

34. Statham, D. (1978) Radicals in Social Work, London, Routledge and Kegan Paul, p. 94.

35. Jordan. B. (1979) Memoirs of a Long-Distance Tight-Rope Walker, in Brandon, D. and Jordan, B. (eds) Creative Social Work, Oxford, Basil Blackwell, pp. 85–96.

36. Jordan, B. (1973) Paupers: The Making of the New Claiming Class, London, Routledge and Kegan Paul.

37. Jordan, B. (1974) Poor Parents: Social Policy and the 'Cycle of Deprivation', London, Routledge and Kegan Paul.

38. Jordan, B. (1976) Freedom and the Welfare State, London, Routledge and Kegan Paul.

39. Jordan, B. (1979) Helping in Social Work, London, Routledge and Kegan Paul.

40. Jordan, B. (1981) Automatic Poverty, London, Routledge and Kegan Paul.

41. Day, P. (1981) Social Work and Social Control, London, Tavistock Publications.

42. Pritchard, C. and Taylor, R. (1978) Social Work: Reform or Revolution? Henley-on Thames, Routledge and Kegan Paul.

43. Halmos, P. (1978) The Personal and the Political: Social Work and Social Action, London, Hutchinson.

44. Day, P. (1981) Social Work and Social Control, London, Tavistock Publications, p. 216.

45. Simpkin, M. (1979) Trapped Within Welfare Surviving Social Work, London, Macmillan Press, p. 20.

46. Wootton, B. (1959) Social Science and Social Pathology, London, Allen and Unwin.

47. Corrigan, P. and Leonard, P. (1978) Social Work Practice Under Capitalism: A Marxist Approach, London, Macmillan Press, p. vii.

48. Butrym, Z. (1976) The Nature of Social Work, London, Macmillan.

49. Morgan, P. (1978) Delinquent Fantasies, London, Temple Smith.

50. Brewer, C. and Lait, J. (1980) Can Social Work Survive, London, Temple Smith.

51. Ivory, M. (2010) The Birth of BASW, Professional Social Work, June, p. 22.

52. Ivory, M. (2010) The Birth of BASW, Professional Social Work, June, p. 23.

53. Bilton, K. (2008) The Formation of the British Association of Social Workers, Meeting of Social Work History Network, 14 February.

54. Heraud, B. (1970) Sociology and Social Work: Perspectives and Problems, Oxford, Pergamon Press, p. 222.

55. Butrym, Z. (1976) The Nature of Social Work, London, Macmillan, p. 131.

56. Bamford, T. (2015) A Contemporary History of Social Work: Learning from the Past, Bristol, Policy Press, pp. 26–27.

57. Bolger, S., Corrigan, P., Docking, J. and Frost, N. (1981) Towards a Socialist Welfare Work, London, Macmillan, p. 68.

58. Bolger, S., Corrigan, P., Docking, J. and Frost, N. (1981) Towards a Socialist Welfare Work, London, Macmillan, pp. 68–69.

59. Bolger, S., Corrigan, P., Docking, J. and Frost, N. (1981) Towards a Socialist Welfare Work, London, Macmillan, p. 70.

60. McLauglin, K. (2008) Social work, politics and society: From radicalism to orthodoxy, Bristol, Policy Press, p. 28.

61. Bamford, T. (2015) A Contemporary History of Social Work: Learning from the Past, Bristol, Policy Press, p. 30.

62. Brake and Bailey (1980) Contributions to a radical social work practice, in Brake, M. and Bailey, R. (eds.) Radical social work in practice, London, Edward Arnold, p. 12.

63. White, T. (2010) The Surprise of My Life, self-published, p. 212.

64. Rogowski, S. (2010) Social Work: The Rise and Fall of a Profession? Bristol, Policy Press.
65. Jones, C. (2011) The best and worst of times: reflections on the impact of radicalism on British social work education in the 1970s, in Lavalette, M. (ed.) Radical Social Work Today: Social Work at the Crossroads, Bristol, Policy Press, p. 39.
66. Jones, C. (2011) The best and worst of times: reflections on the impact of radicalism on British social work education in the 1970s, in Lavalette, M. (ed.) Radical Social Work Today: Social Work at the Crossroads, Bristol, Policy Press, p. 40.
67. Salzberger-Wittenberg, I. (1970) Psycho-Analytic Insight and Relationships: A Kleinian Approach, London, Routledge and Kegan Paul.
68. Timms, N. (1964) Social Casework, London, Routledge and Kegan Paul.
69. Sainsbury, E. (1970) Social Diagnosis in Casework, London, Routledge and Kegan Paul.
70. Heap, K. (1977) Group Theory for Social Workers: An Introduction, Oxford, Pergamon.
71. Douglas, T. (1978) Basic Groupwork, London, Tavistock Publications.
72. Brown, A. (1979) Groupwork, London, Heinemann Educational Books.
73. Thomason, G. (1969) The Professional Approach to Community Work, London, Sands and Co.
74. Jones, D. and Mayo, M. (1974) Community Work One, London, Routledge and Kegan Paul.
75. Jones, D. and Mayo, M. (1975) Community Work Two, London, Routledge and Kegan Paul.
76. Baldock, P (1974) Community Work and Social Work, London, Routledge and Kegan Oaul.
77. Roberts, R. and Nee, R. (1970) (eds) Theories of Social Casework, Chicago, University of Chicago Press.
78. Whittaker, J. (1974) Social Treatment: an approach to interpersonal helping, Chicago, Aldine.

79. Hollis, F. (1970) The Psychosocial Approach to the Practice of Casework, in Roberts, R. and Nee, R. (1970) (eds) Theories of Social Casework, Chicago, University of Chicago Press, pp. 33–76.

80. Jehu, D., Hardiker, P., Yellowly, M. and Shaw, M. (1972) Behaviour Modification in Social Work, London, John Wiley.

81. Jehu, D. (1975) Learning Theory and Social Work, London, Routledge and Kegan Paul.

82. Herbert, H. and Iwaniec, D. (1981) Behavioural Psychotherapy in Natural Homesettings: an Empirical Study Applied to Conduct Disorder and Incontinent Children, Behavioural Psychotherapy, 9, pp. 55–76.

83. Satir, V. (1967) Conjoint Family Therapy, Palo Alto, Science and Behaviour Books.

84. Walrond-Skinner, S. (1976) Family Therapy: The Treatment of Natural Systems, London, Routledge and Kegan Paul.

85. Cross, C, (ed) (1974) Interviewing and Communication in Social Work, London, Routledge and Kegan Paul.

86. Shaw. J. (1974) The Self in Social Work, London, Routledge and Kegan Paul.

87. Davies, M. (1977) Support Systems in Social Work, London, Routledge and Kegan Paul.

88. Reid, W. and Shyne, A. (1969) Brief and Extended Casework, New York, Columbia University Press.

89. Reid, W. and Epstein, L. (1972) Task-Centred Casework, New York, Columbia University Press.

90. Hutten, J. (1977) Short-term Contracts in Social Work, London, Routledge and Kegan Paul.

91. Doel, M. and Marsh, P. (1992) Task-Centred Social Work, Aldershot, Ashgate.

92. Goldstein, H. (1973) Social Work Practice: A Unitary Approach, Columbia, University of South Carolina Press.

93. Gordon, W. (1969) Basic Constructs for an Integrative and Generative Conception of Social Work, in Hearn, G. (ed) The General Systems Approach: Contributions Toward an Holistic Conception of Social Work, New York, Council on Social Work Education, p. 5.

94. Specht, H. and Vickery, A. (1977) (eds) Integrating Social Work Methods, London, George Allen and Unwin.

95. Pincus, A. and Minahan, A. (1973) Social Work Practice: Model and Method, Illinois, Peacock Publishers.

96. Parsloe, P., Goldstein, H., Minahan, A., Pincus, A., Ainsworth, F. and Hunter, J. (1975) (eds) A Unitary Approach to Social Work Practice—implications for education and organisation, Dundee, University of Dundee.

97. Vickery, A. (1977) Use of Unitary Models in Education for Social Work, in Specht, H. and Vickery, A. (1977) (eds) Integrating Social Work Methods, London, George Allen and Unwin.

98. Pincus, A. and Minahan, A. (1973) Social Work Practice: Model and Method, Illinois, Peacock Publishers, p. 54.

99. Pincus, A. and Minahan, A. (1973) Social Work Practice: Model and Method, Illinois, Peacock Publishers, p. 56.

100. Pincus, A. and Minahan, A. (1973) Social Work Practice: Model and Method, Illinois, Peacock Publishers, p. 58.

101. Pincus, A. and Minahan, A. (1973) Social Work Practice: Model and Method, Illinois, Peacock Publishers, p. 61.

102. Compton, B. and Galaway, B. (1975) Social Work Processes, Illinois, The Dorsey Press.

103. Leonard, P. (1975) Towards a Paradigm of Radical Practice, in Bailey, R. and Brake, M. (1975) (eds.) Radical Social Work, London, Edward Arnold, p. 51.

104. Holder, D. and Wardle, M. (1981) Teamwork and the Development of a Unitary Approach, London, Routledge and Kegan Paul, p. 157.

105. Blom-Cooper, L. (1989) Occupational Therapy: An emerging profession in health care, Report of a Commission on Inquiry, London, Duckworth.

106. Mayer, J. and Timms, N. (1970) The Client Speaks, London, Routledge and Kegan Paul.

107. Timms, N. (1973) The Receiving End: Consumer Accounts of Social Help for Children, London, Routledge and Kegan Paul.

108. Sainsbury, E., Nixon, S. and Phillips, D. (1982) Social Work in Focus: Clients' and Social Workers' Perceptions in Long-Term Social Work, London, Routledge and Kegan Paul.

109. Robinson, T. (1978) In Worlds Apart: Professionals and their clients in the welfare state, London, Bedford Square Press.
110. Rees, S. (1978) Social Work Face to Face, London, Edward Arnold.
111. Rees, S. and Wallace, A. (1982) Verdicts on Social Work, London, Edward Arnold, p. 150.
112. Jones, R., Matczak, A., Davies, K. and Byford, I. (2015) Troubled Families: A team around the family, in Davies, K, (ed.) Social work with troubled families: A critical introduction. London, Jessica Kingsley. pp. 124–158.
113. Robinson, T. (1978) In Worlds Apart: Professionals and their clients in the welfare state, London, Bedford Square Press, p. 62.
114. Tutt, N. (1974) Care or Custody: Community Homes and the Treatment of Delinquency, London, Darton, Longman and Todd.
115. Gill, O. (1974) Whitegate: An Approved School in Transition, Liverpool, Liverpool University Press.
116. Walter, J.A. (1078) Sent Away: a study of young offenders in care, Farnborough, Teakfield Limited.
117. Grunsell, R. (1978) Born to be invisible: The story of a school for truants, Basingstoke, Macmillan Education.
118. Corrigan, P. (1979) Schooling the Smash Street Kids, Basingstoke, Macmillan.
119. Parker, H. (1974) View from the Boys, A Sociology of Down-Town Adolescents, Newton Abbott, David and Charles.
120. Gill, O. (1977) Luke Street: Housing Policy, Conflict and the Creation of the Delinquent Area, Basingstoke, Macmillan.
121. Wilson, H. and Herbert, G. (1978) Parents and Children in the Inner City, London, Routledge and Kegan Paul.
122. Fisher, M. (1983) Preface, in Fisher, M. (ed) Speaking of Clients, Sheffield, Joint Unit for Social Services Research, Sheffield University, p. i.
123. Statham, D. (1978) Radicals in Social Work, London, Routledge and Kegan Paul, p. 97.
124. Wilson, E. (1980) Feminism and social work, in Brake, M. and Bailey, R. (eds.) Radical social work in practice, London, Edward Arnold, p. 42.

125. Dominelli, L. (1997) Anti-racist social work: a challenge for white practitioners and educators, Basingstoke: Macmillan.

126. Dominelli, L. and McLeod, E. (1998) Feminist Social Work, Basingstoke, Macmillan.

127. Singh, G. and Masocha, S. (2020) Anti-Racist Social Work: International Perspectives, Basingstoke, Red Globe Press.

128. Bamford, T. (2015) A Contemporary History of Social Work: Learning from the Past, Bristol, Policy Press, p. 98.

129. Grey, E. (1969) Workloads in Children's Departments, London, HMSO.

130. Harris, N. and Palmer, E. (1976) How do social workers spend their time? Community Care, 19 May.

131. Jones, R. (1987) Like Distant Relatives: Adolescents' Perceptions of Social Work and Social Workers, Aldershot, Gower, pp. 22–26.

132. Vickery, A. (1977) Caseload Management, London, National Institute for Social Work.

133. Parsloe, P. (1981) Social Services Area Teams, London, George Allen and Unwin, p. 85.

134. Jones, R., Bhanbhro, S., Grant, R. and Hood, R. (2013) The definition and deployment of differential professional competencies and characteristics in multi-professional health and social care teams, Health and Social Care in the Community, 21.1, pp. 47–58.

135. Barclay Report (1982) Social Workers: Their Role and Tasks, The report of a Working party set up in October 1980, at the request of the Secretary of State for Social Services, by the National In statute for Social Work under the chairmanship of Mr Peter M. Barclay, London, Bedford Square Press, p. vii.

136. Barclay Report (1982) Social Workers: Their Role and Tasks, The report of a Working party set up in October 1980, at the request of the Secretary of State for Social Services, by the National Institute for Social Work under the chairmanship of Mr Peter M. Barclay, London, Bedford Square Press, p. 205.

137. Jordan, B. (1979) Helping in Social Work, London, Routledge and Kegan Paul, p. 1.

138. Barclay Report (1982) Social Workers: Their Role and Tasks, The report of a working party set up in October 1980, at the request of

the Secretary of State for Social Services, by the National Institute for Social Work under the chairmanship of Mr Peter M. Barclay, London, Bedford Square Press, p. 41.

139. Barclay Report (1982) Social Workers: Their Role and Tasks, The report of a Working party set up in October 1980, at the request of the Secretary of State for Social Services, by the National Institute for Social Work under the chairmanship of Mr Peter M. Barclay, London, Bedford Square Press, p. 38.

140. Hadley, R. (1987) A Community Social Worker's Handbook, London, Routledge.

141. Bamford, T. (2015) A Contemporary History of Social Work: Learning from the Past, Bristol, Policy Press, p. 32.

142. Pierson, J. (2011) Understanding Social Work: History and Context, Maidenhead, Open University Press, p. 141.

143. Barclay Report (1982) Social Workers: Their Role and Tasks, The report of a Working party set up in October 1980, at the request of the Secretary of State for Social Services, by the National Institute for Social Work under the chairmanship of Mr Peter M. Barclay, London, Bedford Square Press, pp. 185–186.

144. Parker, R. (1990) Safeguarding Standards, London, National Institute for Social Work.

145. National Institute for Social Work (1992) General Social Services Council Consultation Papers, May, London, National Institute for Social Work.

146. Association of Directors of Social Services (1992) General Social Services Council: ADSS Response to the NISW Consultation Papers, August, Stockport, ADSS.

Chapter 8

1. Pierson, C. (1996) Social Policy, in Marquand, D. and Seldon, A. (eds.) The Ideas that Shaped Post-War Britain, London, Fontana Press, p. 139.

2. Pierson, C. (1996) Social Policy, in Marquand, D. and Seldon, A. (eds.) The Ideas that Shaped Post-War Britain, London, Fontana Press, p. 150.

3. Moore, C. (2013) Margaret Thatcher: The Authorised Biography: Volume One: Not for Turning, London, Allen Lane, p. 480.

4. Thatcher, M. (1995) The Downing Street Years, London, Harper Collins, p. 45.

5. Thatcher, M. (1995) The Downing Street Years, London, Harper Collins, p. 32.

6. Barry, N. (1987) Understanding the Market, in Loney, M. (ed.) The State of the Market: Politics and Welfare in Contemporary Britain, London, Sage, p. 167.

7. Young, H. (1989) One of Us, London, Macmillan, pp. 147–148.

8. Gilmour, I. and Garnett, M. (1998) Whatever Happened To The Tories: The Conservatives Since 1945, London, Fourth Estate, p. 314.

9. Jackson, B. and Wardle, T. (undated) The Battle for Orgreave, Brighton, Vanson Wardle Productions.

10. Lawson, N. (1993) The View from No.11: Memoirs of a Tory Radical, London, Corgi Books, p. 599.

11. Lawson, N. (1993) The View from No.11: Memoirs of a Tory Radical, London, Corgi Books, p. 199.

12. Steadman Jones, D. (2012) Masters of the Universe: Hayek, Friedman, and the birth of Neoliberal Politics, New Jersey, Princeton University Press, p. 63.

13. Freidman, S. and Laurison, D. (2019) The Class Ceiling, Bristol, Policy Press.

14. Aitken, J. (2013) Margaret Thatcher: Power and Personality, London, Bloomsbury, p. 300.

15. Gilmour, I. (1992) Dancing with Dogma: Britain under Thatcherism, London, Simon and Schuster, p. 107.

16. Clark, A. (1998) The Tories: Conservatives and the Nation State 1922–1997, London, Weidenfeld and Nicolson, p. 388.

17. Lawson, N. (1993) The View From No.11: Memoirs of a Tory Radical, London, Corgi Books, p. 201.

18. Crewe, I. (1988) Has the Electorate become more Thatcherite? In Skidelsky, R. (ed.) Thatcherism, London, Chatto and Windus, pp. 35–37.
19. Glennerster, H. (2007) British Social Policy: 1945 to the Present, Oxford, Basil Blackwell, p. 179.
20. Le Grand, J. (1991) The State of Welfare, in Hills, J. (ed.) The State of Welfare: The Welfare State in Britain since 1974, Oxford, Clarendon Press, p. 341.
21. McSmith, A. (2011) No Such Thing as Society: A History of Britain in the 1980s, London, Constable, p. 32.
22. Timmins, N. (1995) The Five Giants: A Biography of the Welfare State, London, Fontana, pp. 376–377.
23. Glennerster, H. (1991) Social Policy since the Second World War, in Hills, J. (ed.) The State of Welfare: The Welfare State in Britain since 1974, Oxford, Clarendon Press, p. 22.
24. Timmins, N. (1995) The Five Giants: A Biography of the Welfare State, London, Fontana, p. 493.
25. Evandrou, M., Falkingham, J. and Glennerster, H. (1991) The Personal Social Services: 'Everyone's Poor Relation but Nobody's Baby', in Hills, J. (ed.) The State of Welfare: The Welfare State in Britain since 1974, Oxford, Clarendon Press, p. 221.
26. Le Grand, J. (1991) The State of Welfare, in Hills, J. (ed.) The State of Welfare: The Welfare State in Britain since 1974, Oxford, Clarendon Press, pp. 340–341.
27. Daines, R., Lyon, K. and Parsloe, P. (1990) Aiming for Partnership, Barkingside, Barnardo's.
28. Evandrou, M., Falkingham, J. and Glennerster, H. (1991) The Personal Social Services: 'Everyone's Poor Relation but Nobody's Baby', in Hills, J. (ed.) The State of Welfare: The Welfare State in Britain since 1974, Oxford, Clarendon Press, p. 228.
29. Bessell, R. (1981) Comment by Robert Bessell, in Goldberg, E.M. and Hatch, S. (eds) A New Look at the Personal Social Services, London, Policy Studies Institute Paper Number 4, p. 13.
30. Hazel, N. (1990) Fostering teenagers: Two innovative schemes in Kent, London, National Foster Care Association.

31. McCarthy, M. (1989) Personal Social Services, in McCarthy, M. (ed.) The New Politics of Welfare: An Agenda for the 1990s? Basingstoke, Macmillan, p. 43.

32. Fowler, N. (1991) Ministers Decide: A Memoir of the Thatcher Years, London, Chapman.

33. Ascher, K. (1987) The Politics of Privatisation: Contracting out Public Services, Basingstoke, Macmillan.

34. Butler, P. (undated) A history of outsourcing, https://www.theguardian.com/society/microsite/outsourcing_/story/0,,933818,00.html.

35. Holman, B. (1993) A New Deal for Social Welfare, Oxford, Lion, p. 16.

36. James, A. (1994) Managing to Care, Harlow, Longman, p. 1.

37. Leat, D. (1993) The Development of Community Care by the Independent Sector, London, Policy Studies Institute, p. 66.

38. Harris, J. (2003) The Social Work Business, London, Routledge, p. 36.

39. Flynn, N. (1990) Public Sector Management, Hemel Hempstead, Harvester Wheatsheaf, p. 68.

40. Rowbottom, R., Hey, A. and Billis, D. (1974) Social Services Departments: Developing Patterns of Work and Organisation, Social Services Organisation Research Unit, Brunel Institute of Organisation and Social Studies, London, Heinemann.

41. Hall, A. and Algie, J. (1974) A Management Game for Social Services, National Institute for Social Work, London, Bedford Square Press.

42. Bamford, T. (1982) Managing Social Work, London, Tavistock Publications.

43. Propper, C., Bartlett, W. and Wilson, D. (1994) Introduction, in Bartlett, W., Propper, C., Wilson, D. and Le Grand, J. (eds) Quasi-Markets in the Welfare State, Bristol, School of Advanced Urban Studies, p. 1.

44. Le Grand, J. and Bartlett, W. (1993) Quasi-markets and social policy, London, Macmillan.

45. Le Grand, J. (2011) Quasi-Market versus State Provision of Public Services: Some Ethical Considerations, Public Reason 3.2, p. 80.

46. Knapp, M. (1989) Private and Voluntary Welfare, in McCarthy, M. (ed.) The New Politics of Welfare, Basingstoke, Macmillan, pp. 235–236.

47. Ascher, K. (1987) The Politics of Privatisation: Contracting out Public Services, Basingstoke, Macmillan, p. xiv.

48. Butt, H. and Palmer, B. (1985) Value for Money in the Public Sector: The Decision-Maker's Guide, Oxford, Basil Blackwell, p. 151.

49. Brooke, R. (1989) Managing the Enabling Authority, Harlow, Longman, p. 24.

50. Hughes, B. (1993) Finance and Management, Community Care, 25 February, p. 18.

51. Holman, B. (1993) A New Deal for Social Welfare, Oxford, Lion, pp. 31–32.

52. Hugman, R. (1991) Organisation and Professionalism: The Social Work Agenda in the 1990s, British Journal of Social Work, 21.3, p. 207.

53. Harris, J. (2003) The Social Work Business, London, Routledge, pp. 74–75.

54. Lipsky, M. (1980) Street-level Bureaucracy: Dilemmas of the Individual in Public Services, New York, Russell Sage Foundation.

55. Salman, S. (2007) The Rule Breakers: The inside story of how to provide good social care, The Guardian, 1 August 2007, pp. 1–3.

56. Parry, N. and Parry, J. (1979) Social work, professionalism and the state, in Parry, N., Rustin, M., and Satyamurti, C. (eds.) Social Work, Welfare and the State, London, Edward Arnold, p. 43.

57. Glastonbury, B., Cooper, D. and Hawkins, P. (1982) Social Work in Conflict, Birmingham, BASW.

Chapter 9

1. Otway, O. (1996) Social work with children: From child welfare to child protection, in Parton, N. (ed.) Social Theory, Social Change and Social Work, London, Routledge, pp. 156–157.

2. Parton, N. (1999) Ideology, Politics and Policy, In Stevenson, O. (ed.) Child Welfare in the United Kingdom 1948–1998, Oxford, Blackwell Science, p. 14.

3. Department of Health and Social Security (1982) Child Abuse: A Study of Inquiry Reports 1973–1981, London, MSO.

4. Brandon, M., Belderson, P., Warren, C., Howe, D., Gardner, R., Dodsworth, J. and Black, J. (2008) Analysing child deaths and serious injury through abuse and neglect: what can we learn? A biennial analysis of serious case reviews 2003–2005, Research Report No DCSF-RR023, London, Department for Children, Schools and Families.

5. Brandon, M., Sidebotham, P., Bailey, S., Belderson, P., Hawley, C., Ellis, C. and Megson, M. (2012) New learning from serious case reviews: a two year report for 2009–2011, Research Report DFE-RR226, London, Department for Education.

6. Sidebotham, P., Brandon, M., Bailey, S., Belderson, P., Dodsworth, J., Garstang, J., Harrison, E., Retzer, A. and Sorensen, P. (2016) Pathways to harm, pathways to protection: a triennial analysis of serious case reviews 2011 to 2014, London, Department for Education.

7. Department of Health and Social Security (1982) Child Abuse: A Study of Inquiry Reports 1973–1981, London, MSO, pp. 65–66.

8. London Borough of Brent (1985) The Report of the Inquiry into the Circumstances Surrounding the Death of Jasmine Beckford, London, London Borough of Brent.

9. London Borough of Lambeth (1987) Whose Child? The Report of the Inquiry into the Death of Tyra Henry, London, London Borough of Lambeth.

10. London Borough of Greenwich (1987) A Child in Mind: Protection of Children in a Responsible Society; The Report of the Commission of Inquiry into the Circumstances Surrounding the Death of Kimberley Carlile, London, London Borough of Greenwich.

11. Munro, E. (2004) The Impact of Child Abuse Inquiries since 1990, in Stanley, N. and Manthorpe, J. (eds) The Age of Inquiry: Learning and blame in health and social care, London, Routledge, p. 77.

12. Munro, E. (2004) The Impact of Child Abuse Inquiries since 1990, in Stanley, N. and Manthorpe, J. (eds) The Age of Inquiry: Learning and blame in health and social care, London, Routledge, p. 78.

13. Rogowski, S. (2010) Social Work: The Rise and Fall of a Profession?, Bristol, Policy Press, p. 74.

14. Report of the Inquiry into Child Abuse in Cleveland 1987 (1988) Cm 412, London, HMSO.

15. Report of the Inquiry into Child Abuse in Cleveland 1987 Short Version Extracted from the Complete Text (1988), Cm 413, London, HMSO, p. 10.

16. Report of the Inquiry into Child Abuse in Cleveland 1987 Short Version Extracted from the Complete Text (1988), Cm 413, London, HMSO, p. 11.

17. Report of the Inquiry into Child Abuse in Cleveland 1987 Short Version Extracted from the Complete Text (1988), Cm 413, London, HMSO, pp. 11–12.

18. Barrow, M. (2017) When did it all go wrong between social work and the media? 21 March, http://www.jkp.com/jkpblog/2017/03/social-work-media/.

19. Donaldson, L. and O'Brien, S. (1995) Press coverage of the Cleveland child sexual abuse enquiry: a source of public enlightenment? Journal of Public Health Medicine, 1 March, 17(1), p. 1.

20. Bell, S. (1988) When Salem came to the Boro: the true story of the Cleveland child abuse crisis, London, Pan.

21. Campbell, B. (1988) Unofficial Secrets: Child Sexual Abuse and the Cleveland Case, London, Virago Press.

22. Richardson, S. and Bacon, H. (1991) (eds.) Child sexual abuse: Whose problem? Reflections from Cleveland, Birmingham, Venture Press, (revised edition 2018, Bristol, Policy Press).

23. Campbell, B. (2020) Official Secrets: Child Sex Abuse from Cleveland to Savile, Bristol, Policy Press, advance publicity.

24. Daily Mail (no author named) (2008) The women who went through an ordeal beyond belief, 24 February, https://www.dailymail.co.uk/femail/article-438208/The-women-went-ordeal-belief.html.

25. Meacher, M. (1987) Child Abuse Cleveland, House of Commons Debate, 9 July, Hansard, vol 119 columns 528–538, https://api.parliament.uk/historic-hansard/commons/1987/jul/09/child-abuse-cleveland.

26. Stevenson, O. (1999) Children in Need and Abused, in Stevenson (ed.) Child Welfare in the UK, Oxford, Blackwell Science, pp. 107–108.

27. Stevenson, O. (1999) Children in Need and Abused, in Stevenson (ed.) Child Welfare in the UK, Oxford, Blackwell Science, p. 108.
28. Department of Health and Social Security and the Welsh Office (1988) Working Together: A guide to arrangements for inter-agency cooperation for the protection of children from abuse, London, HMSO.
29. Clyde, Lord (1992) Inquiry into the Removal of Children from Orkney in February 1991, Edinburgh, HMSO.
30. La Fontaine, J. (1998) Speak of the Devil: Tales of Satanic Abuse in Contemporary England, Cambridge, Cambridge University Press.
31. Otway, O. (1996) Social work with children: From child welfare to child protection, in Parton, N. (ed.) Social Theory, Social Change and Social Work, London, Routledge, p. 156.
32. Children Act (1980) Section3 (1).
33. Rogowski, S. (2016) Social Work with Children and Families, London, Routledge, p. 97.
34. Short Report (1984) Second Report from the Social Services Committee Session 1983–84 Children in Care, Volume 1 Report together with the Proceedings of the Committee, p. xix, London, HMSO.
35. Short Report (1984) Second Report from the Social Services Committee Session 1983–84 Children in Care, Volume 1 Report together with the Proceedings of the Committee, p. xv, London, HMSO.
36. Short Report (1984) Second Report from the Social Services Committee Session 1983–84 Children in Care, Volume 1 Report together with the Proceedings of the Committee, p. xiv, London, HMSO.
37. Short Report (1984) Second Report from the Social Services Committee Session 1983–84 Children in Care, Volume 1 Report together with the Proceedings of the Committee, p. cxiv, London, HMSO.
38. Department of Health and Social Security (1985) Review of Child Care Law: Report to ministers of an interdepartmental working party, September, London, HMSO.

39. Harris, P. (2006) The Making of the Children Act: A Private History, Family Law, December pp. 1054–1059.

40. Department of Health and Social Security (1985) Social Work Decisions in Child Care: Recent Research Findings and their Implications, London, HMSO.

41. Dean, M. (2015) Rupert Hughes: Energetic civil servant determined to improve childcare law, 26 August, The Guardian, p. 33.

42. Hoggett, B. (1977) Social Work Law: Parents and Children, London, Sweet and Maxwell.

43. Hale, Lady B. (2016) 1989 Children Act, Social Work History Network seminar, Kings College, London.

44. Department of Health and Social Security, Home Office, Lord Chancellor's Department, Department of Education and Science, Welsh office, Scottish Office (1987) The Law on Child Care and Family Services, January, London, HMSO.

45. Department of Health and Social Security, Home Office, Lord Chancellor's Department, Department of Education and Science, Welsh office, Scottish Office (1987) The Law on Child Care and Family Services, January, London, HMSO, pp. 4–5, paras 18 and 19.

46. Bottomley, V. (2016) 1989 Children Act, Social Work History Network seminar, Kings College, London.

47. Brown, H.C. (2014) Social Work and Foster Care, Learning Matters, London, Sage, p. 23.

48. Rose, W. (2010) L'Influenza della ricerca di esito nelle politiche perl'infanza nel Regno Unito [The influence of outcomes-based research on child welfare policy in the UK], Studi Zancan, 5, pp. 54–60.

49. Department of Health (2001) The Children Act Now: Messages from Research, London, The Stationary Office, pp. 140–141.

50. Tunstill, J. (2009) 1989 Children Act presentation, Social Work History Network and Making Research Count joint seminar, King's College, London.

51. Parker, R. (1980) (ed.) Caring for Separated Children: Plans, procedures and priorities, London, Macmillan, p. 137.

52. National Institute for Social Work (1988) Residential Care A Positive Choice: report of the Independent Review of Residential Care, London, HMSO.

53. Bullock, R. (1999) The Children Act 1948: Residential Care, in Stevenson, O. (ed.) Child Welfare in the United Kingdom, Oxford, Blackwell, pp. 171–172.

54. Department of Health and Social Security, Home Office, Lord Chancellor's Department, Department of Education and Science, Welsh office, Scottish Office (1987) The Law on Child Care and Family Services, January, London, HMSO, p. 8.

55. Levy, A. and Kahan, B. (1991) The Pindown Experience and the Protection of Children: The Report of the Staffordshire Child Care Inquiry 1990, Staffordshire County Council, p. 1.

56. Kirkwood, A. (1993) The Leicestershire Inquiry 1992, Leicestershire County Council.

57. Waterhouse, R., Clough, M. and le Fleming, M. (2000) Lost in Care: Report of the Tribunal of Inquiry into the abuse of children in acre in the former county council areas of Gwynedd and Clwyd since 1974, London, HMSO.

58. Stanley, N. and Manthorpe, J. (2004) The Age of Inquiries: Learning and blaming in health and social care, London, Routledge.

59. Butler, I. and Drakeford, M. (2003) Scandal, Social Policy and Social Welfare, Bristol, Policy Press.

60. Harris, P. and Bright, M. (2003) The Whistleblower's Story, Paul Harris and Martin Bright investigate how a 12-year-old saga of child abuse and cover-ups has returned to haunt Children's Minister Margaret Hodge, 6 July, https://www.theguardian.com/politics/2003/jul/06/children.childprotection.

61. Routledge, P. (1995) "We got things wrong": Margaret Hodge, the former Islington leader, is finding it politic to eat humble pie, 28 May, https://www.independent.co.uk/voices/we-got-things-wrong-wrong-1621507.html.

62. Walker, D. and Smithrs. R (1999) Borough of Hate and Hit Squads, 19 March, https://www.theguardian.com/politics/1999/mar/19/uk.politicalnews3.

63. Douglas, A. and Philpot, T. (1998) Caring and Coping: A Guide to the Personal Social Services, London, Routledge, pp. 183–189.

64. Utting, W. (1991) Children in the Public Care: A review of residential child care, London, HMSO.

65. House of Commons Health Select Committee (1998) Children Looked After by Local Authorities, https://publications.parliament.uk/pa/cm199798/cmselect/cmhealth/319/31911.htm, para. 181.

66. The Report of the Committee of Inquiry into Selection, Development and Management of Staff in Children's Homes (1992) Choosing with Care, London, HMSO.

67. Bishard, Sir Michael (2004) The Bishard Inquiry Report, London, HMSO.

68. Utting, W. (1997) People like us: the report of the review of the safeguards for children living away from home, London, The Stationery Office, p. 17.

69. Calderdale Social Services Inquiry (1989) An Inquiry into the appointment of Dr R.A. Ryall to the post of director of social services for Calderdale Metropolitan Borough, and the implications of the events which led to his resignation, July, Calderdale, Calderdale Metropolitan Borough Council.

70. Carter, C. (2014) Paedophile Peter Righton advised Government on changes to children's homes, 18 August, https://www.telegraph.co.uk/news/uknews/crime/11040628/Paedophile-Peter-Righton-advised-Government-on-changes-to-childrens-homes.html.

71. BBC (2015) Richard Alston abuse case: Former teacher sentenced, 28 September, https://www.bbc.co.uk/news/uk-england-london-34385091.

Chapter 10

1. National Assistance Act (1948) paragraph 21 (1) (a) London, HMSO.

2. National Assistance Act (1948) paragraph 29 (1) London, HMSO.

3. Chronically Sick and Disabled Persons Act (1970), London, HMSO, paragraph 4 (1).

4. Lord Lloyd of Berwick (1997) Judgments—Reg. v. Gloucestershire C.C. and the Secretary of State for Health. Ex parte Barry and Reg. v. Gloucestershire C.C. and Another. Ex parte Barry (Conjoined Appeals), 20 March, https://publications.parliament.uk/pa/ld199697/ldjudgmt/jd970320/barry01.htm.

5. Harbert, W. (1988) The Welfare Industry, Hadleigh, Holhouse Publications, pp. 89–90.

6. Challis, D. and Davies, B. (1986) Case Management in Community Care, Aldershot, Gower, p. xv.

7. Challis, D., Darton, R., Johnson, L., Stone, M. and Traske, K. (1995) Care Management and Health Care for Older People, Aldershot, Ashgate, p. 2.

8. Means, R., Richards, S. and Smith, R. (third edition 2003) Community Care Policy and Practice, Basingstoke, Palgrave, pp. 49–50.

9. Griffin, J. and Robbins, D. (1993) Introduction in Robbins, D. (ed.) Department of Health 'Community Care Findings From Department of Health Funded Research 1988–1992, London, HMSO, p. xix.

10. Audit Commission (1985) Foreword, in Managing Social Services for the Elderly More Effectively, February, London, HMSO, no page number.

11. Audit Commission (1985) Managing Social Services for the Elderly More Effectively, February, London, HMSO.

12. Audit Commission (1986) Making a Reality of Community Care: A Report of the Audit Commission, London, HMSO.

13. Audit Commission (1992) The Community Revolution: Personal Social Services and Community Care, July, London, HMSO.

14. Audit Commission (1986) Making a Reality of Community Care: A Report of the Audit Commission, London, HMSO, p. 1.

15. Audit Commission (1986) Making a Reality of Community Care: A Report of the Audit Commission, London, HMSO, p. 65

16. Audit Commission (1985) Managing Social Services for the Elderly More Effectively, February, London, HMSO, p. 53.

17. Audit Commission (1986) Making a Reality of Community Care: A Report of the Audit Commission, London, HMSO, pp. 2–3.

18. Timmins, N. (1996) The Five Giants: A Biography of the Welfare State, London, Fontana, p. 417.
19. Audit Commission (1986) Making a Reality of Community Care: A Report of the Audit Commission, London, HMSO, p. 44.
20. Registered Homes Act (1984), London, HMSO.
21. Audit Commission (1985) Managing Social Services for the Elderly More Effectively, February, London, HMSO, pp. 59–60.
22. Audit Commission (1986) Making a Reality of Community Care: A Report of the Audit Commission, London, HMSO, p. 33.
23. Audit Commission (1986) Making a Reality of Community Care: A Report of the Audit Commission, London, HMSO, p. 38.
24. Graham, C. (1994) Obituary: Sir Roy Griffiths, The Independent, https://www.independent.co.uk/news/people/obituary-sir-roy-griffiths-1432347.html.
25. Timmins, N. (1996) The Five Giants: A Biography of the Welfare State, London, Fontana, p. 408.
26. Griffiths, Sir R. (1988) Community Care: Agenda for Action: A Report to the Secretary of State for Social Services by Sir Roy Griffiths, London, HMSO, p. vii.
27. Griffiths, Sir R. (1988) Community Care: Agenda for Action: A Report to the Secretary of State for Social Services by Sir Roy Griffiths, London, HMSO, p. 1.
28. Griffiths, Sir R. (1988) Community Care: Agenda for Action: A Report to the Secretary of State for Social Services by Sir Roy Griffiths, London, HMSO, p. vi.
29. Westland, P. (2011) Care Arrangements: Who Cares? Who Pays?, Social Work History Network Seminar, Department of Health's King's College, London, 5 December, unpublished.
30. ADSS (1988) 'Community Care: Agenda for Action': Response to Sir Roy Griffiths' Report, September, London, ADSS, p. 3.
31. Platt, D. (1989) A Statutory Perspective, in Contracts: Facing the Future, London, National Council for Voluntary Organisations, p. 11.
32. Griffiths, Sir R. (1988) Community Care: Agenda for Action: A Report to the Secretary of State for Social Services by Sir Roy Griffiths, London, HMSO, p. x.
33. Centre for Policy on Ageing (1990) Community life: a code of practice for community care, London, Centre for Policy on Ageing, p. 31.

34. National Institute for Social Work (1898) Community Care Caring for People: A summary of the White Paper, London, National Institute for Social Work Information Service.

35. Smale, G., Tuson, G., Biehal, N. and Marsh, P. (1993) Empowerment, Assessment, Care Management and the Skilled Worker, National Institute for Social Work Practice and Development Exchange, London, HMSO.

36. Department of Health (1990) The National Health Service and Community Care Act 1990: A brief guide, London, Department of Health.

37. Department of Health's Social Services Inspectorate (1991) Care Management and Assessment: Summary of Practice Guidance, London, HMSO.

38. Social Services Inspectorate (1991) Assessment Systems and Community Care, London, Department of Health.

39. KPMG Management Consulting and Department of Health (1992) Implementing Community Care: Improving Independent Sector Involvement in Community Care Planning, London, Department of Health.

40. Social Services Inspectorate (1991) Purchase of Service: Practical Guidance and Practice Materials for Social Services Departments and Other Agencies, London, HMSO.

41. Department of Health's Social Services Inspectorate (1991) The Right to Complain: Practice guidance on complaints procedures in Social Services Departments, London, HMSO.

42. Griffin, J. and Robbins, D. (1993) Introduction in Robbins, D. (ed.) Department of Health 'Community Care Findings From Department of Health Funded Research 1988–1992, London, HMSO.

43. NHS Executive and Social Services Inspectorate (1995) Community Care Monitoring Report 1994: Findings from Local Authority Self Monitoring and NHS Surveys, London, NHS Executive and SSI.

44. Laming, H. and Liddell, A. (1995) Community Care Monitoring: Report of 1994 National Exercises, EL(95)39/ CI(95)7, London, Department of Health.

45. Wistow, G. (1994) Community Care Futures: Inter-Agency Relationships—Stability or Continuing Change, in Titterton,

M. (ed.) Caring for People in the Community: The New Welfare, London, Jessica Kingsley, p. 27.

46. Department of Health and Social Security (1983) Mental Health Act 1983: Memorandum on Parts I to VI, VIII and X, London, HMSO, p. 11.

47. Brammer, A. (2007) Social Work Law: Second Edition, Harlow, Pearson Education, p. 472.

48. Department of Health and the Welsh Office (1983) Mental Health Act 1983: Code of Practice, London, HMSO, p. 6.

49. Department of Health and Social Security (1983) Mental Health Act 1983: Memorandum on Parts I to VI, VIII and X, London, HMSO, p. 3.

50. Means, R., Richards, S. and Smith, R. (third edition 2003) Community Care Policy and Practice, Basingstoke, Palgrave, p. 31.

51. Wistow, G., Knapp, M., Hardy, B., Forder, J., Kendall, J. and Manning, B. (1996) Social Care Markets: Progress and Prospects, Buckingham, Open University Press.

52. Audit Commission (1992) The Community Revolution: Personal Social Services and Community Care, July, London, HMSO, p. 19.

53. Whitely, P. (1992) A social services downer, Community Care.

54. McKinnon, I. (1984) The Scott Controversy: The Daughter: Family bond adds spice to row, 12 May, https://www.independent.co.uk/news/uk/the-scott-controversy-the-daughter-family-bond-adds-spice-to-row-1435304.html.

55. Rose, D. (2015) When disabled people took to the streets to change the law, 7 November, https://www.bbc.co.uk/news/disability-34732084.

56. BBC (2016) The Reunion—Disability Campaigners, 10 April, https://www.bbc.co.uk/programmes/articles/591HbNXpfSw1WF MkPN2fQcY/the-reunion-disability-campaigners-full-programme-transcript-10-april-2016.

57. Campbell, J. and Oliver, M. (1996) Disability Politics: Understanding our past, changing our future, London, Routledge, p. 20.

58. Morris, J. (1993) Independent Lives: Community Care and Disabled People, Basingstoke, Macmillan, p. 21 and p. 23.

59. Mercer, G. (2004) User-led Organisations: Facilitating Independent Living, in Swain, J., French, S., Barnes, C. and Thomas, C. (eds.) Disabling Barriers—Enabling Environments, London, Sage, p. 177.
60. Brindle, D. (2008) Tireless champion of autonomy, 22 October, https://www.theguardian.com/society/2008/oct/21/john-evans.
61. Douglas, A. and Philpot, T. (1998) Caring and Coping: A Guide to Social Services, London, Routledge, p. 121.
62. Ashton, G. (1995) Elderly People and the Law, London, Butterworths, p. 172.
63. Jones, R. (2018) In Whose Interest? The Privatisation of Child Protection and Social Work, Bristol, Policy Press, pp. 232–239.

Chapter 11

1. Seldon, A. (2004) Blair, London, Free Press, p. 433.
2. Draper, D. (1997) Blair's 100 Days, London, Faber and Faber, p. 48.
3. Blair, T. (2011) A Journey, London, Arrow Books, p. 116.
4. Seldon, A. (2004) Blair, London, Free Press, p. 430.
5. Le Grand, J. (2007) Consistent Care Matters: Exploring the Potential of Social Work Practices, http://dera.ioe.ac.uk/7645/1/DFES-00526-2007.pdf.
6. Department for Education and Skills (2006) Care Matters: Transforming the Lives of Children and Young People in Care, https://www.education.gov.uk/consultations/downloadableDocs/6731-DfES-Care%20Matters.pdf.
7. Stanley, N., Austerberry, H., Bilson, A., Farrelly, N., Hargreaves, K., Hollingworth, K., Hussein, S., Ingold, A., Larkins, C., Manthorpe, J., Ridley, J. and Strange, V. (2012) Evaluation of Social Work Practices: Report of the National Evaluation, London, Department for Education.
8. Manthorpe, J., Harris, J., Hussein, S., Cornes, M. and Moriarty, J. (2014) Evaluation of Social Work Practices with Adults: Summary Report, http://www.kcl.ac.uk/sspp/policy-institute/scwru/pubs/2014/reports/Social-Work-Practices-w-Adults-SUMMARY-REPORT-2014.pdf.

9. Jones, C. (2001) Voices From the Front Line: State Social Workers and New Labour, British Journal of Social Work, 13.4, pp. 547–562.

10. Giddens, A. (1998) The Third Way: The Renewal of Social Democracy, Polity Press, Cambridge.

11. Jordan, B. and Jordan, C. (2000) Social Work and Third Way: Tough Love as Social Policy, London, Sage.

12. Jordan, B. (2010) Why The Third Way Failed: Economics, morality and the origins of the 'Big Society', Bristol, Policy Press.

13. Jenkins, S. (2006) Thatcher and Sons: A Revolution in Three Acts, London, Allen Lane, pp. 205–206.

14. Jenkins, S. (2006) Thatcher and Sons: A Revolution in Three Acts, London, Allen Lane, pp. 207–208.

15. Toynbee, P. and Walker, D. (2006) Better or Worse? Has Labour Delivered? London, Bloomsbury, pp. 290–291.

16. Toynbee, P. and Walker, D. (2010) The Verdict: Did Labour Change Britain? London, Granta, p. 265.

17. Secretary of State for Health (1998) Modernising social services: Promoting independence, Improving Protection, Raising Standards, November, Cm 4169, London, The Stationary Office.

18. Dorrell, S. (1997) Better Value for Money in Social Services: A Review of Performance Trends in Social Services in England, Letter to Chairmen of all Social Services Committees in England, 18 February, London, Department of Health.

19. Dobson, F. (1998) Foreword, in Modernising social services: Promoting independence, Improving Protection, Raising Standards, November, Cm 4169, London, The Stationary Office, p. 2.

20. Secretary of State for Health (1998) Modernising social services: Promoting independence, Improving Protection, Raising Standards, November, Cm 4169, London, The Stationary Office, p. 85.

21. Bamford, T. (2015) A Contemporary History of Social Work: Learning from the past, Bristol, Policy Press, p. 32.

22. Parker, R. (1990) Safeguarding Standards, London, National Institute for Social Work.

23. General Social Services Action Group (1992) General Social Services Consultation Papers, May, London, National Institute for Social Work, p. 2.

24. ADSS (1992) General Social Services Council: ADSS Response to the NISW Consultation Papers May 1992, August, Stockport, Association of Directors of Social Services.
25. Bamford, T. (2015) A Contemporary History of Social Work: Learning from the past, Bristol, Policy Press, p. 33.
26. Bamford, T. (2015) A Contemporary History of Social Work: Learning from the past, Bristol, Policy Press, p. 34.
27. Department of Health (1998) Modernising Social Services: Promoting Independence, Improving Protection, Raising Standards, November, Cm 4169, London, The Stationary Office, pp. 65–66.
28. Utting, B. (2010) Bill Pearce and Joan Cooper: Personal Reminiscences, Social Work History Network, October, https://www.kcl.ac.uk/scwru/swhn/uttingonbillpearceandjoancooper.doc.
29. Webb, S. (2001) Some considerations on the validity of evidence-based practice in social work, The British Journal of Social Work, Volume 31, Issue 1, February 2001, pp. 57–79, https://doi.org/10.1093/bjsw/31.1.57.
30. Sheldon, B. (2001) The Validity of Evidence-Based Practice in Social Work: A Reply to Stephen Webb, The British Journal of Social Work, Volume 31, Issue 5, 1 October 2001, pp. 801–809, https://doi.org/10.1093/bjsw/31.5.801.
31. Turner, A. (2019) Academics voice concerns over What Works Centre's family group conferences study, https://www.community-care.co.uk/2019/06/03/academics-voice-concerns-works-centres-family-group-conferences-study/.
32. Pawson, R., Boaz, A., Grayson, L., Long, A. and Barnes, C. (2003) SCIE Knowledge review 03: Types and quality of knowledge in social care, https://www.scie.org.uk/publications/knowledgereviews/kr03.asp.
33. Gray, M., Plath, D. and Webb, S. (2009) Evidence-Based Social Work: A Critical Stance, London, Routledge.
34. Sheldon, B. and Chilvers, R. (2000) Evidence-Based Social Care, Lyme Regis, Russell House Publishing, p. pp. 1–2.
35. Gray, M., Plath, D. and Webb, S. (2009) Evidence-Based Social Work: A Critical Stance, London, Routledge, p. 189.

36. Parkinson, J. (2010) Politicians' love/hate relationship with quangos, https://www.bbc.co.uk/news/uk-politics-11536323.

37. What Works Centre for Children's Social Care (2019) https://whatworks-csc.org.uk/about/.

38. Department of Health (2002) Fair Access to Care Services: Guidance on Eligibility Criteria for Adult Social Care, London, Department of Health, p. 4.

39. HM Government (1999) Local Government Act, London, HMSO.

40. Department of Environment, Transport and Regions (1998) Modernising local government: Improving services through best value, pp. 17–18, London, DETR.

41. Department of Environment, Transport and Regions (1998) Modernising local government: Improving services through best value, p. 17, London, DETR.

42. Department of Environment, Transport and Regions (1998) Modernising local government: Improving services through best value, pp. 5–6, London, DETR.

43. Social Services Inspectorate (2002) Performance Ratings for Social Services in England November 2002 (Refreshed Ratings), London, SSI.

44. Batty, D. (2002) Milburn names worst social services departments, 19 October, https://www.theguardian.com/society/2001/oct/19/socialcare.

45. Community Care (2002) Milburn uses recruitment campaign launch to name and shame councils, 25 October, https://www.communitycare.co.uk/2001/10/25/milburn-uses-recruitment-campaign-launch-to-name-and-shame-councils/.

46. Chief Inspector of Social Services (2002) Modern Social Services: a commitment to reform: The 11th Annual Report of the Chief Inspector of Social Services, London, Department of Health, p. 6.

47. CSCI (2009) The State of Social Care in England 2007–2008, London, Commission for Social Care Inspection.

48. Department of Health (1998) Modernising Health and Social Services: National Priorities Guidance 1999/00–2001/02, September, London, Department of Health, pp. 4–5.

49. Department of Health (1998) Modernising Health and Social Services: National Priorities Guidance 1999/00–2001/02, HSC(98)159:LAC(98)22, London, Department of Health, pp. 3–4.
50. Glasby, J. (2007) Understanding Health and Social Care, Bristol, Policy Press, p. 43.
51. Department of Health (2006) Our health, our care, our say: a new direction for community services, Cm 6737, London, The Stationary Office.
52. Department of Health (2007) Commissioning framework for health and well-being, London, Department of Health.
53. Office of the Deputy Prime Minister (2006) A Sure Start to Later Life: Ending Inequalities for Older People, London, Office of the Deputy Prime Minister.
54. HM Government (2005) Opportunity Age: Meeting the challenges of ageing in the twenty-first century, Cm 6466i, London, HMSO.
55. Department of Health (2005) Independence, Well-being and Choice, London, Department of Health.
56. HM Government (2008) Care, Support, Independence: Meeting the needs of a changing society, London, Department of Health.
57. HM Government (2008) Carers at the heart of twenty-first century families and communities, London, Department of Health.
58. Department of Health (2001) National Service Framework for Older People: Modern Standards and Their Service Models, London, Department of Health.
59. Series, L. (2014) Resource allocation systems: complex and counterproductive, in in Needham, C. and Glasby, J. (eds.) Debates in Personalisation, Bristol, Policy Press.
60. Berseford, P. (2014) Advancing the positives of personalisation/person-centred support: a multi-perspective review, in Needham, C. and Glasby, J. (eds.) Debates in Personalisation, Bristol, Policy Press.
61. Carr, S. and Dittrich, R. (2008) Personalisation: a rough guide, London, Adults' Social Services Report 20, Social Care Institute for Excellence.
62. Windle, K., Wagland, R., Forder, J., D'Amico, F., Janssen, D. and Wistow, G. (2009) National Evaluation of Partnerships for Older

People, Personal Social Services Research Unit, Canterbury, University of Kent.

63. Mencap (1999) Living in Fear: The need to combat bullying of people with a learning disability, London, Mencap.

64. Department of Health (2000) 'No Secrets': Guidance on Developing Multi-Agency Policies and Procedures to Protect Vulnerable Adults from Abuse, HSC 2000/07: LAC (2000)7, London, Department of Health.

65. Commission for Social Care Inspection (2008) Safeguarding Adults: A study of the effectiveness of arrangements to safeguard adults from abuse, London, CSCI, p. 3.

66. Association of Directors of Social Services (2008) Safeguarding Adults: A National Framework of Standards for good practice and outcomes in adult protection work, London, ADSS, p. 3.

67. Glasby, J. (2012) Whose risk is it anyway? Risk and regulation in an era of personalisation, York, Joseph Rowntree Foundation.

68. Glendinning, C., Challis, D. J., Fernandez, J. L., Jacobs, S., Jones, K., Knapp, M., Wilberforce, M. (2008). Evaluation of the Individual Budgets Pilot Programme. Final Report. York: University of York, Social Policy Research Unit.

69. Carr, C. (2010) Enabling risk, ensuring safety: Self-directed support and personal budgets, London, Social Care Institute for Excellence.

70. Manthorpe, J. (2014) Safeguarding, risk and personalisation, in Needham, C. and Glasby, J. (eds.) Debates in Personalisation, Bristol, Policy Press, p. 47.

71. Department of Health (2001) Valuing People: a new strategy for learning disability for the twenty-first Century: A really useful guide to the Government's ideas on how to get services right for all people with learning disabilities, London, Department of Health, p. 28.

72. Buckinghamshire County Council (1998) Independent Longcare Inquiry, Buckingham, Buckinghamshire County Council.

73. Benjamin, A. (2016) Horror stories: Investigations at institutions in Cornwall for people with learning disabilities have revealed appalling levels of abuse, https://www.theguardian.com/society/2006/jul/05/longtermcare.guardiansocietysupplement2.

74. Care Quality Commission (2011) CQC report on Winterbourne View confirms its owners failed to protect people from abuse, https://www.cqc.org.uk/news/releases/cqc-report-winterbourne-view-confirms-its-owners-failed-protect-people-abuse.

75. Dugan, E. (2014) Elderly care home abuse: Shocking footage shows elderly residents being taunted and assaulted at Essex care home, https://www.independent.co.uk/news/uk/home-news/shocking-footage-shows-elderly-residents-being-taunted-and-abused-at-essex-care-home-9303888.html.

76. Morris, S. (2007) Tortured, drugged and killed, a month after the care visits were stopped social workers and police face criticism for failing to spot abuse of vulnerable man, https://www.theguardian.com/society/2007/aug/04/socialcare.crime.

77. Morris, S. (2008) Disabled man's body found in suitcase, https://www.theguardian.com/uk/2008/apr/26/9.

78. The Supreme Court (2014) JUDGMENT: P (by his litigation friend the Official Solicitor) (Appellant) v Cheshire West and Chester Council and another (Respondents); P and Q (by their litigation friend, the Official Solicitor) (Appellants) v Surrey County Council (Respondent), 19 March, Hilary Term [2014] UKSC 19 On appeal from: [2011] EWCA Civ 1257; [2011] EWCA Civ 190, London, Supreme Court.

79. McCulloch, A. and Parker, C. (2004) Mental health inquiries, assertive outreach and compliance: Is there a relationship?, in Stanley, N. and Manthorpe, J. (eds) The Age of the Inquiry: Leaning and blaming in health and social care, London, Routledge.

80. Sheppard, D. (2004) Mental health inquiries 1985–2003, in Stanley, N. and Manthorpe, J. (eds) The Age of the Inquiry: Leaning and blaming in health and social care, London, Routledge.

81. King's Fund (2008) Briefing: Mental Health Act 2007, London, The King's Fund.

82. Turner, J., Hayward, R., Angel, K., Fulford, B., Hall, J. and Millard, C. (2015) The History of Mental Health Services in Modern England: Practitioner Memories and the Direction of Future Research, Medical History, October, 59.4, https://www.ncbi.nlm.nih.gov/pmc/articles/PMC4595954/.

83. Care Quality Commission (2018) Mental Health Act Approved Mental Health Professional Services, March, London, Care Quality Commission.

84. Carson, G. (2018) Approved mental health professional numbers continue decline, Community Care finds, https://www.communitycare.co.uk/2018/02/14/approved-mental-health-professional-numbers-continue-decline-community-care-finds/.

85. Utting, W. (1997) People like us: the report of the review of the safeguards for children living away from home, London, The Stationery Office.

86. HM Government (1998) The Government's Response to the Children's Safeguards Review, Cm 4015, London, The Stationary Office.

87. Stein, M (2009) Quality Matters in Children's Services: Messages from Research, London, Jessica Kingsley, p. 13.

88. Stein, M. (1997) What Works in Leaving Care?, Ilford, Barnardos.

89. Stein, M. (1999) Leaving care: reflections and challenges, in Stevenson, O. (ed.), Child Welfare in the UK, Oxford, Blackwell.

90. Dean, M. (2002) Why children must be heard, https://www.theguardian.com/society/2002/may/01/childrensservices.comment.

91. Become (2019) Become: The charity for children in care and young care leavers, https://www.becomecharity.org.uk/.

92. Coram Voice (2019) Coram Voice: Getting young voices heard, https://coramvoice.org.uk/about-us2/our-history/.

93. Joyce, R. and Sibieta, L. (2013) Labour's Record on Poverty and Inequality, https://www.ifs.org.uk/publications/6738.

94. The Tavistock and Portman NHS Foundation Trust (2019) Family Nurse Partnership National Unit, https://tavistockandportman.nhs.uk/care-and-treatment/our-clinical-services/family-nurse-partnership/.

95. National Institute for Clinical Evidence (undated) The Evidence Base for Family Nurse Partnership, London, NICE.

96. Eisenstadt, N. (2011) Providing a Sure Start: How government discovered early childhood, Bristol, Policy Press, p. 33.

97. HM Treasury (2003) Every Child Matters, Cm 5860, London, Stationary Office.

98. White, S., Hall, C. and Peckover, S. (2009) The Descriptive Tyranny of the Common Assessment Framework: Technologies of Categorization and Professional Practice in Child Welfare, British Journal of Social Work, 39.7, pp. 1197–1217.

99. HM Treasury (2003) Every Child Matters, Cm 5860, London, Stationary Office, p. 9.

100. Laming, L. (2003) The Victoria Climbie Inquiry, Cm 5730, Norwich, The Stationary Office.

101. Home Office (2010) What is a family intervention project? https://webarchive.nationalarchives.gov.uk/20100405142919/http://asb.homeoffice.gov.uk/members/article.aspx?id=8678.

102. Davies, K. (2015) (ed.) Social Work with Troubled Families, London, Jessica Kingsley.

103. Carvel, J. (2002) Blair vows to increase number of adoptions, https://www.theguardian.com/society/2000/dec/22/adoptionand-fostering.health.

104. Department of Health (2002) Adoption a new approach, Cm 5017, London, Norwich, The Stationery Office.

105. Balls, E. (2016) Speaking Out: Lessons in Life and Politics, London, Hutchinson, pp. 284–291.

106. Butler, P. (2011) Sharon Shoesmith wins appeal against sacking over Baby P tragedy: Dismissal of former Haringey council children's boss Sharon Shoesmith was 'tainted by unfairness', court rules.

107. BBC (2014) Baby P: The Untold Story, 27 October.

108. Jones, R. (2014) The Story of Baby P: Setting the Record Straight, Bristol, Policy Press.

109. Shoesmith, S. (2016) Learning From Baby P: The politics of blame, fear and denial, London, Jessica Kingsley.

110. The Leveson Inquiry (2012) Leveson Inquiry: Culture, Practice and Ethics of the Press, https://www.levesoninquiry.org.uk/about/the-report/.

111. Warner, J. (2015) The Emotional Politics of Social Work and Child Protection, Bristol, Policy Press, p. 27.

112. Jones, R. (2014) The Story of Baby P: Setting the Record Straight, Bristol, Policy Press, pp. 286–287.

113. Ahmed, M. (2009) Sun agony aunt defends her place on the Social Work Taskforce, https://www.communitycare.co.uk/2009/01/28/sun-agony-aunt-defends-her-place-on-the-social-work-taskforce/.

114. Social Work Task Force (2009) Building a safe, confident future: The final report of the Social Work Task Force, November, London, Department of Children, Schools and Families.

Chapter 12

1. Tett, G. (2009) Fool's Gold: How Unrestrained Greed Corrupted a Dream, Shattered Global Markets and Unleashed a Catastrophe, London, Little, Brown.

2. Luyendijk, J. (2015) Swimming With Sharks: My Journey into the World of Bankers, London, Guardian Books.

3. Cameron, D. (2019) For the Record, London, William Collins, p. 113.

4. Ussher, K. (2015) Labour did not cause the economic crisis—it must counter the myth that it did, https://www.theguardian.com/commentisfree/2015/may/18/labour-economic-crisis-tories.

5. Rawnsley, A. (2010) The End of the Party: The Rise and Fall of New Labour, Viking, London, pp. 485–486.

6. Darling, A. (2011) Back From The Brink: 1,000 Days At Number 11, London, Atlantic Books, p. 9.

7. Brown, G. (2017) My Life, Our Times, London, Bodley Head, pp. 188–189.

8. Seldon, A. and Lodge, G. (2010) Brown at 10, London, Biteback, p. 166.

9. Sainsbury, D. (2013) Progressive Capitalism: How to Achieve Economic Growth, Liberty and Social Justice, London, Biteback, p. 260.

10. Sainsbury, D. (2013) Progressive Capitalism: How to Achieve Economic Growth, Liberty and Social Justice, London, Biteback, p. 9.

11. Mason, P. (2009) Meltdown: The End of the Age of Greed, London, Verso, pp. vii, x and 171.

12. Seldon, A. and Snowden, P. (2015) Cameron at 10, London, William Collins, p. 41.

13. House of Commons Library (2019) Poverty in the UK: Statistics, https://researchbriefings.parliament.uk/ResearchBriefing/Summary/SN07096.

14. Kentish, B. (2019) Election: Jo Swinson apologises for supporting welfare cuts as part of coalition, https://www.independent.co.uk/news/uk/politics/election-jo-swinson-interview-andrew-neil-liberal-democrats-coalition-welfare-cuts-a9233351.html.

15. Humphries, R., Thorlby, R., Holder, H. Hall, P. and Charles, A. (2016) Social Care for Older People: Home Truths, King's Fund and the Nuffield Trust, London, The King's Fund, p. 3.

16. Scourfield, P. (2011) Cartelization revisited and the lessons of Southern Cross, Critical Social Policy, 32.1, pp. 137–148.

17. Pratley, N. (2017) A shocking way to fund UK care homes, https://www.theguardian.com/business/nils-pratley-on-finance/2017/dec/12/a-shocking-way-to-fund-uk-care-homes.

18. The Royal Commission on Long Term Care (1999) With Respect to Old Age: Long Term Care – Rights and Responsibilities, March, Cm 4192-1, London, The Stationary Office.

19. Secretary of State For Health (1999) The Government's Response to the Health Committee's Report on Long-term Care, July, London, The Stationary Office.

20. Royal Commissioners (2003) Long-Term Care: Statement by Royal Commissioners, September, unpublished.

21. Dickinson, H., Glasby, J., Forder, J. and Beesley, L. (2007) Free personal care in Scotland: a narrative review, British Journal of Social Work, 37.3, pp. 459–474.

22. Dilnot Report (2011) Fairer Care Funding Commission on Funding Care and Support, https://webarchive.nationalarchives.gov.uk/20130201155426/http://www.dilnotcommission.dh.gov.uk/our-report/.

23. Dilnot Report (2011) Fairer Care Funding Commission on Funding Care and Support, p. 74, https://webarchive.nationalarchives.gov.uk/20130201155426/http://www.dilnotcommission.dh.gov.uk/our-report/.

24. Taylor, N. (2016) Five Years Since Dilnot: are we back to square one?, http://www.commissiononcare.org/2016/08/18/five-years-since-dilnot-are-we-back-to-square-one/.

25. Hill, A. (2017) Social care reviewer condemns UK system and calls for new tax: Andrew Dilnot says adult social care system is 'most pernicious means-test' in the British welfare state, https://www.the-guardian.com/society/2017/apr/06/andrew-dilnot-social-care-reviewer-condemns-uk-system-and-calls-for-new-tax.

26. Asthana, A. and Elgot, J. (2017) Theresa May ditches manifesto plan with 'dementia tax' U-turn, 22 May, https://www.theguard-ian.com/society/2017/may/22/theresa-may-u-turn-on-dementia-tax-cap-social-care-conservative-manifesto.

27. Donnelly, L. (2019) NHS chiefs fear hospitals will not cope amid growing social care crisis, https://www.telegraph.co.uk/news/2019/10/07/nhs-chiefs-fear-hospitals-will-not-cope-amid-growing-social/.

28. Labour Party (2019) It's Time for a Change: The Labour Party Manifesto, London, The Labour Party, p. 36.

29. Timmins, N. (2012) Never Again? The story of the 2012 Health and Social Care Act, London, The King's Fund and the Institute for Government.

30. NHS England (2019) Sustainability and transformation partner-ships, https://www.england.nhs.uk/integratedcare/stps/.

31. NHS England (2019) Better Care Fund, https://www.england.nhs.uk/ourwork/part-rel/transformation-fund/bcf-plan/.

32. Bamford, T. (2015) A Contemporary History of Social Work: Learning from the Past, Bristol, Policy Press, p. 136.

33. NHS (2019) NHS Long Term Plan, January, https://www.long-termplan.nhs.uk/.

34. SCIE in collaboration with Integration and Better Care (2019) Practice examples of good practice in integrated care, https://www.scie.org.uk/integrated-care/better-care/practice-examples?utm_campaign=10743278_SCIELine%2024%20July&utm_medium=email&utm_source=SCIE&utm_sfid=0030f0000312GZFAA2&utm_role=Manager%20-%20

learning%20and%20development%2Fworkforce&dm_i=4O5,6E
9KE,UFRPUP,PBNYI,1.

35. Welsh Government (2019) Health and social services transformation fund: projects, https://gov.wales/health-and-social-services-transformation-fund-projects.

36. Northern Ireland Executive (2019) Transformation fund continues to support much-needed change, https://www.northernireland.gov.uk/node/39192.

37. Scottish Government (2019) Health and Social Care integration: progress review, https://www.gov.scot/publications/ministerial-strategic-group-health-community-care-review-progressintegration-health-social-care-final-report/.

38. Department of Health (2010) A Vision for Adult Social Care: Capable Communities and Active Citizens, https://navigator.health.org.uk/content/vision-adult-social-care-capable-communities-and-active-citizens-was-published-department.

39. Butler, P. (2014) Holiday hunger: The charities offering poorer families a lifeline, https://www.theguardian.com/society/2014/oct/24/holiday-hunger-charities-children.

40. McKie, R. (2019) Why is life expectancy faltering?, https://www.theguardian.com/society/2019/jun/23/why-is-life-expectancy-falling.

41. Department of Health (2010) A Vision for Adult Social Care: Capable Communities and Active Citizens, p. 8, https://navigator.health.org.uk/content/vision-adult-social-care-capable-communities-and-active-citizens-was-published-department.

42. Department of Health (2011) Caring for Our Future: Shared Ambitions for Care and Support, https://www.gov.uk/government/publications/caring-for-our-future-shared-ambitions-for-care-and-support%2D%2D2.

43. HM Government (2012) Caring for Our Future: Reforming Care and Support, Cm 8378, London, The Stationary Office, p. 13.

44. HM Government (2010) Recognised, valued and supported: Next steps for the Carers Strategy, London, Department of Health.

45. HM Government (2012) Caring for Our Future: Reforming Care and Support, Cm 8378, London, The Stationary Office, p. 12.

46. Ivory, M. (2014) 'A long time coming': Social workers have their say on the Care Act, https://www.theguardian.com/social-care-network/2015/apr/28/social-work-the-care-act-2015.

47. Snell, J. (2015) A quick guide to the Care Act: An overview of how the legislation affects the provision of social care in England, https://www.theguardian.com/social-care-network/2015/apr/28/-care-act-2014-quick-guide.

48. Hunter, M. (2015) The Care Act makes prevention a duty—but how will councils make it work? Early intervention can help prevent low-level needs escalating into emergencies, yet there are widespread concerns around funding, https://www.theguardian.com/social-care-network/2015/apr/29/the-care-act-makes-prevention-a-duty-but-how-will-councils-make-it-work.

49. Brindle, D. (2014) What are the most important changes to the Care Act? More than 100 amendments were proposed during its passage through parliament, https://www.theguardian.com/social-care-network/2014/jun/05/care-act-most-important-amendments.

50. Toynbee, P. and Walker, D. (2015) Cameron's Coup: How the Tories Took Britain to the Brink, London, Guardian Books, pp. 104–105.

51. Commissioner for Older People for Northern Ireland (2015) Prepared to Care? Modernising Adult Social Care in Northern Ireland, Belfast, Commissioner for Older People for Northern Ireland.

52. Duffy, J., Davidson, G., Basu, S. and Pearson, K. (2016) Modernising Adult Social Care in Northern Ireland, Knowledge Exchange Seminar Series, Northern Ireland assembly.

53. Schwehr, B. (2014) What the Care Act 2014 means for the outsourcing of social work Belinda Schwehr examines provisions for councils to contract out social work functions, assessing how these might be used and the risks they pose, 14 March, https://www.communitycare.co.uk/2014/03/14/care-act-2014-means-outsourcing-social-work/.

54. Campbell, D. (2016) Virgin Care wins £700m contract to run 200 NHS and social care services, 16 November, https://www.theguard-

ian.com/society/2016/nov/11/virgin-care-700m-contract-200-nhs-social-care-services-bath-somerset.

55. Beresford, P. (2014) Despite its promise, the Care Act will give little power to service users, https://www.theguardian.com/social-care-network/2014/dec/02/care-act-2015-service-users-power-social.

56. ADASS (2019) ADASS Budget Survey 2019, https://www.adass.org.uk/adass-budget-survey-2019.

57. Butler, P. (2019) Social care chiefs: funding crisis puts tens of thousands at risk, https://www.theguardian.com/society/2019/jun/26/social-care-funding-crisis-putting-tens-of-thousands-at-risk.

58. NHS Digital (2019) Mental Capacity Act 2005, Deprivation of Liberty Safeguards England 2018–19, https://digital.nhs.uk/data-and-information/publications/statistical/mental-capacity-act-2005-deprivation-of-liberty-safeguards-assessments/england-2018-19.

59. NHS Digital (2019) Safeguarding Adults, England, 2018–19, https://digital.nhs.uk/data-and-information/publications/statistical/safeguarding-adults/annual-report-2018-19-england.

60. Jones, R. (2017) The Story of Baby P: Setting the Record Straight, Bristol, Policy Press.

61. Department for Education (2019) Children looked after in England including adoption: 2018 to 2019, https://www.gov.uk/government/statistics/children-looked-after-in-england-including-adoption-2018-to-2019.

62. Perraudin, F. and McIntyre, N. (2019) Rise in children taken into care pushes 88% of councils over budget: Local authorities overspent on children's services by an estimated £807m in 2017–18, https://www.theguardian.com/society/2019/jan/08/rise-in-children-taken-into-care.

63. Institute for Local Government (2019) Children's Social Care Performance Tracker, https://www.instituteforgovernment.org.uk/publication/performance-tracker-2019/children-social-care.

64. Kelly, E., Lee, T., Sibieta, L, and Waters, T. (2018) Public Spending on Children in England: 2000 to 2020, Institute of Fiscal Studies, June, London, Children's Commissioner for England pp. 34–35.

65. All Party Parliamentary Group for Children (2018) Storing up trouble—a postcode lottery of children's social care, London, National Children's Bureau.

66. Butler, P. (2018) Underfunding to blame for child protection 'crisis', says report: Often only option is to remove them from families, says ex-Tory children's minister, 11 July, https://www.theguardian.com/society/2018/jul/11/underfunding-to-blame-for-child-protection-crisis-says-report.

67. House of Commons Housing, Communities and Local Government Committee (2019) Funding of local authorities' children's services: Fourteenth Report of Session 2017–19, HC 1638, London, House of Commons, p. 70.

68. Jones, R. (2019) In Whose Interest? The Privatisation of Child Protection and Social Work, Bristol, Policy Press, pp. 288–291.

69. Hood, R., Goldacre, A., Grant, R. and Jones, R. (2016) Exploring Demand and Provision in English Child Protection Services, The British Journal of Social Work, Volume 46, Issue 4, 1 June 2016, pp. 923–941, https://doi.org/10.1093/bjsw/bcw044.

70. Bywaters, P., Bunting, L., Davidson, G., Hanratty, J., Mason, W., McCartan, C. and Steils, N. (2016) The relationship between poverty, child abuse and neglect: an evidence review, 3 March, Joseph Rowntree Foundation, https://www.jrf.org.uk/report/relationship-between-poverty-child-abuse-and-neglect-evidence-review.

71. Bilson, A. and Martin, K. (2016) Referrals and Child Protection in England: One in Five Children Referred to Children's Services and One in Nineteen Investigated before the Age of Five, The British Journal of Social Work, Volume 47, Issue 3, 1 April 2017, pp. 793–811, https://doi.org/10.1093/bjsw/bcw054.

72. Webb, C. and Bywater, P. (2018) Austerity, rationing and inequity: trends in children's and young peoples' services expenditure in England between 2010 and 2015, Local Government Studies, 44:3, 391–415, https://doi.org/10.1080/03003930.2018.1430028.

73. University of Huddersfield (2018) Research shows cuts in funding designed to prevent child abuse, https://www.hud.ac.uk/news/2018/february/researchshowscutsinfundingdesignedtopreventchildabuse/.

74. Hood, R., Goldacre, A., Grant, R. and Jones, R. (2016) Exploring Demand and Provision in English Child Protection Services, The British Journal of Social Work, Volume 46, Issue 4, 1 June 2016, p. 1, https://doi.org/10.1093/bjsw/bcw044.

75. Jay, A. (2014) Independent Inquiry into Child Sexual Exploitation in Rotherham (1997–2013), Rotherham, Rotherham Borough Council.

76. BBC (2012) Rochdale grooming trial: Nine found guilty of child sex charges, https://www.bbc.co.uk/news/uk-england-17989463.

77. BBC (2015) Oxfordshire grooming victims may have totalled 373 children, https://www.bbc.co.uk/news/uk-england-oxfordshire-31643791.

78. Sommerlad, N. and McKelvie, G. (2018) Britain's 'worst ever' child grooming scandal exposed: Hundreds of young girls raped, beaten, sold for sex and some even killed, https://www.mirror.co.uk/news/uk-news/britains-worst-ever-child-grooming-12165527.

79. Morris, S. (2014) 13 men guilty of enforced prostitution and rape of vulnerable girls in Bristol, https://www.theguardian.com/uk-news/2014/nov/27/guilty-prostitution-bristol-rape-girls-sex-abuse-somali.

80. IICSA (2020) An inquiry into institutional responses to the sexual exploitation of children by organised networks, https://www.iicsa.org.uk/investigations/child-sexual-exploitation-by-groups-and-gangs.

81. Jones, R., Matczak, A., Davis, K. and Byford, I. (2015) 'Troubled Families': A Team Around the Family, in Davis, K. (ed.) Social Work with Troubled Families: A Critical Introduction, London, Jessica Kingsley, pp. 124–158.

82. The Conservative Party (2007) No More Blame Game – The Future for Children's Social Workers: Conservative Party Commission on Social Workers, October, London, Conservative Party.

83. The Conservative Party (2007), No More Blame Game – The Future for Children's Social Workers: Conservative Party Commission on Social Workers, October, London, Conservative Party, p. 3.

84. Munro, E. (2004) The Impact of Child Abuse Inquiries since 1990, in Stanley, N. and Manthorpe, J. (eds) The Age of Inquiry: Learning and blame in health and social care, London, Routledge, p. 89.

85. Munro, E. (2011) The Munro Review of Child Protection: Final Report: A child-centred system, London, The Stationary Office, pp. 6–7.

86. Munro, E. (2008) interviewed in 'What Happened to Baby P, BBC Panorama, 17 November.

87. McNicoll, A. (2017) Ten years on from Baby P: social work's story, https://www.communitycare.co.uk/2017/08/03/ten-years-baby-p-social-works-story/.

88. Bamford, T. (2015) A Contemporary History of Social Work, Bristol, Policy Press, pp. 160–162.

89. McNicoll, A. (2016) Time to put myths about the College of Social Work closure to bed, https://www.communitycare.co.uk/2016/07/14/time-put-myths-college-social-work-closure-bed.

90. McNicoll, A. (2015) College of Social Work faced £240,000 annual deficit before closure, leaked report reveals, https://www.communitycare.co.uk/2015/06/22/college-social-work-faced-240000-annual-deficit-closure-leaked-report-reveals/.

91. Jones, R. (2019) In Whose Interest? The Privatisation of Child Protection and Social Work, Bristol, Policy Press, pp. 7–51.

92. Butler, P. (2010) Ministers take over 'dysfunctional' Doncaster council: Political feuding, bullying and intimidation are preventing council from serving community, says Audit Commission, https://www.theguardian.com/society/2010/apr/19/doncaster-council-failing-and-dysfunctional.

93. Richardson, H. (2013) 'More child protection takeovers ahead, Gove hints', 12 November, https://www.bbc.co.uk/news/education-24904031.

94. Cameron, D. (2015) 'My vision for a smarter state', 11 September, https://www.gov.uk/government/speeches/prime-minister-myvision-for-a-smarter-state.

95. Jones, R. (2019) In Whose Interest? The Privatisation of Child Protection and Social Work, Bristol, Policy Press, pp. 167–262.

96. Jones, R. (2019) In Whose Interest? The Privatisation of Child Protection and Social Work, Bristol, Policy Press, p. 25.

97. LaingBuisson, COBIC and CICADA (2016) The potential for developing the capacity and diversity of children's social care services in England: Independent research report, December, London, Department for Education.

98. Department for Education (2016) Government response to LaingBuisson's report on the potential for developing the capacity and diversity of children's social care services in England, London, Department for Education.

99. Jones, R. (2019) Outsourcing children's services isn't just wrong – it's a waste of money, https://www.theguardian.com/society/2019/aug/07/outsourcing-childrens-services-wrong-waste-money.

100. Parkes, J. (2019) Children's Services Consultancy Morning Lane Closes, 6 June, https://www.cypnow.co.uk/news/article/children-s-services-consultancy-morning-lane-closes.

101. Jones, R. (2019) In Whose Interest? The Privatisation of Child Protection and Social Work, Bristol, Policy Press, pp. 91–108.

102. Social Work Reform Board (2010) Building a safe and confident future: One year on: Detailed proposals from the Social Work Reform Board, December, London, Department for Education.

103. Department for Education (2014) Knowledge and skills for child and family social work, DFE-00532-2014, London, Department for Education.

104. Department for Education (2019) Guidance: NAAS-national assessment and accreditation system, https://www.gov.uk/government/publications/naas-national-assessment-and-accreditation-system/1-guidance-naas-national-assessment-and-accreditation-system.

105. Association of Directors of Children's Services (2016) ADCS Position Statement: The Assessment and Accreditation of Three New Social Work Statuses, 9 May, http://adcs.org.uk/assets/documentation/ADCS_Position_Statement_The_Assessment_ and_ Accreditation_of_Three_New_Social_Work_Statuses.pdf.

106. McNicoll, A. (2017) 'Social worker accreditation scheme "poor value", directors warn', 14 March, www.communitycare.co.uk/2017/03/14/social-worker-accreditation-scheme-poorvalue-directors-warn.

107. Carter, R. (2017) 'ADASS president warns against splitting social work into "factions"', 12 May, www.communitycare.co.uk/2017/05/12/adass-president-warns-splitting-social-workfactions.

108. British Association of Social Workers (2017) Just 3% of social workers surveyed by BASW England consider NAAS to be value for money, https://www.basw.co.uk/media/news/2017/mar/just-3-social-workers-surveyed-basw-england-consider-naas-be-value-money.

109. House of Commons Education Select Committee (2016) Social Work Reform, July, Third Report of Session 2016–17.

110. Purcell, C. (2020) The Politics of Children's Services Reform: Re-examining Two Decades of Policy Change (1997–2020), Bristol, Policy Press, p. 161.

111. Narey, Sir M. (2014) Making the Education of Social Workers Consistently Effective: Report of Sir Martin Narey's independent review of the education of children's social workers, January, https://www.gov.uk/government/uploads/system/uploads/attachment_data/file/287756/Making_the_education_of_social_workers_consistently_effective.pdf.

112. Narey, Sir M. (2014) Making the Education of Social Workers Consistently Effective: Report of Sir Martin Narey's independent review of the education of children's social workers, January, https://www.gov.uk/government/uploads/system/uploads/attachment_data/file/287756/Making_the_education_of_social_workers_consistently_effective.pdf, p. 43.

113. Croisdale-Appleby, D. (2014) Re-visioning Social Work Education: An Independent Review, February, https://www.gov.uk/government/uploads/system/uploads/attachment_data/file/285788/DCA_Accessible.pdf.

114. British Association of Social Workers (2014) 'Croisdale-Appleby report combines academic rigour with deep understanding of the social work profession', February, https://www.basw.co.uk/news/article/?id=681.

115. Trowler, I. (2015) Social work needs to earn back public trust, https://www.theguardian.com/social-care-network/2015/jul/28/isabelle-trowler-social-work-public-trust-criminal-wilful-neglect.

116. McNicoll, A. (2016) Trowler: New regulator for social workers 'controversial but essential', https://www.communitycare.co.uk/2016/07/08/trowler-new-regulator-social-workers-controversial-essential/.

117. Butler, P. (2014) How Alan Wood became the 'go-to' fixer for child protection, https://www.theguardian.com/society/2014/jul/09/alan-wood-go-to-fixer-child-protection-hackney-social-work.

118. Gove, M. (2013) Michael Gove speech to the NSPCC: getting it right for children in need: Secretary of State for Education Michael Gove delivers a speech on child protection, https://www.gov.uk/government/speeches/getting-it-right-for-children-in-need-speech-to-the-nspcc.

119. Butler, P. (2012) Michael Gove: children at risk of abuse should be put in care more quickly, https://www.theguardian.com/society/2012/nov/16/michael-gove-children-risk-care.

120. Cooper, J. (2013) Gove slams social work education. Education secretary claims social work training is currently dominated by dogma and theories of society, https://www.communitycare.co.uk/2013/11/12/gove-slams-social-work-education/.

121. Paton, G. (2013) Michael Gove: many social workers "not up to the job", https://www.telegraph.co.uk/news/uknews/10442309/Michael-Gove-many-social-workers-not-up-to-the-job.html.

122. Ferguson, H. (2013) No, Mr Gove, social workers don't lack compassion or intellect. They lack time and resources, https://www.theguardian.com/commentisfree/2013/nov/12/gove-social-workers-compassion-intellect-time.

123. Social Work Action Network (2014) In defence of social work: Why Michael Gove is wrong, February, London, Social Work Action Network.

124. Jones, R. (2010) Looking Forward in Waterman, C. (ed.) Take Heed Mr Gove, Great Missenden, IRIS Press, pp. 29–33.

125. Jones, R. (2015) Social work needs a strong independent voice at this time of rapid change, 14 September, Locum Today.

126. Tunstill, J. and Willow, C. (2017) Professional social work and the defence of children's and their families' rights in a period of austerity: A case study, Social Work and Social Sciences Review, 19.1, pp. 40–65.

127. Allison, E. (2015) Carolyne Willow: "We closed the workhouses, let's get rid of child prisons": Children's rights campaigner Carolyne Willow was sent away aged four. That experience spurs her fight to protect minors from custody and incarceration, https://www.theguardian.com/society/2015/feb/11/carolyne-willow-campaigner-child-prisons-childrens-rights.

128. Watson, Lord (2016) Debate on Children and Social Work Bill, Hansard, 8 November, https://hansard.parliament.uk/lords/2016-11-08/debates/5ABC82B8-3486-474C-8A9A-9445BBCD382E/ChildrenAndSocialWorkBill.

129. Lewell-Buck, E. (2017) Debate on Children and Social Work Bill (Lords) Commons Committee Fifth Sitting, https://hansard.parliament.uk/commons/2017-01-10/debates/e6e84821-8912-41b2-b4a0-0850e1a4adf1/ChildrenAndSocialWorkBill.

130. Haynes, L. (2019) Lack of registered social workers on Social Work England board criticised, https://www.communitycare.co.uk/2019/04/18/social-work-englands-failure-appoint-registrants-board-criticised-sector/.

131. Department of Health (2016) Strategic statement for social work with adults in England 2016–2020, https://www.gov.uk/government/publications/vision-for-adult-social-work-in-england.

132. Scottish Government (2019) Review of the Mental Health Act: Future direction of mental health and incapacity legislation, 19 March, https://news.gov.scot/news/review-of-the-mental-health-act.

133. Wessely, S. (2018) Modernising the Mental Health Act: Increasing choice, reducing compulsion, Final report of the Independent Review of the Mental Health Act 1983, p. 7, https://www.gov.uk/government/publications/modernising-the-mental-health-act-final-report-from-the-independent-review.

134. Wessely, S. (2018) Modernising the Mental Health Act: Increasing choice, reducing compulsion, Final report of the Independent Review of the Mental Health Act 1983, p. 10, https://www.gov.uk/government/publications/modernising-the-mental-health-act-final-report-from-the-independent-review.

135. Wessely, S. (2018) Modernising the Mental Health Act: Increasing choice, reducing compulsion, Final report of the Independent Review of the Mental Health Act 1983, p. 21, https://www.gov.uk/government/publications/modernising-the-mental-health-act-final-report-from-the-independent-review.

136. Department of Health and Social Care (2018) Government commits to reform the Mental Health Act, 6 December, https://www.gov.uk/government/news/government-commits-to-reform-the-mental-health-act.

137. Mental Health Today (2019) Government commits to new Mental Health Act delivering advanced "choice and autonomy" to individuals, 14 October, https://www.mentalhealthtoday.co.uk/news/government-policy/government-commits-to-new-mental-health-act-delivering-advance-choice-and-autonomy.

138. House of Commons Library (2019) Adult social care: the Government's ongoing policy review and anticipated Green Paper (England), September 30, https://researchbriefings.parliament.uk/ResearchBriefing/Summary/CBP-8002.

139. Labour Party (2019) It's Time for a Real Change: The Labour Party Maifesto 2019, For the Many Not the Few, London, Labour Party.

140. Vize, R. (2019) This 'bold' Queen's speech lacks the courage to fix society's urgent crises, 20 December, https://www.theguardian.com/society/2019/dec/20/queens-speech-lacks-courage-fix-societys-urgent-crises.

141. Jenkins, S.D. (2019) This was the Queen's speech—as written by Dominic Cummings, 19 December, https://www.theguardian.com/commentisfree/2019/dec/19/johnson-cummings-new-politics-populism-optimism.

142. BBC (2019) UK approves £4bn US takeover of defence company Cobham, 21 December, https://www.bbc.co.uk/news/business-50874181.

Chapter 13

1. Dodd, V. and Grierson, J. (2020) Terrorism police list Extinction Rebellion as extremist ideology. Exclusive: Police scramble to recall guide issued to teachers putting climate activists alongside far-right groups, https://www.theguardian.com/uk-news/2020/jan/10/xr-extinction-rebellion-listed-extremist-ideology-police-prevent-scheme-guidance.

2. Jones, R. (2015) Is 'thought abuse' about to become the fifth category of child abuse? Following a Community Care Live session on radicalisation, social work professor Ray Jones worries about "mission creep" in child protection, https://www.communitycare.co.uk/2015/11/06/thought-abuse-become-fifth-category-child-abuse/.

3. Collinson, P. (2019) Life expectancy falls by six months in biggest drop in UK forecasts. Decline in longevity in England and Wales 'a trend as opposed to a blip', experts say, https://www.theguardian.com/society/2019/mar/07/life-expectancy-slumps-by-five-months.

4. Hiam, L. and McKee, M. (2019) The real scandal behind Britain's falling life expectancy. The health gap between rich and poor is an issue the Tory leadership candidates seem happy to overlook, https://www.theguardian.com/commentisfree/2019/jun/24/britain-life-expectancy-health-gap-rich-poor-tory-leadership.

5. Davis, N. (2018) Life expectancy falling for women in poorest areas of England. Experts say lives are being lost to preventable and treatable diseases as a result of rising poverty, https://www.theguardian.com/society/2018/nov/23/life-expectancy-falling-for-women-in-poorest-areas-of-england.

6. Featherstone, B., White, S. and Morris, K. (2014) Re-Imagining Child Protection: Towards humane social work with families, Bristol, Policy Press, p. 151.

Index[1]

---

[1] Note: Page numbers followed by 'n' refer to notes.

© The Author(s) 2020
R. Jones, *A History of the Personal Social Services in England*,
https://doi.org/10.1007/978-3-030-46123-2

anufacturer's authorised representative in the EU is Springer

Customer Service Centre GmbH, Europaplatz 3, 69115 Heidelberg,

any. If you have any concerns regarding our products, please

ct ProductSafety@springernature.com

d and bound by CPI Group (UK) Ltd, Croydon, CR0 4YY

29/04/2026

02099458-0004